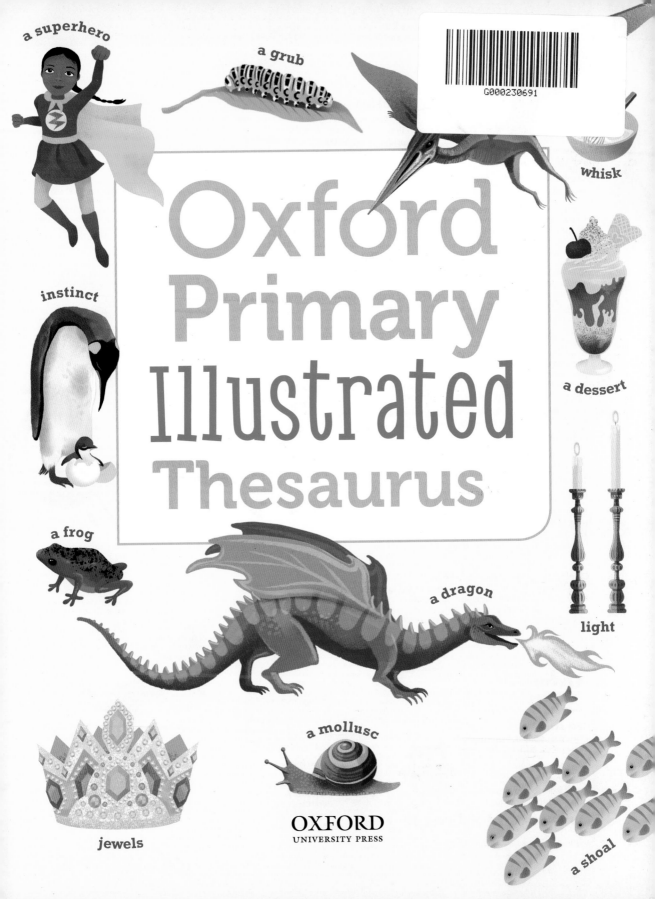

a superhero

a grub

whisk

Oxford Primary Illustrated Thesaurus

instinct

a dessert

a frog

a dragon

light

jewels

a mollusc

OXFORD
UNIVERSITY PRESS

a shoal

OXFORD
UNIVERSITY PRESS

Great Clarendon Street, Oxford, OX2 6DP, United Kingdom

Oxford University Press is a department of the University of Oxford.
It furthers the University's objective of excellence in research,
scholarship, and education by publishing worldwide. Oxford is a
registered trade mark of Oxford University Press in the UK and in
certain other countries

British Library Cataloguing in Publication Data

Data available

ISBN: 978 0 19 276846 9
10 9 8 7 6 5 4 3 2 1

Printed in China

Paper used in the production of this book is a natural,
recyclable product made from wood grown in sustainable forests.
The manufacturing process conforms to the environmental
regulations of the country of origin.

Chief lexicographer Rosalind Combley
The publishers would also like to thank Susan Rennie, Chief lexicographer
of the Oxford Primary Thesaurus 2018 edition.

a longship

a lizard

Oxford OWL

For school
Discover eBooks, inspirational
resources, advice and support

For home
Helping your child's learning
with free eBooks, essential
tips and fun activities

www.oxfordowl.co.uk

Oxford Corpus

You can trust this book
to be up to date, relevant
and engaging because
it is powered by the
Oxford Corpus, a unique
living database of children's
and adults' language.

Contents

a pelican

fry

blend

grate

a triceratops

a samurai

Get to know your thesaurus

guide words
show the first and last word on a page

Hh

Word activity
Every letter begins with a question—you can find the answers in the book.

highlighted letter
shows you which letter you are on

headword
is in blue; it is the word you look up and is in alphabetical order

WORD WEB
gives words that are related to the headword and are useful for project work and story writing

WRITING TIPS
helps you write creatively by suggesting ways to describe how things look, move or sound

literary quotation
shows you how an author has used a word in a story or a poem

A B C D E F G **H** I J K L M N O P Q R S T U V W X Y Z

⚙ Can you think of 5 different words to describe a happy person?

⚙ What word could you use to mean 'happy because you have won'?

⚙ Check the thesaurus to find answers!

habit *NOUN*
*She has a **habit** of playing with her hair.*
• a custom, a practice, a routine, a way

had *(past tense of **have**)*

hair *NOUN*
*Rapunzel's **hair** reached down to the ground.*
• locks, tresses
– A **strand** of hair is a single piece.
– A **lock** of hair is a small bunch or curl.
– A **hank** of hair is a thick bunch or curl.

⚙ **WORD WEB**

HAIR ON AN ANIMAL:
• bristles, a coat, fur, a mane, whiskers
– **Down** is short soft feathers, for example on a duckling.
– **Fleece** is wool on a sheep.
– A **pelt** is an animal skin with fur or hairs on it.

☺ **WRITING TIPS**

You can use these words to describe **hair**:

SOME HAIRSTYLES:
• a braid, a bun, bunches, cornrows, curls, a fringe, a pigtail, a plait, a ponytail, ringlets, a topknot
Brigit's forehead glistened and her hair was curling in little damp ringlets at her temples.—THE HOUNDS OF THE MORRIGAN, Pat O'Shea

TO DESCRIBE LIGHT-COLOURED HAIR:
• blonde, fair, golden, grey, mousy, platinum blonde, silver, strawberry blonde, white

TO DESCRIBE DARK HAIR:
• black, dark, ebony, jet black, raven

TO DESCRIBE BROWN OR RED HAIR:
• auburn, brown, chestnut, fiery, ginger, red, sandy, strawberry blonde

TO DESCRIBE CURLY, THICK OR MESSY HAIR:
• bushy, coarse, curly, dishevelled, frizzy, matted, shaggy, spiky, straggly, tangled, tousled, unkempt, wavy, windswept, wiry
An old man sat inside, a gaunt, pitiful little old man with tousled grey hair.—MIO'S KINGDOM, Astrid Lindgren

TO DESCRIBE THIN, FLAT OR STRAIGHT HAIR:
• fine, floppy, flowing, glossy, greasy, lank, limp, shiny, silky, wispy

TO DESCRIBE SHORT HAIR:
• bristly, cropped, shaved, short, tufty
» *For ways to describe animal hair look at **animal**.*

hairy *ADJECTIVE*
*Mammoths were like elephants with thick **hairy** coats.*
• shaggy, bushy, bristly, woolly, fleecy, furry, fuzzy

handle *NOUN*
*The door **handle** is broken.*
• the grip, the knob
– The **hilt** is the handle of a sword or dagger.

handle *VERB*
❶ *Please don't **handle** the exhibits.*
• to touch, to feel, to hold, to stroke, to fondle

114

cross reference
points you to another headword in this thesaurus where you will find further useful words or information

synonyms
words that mean the same or nearly the same, as the headword

numbered sense
if a word has more than one meaning, they are numbered

word class
tells you what type of word it is, for example *NOUN, VERB, ADJECTIVE* or *ADVERB*

OVERUSED WORD
offers more interesting alternatives for common words such as **big, bit, happy, nice** and **sad**

other forms
shows you tenses and plurals when they are irregular

example sentence
shows you how you might use a word; each meaning of a word has a separate example

opposite
words that are opposite in meaning to the headword; they are also called **antonyms**

label
tells you that certain synonyms are only for *informal* or *formal* use

simile
common similes that are used with a word

alphabet
on every page to help you find your way around the thesaurus easily

❷ *I thought you handled the situation very well.*
• to manage, to deal with, to cope with, to tackle

handsome *ADJECTIVE*
He looked handsome in his suit.
• attractive, good-looking, nice-looking, gorgeous
OPPOSITES ugly, unattractive

handy *ADJECTIVE*
❶ *This gadget is handy for getting lids off jars.*
• useful, helpful, practical
OPPOSITE awkward
❷ *The corner shop is very handy.*
• convenient, accessible, close at hand, nearby
OPPOSITE inaccessible

hang *VERB* hangs, hanging, hung
❶ *I hung the picture on the wall.*
• to fasten, to fix, to attach, to suspend
❷ *A sloth was hanging from the branch.*
• to dangle, to be suspended, to swing, to sway
❸ *His hair hung down over his eyes.*
• to droop, to drop, to flop
➤ **to hang about** or **around**
Some boys were hanging around on the street corner.
• to linger, to loiter, to dawdle
➤ **to hang on to something**
Hang on to the rope.
• to cling on to, to hold on to, to grip, to grasp, to clutch, to clasp
Hang on to your ticket.
• to keep, to retain *(formal)*, to save

happen *VERB*
Did anything interesting happen today?
• to take place, to occur, to arise, to come about, to crop up

happiness *NOUN*
The birthday girl's face glowed with happiness.
• joy, delight, glee, pleasure, contentment, gladness, merriment
— Use **ecstasy** or **bliss** for very great happiness and pleasure.
OPPOSITE sorrow

happy *ADJECTIVE*

OVERUSED WORD
Try to use a more interesting word when you want to say **happy**. Here are some ideas and examples:

TO DESCRIBE A HAPPY MOOD OR HAPPY PERSON:
• cheerful, cheery, joyful, jolly, merry, bright, light-hearted, contented
Laura is always cheerful and bright.
OPPOSITES gloomy, sad

WORDS MEANING VERY HAPPY:
• thrilled, ecstatic, elated, overjoyed
Dax found himself giggling, elated and fizzy with excitement, as if someone had, indeed, given him a new puppy.—SHAPESHIFTER 5: STIRRING THE STORM, Ali Sparkes

FOR HAPPY ABOUT A SUCCESS OR VICTORY:
• triumphant, jubilant, gleeful, delighted
The team came back jubilant after the match.
OPPOSITES disappointed, devastated

FOR A HAPPY TIME OR HAPPY EXPERIENCE:
• enjoyable, joyous, glorious, blissful, heavenly
They spent a glorious summer on the island.
OPPOSITE miserable

TO BE HAPPY TO DO SOMETHING:
• pleased, glad, willing, delighted
I would be glad to help organise the party.
OPPOSITE unwilling

harbour *NOUN*
Several yachts were tied up in the harbour.
• a port, a dock, a mooring, a quay, a pier, a wharf

hard *ADJECTIVE*

OVERUSED WORD
Try to use a more interesting word when you want to say **hard**. Here are some ideas and examples:

FOR HARD GROUND OR A HARD SURFACE:
• solid, firm, compact, rigid, stiff
The ground was solid with frost.
— A common simile is as **hard as a rock**.
OPPOSITE soft

FOR A HARD PULL OR HARD HIT:
• strong, forceful, mighty, heavy, powerful, sharp
— Use **vicious** or **savage** for a hard hit or kick intended to hurt someone.
OPPOSITE light

a b c d e f g **h** i j k l m n o p q r s t u v w x y z

115

phrase
common phrases featuring the headword are also given synonyms

special synonyms
that need more explaining because they have a slightly different meaning or are best for certain special cases

Introduction

This thesaurus has been written with the help of hundreds of great children's books and millions of words of children's own story writing.
It is designed to be used with the *Oxford Primary Illustrated Dictionary* which is aimed at the same age group.

What is the difference between a thesaurus and a dictionary?

A **dictionary** tells you what a word means, so it gives you a **definition** of the word.

A **thesaurus** tells you what other words have the same meaning, so it gives you **synonyms** of a word.

You use a dictionary when you have read or heard a new word and want to know what it means, how to spell it, or some grammar information about it (like the plural of a noun or the past tense of a verb). You use a thesaurus when you want to write or say something yourself and you want to choose the best word.

Here are three good reasons to use your thesaurus:

to find a more interesting word

Are there any other ways to say that someone smiles or laughs? Is there a word for 'to smile unpleasantly' or 'to laugh unpleasantly'? Look up **smile** and **laugh** to find some alternatives.

to find the right word

What do you call a substance that saves you from a **poison**? What are the special words for the **moon** getting bigger or smaller? Are there special names for some **birds'** nests? Look up **poison**, **moon** and **bird** to find out.

to give you ideas for writing

You might want to write a story about a storm at sea. Look up **boat** for the names of parts of a boat and useful verbs for travelling by boat. Look at **storm** for exciting ways to describe a storm. You might also find good ideas at **sea** and **rain**.

There are also lots of tips for making your writing wonderful at the back of this book.

Synonyms

Synonyms are words that mean the same—or nearly the same—as each other, like *big* and *huge*, or *horrible* and *nasty*.

Using different synonyms, rather than using the same words all the time, makes your writing more interesting. Sometimes you can choose from a number of different synonyms without really changing the meaning.

> **Example**
> There are a lot of different words you could choose instead of **good** or **nice**:
>
> The weather was ~~nice~~ *glorious*. The food was ~~nice~~ *delicious*. The people were ~~nice~~ *charming*. In fact, the whole day was ~~nice~~ *wonderful!*

Some synonyms have slightly different meanings or only fit in certain contexts. The thesaurus will help you with these.

> **Example**
> At **clear** the thesaurus tells you that you can use **legible** for writing that is clear.

Other synonyms have a label *formal*, *informal* or *old use*. This helps you to choose different words if you are writing, for example, a formal letter, some informal dialogue, or a story set in the past.

For more tips on different types of writing look at the back of this book.

Overused words

Words like **bad**, **big** and **nice** are very useful and sometimes they are the right word to use (for example, in the *big bad wolf*!). But they can make your writing boring if you use them over and over again, and in this thesaurus, you will find lots of alternatives to these words.

Example

Instead of saying that your character is **bad** at maths, you could describe them as *incompetent*, *appalling* or *abysmal*.

Instead of saying that someone **moves** slowly along, you could say that they *amble*, *dawdle*, *saunter* or *stroll*.

Here is a list of the entries where you will find an OVERUSED WORD panel:

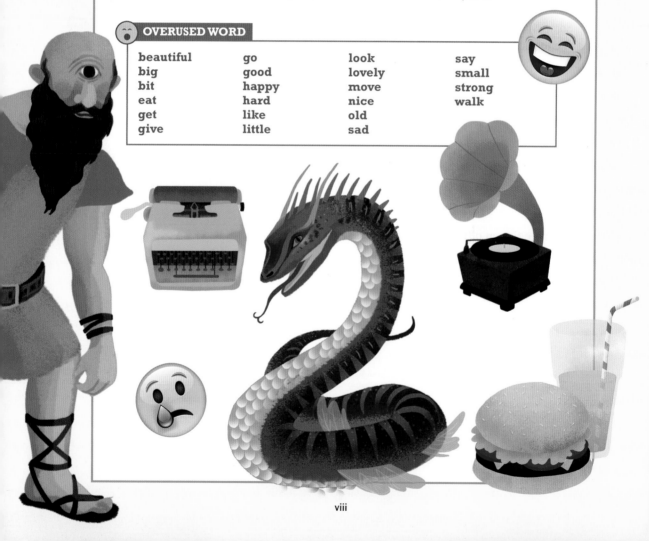

😮 OVERUSED WORD

beautiful	go	look	say
big	good	lovely	small
bit	happy	move	strong
eat	hard	nice	walk
get	like	old	
give	little	sad	

Word Webs

Some words are not synonyms, but relate to the same topic. For example, **building** is a general word but there are many different types of building. These are listed in a Word Web.

Other Word Webs tell you the names for different parts of something, for example the parts of a **castle**, or the parts of a **circle**. They can tell you the names of other things related to the headword, for example things used for riding a **horse**.

Word Webs can help you to find the right word and to be more accurate and interesting in your writing.

Example	you could write:
Instead of writing: *The shop was full of jars of sweets.* *They were many different colours.*	*The shop was full of jars of sweets. They* *were lime green, lavender, rose pink, purple,* *violet, lemon yellow and cherry red.*

These ideas came from the WORD WEBS at **colour** and at **green**, **pink**, **red** and **yellow**.

Here is a list of entries where you will find a WORD WEB:

✦ WORD WEB

aircraft	church	flower	monster	shop
amphibian	circle	food	museum	snake
animal	city	football	music	song
anniversary	cloth	fox	myth	spice
art	clothes	fruit	nut	sport
athletics	colour	game	paper	story
bean	communication	garden	party	superhero
bear	computer	green	pattern	sweet
bed	container	grey	pet	swim
bee	cook	group	pig	tennis
berry	cricket	hair	pink	tent
bicycle	criminal	hat	planet	theatre
bird	cup	herb	plant	time
blue	cupboard	home	poem	tool
boat	dance	horse	poultry	tooth
body	day	house	purple	toy
bone	desert	ice	red	train
book	dinosaur	illness	religion	transport
bridge	disaster	injury	reptile	travel
brown	doctor	insect	restaurant	tree
building	dog	jewel	river	vegetable
bush	door	jewellery	rock	water
cage	drawing	job	room	weapon
candidate	drink	jungle	ruler	wedding
car	environment	kitchen	school	white
card	expression	knife	science	writer
castle	eye	light	sea	writing
cat	farm	magic	seaside	yellow
cattle	feeling	meal	seat	young
cave	fighter	meat	shape	
ceremony	film	medicine	shellfish	
chicken	fish	metal	shoe	

Writing tips

As well as lots of tips for writing at the back of this book, you will find boxes at some headwords full of ideas for writing about a particular animal, event, place, type of weather and so on. These might include interesting adjectives for describing something or verbs for saying what it does.

Examples
At **fire** you will find words for describing a fire and verbs such as *blaze, crackle, spit, glow, leap* and *flare up* for describing what fire does.

At **ghost** you will find words for things a ghost might do and ideas for some spooky places, such as *a crypt, a dungeon* or *a haunted house*.

At **knight** you will find words for things a knight might have, adjectives such as *brave, chivalrous* and *valiant* for describing a knight, and verbs for things that a knight might do.

At the entries for **angry**, **frightened** and **surprised** you will also find suggestions for **idioms** (colourful phrases) to use for describing people's behaviour.

Here is a list of entries where you will find WRITING TIPS:

☺ WRITING TIPS

aircraft	dragon	ice	smell
angry	exclamation	insect	smile
animal	eye	jewel	snake
ball	face	knight	snow
bell	fairy	light	sound
bird	feel	monster	space
boat	fire	moon	storm
body	flavour	mountain	story
building	food	pain	surprised
cat	frightened	pirate	thunder
clothes	ghost	planet	tooth
colour	hair	rain	tree
detective	heat	river	voice
dog	horse	robot	water
		sea	wave
		sky	wind

Throughout the thesaurus you will find brilliant examples of writing from children's authors, to inspire you in your writing—and in your reading!

🔧 Can you think of 5 different words for 'angry'?

🔧 Lots of phrases connected with anger use the idea of heat. Can you think of any?

🔧 Check the thesaurus to find answers!

abandon VERB
*His friends **abandoned** him and went home.*
• to leave, to desert, to forsake, to dump *(informal)*

ability NOUN
❶ *Skin has the **ability** to heal itself.*
• capability, competence
❷ *She is a player with a lot of **ability**.*
• talent, aptitude, skill
• a gift: *He has a real **gift** for drawing.*

able ADJECTIVE
❶ *Will you be **able** to come to my party?*
• allowed, permitted, free, willing
OPPOSITE unable
❷ *He is a very **able** swimmer.*
• competent, capable, expert, skilful, talented, gifted

abolish VERB
*I wish someone would **abolish** homework!*
• to ban, to end, to get rid of, to put an end to, to eliminate

about PREPOSITION
*There were **about** fifty people there.*
• approximately, roughly, around
OPPOSITE exactly
➤ **to be about something**
*The film is **about** a dog called Scruff.*
• to concern, to deal with, to involve

above ADVERB
*An eagle flew high **above**.*
• overhead, in the sky

absent ADJECTIVE
*Why were you **absent** from school yesterday?*
• away, missing
— To be absent from school without permission is to play truant.
OPPOSITE present

absent-minded ADJECTIVE
*He is very **absent-minded** and often forgets things.*
• forgetful, careless, vague, distracted
OPPOSITE alert

absolutely ADVERB
*This floor is **absolutely** filthy!*
• completely, thoroughly, totally, utterly, really

absorb VERB
*A sponge **absorbs** water.*
• to soak up, to take in

absorbed ADJECTIVE
➤ **to be absorbed in something**
*I was so **absorbed** in my book that I forgot the time.*
• to be engrossed in, to be interested in, to be preoccupied with, to be busy with, to concentrate on, to be fascinated by, to be riveted by

absurd ADJECTIVE
*What an **absurd** idea!*
• ridiculous, silly, ludicrous, foolish, nonsensical, idiotic, stupid, unreasonable, illogical
OPPOSITES sensible, reasonable

abuse VERB
❶ *The rescued dog had been **abused** by its owners.*
• to mistreat, to hurt, to harm, to injure
❷ *Some players **abused** the referee.*
• to insult, to swear at, to be rude to
abuse NOUN
*The crowd yelled **abuse**.*
• insults, swear words

accept VERB
❶ *I **accepted** the invitation.*
• to say yes to, to take, to agree to
OPPOSITES to refuse, to decline, to reject
❷ *You have to **accept** the truth.*
• to admit, to acknowledge, to recognise, to resign yourself to
OPPOSITE to deny

above

A
B
C
D
E
F
G
H
I
J
K
L
M
N
O
P
Q
R
S
T
U
V
W
X
Y
Z

acceptable ADJECTIVE
❶ *Something home-made is a very* **acceptable** *present.*
• welcome, agreeable, appreciated, pleasant, pleasing, worthwhile
❷ *This behaviour is not* **acceptable**.
• satisfactory, appropriate, suitable, tolerable
OPPOSITE unacceptable

accident NOUN
❶ *He had an* **accident** *with the paint.*
• a mishap, a disaster, a calamity, a catastrophe
❷ *We saw a car* **accident**.
• a collision, a crash, a smash
— A **pile-up** is a bad accident involving a lot of vehicles.
— A **bump** or a **scrape** is an accident that is not very serious.
➤ **by accident**
I found the clue **by accident**.
• by chance, by luck, by a fluke, accidentally, unintentionally

accidental ADJECTIVE
The damage to the building was **accidental**.
• unintentional, unfortunate, unlucky
OPPOSITE deliberate

accommodate VERB
The hotel can **accommodate** *thirty guests.*
• to house, to shelter, to hold, to take, to provide for

accommodation NOUN
Have you booked your holiday **accommodation** *yet?*
• housing, a home, quarters, premises, a shelter

accompany VERB
I will **accompany** *you to the airport.*
• to escort, to go with, to travel with

accomplish VERB
She **accomplished** *her goal of reading all six books.*
• to achieve, to finish, to complete, to carry out, to perform, to succeed in, to fulfil

account NOUN
I wrote an **account** *of our school trip.*
• a report, a record, a description, a history, a narrative, a story, a chronicle, a log

accumulate VERB
I have **accumulated** *a lot of toys.*
• to collect, to gather, to heap up, to pile up

accurate ADJECTIVE
❶ *We took* **accurate** *measurements of the plant.*
• careful, correct, exact, precise
OPPOSITES inexact, rough
❷ *Is this an* **accurate** *account of what happened?*
• faithful, true, reliable, truthful
OPPOSITES inaccurate, false

ache NOUN
The **ache** *in my tooth is getting worse.*
• pain, soreness, throbbing, discomfort, a pang, a twinge

ache VERB
My legs **ached** *from the long walk.*
• to hurt, to be painful, to be sore, to throb, to smart

achieve VERB
❶ *He* **achieved** *his goal of finishing the book.*
• to accomplish, to succeed in, to carry out, to fulfil
❷ *She* **achieved** *a lot of success as a player.*
• to win, to gain, to earn, to get

acknowledge VERB
❶ *You have to* **acknowledge** *that I'm right.*
• to admit, to accept, to recognise
OPPOSITE to deny
❷ *They never* **acknowledged** *my email.*
• to answer, to reply to, to respond to

act NOUN
❶ *Rescuing the boy from the river was a brave* **act**.
• an action, a deed, a feat, an exploit
— A **stunt** is a risky or dangerous act.
❷ *We saw a comedy* **act**.
• a performance, a show

act VERB
❶ *We must* **act** *to deal with this problem.*
• to do something, to take action
❷ *Stop* **acting** *like a baby!*
• to behave, to carry on

❸ *I acted the part of a pirate in the play.*
• to perform, to play, to portray, to appear as

action NOUN
❶ *The driver's action prevented an accident.*
• an act, a move, a manoeuvre, a deed, an effort
❷ *The film was full of action.*
• drama, excitement, activity, liveliness, energy

active ADJECTIVE
❶ *Mr Aziz is very active for his age.*
• energetic, lively, sprightly, vigorous, busy
❷ *My uncle is an active member of the club.*
• enthusiastic, devoted, dedicated, hard-working
OPPOSITE inactive

activity NOUN
❶ *The town centre was full of activity.*
• action, life, liveliness, excitement, movement, animation
❷ *My mum's favourite activity is gardening.*
• a hobby, an interest, a pastime, a pursuit, an occupation, a task

actual ADJECTIVE
This is the actual ship that Nelson sailed in.
• real, true, very, genuine, authentic

actually ADVERB
What did the teacher actually say to you?
• really, truly, definitely, truthfully, genuinely, in fact

acute ADJECTIVE
❶ *She felt an acute pain in her knee.*
• intense, severe, sharp, piercing, sudden, violent
OPPOSITES mild, slight
❷ *There is an acute shortage of food.*
• serious, severe, urgent, crucial, vital
OPPOSITE unimportant

adapt VERB
He adapted the bike so it was easier to ride.
• to alter, to change, to modify, to adjust, to improve
➤ **to adapt to**
She soon adapted to her new school.
• to adjust to, to become accustomed to, to get used to

add VERB
❶ *What do you get when you add all the amounts?*
• to add up, to total
❷ *Add a little salt and pepper.*
• to mix in, to stir in

additional ADJECTIVE
There are additional toilets downstairs.
• extra, further, more

adjust VERB
You need to adjust the brightness on the screen.
• to alter, to modify, to change, to correct, to put right, to improve
➤ **to adjust to**
I found it hard to adjust to my new school at first.
• to adapt to, to become accustomed to, to get used to

admiration NOUN
I'm full of admiration for her work.
• respect, approval, praise
OPPOSITE contempt

admire VERB
❶ *I admire her courage.*
• to look up to, to have a high opinion of, to respect, to approve of, to value
OPPOSITE to despise
❷ *The travellers stopped to admire the view.*
• to enjoy, to appreciate

admission NOUN
❶ *Admission to the castle is by ticket only.*
• entrance, entry, access, admittance
❷ *We were surprised by his admission of guilt.*
• a confession, a declaration, an acknowledgement
OPPOSITE a denial

admit VERB
❶ *He admitted that he was wrong.*
• to confess, to acknowledge, to accept, to agree
OPPOSITE to deny
❷ *They will not admit you without a ticket.*
• to allow in, to let in, to accept, to take in, to receive
OPPOSITE to exclude

adore VERB
Rosie adores her big sister.
• to love, to worship, to admire

adult NOUN
Adults are not allowed in our club.
• a grown-up
OPPOSITES a young person, a child

adult ADJECTIVE
An adult zebra can run at 80km an hour.
• grown-up, mature, full-size, fully grown
OPPOSITES young, immature

A
B
C
D
E
F
G
H
I
J
K
L
M
N
O
P
Q
R
S
T
U
V
W
X
Y
Z

advance *VERB*
❶ *The army advanced.*
• to move forward, to go forward, to proceed, to progress, to make progress
OPPOSITE to retreat
❷ *Technology advances so quickly.*
• to develop, to improve, to progress, to make progress, to grow, to evolve

advance *NOUN*
There have been amazing technological advances.
• development
• progress: *There has been amazing technological progress.*
➤ **in advance**
Please let us know in advance if you have any allergies.
• beforehand, ahead of time

advantage *NOUN*
Being tall is an advantage in this game.
• a benefit, a help, an aid, an asset
OPPOSITES a disadvantage, a drawback

adventure *NOUN*
❶ *He told us about his latest adventure.*
• an exploit, an escapade, an enterprise, a venture, an expedition, a quest
❷ *They travelled the world in search of adventure.*
• excitement, thrills

adventurous *ADJECTIVE*
I dreamed of being an adventurous explorer.
• bold, brave, daring, fearless, heroic, intrepid, valiant
OPPOSITE unadventurous

advertise *VERB*
We made a poster to advertise the cake sale.
• to promote, to announce, to market

advice *NOUN*
The teacher gave us some useful advice.
• help, guidance, tips, suggestions, recommendations, counsel

advise *VERB*
He advised us to check our work.
• to counsel, to recommend, to suggest, to encourage, to urge

aeroplane *NOUN*
Have you ever flown in an aeroplane?
• a plane, an aircraft

affair *NOUN*
The party was a strange affair.
• an event, an occurrence, an incident, a happening

affect *VERB*
Global warming will affect our climate.
• to have an effect on, to have an impact on, to influence, to change, to modify, to alter

afraid *ADJECTIVE*
❶ *Don't be afraid—it's quite safe.*
• frightened, scared, fearful, alarmed
— Use **terrified** or **petrified** if someone is very afraid.
— Use **anxious** or **apprehensive** if someone is afraid of what might happen.
» *For ideas for writing about being afraid look at* **frightened**.
❷ *I was afraid to speak.*
• hesitant, reluctant, shy

again *ADVERB*
Would you like to try again?
• once more, once again, another time

against *PREPOSITION*
➤ **to be against**
I am against wearing fur.
• to be opposed to, to not be in favour of, to disagree with, to disapprove of
OPPOSITES to be for, to be in favour of

age *NOUN*
The book is set in the age of the Vikings.
• a period, a time, an era, the days

aggressive *ADJECTIVE*
He could be grumpy but he was never aggressive.
• hostile, violent, argumentative, quarrelsome, warlike
OPPOSITE friendly

agile *ADJECTIVE*
Mountain goats are extremely agile.
• nimble, graceful, sprightly, deft, supple, swift
OPPOSITES clumsy, stiff

agitated ADJECTIVE
She rushed in, looking agitated.
• nervous, anxious, restless, fidgety, flustered,
disturbed, upset
OPPOSITES calm, cool

agony NOUN
He screamed in agony when he broke his leg.
• pain, suffering, torture, torment, anguish,
distress

agree VERB
❶ *I'm glad that we agree.*
• to think the same, to have the same view,
to be united, to concur
OPPOSITE to disagree
❷ *I asked him to help us and he agreed.*
• to say yes, to accept, to consent, to be willing
• to undertake to do: *He undertook to help us.*
OPPOSITE to refuse

agreement NOUN
❶ *There was agreement on the need
for longer holidays.*
• consent, unity, harmony, sympathy
OPPOSITE disagreement
❷ *The two sides signed an agreement.*
• a deal, a treaty, an alliance
— A legal agreement is a **contract**.
— An agreement to stop fighting is a **truce**.

aid NOUN
I tidied everything up with the aid of my friends.
• help, support, assistance

aid VERB
We did everything we could to aid them.
• to help, to assist, to support, to collaborate,
to cooperate, to lend a hand

aim NOUN
What was the aim of the experiment?
• a goal, an intention, an objective,
a target, a purpose, an ambition,
a wish

aim VERB
❶ *She aims to be a professional
dancer.*
• to intend, to mean,
to plan, to want,
to wish
❷ *She aimed
her bow and
arrow at the
target.*
• to point, to direct

aim

aircraft NOUN

SOME TYPES OF AIRCRAFT:

• an aeroplane, an airliner, a biplane, a drone,
a glider, a helicopter, a hot-air balloon, a jet,
a jumbo jet

SOME PARTS OF AIRCRAFT:

• the cabin, the cockpit, a fin, the fuselage, the
hold, a joystick, the nose, a propeller, a rudder,
the tail, the undercarriage, a wing

a drone

an aeroplane

a helicopter

😊 **WRITING TIPS**

Here are some useful words for writing about
aircraft:
• *The aeroplane was **flying** high above the clouds.*
• *The jumbo jet **soared** up into the sky.*
• *Our plane **took off** at six o'clock and **landed**
at ten o'clock.*
• *The aeroplane **touched down** and then **taxied**
along the **runway**.*
• *The **pilot** set a **course** for home.*
The aircraft stayed very low, following the coastline.
—SHARK ISLAND, David Miller

a
b
c
d
e
f
g
h
i
j
k
l
m
n
o
p
q
r
s
t
u
v
w
x
y
z

alarm VERB
The noise **alarmed** her.
• to frighten, to startle, to scare, to panic, to agitate, to distress, to shock, to upset, to worry
OPPOSITE to reassure

alarm NOUN
❶ Did you hear the **alarm**?
• a signal, a siren, a warning bell
❷ The sudden noise filled me with **alarm**.
• fright, fear, panic, anxiety, worry, distress, nervousness, terror, uneasiness

a siren

alert ADJECTIVE
The guards were told to stay **alert** at all times.
• watchful, sharp, observant, on the lookout, ready, wary

alert VERB
We **alerted** them to the danger.
• to warn, to make aware, to inform

alien ADJECTIVE
The desert landscape looked **alien** to us.
• strange, foreign, unfamiliar, different, exotic
OPPOSITE familiar

alien NOUN
I wrote a story about **aliens** from another galaxy.
• extraterrestrial, alien life form

alike ADJECTIVE
All the houses in the street looked **alike**.
• similar, the same, identical
OPPOSITE different

alive ADJECTIVE
Fortunately, my goldfish was still **alive**.
• living, existing, in existence, surviving, breathing
OPPOSITE dead

allocate VERB
They **allocated** us each a desk.
• to assign, to allow, to set aside, to reserve

allow VERB
❶ They don't **allow** skateboards in the playground.
• to let: They don't **let** us use skateboards in the playground.
• to permit, to authorise, to approve of, to agree to, to consent to, to give permission for
OPPOSITE to forbid
❷ Have you **allowed** enough time for the journey?
• to allocate, to set aside, to assign, to grant

allowed ADJECTIVE
Dogs are not **allowed** on this beach.
• permitted, accepted, acceptable, all right, legitimate

all right ADJECTIVE
❶ The food was **all right**.
• satisfactory, acceptable, reasonable, fairly good
❷ The survivors appeared to be **all right**.
• well, unhurt, unharmed, uninjured, safe
❸ Is it **all right** to play music in here?
• acceptable, allowed, permitted

almost ADVERB
I have **almost** finished my book.
• nearly, practically, just about, virtually, not quite

alone ADJECTIVE ADVERB
❶ Did you go to the party **alone**?
• on your own, by yourself, unaccompanied
❷ Zoe had no friends and felt very **alone**.
• lonely, friendless, isolated, solitary, desolate

also ADVERB
We need some bread, and **also** more butter.
• in addition, besides, additionally, too, furthermore, moreover

altogether ADVERB
❶ Our house has five rooms **altogether**.
• in all, in total
❷ I soon forgot about it **altogether**.
• completely, entirely, absolutely, totally, utterly

always ADVERB
❶ The sea is **always** in motion.
• constantly, continuously, endlessly, eternally, forever, perpetually
❷ This bus is **always** late.
• consistently, continually, invariably, persistently, regularly, repeatedly

amaze VERB
It **amazes** me to think that the earth is billions of years old.
• to astonish, to astound, to surprise, to stun, to shock, to stagger, to startle

amazement NOUN
Everyone stared at me in **amazement**.
• astonishment, surprise
— Use **wonder** when you feel amazement and admiration.
— Use **awe** when you feel amazement, admiration and a little fear.
— Use **shock** when you feel amazement at something bad.

amazing ADJECTIVE
The Northern Lights are an amazing sight.
• astonishing, astounding, staggering, remarkable, surprising, extraordinary, incredible, breathtaking, sensational, tremendous, wonderful

ambition NOUN
❶ *My ambition is to play tennis at Wimbledon.*
• a goal, an aim, an intention, an objective, a target, a desire, a dream, a wish, a hope
❷ *She has a lot of ambition and should do well.*
• enthusiasm, zeal, eagerness

ambitious ADJECTIVE
❶ *He is very ambitious and wants to be a doctor.*
• enthusiastic, committed, keen, eager
OPPOSITE unambitious
❷ *I think your plan is too ambitious.*
• challenging, optimistic, grand
OPPOSITE unambitious

amount NOUN
❶ *He paid me the correct amount.*
• sum, total
❷ *There's a large amount of paper in the cupboard.*
• quantity, supply, volume, mass, bulk

amphibian NOUN

WORD WEB

SOME ANIMALS
WHICH ARE AMPHIBIANS:

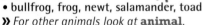
a newt

• bullfrog, frog, newt, salamander, toad
» *For other animals look at* **animal**.

amuse VERB
The kitten's antics amused us.
• to make someone laugh, to make someone smile, to entertain, to divert, to cheer someone up

amusement NOUN
❶ *His behaviour caused a lot of amusement.*
• laughter, mirth, entertainment
❷ *Puppet shows were a popular amusement.*
• a pastime, a recreation, an entertainment, a diversion, a hobby, a leisure activity

analyse VERB
We analysed the results of our experiment.
• to examine, to assess, to study, to investigate, to scrutinise

ancestor NOUN
Our family's ancestors came from France.
• a predecessor, a forefather
OPPOSITE a descendant

ancient ADJECTIVE
In ancient times, our ancestors were hunters.
• early, primitive, olden
— Use **prehistoric** for the times before written records were kept.
— Use **classical** to describe things from the time of the ancient Greeks and Romans.
OPPOSITES modern, recent

anger NOUN
I was filled with anger when I read her letter.
• rage, fury, outrage, wrath (old use)
— An outburst of anger is a **tantrum** or a **fit of temper**.

angle NOUN
Let's look at the problem from a different angle.
• a viewpoint, a point of view, a perspective

angry ADJECTIVE
She was angry when she saw the mess.
• furious, enraged, fuming, infuriated, indignant, irate, livid, mad (informal), in a rage, in a temper, seething
— Use **cross** or **annoyed** if someone is slightly angry.
— Use **berserk** or **in a frenzy** if someone is very angry and out of control.
OPPOSITE calm
➤ **to make someone angry**
His rude attitude made me angry.
• to enrage, to infuriate, to madden, to annoy, to irritate, to vex, to antagonise, to provoke, to make someone's blood boil (informal), to make someone see red (informal), to drive someone mad (informal)

WRITING TIPS

Here are some things someone might do if they feel **angry**:
• to blow a fuse, to blow your top, to fly off the handle, to have a face like thunder, to glare, to glower, to scowl, to have steam coming out of your ears, to hit the roof, to see red
Well, that did it! I saw red. And before I was able to stop myself, I did something I never meant to do. I PUT THE MAGIC FINGER ON THEM ALL!—THE MAGIC FINGER, Roald Dahl
» *For ideas for writing about being angry look at* **say**.

A B C D E F G H I J K L M N O P Q R S T U V W X Y Z

animal NOUN

*Wild **animals** roam freely in the safari park.*

• a creature, a beast, a brute

— A word for wild animals in general is **wildlife**.

🕸 **WORD WEB**

SOME TYPES OF ANIMALS:

• an amphibian, a bird, a crustacean, a fish, an insect, a mammal, a marsupial, a mollusc, a reptile, a rodent

— An animal that has a backbone is a **vertebrate**.

— An animal that does not have a backbone is an **invertebrate**

— An animal that eats meat is a **carnivore**.

— An animal that eats plants is a **herbivore**.

— An animal that eats meat and plants is an **omnivore**.

» *For examples of types of animals look at* **amphibian**, **bird**, **fish**, **insect** *and* **reptile**.

SOME WILD ANIMALS FOUND IN BRITAIN:

• badger, bat, deer, dormouse, fox, grass snake, hare, hedgehog, mole, mouse, otter, rabbit, rat, shrew, squirrel, stoat, vole, weasel

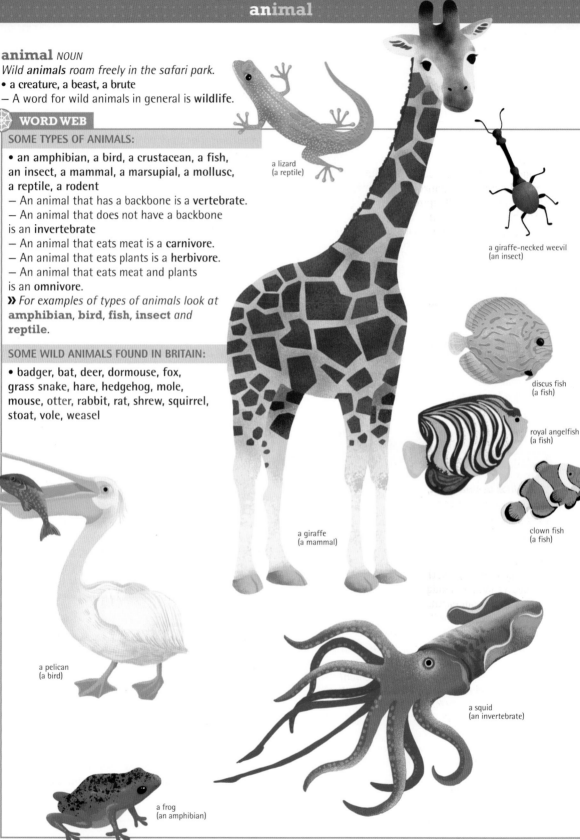

a lizard
(a reptile)

a giraffe-necked weevil
(an insect)

discus fish
(a fish)

royal angelfish
(a fish)

clown fish
(a fish)

a giraffe
(a mammal)

a pelican
(a bird)

a squid
(an invertebrate)

a frog
(an amphibian)

a snail
(a mollusc)

SOME LAND ANIMALS FOUND IN OTHER COUNTRIES:

• aardvark, anteater, antelope, ape, armadillo, baboon, bear, beaver, bison, boar, buffalo, camel, cheetah, chimpanzee, chipmunk, donkey, echidna, elephant, elk, gazelle, giraffe, gorilla, grizzly bear, hippopotamus or hippo, hyena, jackal, jaguar, kangaroo, koala, leopard, lion, llama, lynx, meerkat, mongoose, monkey, moose, orangutan, panda, panther, platypus, polar bear, porcupine, reindeer, rhinoceros or rhino, skunk, tapir, tiger, wallaby, warthog, wildebeest, wolf, wombat, yak, zebra

SOME ANIMALS THAT LIVE IN THE SEA:

• dolphin, killer whale or orca, manatee, narwhal, porpoise, seal, sea lion, walrus, whale

PARTS OF AN ANIMAL'S BODY:

• antler, claw, fang, foreleg, hind leg, hoof, horn, jaws, mane, muzzle, paw, snout, tail, trotter, tusk, whisker, fur, coat, fleece, hide, pelt
» For animals found on a farm look at **farm**.
» For animals kept as pets look at **pet**.
» Also look at **bear, cat, cattle, deer, dog, horse, pig** and **sheep**.
» For groups of animals look at **group**.

HOMES OF WILD ANIMALS:

• den, lair
— A badger lives in a **sett**.
— A beaver lives in a **lodge**.
— A fox lives in an **earth**.
— An otter lives in a **holt**.
— A rabbit lives in a **burrow** or **warren**.
— A squirrel lives in a **drey**.

SOUNDS MADE BY ANIMALS:

• bark, bay, bellow, buzz, gnash, growl, grunt, hiss, howl, jabber, oink, purr, roar, snap, snarl, snort, snuffle, squeak, trumpet, whimper, whine, woof, yap, yelp, yowl
— A sheep **bleats**.
— A donkey **brays**.
— A frog **croaks**.
— Cattle **low** or **moo**.
— A cat **mews** or **miaows**.
— A horse **neighs** or **whinnies**.

😀 WRITING TIPS

TO DESCRIBE HOW AN ANIMAL MOVES:

You can use these words to describe an **animal**:
• to bound, to creep, to crouch, to dart, to frisk, to gallop, to hop, to leap, to lumber, to nuzzle, to pad, to pounce, to roam, to scuttle, to skip, to slink, to slither, to spring, to stampede, to trot, to waddle, to wallow
The hounds started to spread out in a circle around him. They were growling and snapping, looking for a chance to pounce.—HERE BE MONSTERS, Alan Snow

TO DESCRIBE AN ANIMAL'S SKIN OR COAT:

• fluffy, furry, glistening, glossy, hairy, leathery, matted, mottled, prickly, scaly, shaggy, shiny, silky, sleek, slimy, slippery, smooth, spiky, spotted, striped, woolly

anniversary NOUN

✸ WORD WEB

— The anniversary of the day you were born is your **birthday**.
— The anniversary of the day someone was married is their **wedding anniversary**.

SPECIAL WEDDING ANNIVERSARIES:

• silver wedding (25 years), ruby wedding (40 years), golden wedding (50 years), diamond wedding (60 years)

SPECIAL ANNIVERSARIES:

• centenary (100 years), bicentenary (200 years), tercentenary (300 years), quatercentenary (400 years), quincentenary (500 years), millenary (1000 years)

announce VERB

*The head **announced** that sports day was cancelled.*
• to declare, to state, to proclaim, to pronounce

annoy VERB

❶ *It **annoys** her when I'm late.*
• to irritate, to displease, to infuriate, to bother, to vex, to upset, to offend, to get on someone's nerves *(informal)*, to drive someone mad *(informal)*
OPPOSITE to please
❷ *Please don't **annoy** me while I'm working.*
• to pester, to bother, to disturb, to harass, to interrupt, to badger, to plague, to trouble

a
b
c
d
e
f
g
h
i
j
k
l
m
n
o
p
q
r
s
t
u
v
w
x
y
z

annoying *ADJECTIVE*
*My brother has a lot of **annoying** habits.*
• irritating, maddening, infuriating, provoking, tiresome, vexing, troublesome

answer *NOUN*
❶ *Did you get an **answer** to your question?*
• a reply, a response, a reaction, an acknowledgement
— A quick or angry answer is a **retort**.
❷ *The **answers** to the quiz are at the back.*
• a solution, an explanation

answer *VERB*
*I called out but nobody **answered**.*
• to give an answer, to reply, to respond, to react
— To **retort** is to answer quickly or angrily.
— To **acknowledge** a message or question is to let someone know that you have received it.

anticipate *VERB*
*We **anticipate** a difficult match.*
• to expect, to predict, to forecast, to be prepared for

anxiety *NOUN*
*We waited for news with a growing sense of **anxiety**.*
• concern, worry, fear, nervousness, tension, stress, uncertainty, doubt
OPPOSITES calmness, calm

anxious *ADJECTIVE*
❶ *Are you **anxious** about your exams?*
• nervous, worried, apprehensive, concerned, preoccupied, uneasy, fearful, tense, troubled
OPPOSITE calm
❷ *I'm **anxious** to do my best.*
• eager, keen, impatient, enthusiastic, willing

apologise *VERB*
*He **apologised** for his behaviour.*
• to make an apology, to say sorry, to express regret, to repent

apparent *ADJECTIVE*
*There was no **apparent** reason for the crash.*
• obvious, evident, clear, noticeable, detectable, conspicuous, recognisable, visible
OPPOSITES concealed, unclear

appeal *VERB*
➤ **to appeal for**
*They **appealed for** our help.*
• to request, to beg for, to plead for, to entreat
➤ **to appeal to**
*That kind of music doesn't **appeal to** me.*
• to attract, to interest, to fascinate, to tempt

appeal *NOUN*
*The school made an **appeal** for help from parents.*
• a plea, a request, a call, a cry

appear *VERB*
❶ *Snowdrops **appear** in the spring.*
• to come out, to become visible, to be seen, to come into view, to arrive
— To **emerge** is to appear from inside or behind something.
— To **surface** is to appear from underneath something.
— To **loom** is to appear as something large and threatening.
OPPOSITE to disappear
❷ *She **appeared** tired.*
• to seem, to look

appearance *NOUN*
❶ *They were startled by the **appearance** of a ghost.*
• arrival, approach, entrance, emergence
OPPOSITE disappearance
❷ *Mr Hogweed had a grim **appearance**.*
• an air, a bearing, a look

applaud *VERB*
*The audience laughed and **applauded**.*
• to clap, to cheer
OPPOSITE to boo

apply *VERB*
❶ *She **applied** for a job in a shop.*
• to make an application for, to ask for, to request
❷ *The rules **apply** to everyone.*
• to be relevant for, to relate to, to refer to
❸ *Don't forget to **apply** sunscreen.*
• to put on, to rub on, to use

appoint *VERB*
*The school governors **appointed** a new teacher.*
• to choose, to select, to nominate, to name

appointment *NOUN*
*I have an **appointment** at the dentist's.*
• an arrangement, an engagement

appreciate *VERB*
❶ *He **appreciates** good music.*
• to enjoy, to relish, to like, to love, to value, to admire
❷ *I **appreciate** how difficult it is for you.*
• to understand, to grasp, to realise, to see, to recognise, to acknowledge

apprehensive *ADJECTIVE*
*Are you **apprehensive** about your exams?*
• worried, anxious, nervous, tense, uneasy, uncertain, troubled, frightened, fearful

approach *VERB*
❶ *He **approached** the dog nervously.*
• to draw near to, to come near to, to come up to, to move towards, to advance on
❷ *The day of the match was **approaching**.*
• to come close, to draw near, to near

approach *NOUN*
❶ *We could hear the **approach** of heavy footsteps.*
• the arrival, the advance, the coming near
❷ *I like her positive **approach**.*
• an attitude, a manner, a style, a method, a way

appropriate *ADJECTIVE*
*Those jeans are not **appropriate** for a job interview.*
• suitable, proper, right, correct, in good taste
OPPOSITE inappropriate

approve *VERB*
➤ **to approve of**
*Her family did not **approve of** her boyfriend.*
• to like, to welcome, to appreciate, to agree with, to admire, to praise, to respect, to favour, to commend
OPPOSITE to disapprove of

approximate *ADJECTIVE*
*What is the **approximate** width of the room?*
• rough, estimated, inexact
OPPOSITES exact, precise

approximately *ADVERB*
*The film will finish at **approximately** five o'clock.*
• roughly, about, around, round about, close to, more or less
OPPOSITES exactly, precisely

aptitude *NOUN*
*He has a remarkable **aptitude** for music.*
• a talent, a gift, an ability, a skill

area *NOUN*
❶ *There are a lot of shops in this **area**.*
• a district, a neighbourhood, a region, a zone, a vicinity
❷ *From the plane we saw a big **area** of desert.*
• an expanse, a stretch
— A small area is a **patch**.

argue *VERB*
❶ *She and her sister are always **arguing**.*
• to quarrel, to disagree, to differ, to debate, to clash, to fight, to have an argument, to fall out, to squabble
OPPOSITE to agree
❷ *She **argued** that it was impossible.*
• to claim, to maintain, to reason, to suggest

argument *NOUN*
*They had an **argument** over who should pay.*
• a disagreement, a quarrel, a dispute, a row, a clash, a squabble, a fight, a debate
— A feud is a bitter argument between people or families that lasts a long time.

arise *VERB*
*A problem **arose**.*
• to occur, to emerge, to develop, to appear, to come up, to happen

aroma *NOUN*
*The **aroma** of lavender filled the air.*
• a smell, a scent, an odour, a fragrance, a perfume

around *PREPOSITION*
❶ *The mermaid wore a coral necklace **around** her neck.*
• about, round, encircling, surrounding
❷ *There were **around** a hundred people in the audience.*
• about, approximately, roughly, more or less

arrange *VERB*
❶ *We **arranged** the chairs in rows.*
• to place, to set out, to order, to put in order, to group, to organise, to sort
❷ *Mum **arranged** a party for my birthday.*
• to plan, to organise, to prepare, to set up
❸ *I **arranged** to meet her after school.*
• to plan, to agree, to fix up

arrangement *NOUN*
❶ *They made an **arrangement** to meet.*
• an agreement, an appointment, a plan, a deal
❷ *We changed the **arrangement** of the chairs.*
• the organisation, the layout, the order, the grouping

arrest *VERB*
*The police **arrested** two men.*
• to seize, to capture, to detain, to catch, to take into custody

arrive *VERB*
*When is the train due to **arrive**?*
• to appear, to come, to come in, to turn up,
• to reach: *What time are we due **to reach** the station?*
— When a plane arrives, it lands or touches down.

arrogant *ADJECTIVE*
*His **arrogant** manner annoys me.*
• boastful, conceited, proud, haughty, pompous, superior, vain, cocky *(informal)*
OPPOSITE modest

A
B
C
D
E
F
G
H
I
J
K
L
M
N
O
P
Q
R
S
T
U
V
W
X
Y
Z

art NOUN

WORD WEB

SOME TYPES OF ART, CRAFT AND DESIGN:

• animation, ceramics, cartoon, collage, crochet, design, drawing, embroidery, engraving, fine art, graphics, illustration, jewellery, knitting, metalwork, modelling, mosaics, painting, photography, pottery, printing, screen printing, sculpture, sewing, sketching, stencilling, tapestry, textiles, watercolour, weaving, woodwork

ceramics

SOME ARTISTS AND CRAFTSPEOPLE:

• animator, cartoonist, designer, graphic artist, graphic designer, illustrator, jeweller, painter, photographer, potter, printer, sculptor, weaver

article NOUN
❶ *They sell various household **articles**.*
• an item, an object, a thing
❷ *I wrote an **article** for the school magazine.*
• a report, a piece, a column, an essay

artificial ADJECTIVE
❶ *Organic gardeners don't use **artificial** fertilisers.*
• man-made, manufactured
OPPOSITE natural
❷ *She had an **artificial** flower in her hair.*
• imitation, fake, false
OPPOSITES genuine, real

artistic ADJECTIVE
*Mum's flower arrangements are very **artistic**.*
• creative, imaginative, attractive, beautiful

ascend VERB
*He slowly **ascended** the mountain.*
• to climb, to go up, to mount, to scale, to move up, to rise up
OPPOSITE to descend

ascent NOUN
*The bus moved slowly up the steep **ascent**.*
• a climb, a rise, a slope, a hill, a gradient, an incline, a ramp
OPPOSITE a descent

ashamed ADJECTIVE
*He was **ashamed** because of what he had done.*
• sorry, repentant, remorseful, embarrassed, humiliated
OPPOSITES unashamed, unrepentant

ask VERB
*He **asked** me about my family.*
• to question, to enquire
*He **enquired** about my family.*
— To **consult** someone is to ask them about a subject they know a lot about.
➤ **to ask for**
*Oliver **asked for** more food.*
• to request, to demand, to beg for, to appeal for, to plead for

asleep ADJECTIVE
*I didn't hear the phone because I was **asleep**.*
• sleeping, dozing, having a nap, napping, snoozing, resting, slumbering *(old use)*
— An animal asleep for the winter is **hibernating**.
OPPOSITE awake
➤ **to fall asleep**
*We waited until the giant **fell asleep**.*
• to drop off, to doze off, to nod off

aspect NOUN
*What are the most interesting **aspects** of your job?*
• a part, a feature, an element, a quality, a detail

assemble VERB
❶ *A crowd **assembled** to watch the rescue.*
• to gather, to come together, to converge, to accumulate, to flock, to meet
OPPOSITE to disperse
❷ *He **assembled** the bookcase from a kit.*
• to put together, to build, to construct

assent NOUN
*The head teacher gave her **assent** to the plan.*
• agreement, approval, consent, permission
OPPOSITE refusal

assess VERB
*The test will **assess** your knowledge of French.*
• to judge, to gauge, to measure, to estimate, to grade

asset NOUN
*Good health is a great **asset**.*
• an advantage, a benefit, a help, an aid

assign VERB
*He **assigned** the difficult jobs to the older children.*
• to allocate, to give, to hand out, to distribute

assignment NOUN
*The spy was given a tough **assignment**.*
• a job, a task, a piece of work, a mission, a project, a duty, a responsibility

assist VERB
He offered to assist me with the work.
• to help, to aid, to support
OPPOSITE to hinder

assistance NOUN
Do you need any assistance with organising the trip?
• help, aid, support, backing

assistant NOUN
The magician was training a new assistant.
• a helper, a partner, a colleague, a supporter, a deputy

association NOUN
❶ *We have started a junior tennis association.*
• an organisation, a club, a society, a group, a league, a union, an alliance
❷ *There is a strong association between smoking and cancer.*
• a link, a connection, a relationship

assorted ADJECTIVE
The sweets come in assorted flavours.
• various, different, mixed, diverse, several

assortment NOUN
There was an assortment of sandwiches.
• a variety, a mixture, a selection, a range, a choice

assume VERB
I assume you know each other.
• to suppose, to presume, to imagine, to believe, to guess, to expect, to think

astonish VERB
It astonished me to see so many people there.
• to amaze, to astound, to surprise, to stun, to shock, to stagger, to startle

astonished ADJECTIVE
I was astonished by how much it cost.
• amazed, astounded, dumbfounded, surprised, stunned, shocked, speechless, staggered, startled, taken aback

ate (past tense of eat)

athletic ADJECTIVE
You need to be athletic to run a marathon.
• fit, active, energetic, strong, muscular, powerful, vigorous
OPPOSITES feeble, puny

assorted

athletics NOUN

discus

WORD WEB

SOME ATHLETIC EVENTS:

• cross-country, discus, javelin, shot-put, high jump, long jump, marathon, pole vault, sprint, hurdles, relay

SOME PEOPLE WHO TAKE PART IN ATHLETICS:

• an athlete, a runner, a sportsman or sportswoman, a cross-country runner, a sprinter, a hurdler, a high jumper, a long jumper, a pole vaulter
» *For ideas for writing about athletics look at sport.*

atmosphere NOUN
❶ *The atmosphere on Mars is unbreathable.*
• air, gases, environment
❷ *The place had a happy atmosphere.*
• a feeling, a mood, a spirit, an air

attach VERB
Attach this label to the parcel.
• to fasten, to fix, to join, to tie, to stick, to secure, to connect, to link
OPPOSITE to detach

attack VERB
The travellers were attacked by a bear.
• to assault, to set upon
— To **charge** is to suddenly rush towards someone to attack them.
— To **ambush** someone is to attack them suddenly from a hidden place.
— To **bombard** a place is to attack it with a lot of bullets or bombs.
— To **storm** or **raid** a place is to attack and rush into it suddenly.
— To **invade** is to enter and attack someone else's territory.

attack NOUN
The pirates' attack took us by surprise.
• an assault, a raid, a strike
— An **ambush** is a surprise attack from a hidden place.
— An **invasion** is an attack in which an army enters someone else's territory.

attempt VERB
They will attempt to break the record.
• to try, to endeavour, to strive, to seek, to aim, to make an effort

attempt *NOUN*
My first attempt to hit the target failed.
• a try, a go, an effort
— A **venture** or an **enterprise** is an attempt to do something new or difficult.

attend *VERB*
You must attend school regularly.
• to go to, to be present at, to appear at
➤ **to attend to**
She had some business to attend to.
• to take care of, to deal with, to sort out, to see to

attention *NOUN*
I was giving all my attention to my work.
• concentration, care, focus, consideration, thought, awareness
➤ **to pay attention to**
Please pay attention to the safety instructions.
• to listen to, to heed, to concentrate on, to focus on, to be aware of

attitude *NOUN*
She always has a very positive attitude.
• an approach, an outlook, a disposition, a view, a point of view, a viewpoint, a position

attract *VERB*
❶ *Does the idea of travelling in space attract you?*
• to interest, to appeal to, to fascinate, to tempt
❷ *Baby animals attract big crowds at the zoo.*
• to draw, to pull in
OPPOSITE to repel

attractive *ADJECTIVE*
❶ *Do you think the singer is attractive?*
• beautiful, good-looking, lovely
— An attractive man or boy is **handsome**.
— An attractive girl or woman is **pretty**.
— Someone who is very attractive is **gorgeous** or **stunning**.
— Someone or something that is attractive and exciting is **glamorous**.
OPPOSITE unattractive
❷ *It was a very attractive offer.*
• appealing, agreeable, interesting, desirable, tempting, irresistible

audience *NOUN*
The audience clapped and cheered.
• crowd, spectators
— A TV programme's **viewers** are its audience.
— A radio programme's **listeners** are its audience.

authority *NOUN*
She has the authority to spend money on behalf of the club.
• the power, the right, permission, approval

available *ADJECTIVE*
There is paper available for you to use.
• spare, free, on hand, accessible, at your disposal
OPPOSITE unavailable

average *ADJECTIVE*
It was an average kind of day at school.
• everyday, ordinary, normal, typical, usual, regular, commonplace, familiar
OPPOSITES special, extraordinary

avid *ADJECTIVE*
My sister is an avid reader.
• keen, eager, enthusiastic, passionate, fervent

avoid *VERB*
❶ *I avoid her when she's in a bad mood.*
• to get out of the way of, to keep away from, to keep clear of, to steer clear of
❷ *How did you manage to avoid the washing-up?*
• to escape, to evade, to get out of, to dodge

awake *ADJECTIVE*
I was awake for hours in the night.
• wide awake, restless, sleepless, conscious
OPPOSITE asleep

award *NOUN*
Her story won an award.
• a prize, a trophy, a medal

a trophy

aware *ADJECTIVE*
➤ **aware of**
The spy was aware of the dangers of the mission.
• conscious of, familiar with, informed about
OPPOSITE ignorant of

awful *ADJECTIVE*
What happened was really awful.
• dreadful, terrible, horrible, appalling, abominable, dire, abysmal
》 *For ideas for writing about being awful look at* **bad**.

awkward *ADJECTIVE*
❶ *The parcel was an awkward shape.*
• difficult, inconvenient, bulky, unmanageable, unwieldy
OPPOSITE convenient
❷ *We found ourselves in a very awkward situation.*
• difficult, tricky, troublesome, challenging
OPPOSITES straightforward, simple
❸ *I felt awkward as I didn't know anyone.*
• embarrassed, uncomfortable, uneasy, out of place
OPPOSITES comfortable, at ease

 How many different types of boat can you think of?

 Do you know the special words for 'left' and 'right' on a boat?

 Check the thesaurus to find answers!

baby NOUN
• an infant, a child
— A **newborn** is a baby who has just been born.
— A **toddler** is a baby who is learning to walk.

back NOUN
We always sit at the **back** of the bus.
• end, rear, tail end
— The back of a ship is the **stern**.
— The back of something with two sides is the **reverse**.
OPPOSITE front

back ADJECTIVE
The **back** door was locked.
• rear
— The back section of something long such as a plane is the **tail** section.
— The back legs of an animal are its **hind** legs.
OPPOSITE front

back VERB
➤ **to back away**
When the dog growled, he **backed away**.
• to retreat, to reverse, to move back, to recoil, to retire
OPPOSITE to approach
➤ **to back someone up**
Will you **back** me **up**?
• to support, to help, to stand up for, to stick up for

background NOUN
❶ I drew a horse with hills in the **background**.
OPPOSITE foreground
❷ Let me explain the **background** to the story.
• circumstances, lead-up
❸ I don't know anything about her **background**.
• family, childhood, upbringing

bad ADJECTIVE

😮 **OVERUSED WORD**

Try to use a more interesting word when you want to say **bad**. Here are some ideas and examples:

FOR A BAD PERSON OR CREATURE:
• wicked, evil, cruel, malevolent, malicious, vicious, mean, nasty, beastly, monstrous, horrible, horrid, deplorable, detestable, loathsome, immoral, diabolical
— Use **corrupt** for someone who uses their power in a bad way.
— Use **infamous** or **notorious** for someone who is well known for something bad.
Mrs Twit may have been ugly and she may have been beastly, but she was not stupid.—THE TWITS, Roald Dahl
— A bad person is a **rogue** or a **villain**.
OPPOSITES good, virtuous

a monstrous basilisk

FOR BAD BEHAVIOUR:
• naughty, mischievous, disobedient, disgraceful
That mischievous kitten drank my milk!
— A naughty person is a **rascal**.

FOR A BAD ACCIDENT, ILLNESS OR PAIN:
• serious, severe, grave, acute, major, terrible, appalling, dire
I remembered how Halfgrim had killed my father and the sorrow was so acute I was nearly sick.—SIGRUN'S SECRET, Marie-Louise Jensen
OPPOSITES minor, slight

FOR A BAD EXPERIENCE OR BAD NEWS:
• unpleasant, unwelcome, disagreeable, horrible, awful, terrible, dreadful, dire, horrific, appalling, shocking, hideous, disastrous, ghastly, frightful, abominable, diabolical
He'd been threatened with all sorts of dire punishments including being locked out for the night.—OLGA CARRIES ON, Michael Bond
— A very bad experience is an **ordeal**.
OPPOSITES good, pleasant

FOR A BAD PERFORMANCE OR BAD WORK:
• poor, weak, inferior, unsatisfactory, incompetent, awful, appalling, hopeless, terrible, useless, abysmal, rubbish *(informal)*
The story is good but the handwriting is appalling.
OPPOSITES good, skilled

FOR A BAD HABIT OR SOMETHING THAT IS BAD FOR YOU:

• harmful, damaging, dangerous, undesirable, unhealthy

Too much sugar is harmful.

OPPOSITES good, healthy

FOR FOOD THAT HAS GONE BAD:

• mouldy, decayed, spoiled
– Use **off** for meat, fish and milk.
– Use **sour** for milk or cream.
– Use **rotten** for fruit and vegetables.
The bread has gone mouldy.

OPPOSITE fresh

» *To describe bad smells look at* **smell**.
» *To describe food that tastes bad look at* **food**.
» *To say that someone feels bad about something look at* **guilty**.
» *To talk about bad timing look at* **inconvenient**.

bad-tempered *ADJECTIVE*
Trolls are always bad-tempered before breakfast.
• cross, grumpy, irritable, moody, quarrelsome, sullen, contrary
OPPOSITE good-tempered

bag *NOUN*
I put my wet clothes in a plastic bag.
• a sack, a handbag, a shoulder bag
– A **carrier bag** is a plastic or paper bag for putting shopping in.
– A **satchel** is a bag with a long strap, especially for books.
– A **briefcase** is a flat, usually hard bag for papers.
– A **holdall** or a **sports bag** is a large soft bag for sports clothes.
– A bag you carry on your back is a **backpack** or a **rucksack**.

baggy *ADJECTIVE*
The clown wore a pair of baggy trousers.
• loose, large, loose-fitting, roomy

bake *VERB*
» *For ways to cook things look at* **cook**.

ball *NOUN*
He rolled the pastry into a ball.
• a sphere, a globe
» *For games played with a ball look at* **sport**.

ban *VERB*
❶ *Smoking is banned in public places.*
• to forbid, to prohibit, to abolish, to outlaw
OPPOSITES to allow, to permit

❷ *She was banned from the competition.*
• to exclude, to disqualify, to eliminate

band *NOUN*
❶ *I play trumpet in the school band.*
• a group, an orchestra
❷ *They were attacked by a band of robbers.*
• a gang, a company, a group, a crew
❸ *The team captain wears a red band on his arm.*
• a strip, a stripe

bandit *NOUN*
Bandits used to live in these mountains.
• a robber, a brigand, a thief, an outlaw, a highwayman, a pirate, a buccaneer

bang *NOUN*
❶ *There was a loud bang as the balloon burst.*
• a blast, a boom, a crash, a thud, a thump, a pop, an explosion
» *For other types of noise look at* **sound**.

❷ *He got a bang on the head and felt dizzy.*
• a bump, a blow, a hit, a knock, a thump, a smack, a whack, a wallop *(informal)*

bang *VERB*
❶ *Someone was banging on the door.*
• to hammer, to pound, to knock, to thump
❷ *She fell and banged her knee.*
• to hit, to bump, to bash, to knock, to whack

banish *VERB*
The king's brother was banished forever.
• to exile, to expel, to send away, to eject

bank *NOUN*
❶ *They walked along the bank of the river.*
• the edge, the side, the shore, the margin
❷ *We rolled down a grassy bank.*
• a slope, a mound, a ridge, an embankment

bar *NOUN*
❶ *The window had iron bars across it.*
• a rod, a pole, a rail, a stake, a beam, a girder
❷ *Did you eat the whole bar of chocolate?*
• a block, a slab, a chunk, a wedge, a brick
— A bar of soap is a **cake**.
— A bar of gold or silver is an **ingot**.

ingots

bare *ADJECTIVE*
❶ *It's too cold to have bare arms.*
• naked, nude, exposed,
uncovered, unclothed, undressed
❷ *We slept outside on the bare mountain.*
• bleak, barren
❸ *The room was bare.*
• empty, unfurnished

barely *ADVERB*
We barely had time to eat.
• hardly, scarcely, only just

bargain *NOUN*
❶ *The jacket was a bargain.*
• a good buy, a special offer
— If something is a bargain, it is **good value**.
❷ *We made a bargain to help each other.*
• a deal, an agreement, a promise

bargain *VERB*
He refused to bargain with them.
• to argue, to do a deal, to haggle, to negotiate

barge *VERB*
➤ **to barge in**
He barged in right in the middle of the lesson.
• to interrupt, to push your way in, to shove your way in, to storm in
➤ **to barge into**
A woman barged into me with her shopping trolley.
• to bump into, to bash into, to shove, to collide with

bark *VERB*
The guard dog began to bark.
• to woof, to yap, to yelp, to growl, to snarl

barrel *NOUN*
The smugglers carried barrels of gunpowder.
• a cask, a tub, a butt, a drum

barren *ADJECTIVE*
All we could see was acres of barren land.
• dry, dried-up, arid, bare, bleak, lifeless, infertile
OPPOSITES fertile, lush

barrier *NOUN*
❶ *Spectators were asked to stay behind the barrier.*
• a wall, a fence, a railing, a barricade
❷ *His shyness was a barrier to making friends.*
• an obstacle, a hurdle, a drawback, a hindrance

base *NOUN*
❶ *The footprints stop at the base of the pyramid.*
• the bottom, the foot
❷ *We built the model on a wooden base.*
• a foundation, a support
— A base under a statue is a **pedestal** or **plinth**.
❸ *The explorers returned to their base.*
• a headquarters, a camp, a station, a depot

basic *ADJECTIVE*
❶ *These are the basic moves in ice skating.*
• main, chief, principal, key, central, essential, crucial
❷ *They just have a few basic tools.*
• elementary, simple, primitive, crude
OPPOSITE advanced

basically *ADVERB*
These two systems are basically the same.
• essentially, in essence

basin *NOUN*
Fill a basin with soapy water.
• a sink, a bowl, a dish

basis *NOUN*
What is the basis of your argument?
• the starting point, the foundation, the core

basket *NOUN*
— A basket of food is a **hamper**.
— A basket on a bicycle is a **pannier**.

bat *NOUN*
A bat is used in cricket, rounders and baseball.
— In tennis and badminton, you use a **racket**.
— In golf, you use a **club**.
— In snooker, you use a **cue**.
— In hockey, you use a **stick**.

batter *VERB*
Waves battered against the rocks.
• to beat, to pound, to hammer, to thump

battle *NOUN*
❶ *Many were killed in the battle.*
• a fight, a clash, a conflict, combat, action
❷ *She faced a tough battle to raise the money she needed.*
• a struggle, a fight, a campaign

bay *NOUN*
Dolphins were swimming in the bay.
• a cove, an inlet, a gulf, a harbour

a
b
c
d
e
f
g
h
i
j
k
l
m
n
o
p
q
r
s
t
u
v
w
x
y
z

beach NOUN

We found these shells on the beach.

• the sands, the seashore, the seaside, the shore, the shingle

» *For things you might see or do on a beach look at* **seashore** *and* **seaside**.

beam NOUN

❶ *Wooden beams ran across the ceiling.*

• a bar, a timber, a plank, a post, a pole, a rafter, a spar, a strut, a support

❷ *A beam of sunlight entered the cave.*

• a ray, a shaft, a stream, a gleam

beam VERB

We all beamed at the camera.

• to grin, to smile broadly

OPPOSITES to frown, to scowl

bean NOUN

kidney beans

⊛ **WORD WEB**

SOME TYPES OF BEAN:

• a broad bean, a green bean, a kidney bean, a runner bean, a soya bean

bear NOUN

⊛ **WORD WEB**

SOME TYPES OF BEAR:

• a black bear, a brown bear, a grizzly bear, a polar bear

— Koalas, **pandas** and **wombats** are similar to bears (although they are not actually bears).

— A toy bear is a **teddy bear.**

— A young bear is a **cub.**

— A bear lives in a **den** and **hibernates** in winter.

» *For other animals look at* **animal**.

bear VERB bears, bearing, bore, born or borne

❶ *The rope won't bear my weight.*

• to carry, to support, to hold, to take

❷ *The gravestone bears an inscription.*

• to display, to show, to have

❸ *The pain was too much to bear.*

• to put up with, to cope with, to stand, to suffer, to tolerate, to endure

beast NOUN

They heard a wild beast howl.

• an animal, a creature, a brute

— A **monster** is a large or frightening beast, especially one that only exists in stories.

beat VERB beats, beating, beat, beaten

❶ *I beat my brother at chess.*

• to defeat, to conquer, to vanquish, to win against, to overcome

— To **thrash** someone is to beat them very easily.

❷ *It's cruel to beat animals.*

• to hit, to strike, to thrash, to batter, to whip, to flog

❸ *Beat the eggs and milk together.*

• to whisk, to whip, to blend, to mix, to stir

❹ *Can you feel your heart beating?*

• to pulse

— If your heart **pounds**, **thumps** or **hammers**, it seems to beat very hard, for example because you are frightened.

beat NOUN

❶ *We clapped to the beat of the music.*

• a rhythm

❷ *Can you feel the beat of your heart?*

• a pulse, a throb

beautiful ADJECTIVE

😮 **OVERUSED WORD**

Try to use a more interesting word when you want to say **beautiful**. Here are some ideas and examples:

FOR A BEAUTIFUL PERSON:

• attractive, good-looking, lovely, charming

— Use **gorgeous** or **stunning** for someone who is very beautiful.

— Use **pretty** for an attractive girl or woman.

— Use **handsome** for an attractive man or boy.

— Use **glamorous** for someone who looks beautiful and rich.

— Use **radiant** for someone who looks beautiful and happy.

— Use **elegant** for someone who dresses and behaves beautifully.

— Use **graceful** for someone who moves in a beautiful way.

This balcony belonged to an attractive middle-aged lady called Mrs Silver . . . And although she didn't know it, it was she who was the object of Mr Hoppy's secret love.–ESIO TROT, Roald Dahl

OPPOSITES ugly, unattractive

FOR A BEAUTIFUL SIGHT:

• glorious, gorgeous, magnificent, splendid, spectacular, breathtaking

— Use **picturesque** for a place that is pretty and charming.

18

— Use **exquisite** for something delicate and beautiful: *an **exquisite** lace tablecloth*
They were travelling through spectacular mountain scenery: soaring peaks, snowcovered slopes, and thick forests of pine trees.—DRAGONFLY, Julia Golding

beauty NOUN
❶ *The film star was famous for her **beauty**.*
• attractiveness, prettiness, loveliness, charm
— Use **glamour** if someone looks beautiful and rich.
`OPPOSITE` ugliness
❷ *I was amazed by the **beauty** of the mountains.*
• splendour, magnificence, glory, loveliness

beckon VERB
*The guard was **beckoning** me to approach.*
• to signal, to gesture, to motion

become VERB becomes, becoming, became, become
❶ *I soon **became** frustrated with the video game.*
• to begin to be, to get, to grow, to turn
❷ *Eventually, the tadpoles will **become** frogs.*
• to grow into, to change into, to develop into, to turn into

bed NOUN

 WORD WEB

SOME TYPES OF BED:

— A bed for a baby is a **cot**, a **cradle** or a **crib**.
— Two single beds one above the other are **bunk beds**.
— A bed on a ship or train is a **berth**.
— A bed made of net or cloth hung up above the ground is a **hammock**.
— A **four-poster bed** is a bed with curtains around it.

bee NOUN

 WORD WEB

SOME TYPES OF BEE:

• a **bumblebee**, a **honeybee**, a **queen** (bee), a **worker** (bee)
— A male bee that does not work is a **drone**.
— A young bee after it hatches is a **larva**.
— A group of bees is a **swarm** or a **colony**.
— A place where bees live is a **hive**.
— A person who looks after bees and collects their honey is a **beekeeper**.
» *For other insects look at **insect**.*

before ADVERB
❶ *Have you used a camera **before**?*
• previously, in the past, earlier, sooner
— To happen before something else is to **precede** it: *What **preceded** this incident?*
`OPPOSITE` later
❷ *Those people were **before** us in the queue.*
• in front of, ahead of
— To come or go before something or someone else is to **precede** them: *He allowed the Princess to **precede** him into the room.*
`OPPOSITE` after

beg VERB
*He **begged** me not to let go of the rope.*
• to ask, to plead with, to entreat, to implore

begin VERB begins, beginning, began, begun
❶ *The hunters **began** their search at dawn.*
• to start, to commence, to embark on, to set about
`OPPOSITES` to end, to finish, to conclude
❷ *When did the trouble **begin**?*
• to start, to commence, to arise, to emerge, to appear, to originate
`OPPOSITES` to end, to stop, to cease

beginner NOUN
*This swimming class is for **beginners**.*
• a learner, a starter, a novice
— A beginner in a trade or a job is an **apprentice** or a **trainee**.
— A beginner in the police or army is a **cadet** or a **recruit**.

beginning NOUN
*I liked the **beginning** of the story.*
• the start, the opening, the commencement
— A section at the beginning of a book or film is an **introduction**, **preface** or **prologue**.
— The way that something first begins is its **origin**: *What is the **origin** of this custom?*
— The beginning of something new that did not exist before is its **appearance** or **emergence**: *We saw the **emergence** of many new technologies.*
— The beginning of an organisation or business is its **establishment**, **founding** or **setting up**: *She has worked for the charity since its **founding**.*
`OPPOSITES` the end, the ending

behave VERB
❶ *He was **behaving** very strangely.*
• to act, to react
❷ *If you let me come, I promise to **behave**.*
• to behave yourself, to be good, to be on your best behaviour

A
B
C
D
E
F
G
H
I
J
K
L
M
N
O
P
Q
R
S
T
U
V
W
X
Y
Z

behaviour NOUN
I give my puppy treats for good behaviour.
• conduct, manners, attitude

being NOUN
They looked like beings from another planet.
• a creature, an individual, a person

belief NOUN
❶ *She was a woman of strong religious beliefs.*
• a faith, a principle
❷ *It is my belief that he stole the money.*
• an opinion, a view, a conviction, a feeling, a notion, a theory

believe VERB
❶ *I don't believe anything he says.*
• to accept, to have faith in, to rely on, to trust
OPPOSITES to disbelieve, to doubt
❷ *I believe they used to live in Canada.*
• to think, to understand, to reckon

bell NOUN

WRITING TIPS

You can use these words to describe the sound of a **bell**:
• to chime, to ring, to jingle, to jangle
— To **clang** is to make a loud heavy ringing sound.
— To **tinkle** is to make a light high ringing sound.
— To **toll** is to ring slowly and repeatedly with a low sound.
— To **peal** is to ring loudly.
— The **peal** of bells is a loud ringing sound, for example from a church.
They wore round hats ... with little bells around the brims that tinkled sweetly as they moved.
—THE WONDERFUL WIZARD OF OZ, L. Frank Baum

belong VERB
❶ *This ring belonged to my grandmother.*
• to be owned by
❷ *I belong to the drama club.*
• to be a member of, to be in, to have joined

belongings NOUN
Don't leave any belongings on the bus.
• possessions, property, things

belt NOUN
The prince wore a belt of pure gold.
• a girdle, a sash, a strap, a band

bend VERB bends, bending, bent
❶ *The trees bent in the wind.*
• to curve, to bow *(rhymes with* cow*)*, to twist, to turn, to arch, to warp
— Something that bends easily is flexible.
OPPOSITE to straighten
❷ *She bent to tie her shoelace.*
• to bend down, to stoop, to crouch, to hunch, to lean over
— To **bow** or **nod** your head is to bend it downwards.
— To **duck** is to bend down suddenly to avoid being hit by something.

bend NOUN
There is a bend in the road.
• a curve, a turn, an angle, a corner, a twist, a zigzag

benefit NOUN
❶ *Exercise has a lot of benefits.*
• an advantage, a reward, a use, a good point
OPPOSITES a disadvantage, a drawback
❷ *I'm doing this for your benefit.*
• welfare, sake

benefit VERB
The rain will benefit gardeners.
• to help, to aid, to assist, to be good for
OPPOSITES to harm, to hinder

bent ADJECTIVE
❶ *After the crash, the car was a mass of bent metal.*
• curved, twisted, warped, distorted, crooked, coiled, buckled, folded, gnarled
❷ *The old man had a bent back.*
• crooked, hunched, curved, arched, bowed *(rhymes with* loud*)*
OPPOSITE straight

berry NOUN

WORD WEB

SOME TYPES OF BERRY:

• a blackberry, a blackcurrant, a blueberry, a cranberry, a currant, an elderberry, a gooseberry, a mulberry, a raspberry, a redcurrant, a strawberry

mulberries

besides ADVERB
❶ *No one knows the secret, besides you and me.*
• in addition to, as well as, apart from, other than
❷ *It's too cold to go out. Besides, it's dark now.*
• also, in addition, additionally, furthermore, moreover

best ADJECTIVE
She is our best goalkeeper.
• top, leading, finest, foremost, supreme, prime, primary, ultimate, star
OPPOSITE worst

bet *VERB* **bets, betting, bet** or **betted**

❶ *I bet you 50 pence that it will snow tomorrow.*
• to gamble, to wager, to stake, to risk

❷ *I bet my brother will forget my birthday.*
• to feel sure, to be certain, to be positive, to expect

betray *VERB*

He betrayed us by telling the enemy our plan.
• to be disloyal to, to be a traitor to, to cheat, to let down
— Someone who betrays you is a **traitor**.
— To betray your country is to commit **treason**.

better *ADJECTIVE*

❶ *Which of these songs do you think is better?*
• superior, preferable
— If one thing or person is better than another, you can say that they **surpass** them or **outdo** them: *All her books are good, but the last one outdid all the rest.*

❷ *I had a cold, but I'm better now.*
• recovered, cured, healed, improved, well

beware *VERB*

Beware! There are pickpockets.
• to be careful, to watch out, to look out, to take care, to be on your guard
➤ **beware of**
Beware of the bull.
• to watch out for, to mind, to heed, to keep clear of

bewilder *VERB*

The instructions bewildered me.
• to confuse, to puzzle, to baffle, to mystify, to perplex

bicycle *NOUN*
• a bike, a cycle

a penny-farthing

🕸 **WORD WEB**

SOME TYPES OF BICYCLE:

• a mountain bike, a racing bike, a road bike
— A **tandem** is a bicycle with seats for two people, one behind the other.
— A **tricycle** or **trike** is a bicycle with three wheels.
— A **unicycle** is a bicycle with one wheel.
— A **penny-farthing** was a type of bicycle used in the past, with one very large and one very small wheel.
— Someone who rides a bicycle is a **cyclist**.

big *ADJECTIVE*

😮 **OVERUSED WORD**

Try to use a more interesting word when you want to say **big**. Here are some ideas and examples:

FOR SOMETHING BIG IN SIZE, WEIGHT OR POWER:

• large, huge, enormous, massive, great, gigantic, tremendous, terrific, colossal, mammoth, humungous *(informal)*, ginormous *(informal)*
OPPOSITES small, little, tiny
At the very same moment a colossal explosion erupted below.—TOM SCATTERHORN: THE FORGOTTEN ECHO, Henry Chancellor

FOR A BIG PERSON OR BIG CREATURE:

• giant, hefty, burly, mighty, monstrous, towering, looming
Alazandr turned to these monstrous insects hacking quickly through the trees.—LYDIA'S TIN LID DRUM, Neale Osborne

FOR A BIG DISTANCE OR BIG AREA:

• immense, vast, infinite
A vast stretch of ocean lay before them.

FOR SOMETHING BIG INSIDE:

• roomy, spacious
Inside, the spaceship was surprisingly roomy.
OPPOSITE cramped

FOR A BIG MEAL OR BIG PORTION:

• hearty, considerable, substantial, generous
We each got a generous helping of porridge.
OPPOSITE meagre

FOR A BIG DECISION OR BIG PROBLEM:

• important, significant, major, serious, grave
They took grave risks and failed.
—THE CHIMERA'S CURSE, Julia Golding
OPPOSITES insignificant, minor

a towering Cyclops

bind *VERB* **binds, binding, bound**
*We **bound** the sticks together with some rope.*
• to attach, to fasten, to tie, to secure, to join, to lash, to connect

bird *NOUN*

 WORD WEB

— A female bird is a **hen**.
— A male bird is a **cock**.
— A young bird is a **chick** or **fledgling**.
— A person who studies birds is an **ornithologist**.

SPECIAL NAMES:

— A female peacock is a **peahen**.
— A young duck is a **duckling**.
— A young goose is a **gosling**.
— A young puffin is a **puffling**.
— A young swan is a **cygnet**.
— An eagle's nest is an **eyrie**.
— A place where rooks nest is a **rookery**.

SOME COMMON BRITISH BIRDS:

• blackbird, blue tit, chaffinch, crow, cuckoo, dove, goldfinch, jackdaw, jay, lark, magpie, martin, nightingale, peewit, pigeon, raven, robin, rook, skylark, sparrow, starling, swallow, swift, thrush, tit, wagtail, woodpecker, wren

BIRDS OF PREY:

• buzzard, eagle, falcon, hawk, kestrel, kite, osprey, owl, vulture

a buzzard

FARM AND GAME BIRDS:

• chicken, duck, goose, grouse, partridge, pheasant, quail, turkey
— Birds kept by farmers are called **poultry**.

SEA AND WATER BIRDS:

• albatross, auk, coot, cormorant, crane, duck, gannet, goose, gull, heron, kingfisher, lapwing, moorhen, pelican, penguin, plover, puffin, seagull, stork, swan

BIRDS FROM OTHER COUNTRIES:

• budgerigar, canary, cockatoo, emu, flamingo, hummingbird, kiwi, kookaburra, macaw, ostrich, parakeet, parrot, peacock, toucan

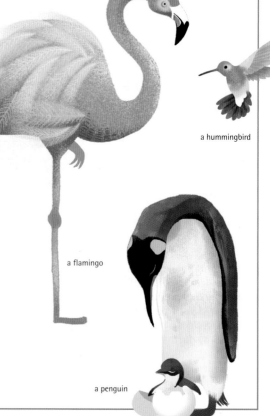

a hummingbird

a flamingo

a peacock

a penguin

22

a
b
c
d
e
f
g
h
i
j
k
l
m
n
o
p
q
r
s
t
u
v
w
x
y
z

WRITING TIPS

Here are some useful words for writing about **birds**:

TO DESCRIBE HOW A BIRD MOVES:

• to dart, to flit, to flutter, to fly, to hover, to glide, to soar, to swoop, to hop, to peck, to perch
— When a bird cleans its feathers, it **preens**.
— When a bird sits somewhere to sleep, it **roosts**.
The post owls arrived, swooping down through rain-flecked windows, scattering everyone with droplets of water.
—HARRY POTTER AND THE HALF-BLOOD PRINCE, J. K. Rowling

TO DESCRIBE NOISES A BIRD MAKES:

• to tweet, to twitter, to chirp, to cheep, to sing, to pipe, to warble, to call, to screech, to shriek, to squawk
— An owl **hoots**.
— A pigeon or a dove **coos**.
— A hen **clucks**.
— A duck **quacks**.
— A goose **honks**.
— A turkey **gobbles**.

bit NOUN
Would you like another bit of cake?
• a piece, a portion, a part, a section, a segment, a share, a slice
➤ **a bit**
These jeans are a bit small.
• slightly, a little, rather, fairly, quite

OVERUSED WORD

Try to use a more interesting word when you want to say **bit**. Here are some ideas and examples:

FOR A LARGE BIT OF SOMETHING:

• a chunk, a lump, a hunk, a wedge, a slab, a block
And they all went over to the tunnel entrance and began scooping out great chunks of juicy, golden-coloured peach flesh.—JAMES AND THE GIANT PEACH, Roald Dahl

FOR A SMALL BIT OF SOMETHING:

• a fragment, a scrap, a particle, a speck
— A **sliver** is a small thin bit.
— A **chip** is a small bit that has broken off something.
— A **shred** is a small bit torn off something.
— A **dash**, **splash** or **spot** is a small bit of liquid.
— A **dab** is a small bit of a liquid or soft substance.
— A **pinch** is a small bit of a powder.
The vase . . . smashed against the wall behind him, and then rained down in tiny fragments.—OLAF THE VIKING PIG WHO WOULD BE KING, Martin Conway

FOR A BIT OF FOOD:

• a morsel, a crumb, a bite, a nibble, a taste, a mouthful
He begged them for a morsel of cake.

bite VERB bites, biting, bit, bitten
❶ *I bit a chunk out of my apple.*
• to chew, to crunch, to munch, to nibble, to gnaw
» *For other ways to eat look at* **eat**.

❷ *I was afraid the dog would bite.*
• to nip, to snap
— When an insect bites, it **stings**.

bitter ADJECTIVE
❶ *The medicine had a bitter taste.*
• sharp, acrid, sour, acid, tart
OPPOSITE sweet
❷ *There was a bitter wind.*
• biting, cold, freezing, icy, piercing, raw, wintry
OPPOSITE mild
❸ *His brother was still bitter about the quarrel.*
• resentful, angry
— To be bitter about something is to **bear a grudge**.

bizarre ADJECTIVE
'Whiskers' is a bizarre name for a goldfish!
• odd, strange, peculiar, weird, extraordinary
OPPOSITE ordinary

black ADJECTIVE, NOUN
❶ *She had shiny black hair.*
• coal-black, jet-black, pitch-black, ebony, raven
— You can say something is **as black as coal**, **as black as pitch** or **as black as night**.
❷ *The sky was black.*
• dark, pitch-black, pitch-dark, moonless, starless
OPPOSITES light, bright

blame VERB
Don't blame me if you miss the bus.
• to accuse, to criticise, to put the blame on, to condemn, to reproach

bland ADJECTIVE
This cheese has a really bland taste.
• mild, dull, weak
OPPOSITES strong, pungent

blank ADJECTIVE
❶ *I have one blank page left.*
• empty, bare, clean, plain
❷ *She gave us a blank look.*
• vacant, expressionless, emotionless

blanket NOUN
❶ *The baby was wrapped in a **blanket**.*
• a cover, a bedspread, a quilt, a rug
❷ *A **blanket** of snow covered the lawn.*
• a covering, a layer, a sheet, a mantle

blast NOUN
*A **blast** of cold air came through the door.*
• a gust, a rush, a draught, a burst

blatant ADJECTIVE
*Do you expect me to believe such a **blatant** lie?*
• obvious, shameless, brazen

blaze NOUN
*Firefighters fought the **blaze** for hours.*
• a fire, flames, an inferno

blaze VERB
*Within a few minutes the campfire was **blazing**.*
• to burn brightly, to flare up

bleak ADJECTIVE
❶ *The countryside was **bleak** and barren.*
• bare, barren, desolate, empty, exposed
❷ *The future looks **bleak** for the club.*
• gloomy, hopeless, depressing, dismal, grim, miserable
OPPOSITE promising

blend VERB
Blend the flour with a tablespoon of water.
• to beat together, to mix, to combine, to stir together, to whip, to whisk

blend NOUN
*This paint colour is a **blend** of red, yellow and white.*
• a mixture, a mix, a combination

blew (past tense of **blow**)

bliss NOUN
*Having a whole day off school was sheer **bliss**.*
• joy, delight, pleasure, happiness, ecstasy
OPPOSITE misery

blob NOUN
*The alien left **blobs** of green slime on the carpet.*
• a drop, a lump, a spot, a dollop

block NOUN
❶ *A **block** of ice fell from the glacier.*
• a chunk, a hunk, a lump, a slab, a brick, a piece
❷ *There must be a **block** in the pipe.*
• a blockage, a jam, an obstacle

block VERB
❶ *Leaves had **blocked** the drain.*
• to clog, to jam, to plug, to stop up
❷ *Something was **blocking** my messages so they could not get through.*
• to bar, to hinder, to cut off, to intercept, to stop

bloom NOUN
*The pear tree was covered in white **blooms**.*
• a flower, a bud
— Blossom is a mass of flowers or blooms.

bloom VERB
*The daffodils **bloomed** early this year.*
• to blossom, to flower, to open
OPPOSITE to fade

blot NOUN
*The old map was covered with ink **blots**.*
• a spot, a mark, a blob, a splodge, a smudge, a smear, a stain

blot VERB
➤ **to blot something out**
*A dark cloud **blotted out** the sun.*
• to block, to cover, to conceal, to hide, to mask, to obscure

blow VERB blows, blowing, blew, blown
❶ *The wind was **blowing** from the east.*
• to blast, to gust, to puff
❷ *The flags **blew** in the wind.*
• to wave, to flap, to flutter, to billow
➤ **to blow up**
❶ *I need to **blow up** the tyres on my bike.*
• to inflate, to pump up, to fill
❷ *The soldiers tried to **blow up** the enemy hideout.*
• to bomb, to explode, to blast, to destroy

blow NOUN
*He was knocked out by a **blow** on the head.*
• a knock, a bang, a bash, a hit, a punch, a slap, a smack, a thump, a whack

blown (past participle of **blow**)

blue ADJECTIVE, NOUN

 WORD WEB

SOME SHADES OF BLUE:

• azure, indigo, navy blue, royal blue, sapphire, sky-blue, turquoise

blunt ADJECTIVE
❶ *This pencil is **blunt**.*
• dull
OPPOSITES sharp, pointed
❷ *Her reply to my question was very **blunt**.*
• frank, direct, plain, tactless
OPPOSITE tactful

blur ADJECTIVE
*The day passed in a **blur**.*
• a daze, a haze, a mist

blur VERB
*Tears **blurred** my vision.*
• to cloud, to obscure

blurry ADJECTIVE
*The photograph is **blurry**.*
• blurred, indistinct, unclear, fuzzy, hazy,
out of focus, vague
OPPOSITES clear, distinct

blush VERB
*I **blushed** with embarrassment.*
• to flush, to go red, to redden, to colour
— You can say that someone's cheeks **burn** when
they blush.

board NOUN
*The table top was made from a wooden **board**.*
• a plank, a panel, a beam, a timber
» For board games look at **game**.

board VERB
*We **boarded** the plane for New York.*
• to get on, to enter, to embark

boast VERB
*The knight was always **boasting** about his
exploits.*
• to brag, to show off, to gloat, to swagger

boat NOUN
*Several fishing **boats** were moored in the harbour.*
• a ship, a craft, a vessel

 **WORD WEB**

SOME TYPES OF BOAT OR SHIP:

• a barge, a canoe, a dinghy, a ferry, a fishing
boat, a galleon, a hovercraft, a houseboat,
a junk, a kayak, a lifeboat, a liner, a longship,
a motorboat, a raft, a rowing boat, a sailing
boat, a schooner, a speedboat, a steamship or
steamer, a submarine, a tanker, a trawler,
a warship, a yacht

WORDS FOR PARTS OF A BOAT OR SHIP:

• the anchor, the bridge, a cabin, the crow's
nest, the deck, the engine room, a funnel,
a gangplank, a gangway, the helm, the hull,
the jib, the keel, a mast, a porthole, a propeller,
the rigging, the rudder, a sail, a spar, the tiller
*The ocean rushes beneath us, a constant stream
of white noise. Waves slap against Moana's hull,
like a heartbeat.*—WHITE DOLPHIN, Gill Lewis

SPECIAL NAMES:

— The front part of a boat is the bow or **prow**.
— The back part of a boat is the **stern**.
— A bed on a boat is called a **berth**.
— The left-hand side of a boat is called **port**.
— The right-hand side of a boat is called **starboard**.

 WRITING TIPS

Here are some useful words for writing about
how a boat moves:
• to sail, to steam, to drift, to float, to glide,
to bob, to roll
— If a boat turns over, it **capsizes**.
— The **wake** of a boat is the trail it leaves in the water.
*So the boat was left to drift down the stream as
it would, till it glided gently in among the waving
rushes.*—ALICE THROUGH THE LOOKING-GLASS, Lewis Carroll

SOME WORDS FOR WRITING ABOUT SAILING
OR TRAVELLING IN A BOAT:

• to launch, to cast off, to navigate, to pilot,
to paddle, to row
— To **stow away** on a boat is to hide and secretly
travel on it.
— To **moor** a boat is to tie it up.
— To **scuttle** a boat is to deliberately sink it.

bob VERB
*A plastic duck **bobbed** up and down in the water.*
• to bounce, to float, to toss, to wobble

body NOUN

 WORD WEB

— The main part of your body except your head,
arms and legs is your **torso**.
— The dead body of a person is a **corpse**.
— The dead body of an animal is a **carcass**.
— The study of the human body is **anatomy**.
— The adjective **physical** means 'relating to the body':
*Is it a **physical** problem?*

a
b
c
d
e
f
g
h
i
j
k
l
m
n
o
p
q
r
s
t
u
v
w
x
y
z

bog NOUN
*We felt our boots sinking into the **bog**.*
• a swamp, a marsh, quicksand

boil VERB
*The water must be **boiling** before you add the pasta.*
• to bubble, to seethe, to steam
» *For ways to cook food look at* **cook**.

bold ADJECTIVE
❶ *It was a **bold** move to attack the fortress.*
• brave, courageous, daring, adventurous, ambitious, confident, fearless, heroic, valiant, intrepid, plucky
OPPOSITE timid
❷ *Use **bold** colours for your poster.*
• striking, strong, bright, loud, showy, conspicuous, noticeable, prominent
OPPOSITES inconspicuous, subtle

bolt VERB
❶ *She **bolted** for the exit.*
• to flee, to dash, to dart, to sprint, to run, to rush
❷ *Did you remember to **bolt** the door?*
• to fasten, to latch, to lock, to secure, to bar

bone NOUN

 WORD WEB

SOME BONES IN THE HUMAN BODY:

— The bones of your body are your **skeleton**.
• backbone or spine, collarbone, pelvis, ribs, shoulder blade, skull

book NOUN
• a text, a publication
— One book is a **copy** or an **edition**.
— One book which is part of a set is a **volume**.
— A book with hard covers is a **hardback**.
— A book with soft covers is a **paperback**.
— A thin book with paper covers is a **booklet**, **leaflet** or **pamphlet**.

 WORD WEB

SOME TYPES OF BOOK:

• an annual, an anthology, an atlas, an audiobook, an autobiography, a biography, a brochure, a catalogue, a comic or comic book, a diary, a dictionary, a directory, an e-book, an encyclopedia, a manual, a notebook, a novel, a picture book, a reading book, a reference book, a story book, a textbook, a thesaurus

book VERB
*Have you **booked** a seat on the train?*
• to reserve, to order, to arrange

boom VERB
*The head teacher's voice **boomed** along the corridor.*
• to shout, to roar, to bellow, to blast, to thunder, to resound

boost VERB
*Scoring a goal really **boosted** our morale.*
• to raise, to improve, to increase, to help, to encourage, to enhance
OPPOSITE to lower

boot NOUN
» *For types of shoe or boot look at* **shoe**.

border NOUN
❶ *The town is on the **border** between France and Germany.*
• a boundary, a frontier
❷ *I drew a thin line around the **border** of the picture.*
• the edge, the margin, the perimeter
— A decorative border around the top of a wall is a **frieze**.
— A decorative border on fabric is a **frill**, **fringe** or **trim**.
— A border around the bottom of a piece of clothing is a **hem**.

bore (*past tense of* **bear**)

bored ADJECTIVE
*I was **bored** and started looking out of the window.*
• uninterested, uninspired, restless
➤ **be bored of**
*I'm **bored of** this game now.*
• be tired of, be fed up with, have had enough of

boring ADJECTIVE
*The film was so **boring** I fell asleep.*
• dull, dreary, tedious, tiresome, unexciting, uninteresting, unimaginative, unoriginal, uninspiring, bland
— Use **monotonous** for something that is boring because it always stays the same.
OPPOSITES interesting, exciting

SOME PARTS OF A BOOK:

• an appendix, a bibliography, a blurb, a chapter, the contents, the cover, a dedication, an illustration, an index, an introduction, the jacket, a preface, the title page

born (also **borne**) (past participle of **bear**)

borrow VERB
Can I borrow your pencil?
• to use, to take
OPPOSITE to lend

boss NOUN
❶ *Who is the boss here?*
• the chief, the head, the leader, the owner,
the proprietor, the person in charge
❷ *Her boss said she could have the day off.*
• an employer, a manager, a supervisor, a director

bossy ADJECTIVE
Stop being so bossy.
• domineering, bullying, controlling

bother VERB
❶ *Would it bother you if I played some music?*
• to upset, to annoy, to irritate, to worry, to vex
❷ *Sorry to bother you, but I need some help.*
• to disturb, to interrupt, to trouble, to pester
— To **harass** someone is to keep bothering them
when they do not want you to.
❸ *He didn't bother to apologise.*
• to make an effort, to take the
trouble, to concern yourself

bother NOUN
*I'm sorry for all the bother
I caused.*
• trouble, inconvenience,
disturbance, upheaval,
annoyance, difficulty,
hassle (informal)

bottle NOUN
Bring a bottle of water with you.
• a flask, a jar

bottom NOUN
❶ *We camped at the bottom of the mountain.*
• the foot, the base
OPPOSITES the top, the summit
❷ *The wreck sank to the bottom of the sea.*
• the bed, the floor
OPPOSITE the surface
❸ *A wasp stung me on the bottom.*
• the backside, the behind, the buttocks, the rear,
the rump

bought (past tense of **buy**)

bounce VERB
The ball bounced twice before it reached the net.
• to rebound, to ricochet, to deflect

bound (past tense of **bind**)

bound ADJECTIVE
❶ *It's bound to rain at the weekend.*
• certain, sure
❷ *The accident was bound to happen.*
• destined, doomed, fated
➤ **bound for**
The space rocket was bound for Mars.
• going to, heading for, making for, travelling
towards, off to

bound VERB
The puppies bounded across the lawn.
• to leap, to bounce, to jump, to spring, to skip,
to frisk

boundary NOUN
The lamp post marks the boundary of Narnia.
• the border, the frontier, the edge, the end,
the limit, the perimeter, the dividing line

bowl NOUN
There was a bowl of fresh fruit on the table.
• a basin, a dish

box NOUN
We took the toys out of the box.
• a case, a chest, a crate, a carton, a packet
— A **trunk** is a large box for luggage.

boy NOUN
• a lad, a youngster, a youth,
a kid (informal), a child, a teenager,
a teen

brag VERB
She was bragging about her victory.
• to show off, to boast, to gloat

a brain

brain NOUN
You'll need to use your brain to solve this riddle.
• intelligence, mind, reason, sense, wit

branch NOUN
A robin perched on a branch of the tree.
• a bough, a limb

branch VERB
Follow the track until it branches into two.
• to divide, to fork

brand NOUN
Which brand of ice cream do you like?
• a make, a kind, a sort, a type, a variety, a label
— A **trademark** is the official name of a brand.
— A **logo** is a symbol or design used by a brand.

a b c d e f g h i j k l m n o p q r s t u v w x y z

brandish VERB
Captain Hook **brandished** his cutlass at the crew.
• to flourish, to wield, to wave

brave ADJECTIVE
It was **brave** of you to stand up to the bullies.
• courageous, heroic, valiant, fearless, daring, bold, gallant, intrepid, plucky
— You can say that someone is as **brave** as a lion or lion-hearted.
OPPOSITE cowardly

bravery NOUN
She won a medal for **bravery**.
• courage, heroism, valour, fearlessness, boldness, daring, nerve
OPPOSITE cowardice

break VERB breaks, breaking, broke, broken
❶ The vase fell off the shelf and **broke**.
• to crack, to get broken
— Use **smash**, **shatter** or **splinter** when something breaks into a lot of sharp pieces.
— Use **chip** when a small piece breaks off something.
— Use **crumble** when something breaks into many small pieces.
— Use **snap** when something hard breaks in two.
— Use **split** when something bursts or breaks in two.
❷ My brother **broke** my phone.
• to damage, to wreck, to ruin
❸ The burglar was arrested for **breaking** the law.
• to disobey, to disregard, to go against
❹ In her last race, she **broke** the world record.
• to beat, to exceed, to surpass, to outdo
➤ to break down
Our car **broke down** on the motorway.
• to fail, to go wrong, to stop working
➤ to break off
She **broke off** for a moment, then started speaking again.
• to pause, to stop
➤ to break out
Fighting **broke out**.
• to begin, to start, to spread
➤ to break up
The crowd started to **break up**.
• to disperse, to disintegrate, to dissolve, to come apart

break NOUN
❶ Let's take a **break**.
• a pause, an interval, a rest
— Use a **lull** for a short period of quiet or calm:
There was a **lull** in the storm.

❷ I saw a **break** in the cloud.
• a gap, an opening, a hole, a crack, a split, a rift
— A **fracture** is a break in a bone.
— A **fissure** is a narrow break in rock.

breakthrough NOUN
Scientists have made a **breakthrough** in medicine.
• an advance, a leap forward, a discovery, a development, a revolution, progress
OPPOSITE a setback

breath NOUN
❶ There wasn't a **breath** of wind.
• a breeze, a puff, a waft
❷ Take a deep **breath**.
— A breath in is an **inhalation**.
— A breath out is an **exhalation**.

breathe VERB
• to respire
— To breathe in is to **inhale**.
— To breathe out is to **exhale**.
— To breathe heavily when you have been running is to **pant**, to **puff** or to **gasp**.
— The formal word for breathing is **respiration**.

breathless ADJECTIVE
Leo was **breathless** after the race.
• out of breath, gasping, panting, puffing, tired out, wheezing

breed VERB breeds, breeding, bred
Salmon swim upstream to **breed** every year.
• to reproduce, to have young, to multiply

breed NOUN
What **breed** of dog is that?
• a kind, a sort, a type, a variety
— A dog from a single breed is a **pedigree** dog.

bridge NOUN

WORD WEB

— A **footbridge** is a bridge for people to walk over.
— A **flyover** is a bridge that carries a road over another road.
— An **aqueduct** is a bridge that carries water across a valley.
— A **viaduct** is a bridge that carries a road or railway across a valley.
— A **drawbridge** is a bridge across the moat of a castle.
— A **gangway** is a movable bridge for getting on or off a ship.

brief *ADJECTIVE*
❶ *We paid them a brief visit.*
• short, quick, hasty, fleeting, temporary, momentary
❷ *Give me a brief account of what happened.*
• short, concise, abbreviated, compact
OPPOSITES long, lengthy

bright *ADJECTIVE*
❶ *We saw the bright lights of the town in the distance.*
• shining, brilliant, blazing, dazzling, glaring, gleaming
OPPOSITES dull, dim, faint
❷ *Bright colours will make the poster stand out.*
• strong, intense, bold, vivid, showy, gaudy
— Colours that shine in the dark are **luminous** or **fluorescent**.
OPPOSITES dull, faded, pastel
❸ *Her teachers thought she was very bright.*
• clever, intelligent, gifted, sharp, smart, quick, brainy *(informal)*
❹ *It was a cold bright day.*
• sunny, clear, fine, light
OPPOSITES dull, overcast, dark

brighten *VERB*
➤ **to brighten up**
She brightened up when she saw us.
• to cheer up, to light up, to liven up

brilliant *ADJECTIVE*
❶ *Brunel was a brilliant engineer.*
• clever, exceptional, outstanding, gifted, talented
OPPOSITES incompetent, talentless
❷ *The fireworks gave off a brilliant light.*
• bright, blazing, dazzling, glaring, gleaming, glittering, glorious, shining, splendid, vivid
OPPOSITES dim, dull, faint
❸ *(informal) I saw a brilliant film last week.*
• excellent, marvellous, outstanding, wonderful, superb, fantastic, fabulous
» *Look at* **good**.

brim *NOUN*
I filled my glass to the brim.
• the top, the rim, the edge, the brink, the lip

bring *VERB* **brings, bringing, brought**
❶ *Can you bring the shopping in from the car?*
• to carry, to fetch, to get, to deliver, to transport
❷ *His dad brought him to the party.*
• to escort, to come with, to conduct, to guide, to lead
➤ **to bring something about**
The new coach brought about some changes.
• to cause, to create, to introduce, to produce, to be responsible for, to generate

➤ **to bring someone up**
In the story, Tarzan is brought up by apes.
• to rear, to raise, to care for, to look after, to nurture, to educate
— To **foster** a child is to look after them in your home for a while because their parents cannot.
— To **adopt** a child is to bring them into your home and make them legally your own.

brisk *ADJECTIVE*
She goes for a brisk walk every morning.
• quick, lively, energetic, vigorous
OPPOSITES slow, leisurely

brittle *ADJECTIVE*
The leaves were dry and brittle.
• breakable, fragile, delicate, frail
OPPOSITE flexible

broad *ADJECTIVE*
❶ *We walked along the broad avenue.*
• wide, open, large, roomy, spacious, vast, extensive
OPPOSITE narrow
❷ *Just give me a broad outline of what happened.*
• general, rough, vague, loose, indefinite, imprecise
OPPOSITES specific, detailed

brochure *NOUN*
We looked through a holiday brochure.
• a leaflet, a pamphlet, a booklet, a catalogue

broke *(past tense of* **break***)*

broken *ADJECTIVE*
Don't use that computer—it's broken.
• faulty, defective, damaged, out of order
OPPOSITE working

brought *(past tense of* **bring***)*

brown *ADJECTIVE, NOUN*

🌐 **WORD WEB**

SOME SHADES OF BROWN:
• beige, chestnut, chocolate, fawn, hazel, khaki, tan, tawny

brush *VERB*
❶ *Brush your hair.*
• to groom, to comb, to tidy
— To brush your teeth is to **clean** them.
— To brush the floor is to **sweep** it.
❷ *A bird brushed my cheek as it flew past.*
• to touch, to make contact with, to caress, to swipe, to scrape

a
b
c
d
e
f
g
h
i
j
k
l
m
n
o
p
q
r
s
t
u
v
w
x
y
z

brutal ADJECTIVE
The bandits launched a **brutal** attack.
• savage, vicious, cruel, bloodthirsty, bloody, ferocious, inhuman, callous, merciless, pitiless, ruthless
OPPOSITE gentle

bubble NOUN
— Use foam or **froth** for bubbles on top of a liquid.
— Use **lather** or **suds** for bubbles made by soap or detergent.
— Use **fizz** or **effervescence** for the bubbles in a fizzy drink.

bubble VERB
A green liquid **bubbled** in the witch's cauldron.
• to boil, to seethe, to gurgle, to froth, to foam

buckle NOUN
The pirate wore a belt with a large silver **buckle**.
• a clasp, a fastener, a fastening, a clip, a catch

buckle VERB
Please **buckle** your seat belts.
• to fasten, to secure, to clasp, to clip, to do up

a bud

bud NOUN
Buds are appearing on the apple trees.
• a shoot, a sprout

budge VERB
The window was stuck and wouldn't **budge**.
• to give way, to move, to shift, to stir

bug NOUN
❶ There are lots of **bugs** in the garden.
• an insect, a minibeast, a pest
❷ (informal) She was off school with a stomach **bug**.
• an infection, a virus, a germ, a disease, an illness
❸ There are a few **bugs** in the computer program.
• a fault, an error, a defect

bug VERB
The spy **bugged** their phone conversations.
• to tap, to record, to listen in to, to intercept

build VERB builds, building, built
Dad is going to **build** a shed in the garden.
• to construct, to erect, to put together, to put up, to set up, to assemble, to create
➤ **to build up**
The excitement was starting to **build up** before the game.
• to increase, to intensify, to rise, to grow, to mount up

building NOUN
The new **building** will have seven storeys.
• a construction, a structure, a dwelling

⬡ WORD WEB

BUILDINGS WHERE PEOPLE LIVE:

• an apartment, a bungalow, a cabin, a castle, a chalet, a cottage, a farmhouse, a flat, a house, a hut, a mansion, a palace, a shack, a skyscraper, a tower block, a villa

BUILDINGS WHERE PEOPLE WORSHIP:

• a cathedral, a chapel, a church, a gurdwara, a mosque, a pagoda, a shrine, a synagogue, a temple

OTHER TYPES OF BUILDING:

• an amphitheatre, a barn, a cafe, a cinema, a factory, a fire station, a fort, a garage, a gallery, a greenhouse, a hotel, a library, a lighthouse, a mill, a museum, an observatory, an office block, a pavilion, a police station, a post office, a power station, a prison, a restaurant, a school, a shed, a shop, a stable, a theatre, a tower, a warehouse, a windmill

bulge VERB
The creature's eyes **bulged** out of its head.
• to stick out, to swell, to protrude

bulge NOUN
There was a large **bulge** in the robber's sack.
• a bump, a hump, a lump, a swelling

bully VERB
Some of the children were afraid of being **bullied**.
• to persecute, to torment, to intimidate, to terrorise, to threaten, to push around

bump VERB
He **bumped** his knee on the table.
• to hit, to knock, to strike, to bang, to bash

bump NOUN
❶ We felt a **bump** as the plane landed.
• a thump, a thud, a jolt, a bang, a blow, a knock
❷ How did you get that **bump** on your head?
• a lump, a swelling, a bulge

bumpy ADJECTIVE
❶ The car jolted up and down on the **bumpy** road.
• rough, uneven, irregular, lumpy
OPPOSITES smooth, even
❷ We had a **bumpy** ride.
• bouncy, jerky, jolting, lurching

bunch *NOUN*
❶ *The caretaker jangled a **bunch** of keys.*
• a bundle, a cluster, a collection, a set
❷ *She gave me a **bunch** of flowers.*
• a bouquet, a posy, a spray, a sheaf

bundle *NOUN*
*I found a **bundle** of old newspapers.*
• a bunch, a batch, a pile, a stack, a collection
— A **bale** is a large bundle of hay, straw, paper or cloth tied together.
— A **sheaf** is a bundle of papers or a bundle of corn stalks tied together.

bundle *VERB*
❶ *We **bundled** up the papers that were on the desk.*
• to pack, to tie, to fasten, to bind
❷ *The police **bundled** him into the back of their car.*
• to push, to shove, to jostle

burglar *NOUN*
*The **burglars** must have got in through the window.*
• a robber, a thief, an intruder

burn *VERB* **burns, burning, burnt** or **burned**
❶ *We could see fires **burning** in the distance.*
• to be alight, to be on fire, to blaze, to flame, to flare, to flicker
— To burn without flames is to **glow** or **smoulder**.
❷ *They **burned** the dead leaves on a bonfire.*
• to set fire to, to set alight
— To **kindle** or **ignite** something is to start it burning.
— To **scorch** or **singe** something is to damage it slightly with fire.
— To **scald** someone is to burn them with boiling liquid or steam.

burrow *NOUN*
*The field was full of rabbit **burrows**.*
• a hole, a tunnel
— A **warren** is an area of ground with many burrows.
— An **earth** is a fox's or badger's burrow.
» *For other animal homes look at **animal**.*

burrow *VERB*
*Rabbits have been **burrowing** under the fence.*
• to tunnel, to dig, to excavate

a mole burrowing

burst *VERB* **bursts, bursting, burst**
*The balloon **burst** with a bang.*
• to split, to pop, to puncture, to break, to tear

bury *VERB*
*The letter was **buried** under a pile of rubbish.*
• to cover, to conceal, to hide

bush *NOUN*
*We hid in the **bushes**.*
• a shrub

gorse

✦ **WORD WEB**

SOME TYPES OF BUSH:

• a bramble, a briar, a gooseberry bush, gorse, heather, a laurel, a lilac
— **Scrub** is land covered with bushes and low trees.

bushy *ADJECTIVE*
*The troll had **bushy** green eyebrows.*
• hairy, thick, dense, shaggy, bristly

business *NOUN*
❶ *My mum runs her own **business**.*
• a company, a firm, an organisation
❷ *She wants to work in **business**.*
• trade, buying and selling, commerce
❸ *I'd like to go into the travel **business**.*
• industry, trade, profession, career
❹ *What I do in my spare time is not your **business**.*
• affair, concern, interest

bustle *VERB*
*He **bustled** about making tea.*
• to rush, to dash, to hurry, to scurry, to scuttle

busy *ADJECTIVE*
❶ *Mum is **busy** making my birthday cake just now.*
• occupied, engaged, employed, working
— Use **absorbed** or **engrossed** for someone who is busy and very interested in what they are doing.
— You can say someone is **as busy as a bee**.
OPPOSITE idle
❷ *I've had a very **busy** day.*
• active, energetic, full, lively
OPPOSITES quiet, inactive
❸ *Town is always really **busy** on Saturdays.*
• crowded, bustling, lively, swarming, swamped
OPPOSITES quiet, empty

buy *VERB* **buys, buying, bought**
*I'm saving up to **buy** a skateboard.*
• to get, to pay for, to purchase, to acquire
OPPOSITE to sell

buzz *NOUN, VERB*
» *For various sounds look at **sound**.*

a
b
c
h
i
j
k
l
m
n
o
p
q
r
s
t
u
v
w
x
y
z

⚙ Can you think of some different ways to say 'blue', 'pink', 'red' or 'yellow'?

⚙ Check the thesaurus to find answers!

cabin NOUN
The outlaws hid in a cabin in the woods.
• a hut, a shack, a shed, a lodge, a chalet, a shelter

cable NOUN
❶ *The tent was held down with strong cables.*
• a rope, a cord, a line, a chain
❷ *Don't trip over the computer cable.*
• a flex, a lead, a wire, a cord

cafe NOUN
We had lunch in a cafe overlooking the river.
• a coffee shop, a canteen, a cafeteria, a buffet, a snack bar
» *For other places to eat look at* **restaurant**.

cage NOUN

🕸 **WORD WEB**

– A **hutch** is a cage for a pet rabbit or guinea pig.
– A **pen** is a cage or enclosure for farm animals.
– A **coop** is a cage or enclosure for chickens.
– An **aviary** is a large cage or enclosure for birds.

cake NOUN
Would you like a piece of cake?
• a sponge
– A **cupcake** or **fairy cake** is a small sponge cake with icing or cream on it.
– A **muffin** is a small sponge cake with fruit or chocolate in it.
– A **scone** is a small plain cake, often eaten with jam.
– A **gateau** is a rich cream cake.

calculate VERB
I calculated that it would take an hour to walk home.
• to work out, to figure out, to reckon, to add up, to count, to total
– To **estimate** something is to calculate it approximately.

call VERB
❶ *'Is anyone there?' I called.*
• to cry, to exclaim, to shout, to yell
» *For other ways to say something look at* **say**.
❷ *They called the baby Jessica.*
• to name
– Use **entitle** or **title** for naming something such as a book or film: *I entitled my story 'The Storm'.*
❸ *The head teacher called me to her office.*
• to summon, to send for, to order, to invite
❹ *I called my mum and asked her to pick me up.*
• to phone, to ring, to telephone

call NOUN
We heard a call for help.
• a cry, an exclamation, a scream, a shout, a yell

calm ADJECTIVE
❶ *Please try to stay calm.*
• cool, patient, relaxed, placid, serene, tranquil, dignified, sober, unemotional
OPPOSITES anxious, excited
❷ *The sea was calm.*
• smooth, still, flat, motionless
OPPOSITES rough, choppy
❸ *You can't fly a kite on such a calm day.*
• still, quiet
OPPOSITES windy, stormy

came (past tense of **come**)

camp NOUN
It was dark when they reached their camp.
• a campsite, a camping ground, a base
– A military camp is an **encampment**.

campaign NOUN
Will you join our campaign against plastic pollution?
• a movement, a drive, a fight, a battle, an effort, a struggle

campaign VERB
They are campaigning against animal cruelty.
• to struggle, to fight, to battle, to demand action

cancel VERB
We had to cancel the race because of the weather.
• to abandon, to call off, to scrap
– To **postpone** or **put off** something is to cancel it, but rearrange it for later.

candidate NOUN

WORD WEB

— A candidate for a job is an **applicant**.
— A candidate to win a contest or prize is a **competitor** or **contestant**.

cap NOUN

Who left the cap off the toothpaste?
• a cover, a lid, a top
» *For various kinds of hat look at* **hat**.

capable ADJECTIVE

She is a capable organiser.
• competent, able, skilful, effective
OPPOSITE incompetent
➤ **to be capable of**
Are computers capable of learning?
• to be able to: *Are computers able to learn?*
• can: *Can computers learn?*
OPPOSITE to be incapable of

capacity NOUN

What is the capacity of this glass?
• the size, the volume, the extent
» *For more words for size look at* **size**.

cape NOUN

❶ *The lady wore a cape of black velvet.*
• a cloak, a shawl, a wrap, a robe, a mantle *(old use)*
❷ *We could see the island from the cape.*
• the headland, the point, the head

capital NOUN

❶ *Paris is the capital of France.*
• the capital city, the centre of government
❷ *The name should start with a capital.*
• a capital letter, an upper-case letter, a block capital

capsize VERB

The canoe capsized when it hit a rock.
• to overturn, to tip over, to turn over, to keel over

capsule NOUN

❶ *This capsule contains poison.*
• a pill, a tablet, a lozenge
❷ *The space capsule is designed to orbit Mars.*
• a module, a pod
» *For other words to do with space travel look at* **space**.

captain NOUN

The captain brought his ship safely into harbour.
• the commander, the pilot, the master, the skipper *(informal)*

captive ADJECTIVE

The pirates held the crew captive for ten days.
• imprisoned, captured, in captivity, detained, jailed
OPPOSITES free, released

captive NOUN

The captives were thrown into the dungeon.
• a prisoner
— A **hostage** is someone who is held captive until a demand is met.

captivity NOUN

The prisoners were released from captivity.
• imprisonment, confinement, detention
OPPOSITE freedom

capture VERB

❶ *The bank robbers were captured by police this morning.*
• to catch, to arrest, to seize, to take prisoner
❷ *The castle has never been captured by enemy forces.*
• to occupy, to seize, to take, to take over, to win

car NOUN

WORD WEB

SOME TYPES OF CAR:

• a convertible, an electric car, an estate car, a four-wheel drive, a hatchback, a Jeep *(trademark)*, a limousine or limo *(informal)*, a patrol car or police car, a people carrier, a racing car, a saloon, a sports car, an SUV, a taxi, a van, a vintage car

SOME PARTS OF A CAR:

• the bonnet, the boot, the brakes, the bumper, the clutch, the dashboard, the exhaust, the fuel tank, the gears, the headlights or headlamps, the ignition, the seat belts, the tyres, the wheels, the windscreen, the windscreen wipers
» *For other vehicles look at* **transport**.

WRITING TIPS

Here are some useful words for writing about **cars**:
• to steer, to drive, to reverse, to swerve, to skid, to crash, to collide, to bump, to honk, to hoot, to accelerate, to speed, to zoom, to race, to fly, to brake, to slow down, to crawl, to pull over
— *If a car stops suddenly you can say it* **screeches to a halt**.

The little car swerved violently off the road, leaped through the gap, hit the rising ground, bounced high in the air, then skidded round sideways behind the hedge and stopped.—DANNY THE CHAMPION OF THE WORLD, Roald Dahl

card *NOUN*
❶ *I made a stencil out of card.*
• cardboard, paper
❷ *I sent her a card to say thank you.*
• a greetings card, a postcard, a note
— A card for someone's birthday is a **birthday card**.

care *VERB*
I don't care who wins.
• to mind, to bother, to worry, to be interested, to be bothered, to be worried
➤ **to care for**
You have to care for the young plants.
• to take care of, to look after, to attend to, to tend, to nurse

care *NOUN*
❶ *I gave a lot of care to my work.*
• attention, thought
• effort: *I put a lot of effort into my work.*
[OPPOSITE] carelessness
❷ *I forgot all my cares.*
• worries, anxieties, troubles, concerns, burdens, responsibilities, sorrow, stress
➤ **to take care of**
My granny takes care of me after school.
• to care for, to look after, to mind, to watch over, to attend to, to be responsible for

career *NOUN*
He dreamed of a career as a writer.
• a job, an occupation, a profession, a trade, work, employment
» *For various careers look at* **job**.

careful *ADJECTIVE*
❶ *You must be more careful with your spelling.*
• accurate, conscientious, thorough, thoughtful, precise, methodical
[OPPOSITES] careless, inaccurate
❷ *I am always careful when I cross the road.*
• attentive, watchful, alert, cautious, prudent, wary
[OPPOSITES] careless, inattentive
➤ **to be careful**
Please be careful with those scissors.
• to take care, to be on your guard, to look out, to watch out

careless *ADJECTIVE*
❶ *This is a very careless piece of work.*
• messy, untidy, thoughtless, inaccurate, shoddy, sloppy
[OPPOSITES] careful, accurate
❷ *I was careless and cut my finger.*
• inattentive, thoughtless, absent-minded, irresponsible, reckless
[OPPOSITES] careful, attentive

caress *VERB*
The woman gently caressed her child's hair.
• to stroke, to touch, to smooth

cargo *NOUN*
Some planes carry cargo instead of passengers.
• goods, freight, merchandise

carnival *NOUN*
The whole village comes out for the annual carnival.
• a fair, a festival, a fete, a gala, a parade, a procession, a show, a celebration, a pageant

carry *VERB*
❶ *I helped Mum to carry the shopping to the car.*
• to take, to transfer, to lift, to fetch, to bring
❷ *Aircraft carry passengers and goods.*
• to transport, to convey
➤ **to carry on**
We carried on playing in spite of the rain.
• to continue, to go on, to persevere, to persist, to keep on
➤ **to carry something out**
They carried out an experiment.
• to perform, to do, to execute, to accomplish, to achieve, to complete, to finish

carve *VERB*
Some shapes were carved into the rock.
• to cut, to shape, to engrave, to inscribe

case *NOUN*
❶ *What's in those cases?*
• a box, a chest, a crate, a carton, a container
❷ *I'm packing my case to go on holiday.*
• a suitcase, a trunk, a bag
— Your **luggage** is one or more cases that you take on a journey.
❸ *It was a clear case of mistaken identity.*
• an instance, an occurrence, an example, a situation
❹ *She was working on a murder case.*
• an inquiry, an investigation, a court case

cash *NOUN*
How much cash do you have?
• money, change, coins, notes, currency

castle NOUN
*They fought to defend the **castle**.*
• a fortress, a fort, a stronghold

🕸 WORD WEB

PARTS OF A CASTLE:

• the battlements, a courtyard, a drawbridge, a dungeon, the gate, the keep, the moat, a parapet, a portcullis, a tower, a turret, the walls

Tiuri stood in the rain, looking at the river and the castle. An open drawbridge led to the gate, which was positioned between two large towers.—THE LETTER FOR THE KING, Tonke

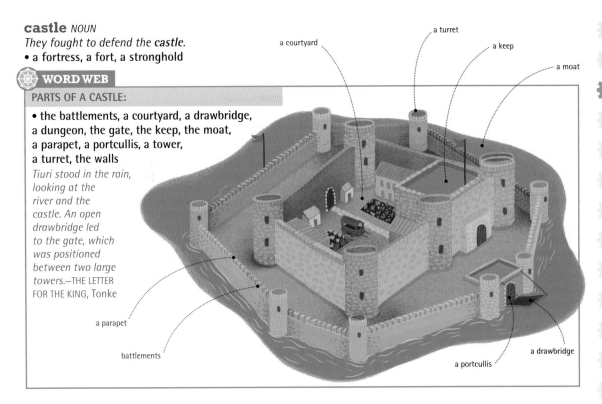

a courtyard
a turret
a keep
a moat
a parapet
battlements
a portcullis
a drawbridge

casual ADJECTIVE
❶ *It was just a **casual** remark, so don't take it too seriously.*
• accidental, chance, unexpected, unintentional, unplanned
OPPOSITE deliberate
❷ *The restaurant had a **casual** atmosphere.*
• informal, relaxed, easy-going
OPPOSITE formal

cat NOUN

🕸 WORD WEB

— A young cat is a **kitten**.
— A male cat is a **tom**.
— A cat with streaks in its fur is a **tabby**.
— A word meaning 'to do with cats' is **feline**.

SOME BREEDS OF CAT:

• an Abyssinian, a Burmese, a Manx cat, a Persian cat, a Siamese cat

SOME WILD ANIMALS OF THE CAT FAMILY:

• a cheetah, a jaguar, a leopard, a lion, a lynx, an ocelot, a panther, a puma, a tiger, a wildcat
» *Look at **animal**.*

😃 WRITING TIPS

Here are some useful words for writing about **cats**:

SOUNDS MADE BY CATS:

• to mew, to miaow, to purr, to hiss

HOW CATS MOVE:

• to pad, to slink, to stalk, to prowl, to crouch, to pounce

DESCRIBING CATS' FUR:

• sleek, silky, soft
The cat stared at her with its round golden eyes and droopy white whiskers. It started to purr.
—TILLY'S MOONLIGHT FOX, Julia Green

catastrophe NOUN
*The drought is a **catastrophe** for farmers.*
• a disaster, a calamity, a tragedy, a misfortune, a mishap

catch VERB catches, catching, caught
❶ *My friends yelled at me to **catch** the ball.*
• to grab, to seize, to intercept, to grasp, to grip, to clutch, to hang on to, to hold, to snatch, to take

② *One of the anglers **caught** a fish.*
• to hook, to net, to trap
③ *The police soon **caught** the thief.*
• to arrest, to capture, to corner
④ *I **caught** him cheating.*
• to discover, to spot, to see
⑤ *I hope you don't **catch** my cold.*
• to become infected by, to contract, to get
⑥ *We **catch** the bus to school.*
• to get, to get on

catch NOUN
*All the windows are fitted with safety **catches**.*
• a fastening, a latch, a lock, a bolt, a hook

catching ADJECTIVE
*Chickenpox is **catching**.*
• contagious, infectious

category NOUN
*I won first prize in the under-10s **category**.*
• a group, a section, a class, a division, a set

cattle NOUN

 WORD WEB

– Male cattle are **bulls**.
– Female cattle are **cows**.
– Young cattle are **calves**.
– Meat from a cow is **beef**.
– Meat from a calf is **veal**.
– When cattle make a sound, they **moo** or **low**.
– A word meaning 'to do with cattle' is **bovine**.
– Farm animals in general are **livestock**.

caught (past tense of **catch**)

cause VERB
① *A single spark could **cause** an explosion.*
• to bring about, to lead to, to trigger, to generate, to give rise to, to result in
② *His idea **caused** a lot of excitement.*
• to create, to start, to provoke, to arouse, to stimulate, to inspire

cause NOUN
① *What was the **cause** of the trouble?*
• the origin, the source, the start
• the reason: *What was the **reason** for the trouble?*
② *You've got no **cause** to complain.*
• grounds, a basis, a motive, a reason

caution NOUN
① *You should proceed with **caution**.*
• care, attention, watchfulness, wariness
② *The traffic warden let him off with a **caution**.*
• a warning, a telling-off

cautious ADJECTIVE
*My grandad is a **cautious** driver.*
• careful, attentive, watchful, wary, hesitant
OPPOSITE reckless

cave NOUN
*The **cave** walls were covered with prehistoric paintings.*
• a cavern, a pothole, an underground chamber

 WORD WEB

PARTS AND FEATURES OF A CAVE:
– The entrance to a cave is the **mouth**.
– The top of a cave is the **roof** and the bottom is the **floor**.
– A **stalactite** hangs from the roof of a cave.
– A **stalagmite** rises from the floor of a cave.

cease VERB
*The fighting **ceased** at midnight.*
• to come to an end, to end, to finish, to stop, to halt
OPPOSITE to begin

celebrate VERB
① *After the game the team were all **celebrating**.*
• to rejoice, to be happy, to cheer, to enjoy yourself, to have a good time
② *How do you **celebrate** Christmas?*
• to commemorate, to observe, to mark

celebration NOUN
*After we won, the **celebration** went on all day.*
• a party, a feast, a carnival, a festival, festivities

celebrity NOUN
*Lots of **celebrities** eat at that restaurant.*
• a famous person, a VIP, a star, a personality

cellar NOUN
*There is a **cellar** underneath the house.*
• a basement, a vault

cemetery NOUN
*A famous author is buried in the local **cemetery**.*
• a graveyard, a burial ground, a churchyard

central ADJECTIVE
① *We are now in the **central** part of the building.*
• middle, core, inner, interior
OPPOSITE outer
② *Who are the **central** characters in the story?*
• chief, main, major, principal, important, crucial, essential, fundamental, vital
OPPOSITE unimportant

centre *NOUN*
❶ *The centre of the planet is very hot.*
• the core, the interior, the inside, the middle
— The centre of a target is the **bullseye**.
— The centre of a wheel is the **hub**.
— The centre of an atom or cell is the **nucleus**.
OPPOSITES the edge, the outside, the surface
❷ *She works in the centre of town.*
• the middle, the heart
OPPOSITES the edge, the outskirts

ceremony *NOUN*
*We watched the ceremony of the opening
of Parliament.*
• a rite, a ritual, formalities

 **WORD WEB**

SOME CEREMONIES:

• an awards ceremony, a baptism, a christening,
a bar mitzvah, a bat mitzvah, a coronation,
a funeral, an opening ceremony, a presentation,
a prize-giving, a wedding

certain *ADJECTIVE*
❶ *I'm certain it was him.*
• confident, convinced, positive, sure, definite
OPPOSITE uncertain
❷ *Her new book is certain to be a bestseller.*
• bound, sure
❸ *They are headed for certain disaster.*
• inevitable, definite, undoubtable, unavoidable
❹ *There are certain things you can do to stay healthy.*
• particular, specific, some

certainly *ADVERB*
You will certainly succeed.
• definitely, undoubtedly, unquestionably,
without a doubt

certificate *NOUN*
At the end of the course, you will receive a certificate.
• a diploma, a document, a licence

chain *NOUN*
❶ *The anchor was attached to a chain.*
• a cable
— A **necklace** is a chain you wear around your neck.
— **Bonds** are chains used to tie someone up.
— One ring in a chain is a **link**.
❷ *This began a strange chain of events.*
• a series, a sequence, a succession, a string

chair *NOUN*
» *For furniture to sit on look at* **seat**.

challenge *VERB*
I challenged Jo not to eat sweets for a week.
• to dare, to defy, to issue a challenge

challenging *ADJECTIVE*
This is a very challenging task.
• ambitious, difficult, hard, tricky
OPPOSITES easy, unchallenging

champion *NOUN*
She is the current world champion at ice skating.
• title-holder, prizewinner, victor, winner, conqueror

championship *NOUN*
Fifteen schools took part in the karate championship.
• a competition, a contest, a tournament

chance *NOUN*
❶ *This is a chance to try a new sport.*
• an opportunity, a possibility, a time, an occasion
❷ *There is no chance she will agree.*
• a possibility, a likelihood, a probability, a prospect
— A chance of something bad is a **risk** or **danger**.
❸ *We met by chance.*
• coincidence, accident, luck, fate, a fluke

change *VERB*
❶ *I changed my design because it didn't work.*
• to alter, to modify, to reorganise, to adjust,
to adapt, to revise, to vary
— If you **revolutionise** or **transform** something, you
make a very big or complete change to it.
❷ *The town has changed a lot.*
• to alter, to become different, to develop, to grow
— If something **transforms**, it changes completely.
— If something **evolves**, it changes gradually.
❸ *Can I change seats?*
• to exchange, to swap, to switch
➤ **to change into**
Tadpoles change into frogs.
• to become, to turn into, to develop into,
to grow into, to evolve into

change *NOUN*
We made some changes to the plan.
• an alteration, a modification, a revision,
an adjustment, a development, a shift
— Use **transformation** or **revolution** for a very big
change.
— Use **evolution** for a gradual change.
— Use **metamorphosis** for a complete physical change.

channel *NOUN*
❶ *The rainwater runs along this channel.*
• a ditch, a duct, a gully, a gutter, a groove,
a furrow, a trough
❷ *How many TV channels do you get?*
• a station

a
b
c
d
e
f
g
h
i
j
k
l
m
n
o
p
q
r
s
t
u
v
w
x
y
z

chaos NOUN
After the earthquake, the city was in chaos.
• confusion, disorder, mayhem, uproar, upheaval, tumult, turmoil, havoc, pandemonium
OPPOSITE order

chaotic ADJECTIVE
The hall was chaotic, with people rushing everywhere.
• confused, disorderly, disorganised, topsy-turvy, untidy, unruly, riotous, in turmoil
OPPOSITES orderly, organised

character NOUN
❶ *Her character is quite different from her sister's.*
• a personality, a temperament, a nature, a disposition
❷ *Who was your favourite character in the film?*
• a part, a role
» *Look at* **story**.

characteristic NOUN
Humour is one of her main characteristics.
• a feature, a peculiarity, a trait

characteristic ADJECTIVE
He replied with his characteristic enthusiasm.
• typical, distinctive, recognisable, particular, special, unique, usual

charge NOUN
The admission charge is five euros.
• a price, a rate, a fee, a payment
— The charge for using public transport is the **fare**.
➤ **to be in charge of**
An experienced sailor was in charge of the crew.
• to manage, to lead, to command, to direct, to supervise, to run, to be responsible for

charge VERB
❶ *The library charges ten pence for a photocopy.*
• to ask
❷ *The bull charged.*
• to attack, to assault, to rush, to lunge, to stampede

charm NOUN
❶ *She has a lot of charm.*
• attractiveness, appeal
❷ *The sorcerer recited a magic charm.*
• a spell
» *For other words to do with magic look at* **magic**.

charm VERB
Winnie the Pooh has charmed readers all over the world.
• to delight, to enchant, to bewitch, to entrance, to fascinate, to please

charming ADJECTIVE
We saw a charming little village.
• delightful, attractive, pleasant, pleasing, picturesque, quaint, appealing

chart NOUN
❶ *This chart shows the heights of the children in the class.*
• a diagram, a graph, a table
❷ *The explorer stopped to consult his chart.*
• a map, a plan

chase VERB
The wolves chased a deer through the forest.
• to pursue, to run after, to follow, to track, to trail, to hunt

chase NOUN
After a long chase, they caught the thief.
• a pursuit

chat VERB
Stop chatting and get on with your work.
• to chatter, to natter, to talk
— To **gossip** means to talk about other people.

chat NOUN
I rang my friend for a chat.
• a talk, a conversation, a gossip

cheap ADJECTIVE
We got a cheap flight to London.
• inexpensive, affordable, bargain, cut-price, good value, low-cost, reasonable

cheat VERB
❶ *He was accused of cheating in the test.*
• to copy, to be dishonest, to break the rules
❷ *She was cheated out of her money.*
• to deceive, to trick, to fool, to con (informal), to hoax

cheat NOUN
Don't trust him—he's a cheat.
• a cheater, a deceiver, a liar, a fraud, a hoaxer

check VERB
❶ *Have you checked your work carefully?*
• to examine, to inspect, to look over, to scrutinise
❷ *Check that the door is locked.*
• to make sure, to ensure, to verify
❸ *If you don't know the spelling, check the dictionary.*
• to consult, to refer to

check NOUN
I need to run some checks on the computer.
• a test, an examination, an inspection, a check-up

cheeky *ADJECTIVE*
Don't be so cheeky!
• disrespectful, impertinent, impudent, impolite, insolent, insulting, saucy, rude
OPPOSITE respectful

cheer *VERB*
We cheered when our team scored a goal.
• to clap, to applaud, to shout, to yell
OPPOSITES to jeer, to boo
➤ **to cheer up**
He cheered up when he saw the food.
• to become more cheerful, to brighten up
➤ **to cheer someone up**
The good news cheered me up.
• to comfort, to console, to delight, to please, to encourage

cheerful *ADJECTIVE*
The sun was shining, and we set out in a cheerful mood.
• happy, good-humoured, light-hearted, merry, jolly, jaunty, jovial, joyful, joyous, positive, optimistic, glad, lively, bright, animated, buoyant, elated
OPPOSITE sad

chemist *NOUN*
The chemist gave me some medicine.
• pharmacist
— A chemist's shop is a **pharmacy**.

chest *NOUN*
I found some old books in a chest in the attic.
• a box, a crate, a case, a trunk

chew *VERB*
She was chewing a sandwich.
• to eat, to gnaw, to munch, to bite, to crunch
» *For other ways to eat look at* **eat**.

chicken *NOUN*

🕸 **WORD WEB**

— A female chicken is a **hen**.
— A male chicken is a **rooster** or a **cock**.
— A young male chicken is a **cockerel**.
— A baby chicken is a **chick**.
— Chickens and other birds kept for eggs and meat are **poultry** or **fowl**.

a chest

a rooster or a cock

a hen

chief *NOUN*
The pirates chose Redbeard as their chief.
• a leader, a ruler, a head, a commander, a captain, a master, a boss
chief *ADJECTIVE*
❶ *He was the queen's chief advisor.*
• head, senior
❷ *The chief thing to remember is wear gloves.*
    • main, central, key, principal, crucial, basic, essential, important, vital, major, primary, foremost
    OPPOSITES unimportant, minor

child *NOUN*
❶ *He is only a child.*
• a boy or girl, a kid *(informal)*, a youngster, a youth, a young person
— A **juvenile** or a **minor** is someone who is not yet an adult, especially according to the law.
OPPOSITE an adult
❷ *Do you have any children?*
• a son or daughter, offspring

childhood *NOUN*
He spent his childhood in France.
• youth, boyhood or girlhood
— The time when someone is a baby is their **babyhood** or their **infancy**.
— The time when someone is a teenager is their **adolescence** or their **teens**.
OPPOSITE adulthood

childish *ADJECTIVE*
It's childish to make rude noises.
• babyish, immature, juvenile, infantile
OPPOSITE mature

chilly *ADJECTIVE*
It's chilly, so wrap up well.
• cold, cool, frosty, icy, crisp, fresh, raw, wintry
OPPOSITE warm

chip *NOUN*
❶ *Some chips of paint had come off the door.*
• a bit, a piece, a fragment, a scrap, a sliver, a splinter, a flake, a shaving
❷ *This mug's got a chip in it.*
• a crack, a notch, a flaw
chip *VERB*
I chipped a cup while I was washing up.
• to crack, to damage, to break

a b c d e f g h i j k l m n o p q r s t u v w x y z

choice NOUN
❶ *You've made a good choice.*
• a selection, a preference, a pick, a vote
❷ *I had no choice but to agree.*
• an alternative, an option
❸ *There is a great choice of books in the library.*
• a range, a selection, an assortment, an array, a variety, a mixture

choke VERB
❶ *I feel like this tie is choking me.*
• to strangle, to suffocate, to stifle, to throttle
❷ *Thick fumes made the firefighters choke.*
• to cough, to gasp

choose VERB chooses, choosing, chose, chosen
❶ *Which flavour did you choose?*
• to select, to pick, to decide on, to opt for, to prefer
❷ *We chose a new class captain.*
• to select, to appoint, to nominate, to name, to elect, to vote for

chop VERB
❶ *Chop the celery into pieces.*
• to cut, to split, to slice, to dice, to mince
❷ *They chopped down the undergrowth to make a path.*
• to hack, to slash
— To chop down a tree is to **fell** it.

chubby ADJECTIVE
The baby has chubby cheeks.
• plump, tubby, podgy

chunk NOUN
I bit a chunk out of my apple.
• a piece, a portion, a lump, a block, a hunk, a slab, a wedge

church NOUN

WORD WEB

— A **cathedral** is a large and important church.
— An **abbey** is a church with buildings where monks or nuns live or lived.
— A **chapel** is a small church or part of a large church.
» *For other places of worship look at* **building**.

PARTS OF A CHURCH:

• an aisle, a churchyard, a crypt, a font, a pulpit, a spire, a steeple

circle NOUN
We arranged the chairs in a circle.
• a ring, a round, a hoop
— A **coil** is a circle of wire or rope.
— A **disc** is a flat solid circle.
— An **oval** or an **ellipse** is an egg shape.
— A **sphere** is a three-dimensional round shape.
» *For other shapes look at* **shape**.

WORD WEB

PARTS OF A CIRCLE:

— The **circumference** of a circle is the line or distance around its edge.
— An **arc** is part of the circumference of a circle.
— The **diameter** is the distance across a circle through the centre.
— The **radius** is the distance from the centre to the circumference of a circle.
— A **quadrant** is a quarter of a circle.
— A **semicircle** is half a circle.

circle VERB
❶ *The vultures circled overhead.*
• to turn, to go round, to revolve, to rotate, to wheel
❷ *The space probe circled Mars.*
• to orbit, to revolve around

circumference NOUN
There is a fence around the circumference of the field.
• the perimeter, the border, the boundary, the edge, the fringe

citizen NOUN
The citizens of New York are proud of their city.
• a resident, an inhabitant

city NOUN

WORD WEB

— The main city of a country or region is the **capital**.
— An area of houses outside the central part of a city is the **suburbs**.
— A word meaning 'to do with a town or city' is **urban**.
» *Look at* **town**.

civilisation NOUN
We are studying the civilisation of ancient Egypt.
• a culture, a society

civilised *ADJECTIVE*
*Trolls seldom behave in a **civilised** manner.*
• polite, well-behaved, well-mannered, orderly, cultured, sophisticated, refined
OPPOSITE uncivilised

claim *VERB*
❶ *She **claims** she is an expert.*
• to declare, to assert, to state, to maintain, to argue, to insist
❷ *You can **claim** your prize here.*
• to ask for, to request, to demand, to collect

clang *NOUN, VERB*
» For various sounds look at **sound**.

clank *NOUN, VERB*
» For various sounds look at **sound**.

clap *VERB*
*The audience **clapped** loudly.*
• to applaud, to cheer

clash *VERB*
❶ *The cymbals **clashed**.*
• to crash, to resound
❷ *The two armies **clashed**.*
• to fight, to get into conflict, to confront one another

clash *NOUN*
❶ *The **clash** of cymbals made me jump.*
• a crash, a bang
❷ *There was a **clash** between rival supporters at the match.*
• a fight, a battle, a confrontation, a conflict

clasp *VERB*
❶ *My little brother **clasped** my hand.*
• to grasp, to grip, to hold, to squeeze, to cling to
❷ *She **clasped** him in her arms.*
• to embrace, to hug

clasp *NOUN*
*The cloak was held in place by a gold **clasp**.*
• a fastener, a fastening, a clip, a buckle

class *NOUN*
❶ *There are 26 children in our **class**.*
• a form, a set, a group
— The other pupils in your class are your **classmates**.
❷ *There are many different **classes** of plants.*
• a category, a group, a classification, a division, a set, a sort, a type, a kind

classic *ADJECTIVE*
*This is a **classic** film.*
• well-regarded, excellent, first-class, exceptional, fine, great, admirable, respected
OPPOSITE ordinary

clean *ADJECTIVE*
❶ *Can you bring me a **clean** cup, please?*
• washed, fresh
— Use **spotless** or **immaculate** if something is perfectly clean.
— Use **hygienic** if something is clean and free of germs.
OPPOSITE dirty
❷ *They have no **clean** water to drink.*
• pure, clear, fresh, unpolluted, uncontaminated
OPPOSITES polluted, contaminated
❸ *I started again with a **clean** piece of paper.*
• blank, unused, empty, fresh, new
OPPOSITE used

clean *VERB*
❶ *We **cleaned** the house from top to bottom.*
• to wash, to wipe, to sweep, to tidy
» Look at **wash** and **wipe**.
OPPOSITES to dirty, to mess up
❷ *The nurse **cleaned** the wound.*
• to cleanse, to bathe
OPPOSITES to infect, to contaminate

clear *ADJECTIVE*
❶ *She gave nice **clear** instructions.*
• understandable, plain, simple, straightforward, unambiguous
OPPOSITES confusing, ambiguous
❷ *The picture is not very **clear**.*
• distinct, visible, recognisable, sharp, in focus
— Use **legible** for writing that is clear.
OPPOSITES unclear, fuzzy
❸ *Try to speak in a **clear** voice.*
• distinct, audible
— A common simile is **as clear as a bell**.
OPPOSITE muffled
❹ *The difference between them was **clear**.*
• obvious, evident, unmistakable
❺ *We saw fish swimming in the **clear** pool.*
• clean, pure, colourless, transparent
— A common simile is **as clear as crystal**.
OPPOSITE opaque
❻ *The sky was **clear**.*
• cloudless
— A clear day is **sunny** or **bright**.
— A clear night is **moonlit** or **starlit**.
OPPOSITES cloudy, overcast
❼ *Make sure the path is **clear**.*
• open, empty, free, unblocked
OPPOSITE blocked

a b c d e f g h i j k l m n o p q r s t u v w x y z

clear VERB
❶ *Will you clear your things off the table?*
• to get rid of, to tidy, to remove, to take away, to shift
❷ *The plumber cleared the drain.*
• to unblock, to unclog, to clean out, to open up
❸ *The fog cleared slowly.*
• to disappear, to vanish, to disperse, to evaporate, to melt away
❹ *The forecast said that the weather will clear.*
• to become clear, to brighten, to brighten up
❺ *The runners cleared the first hurdle.*
• to pass over, to get over, to jump over, to leap over, to vault, to vault over

clever ADJECTIVE
❶ *She's very clever and she does well at school.*
• intelligent, bright, quick, gifted, able, smart, brainy *(informal)*
OPPOSITE unintelligent
❷ *He came up with a clever idea.*
• brilliant, bright, ingenious, inspired, inventive, effective
❸ *The clever fox tricked them all.*
• cunning, crafty, sly, sharp, shrewd, wily

cliff NOUN
The car rolled over the edge of a cliff.
• a crag, a precipice, a rock face

climax NOUN
The climax of the film is a stunning car chase.
• the high point, the highlight

climb VERB
❶ *It took us several hours to climb the mountain.*
• to ascend, to clamber up, to go up, to scale, to mount
❷ *The plane climbed into the clouds.*
• to lift off, to soar, to take off
❸ *The road climbs steeply up.*
• to rise, to slope

climb NOUN
It's a steep climb up to the castle.
• an ascent, a hill, a gradient, a rise, a slope, an incline

cling VERB clings, clinging, clung
➤ **to cling to**
The baby koala clung to its mother.
• to clasp, to grasp, to clutch, to embrace, to hug

clip NOUN
I held my hair back with a clip.
• a fastener, a clasp, a grip, a pin

clip VERB
❶ *The sheets of paper were clipped together.*
• to fasten, to pin, to staple
❷ *Dad clipped the hedge.*
• to cut, to trim
— To cut parts off a tree or bush is to **prune** it.

cloak NOUN
The girl wrapped her cloak tightly around herself.
• a cape, a wrap, a mantle *(old use)*

clock NOUN
» *For instruments used to measure time look at* **time**.

close *(say* klohss*)* ADJECTIVE
❶ *Our house is close to the shops.*
• near, nearby, not far
OPPOSITES far, distant
❷ *Anisha and I are close friends.*
• intimate, dear, devoted, fond
❸ *Pay close attention.*
• careful, thorough, detailed
❹ *It was a very close race.*
• equal, even, level, well-matched

close *(say* klohz*)* VERB
Don't forget to close the lid.
• to shut, to fasten, to seal, to secure
— Use **slam** when someone closes something noisily.
OPPOSITE to open

cloth NOUN
The curtains were made of striped cotton cloth.
• fabric, material
— A general word for cloth is textiles.

> **WORD WEB**

SOME TYPES OF CLOTH:

• canvas, corduroy, cotton, denim, felt, flannel, gauze, lace, linen, muslin, satin, silk, tartan, tweed, velvet, wool

tartan
tweed
corduroy
silk
linen
denim

clothes NOUN
He has a lot of clothes.
• clothing, garments
— An **outfit** is a set of clothes worn together.
— A **uniform** is a special set of clothes worn for school or work.
— A **costume** is a set of clothes worn to look like someone else: *I wore a pirate costume to the party.*

WORD WEB

SOME ITEMS OF CLOTHING:

• a blouse, a cardigan, a dress, dungarees, a fleece, a frock, a gown, a hijab, a hoodie, jeans, a jersey, a jumper, a kilt, a kimono, leggings, a pinafore, a polo shirt, a pullover, a robe, a sari, a shirt, shorts, a skirt, a smock, a suit, a sweater, a sweatshirt, a tracksuit, trousers, trunks, a T-shirt, a tunic, a waistcoat

buttons

OUTER CLOTHES:

• an anorak, an apron, a blazer, a cape, a cloak, a coat, a dressing gown, a duffel coat, a jacket, overalls, an overcoat, a parka, a raincoat, a shawl
» *Look at* **hat** *and* **shoe**.

PARTS OF A GARMENT:

• a bodice, a button, a collar, a cuff, a hem, a lapel, a pocket, a seam, a sleeve, a waistband, a zip

WRITING TIPS

You can use these words to describe **clothes**:
• baggy, casual, drab, fashionable, fine, formal, frilly, glamorous, loose, old-fashioned, ornate, ragged, roomy, scruffy, shabby, smart, stylish, tattered, tatty, threadbare, tight, worn

The stranger was wearing an extremely shabby set of wizard's robes which had been darned in several places.—HARRY POTTER AND THE PRISONER OF AZKABAN, J. K. Rowling

cloud NOUN
A cloud of steam billowed from the kettle.
• a billow, a puff, a haze, a mist, a wisp

cloudy ADJECTIVE
❶ *The day was cold and cloudy.*
• dull, overcast, grey, dark, dismal, gloomy, sunless
OPPOSITE cloudless
» *Look at* **weather**.
❷ *We couldn't see any fish in the cloudy water.*
• muddy, murky, hazy, milky
OPPOSITES clear, transparent

club NOUN
❶ *Would you like to join our book club?*
• a group, a society, an association, an organisation
❷ *The warrior held a wooden club.*
• a stick, a baton, a truncheon
» *Look at* **bat**.

clue NOUN
Shall I give you a clue?
• a hint, a suggestion, a tip, an idea
» *Look at* **detective**.

clump NOUN
The owl flew into a clump of trees on the hill.
• a group, a cluster
—A **tuft** is a clump of grass or hair.

clumsy ADJECTIVE
The clumsy gnome was always breaking things.
• careless, awkward, accident-prone, graceless
OPPOSITE graceful

clutch VERB
The mountaineer clutched his rope.
• to catch, to clasp, to cling to, to grab, to grasp, to grip, to hang on to, to hold on to, to seize, to snatch

clutter NOUN
We'll have to clear up all this clutter.
• mess, muddle, junk, litter, rubbish

coach NOUN
❶ *We went on the trip by coach.*
• bus
» *For other vehicles look at* **transport**.
❷ *The football team has a new coach.*
• a trainer, an instructor

coach VERB
He was coached by a former champion.
• to train, to teach, to instruct

coarse ADJECTIVE
The blanket was made of coarse woollen material.
• rough, harsh, scratchy, bristly
OPPOSITES soft, smooth

coast NOUN
After the disaster, oil was washed up along the coast.
• the coastline, the shore
» *Look at* **seashore**.

coat NOUN
❶ *The fox had a reddish-brown coat.*
• fur, hair, a pelt
— Use **fleece** for a sheep's coat.
» *For garments look at* **clothes**.
❷ *The front door needs a coat of paint.*
• a layer, a coating, a covering

coat VERB

*We ate marshmallows **coated** with chocolate.*

• to cover, to spread, to glaze

code NOUN

❶ *The message was written in **code**.*

— To put a message in code is to **encode** or **encrypt** it.

— To understand a code is to **decode**, **decipher** or **crack** it.

❷ *We are learning to write computer **code**.*

• programs, software

code VERB

*We are learning to **code**.*

• to program, to write software

coil NOUN

*He picked up a **coil** of rope.*

• a spiral, a twist, a loop, a curl, a circle

coil VERB

*The snake **coiled** around a branch.*

• to curl, to loop, to roll, to spiral, to turn, to twist, to twirl, to wind, to writhe

coin NOUN

*Do you have any **coins**?*

• change

— A **token** is a plastic or metal coin that can be used to make something work.

coincidence NOUN

*It was a **coincidence** that we saw him there.*

• an accident, a fluke, chance, luck

cold ADJECTIVE

❶ *It's **cold** today.*

• chilly

— Use **cool** for slightly cold weather.

— Use **crisp** for pleasantly cold dry weather.

— Use **freezing** or **bitter** for very cold weather.

— Use **frosty**, **icy**, **snowy** or **wintry** when there is frost, ice or snow.

— A common simile is **as cold as ice**.

OPPOSITES hot, warm

❯❯ *Look at **weather**.*

❷ *I was **cold** in spite of my woolly hat.*

• freezing, frozen, chilly, shivering

OPPOSITES warm, hot

❸ *She gave me a **cold** stare.*

• unfriendly, hostile, unkind, cruel, icy, heartless, indifferent, uncaring

OPPOSITES warm, friendly

collapse VERB

❶ *Many buildings **collapsed** in the earthquake.*

• to fall down, to fall in, to cave in, to give way, to crumble, to crumple, to buckle, to disintegrate, to tumble down

❷ *Some of the runners **collapsed** in the heat.*

• to faint, to pass out, to fall over, to keel over

colleague NOUN

*She discussed the plan with her **colleagues**.*

• a co-worker, a workmate, a teammate, an associate, a partner

collect VERB

❶ *Squirrels **collect** nuts for the winter.*

• to gather, to accumulate, to store up, to hoard, to pile up, to bring together

❷ *A crowd **collected** to watch the fire.*

• to assemble, to gather, to come together, to converge

OPPOSITES to scatter, to disperse

❸ *Dad came to **collect** me.*

• to fetch, to pick up, to get

OPPOSITE to drop off

collection NOUN

*She has a big **collection** of stickers.*

• an assortment, a set, a hoard, a pile

college NOUN

❯❯ *For places where people study look at **education**.*

collide VERB

➤ **to collide with**

*The runaway trolley **collided with** a wall.*

• to bump into, to crash into, to run into, to smash into, to knock into, to hit, to strike

collision NOUN

*His car was involved in a **collision**.*

• a crash, a bump, a smash, a knock, an accident

— A **pile-up** is a collision involving a lot of vehicles.

colour NOUN

*What do you call that **colour**?*

• a shade, a hue, a tint, a tone

✦ **WORD WEB**

NAMES OF VARIOUS COLOURS:

• black, blue, brown, cream, gold, golden, green, grey, lavender, orange, pink, purple, red, silver, turquoise, violet, white, yellow

— The colours red, yellow and blue are known as **primary colours**.

❯❯ *For shades of colours look at **black**, **blue**, **brown**, **green**, **grey**, **pink**, **purple**, **red**, **white** and **yellow**.*

WRITING TIPS

Here are some useful words for describing **colour**:

TO DESCRIBE A PALE COLOUR:

• delicate, dull, faded, faint, light, pale, pallid, pastel, soft
The west was a glory of soft, mingled hues, and the pond reflected them all in still softer shadings.—ANNE OF GREEN GABLES, L. M. Montgomery

TO DESCRIBE A STRONG COLOUR:

• bright, brilliant, deep, loud, rich, strong, vivid
—Use **luminous**, **fluorescent** or **neon** for a colour that is so bright it shines in the dark.
*My bike helmet is **fluorescent** orange.*

colour VERB
*I **coloured** the icing deep pink.*
• to paint, to dye, to tint

colourful ADJECTIVE
❶ *Everyone wore **colourful** clothes.*
• multicoloured, bright, showy, brilliant
OPPOSITE dull
❷ *The book gives a **colourful** account of life on an island.*
• exciting, interesting, lively, vivid, striking
OPPOSITE dull

column NOUN
❶ *The roof of the temple was supported by stone columns.*
• a pillar, a post, a support, a shaft
❷ *A **column** of soldiers was crossing the desert.*
• a line, a file, a procession, a row
❸ *She writes a **column** in the school magazine.*
• an article, a piece, a report, a feature

combine VERB
❶ ***Combine** the flour and water.*
• to mix, to blend, to stir together, to add together
OPPOSITE to separate
❷ *We **combined** to make one big group.*
• to join together, to come together, to merge, to mingle, to unite, to converge
OPPOSITE to split

come VERB comes, coming, came, come
❶ *The bus is **coming**.*
• to arrive, to approach, to draw near, to turn up, to appear
OPPOSITE to go
❷ *They **come** to school by bike.*
• to travel to, to get to, to reach, to attend
OPPOSITE to leave
❸ *Would you like to **come** to my house?*
• to visit, to go to

❹ *At last the day **came** for the party.*
• to arrive, to happen, to come round
— When night comes, it **falls**: *Night **fell** and the little town was quiet.*

comfort NOUN
❶ *My friends brought me a lot of **comfort** when I was ill.*
• consolation, support, encouragement, reassurance, relief
❷ *The hotel provides everything for your **comfort**.*
• welfare, well-being, ease, contentment

comfort VERB
*The coach tried to **comfort** the team after they lost.*
• to console, to cheer someone up, to calm someone down, to reassure, to encourage, to soothe

comfortable ADJECTIVE
❶ *This bed is very **comfortable**.*
• cosy, snug, relaxing, soft, easy
OPPOSITE uncomfortable
❷ *I was very **comfortable** on the sofa.*
• cosy, relaxed, snug, contented, settled, at ease
OPPOSITE uncomfortable

comic (also **comical**) ADJECTIVE
*We laughed at his **comic** remarks.*
• amusing, humorous, funny, witty
— Use **hilarious** or **hysterical** *(informal)* to mean very funny.
— Use **ironic** or **sarcastic** when someone says the opposite of what they mean in order to be funny.
OPPOSITE serious

command NOUN
❶ *The general gave the **command** to attack.*
• an order, an instruction, a decree
❷ *Who is in **command** here?*
• charge, control, authority, power

command VERB
❶ *The king **commanded** them to fight.*
• to order, to instruct, to direct, to tell
❷ *The captain **commands** the crew.*
• to control, to direct, to be in charge of, to head, to lead, to manage, to supervise

comment NOUN
*Do you want to make any **comments** about the story?*
• a remark, a statement, an observation, an opinion

commitment NOUN
❶ *Our team has the **commitment** to win.*
• determination, dedication, enthusiasm, keenness, passion, resolution

a
b
c
d
e
f
g
h
i
j
k
l
m
n
o
p
q
r
s
t
u
v
w
x
y
z

② *I've made a **commitment** to help my grandma on Saturday.*
• a promise, a pledge, a guarantee, an engagement
— A **vow** or an **oath** is a very serious commitment.
— To make a commitment is to **commit yourself** to something.

common ADJECTIVE
❶ *The robin is a **common** bird.*
• commonplace, everyday, normal, ordinary, familiar, well-known
OPPOSITE rare
❷ *Earthquakes are quite **common** there.*
• frequent, commonplace, widespread, usual, normal
OPPOSITES rare, infrequent
❸ *'Hello' is a **common** way to greet people.*
• typical, usual, regular, routine, standard, everyday, customary, conventional, traditional
OPPOSITES uncommon, unusual
❹ *We have a **common** interest in music.*
• shared, mutual, joint

commotion NOUN
*The crowd was causing a **commotion** outside.*
• a disturbance, a row, a fuss, a din, a racket, a riot, an uproar, an upheaval, trouble, disorder, unrest, agitation, turmoil, chaos, pandemonium

communicate VERB
❶ *You can **communicate** your feelings with your expression.*
• to express, to make known, to indicate, to convey, to get across
❷ *We usually **communicate** by instant message.*
• to contact each other, to correspond, to be in touch, to talk

communication NOUN
❶ *Dolphins use sound for **communication**.*
• communicating, contact, understanding each other
❷ *He received a **communication** from headquarters.*
• a message, a dispatch, a transmission, a report

community NOUN
*My uncle grew up in a farming **community**.*
• a neighbourhood, a settlement, a colony, an area

companion NOUN
*His dog was his trusted **companion**.*
• a friend, a partner, a comrade, a mate *(informal)*, a pal *(informal)*

company NOUN
❶ *My cousin works for a computer **company**.*
• a business, a firm, a corporation, an organisation, an establishment
❷ *I was lonely and wanted some **company**.*
• companionship, friendship

compare VERB
*We **compared** the two pictures.*
• to contrast, to relate, to set side by side
➤ compared with
*These sums are so easy **compared with** the other ones.*
• in comparison to, in contrast to, in relation to

comparison NOUN
❶ *I put the two colours side by side for **comparison**.*
• comparing, contrast
❷ *There's no **comparison** between their team and ours.*
• a similarity, a resemblance, a likeness, a match

compete VERB
*Five schools will be **competing** in the tournament.*
• to participate, to take part, to enter, to play, to perform
➤ to compete against
*We are **competing against** a strong team.*
• to oppose, to play against, to challenge

competent ADJECTIVE
*She is a **competent** driver.*
• able, capable, skilful, skilled, accomplished, experienced
OPPOSITE incompetent

competition NOUN
❶ *Let's have a **competition** to see who can finish first.*
• a contest, a challenge, a race, a game
❷ *We won a maths **competition**.*
• a tournament, a championship

competitor NOUN
*The **competitors** lined up for the start of the race.*
• a contestant, a challenger, a participant, an opponent, a rival

complain VERB
*She is always **complaining**.*
• to moan, to grumble, to whinge, to grouse
➤ to complain about
*I wrote a letter **complaining about** the noise.*
• to protest about, to object to, to criticise, to oppose, to campaign against
OPPOSITE to praise

complaint NOUN
They got a lot of complaints about the noise.
• a criticism, an objection, a protest, a moan, a grumble
• an outcry: *There was an outcry about the noise.*

complement VERB
That shade of green complements your eyes.
• to match, to go with, to suit

complete ADJECTIVE
❶ *Have you got a complete set of cards?*
• whole, entire, full, intact
OPPOSITE incomplete
❷ *Now our mission is complete.*
• finished, completed, ended, accomplished, concluded
OPPOSITE unfinished
❸ *The room was a complete mess.*
• total, utter, absolute, downright, thorough, sheer

complete VERB
We have completed all the tasks on the sheet.
• to finish, to carry out, to end, to conclude, to accomplish

completely ADVERB
❶ *Have you completely finished?*
• totally, absolutely, wholly, fully, entirely
❷ *I was completely shocked.*
• totally, utterly, absolutely, really, thoroughly

complex ADJECTIVE
This is a complex task.
• complicated, difficult, tricky, elaborate, detailed, intricate
OPPOSITE simple

complicated ADJECTIVE
The plot of the film is very complicated.
• complex, intricate, elaborate, sophisticated, difficult
OPPOSITES simple, straightforward

component NOUN
The factory makes components for cars.
• a part, a bit, a piece, a section

comprehend VERB
The crowd couldn't comprehend what was happening.
• to understand, to grasp, to work out, to figure out, to follow, to appreciate

compulsory ADJECTIVE
The wearing of seat belts is compulsory.
• required, obligatory, necessary
OPPOSITE optional

computer NOUN

✦ WORD WEB

SOME KINDS OF COMPUTER:
• a desktop, a laptop, a notebook, a PC, a smartphone, a tablet

SOME PARTS OF A COMPUTER SYSTEM:
• a chip, a console, the desktop, a disk, the display, a drive, the hard disk, a joystick, a keyboard, a keypad, a monitor, a mouse, a printer, the screen, a terminal, a touchscreen

OTHER TERMS USED IN COMPUTING:
• an app, an application, an attachment, a backup, a bookmark, broadband, a browser, a bug, a byte, code, a cursor, data, a database, a directory, a document, a download, an email, a file, a folder, a font, a function, graphics, hardware, an icon, input, the Internet, a kilobyte, a megabyte, memory, a menu, a network, offline, online, output, a printout, a program, RAM, ROM, a search, a search engine, software, virtual reality, a virus, a website, a window, Wi-Fi, wireless

SOME THINGS YOU DO WITH A COMPUTER:
• to back up, to boot up, to browse, to click, to close, to code, to connect, to copy and paste, to crash, to email, to hack (into), to install, to log in, to log out, to open, to program, to reboot, to save, to scroll, to search, to select, to sort, to spellcheck, to stream, to surf (the Internet), to undo, to upload

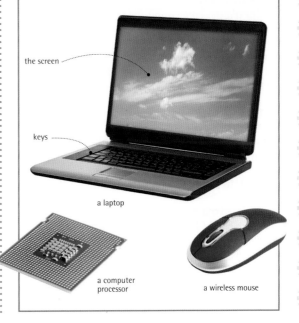

the screen

keys

a laptop

a computer processor

a wireless mouse

conceited *ADJECTIVE*
He was so conceited when he won first prize!
• boastful, arrogant, proud, vain, self-satisfied,
pompous, haughty
OPPOSITE modest

concentrate *VERB*
I had to concentrate to follow the story.
• to be attentive, to pay attention, to focus,
to think hard

concept *NOUN*
The story is about the concept of time travel.
• an idea, a thought, a notion

concern *VERB*
❶ *It concerns me that we are destroying the rainforests.*
• to worry, to bother, to distress, to trouble, to upset
❷ *This doesn't concern you.*
• to affect, to involve, to relate to, to be relevant to,
to be important to, to matter to

concern *NOUN*
❶ *Climate change is a great concern for us.*
• a worry, an anxiety, a fear, a problem
❷ *My private life is not your concern.*
• affair, business

concerned *ADJECTIVE*
I am a bit concerned about what has happened to him.
• worried, anxious, troubled, upset, bothered,
preoccupied, distressed

concerning *PREPOSITION*
We got a letter concerning the trip.
• about, regarding, relating to, with regard to

concert *NOUN*
The jazz band is giving a concert tonight.
• a performance, a show

conclude *VERB*
❶ *They concluded that he was guilty.*
• to decide, to deduce, to infer, to form the opinion,
to gather, to work out
❷ *He concluded his speech with a joke.*
• to end, to finish, to complete, to round off

conclusion *NOUN*
❶ *At the end of the experiment we wrote our
conclusion.*
• findings, a judgement, an opinion, a verdict,
a deduction, a decision
❷ *The conclusion of the film was a bit puzzling.*
• the end, the ending, the close

condemn *VERB*
The manager condemned the behaviour of the players.
• to criticise, to disapprove of, to denounce,
to reproach
OPPOSITE to praise

condition *NOUN*
❶ *Is your bike in good condition?*
• a state, repair
❷ *A dog needs exercise to stay in good condition.*
• fitness, health, shape
❸ *They were living in very bad conditions.*
• circumstances, surroundings, a situation
➤ **on condition that**
*You can paint on condition that you clean up
afterwards.*
• provided, providing that, only if

conduct *VERB*
❶ *We conducted an experiment.*
• to carry out, to perform, to do, to organise, to run
❷ *Mrs Patel conducts the choir.*
• to lead, to direct
❸ *Metal conducts heat.*
• to transmit, to transfer, to pass along

conduct *NOUN*
Your conduct during the trip was excellent.
• behaviour, manners, attitude

confess *VERB*
The goblin confessed that he had stolen the gold.
• to admit, to own up, to acknowledge, to reveal,
to disclose

confidence *NOUN*
❶ *I wish I had her confidence.*
• self-confidence, self-assurance, self-belief, boldness
❷ *I have confidence in you.*
• faith, trust, belief, hope, optimism
OPPOSITE doubt

confident *ADJECTIVE*
❶ *She seems very confident.*
• self-confident, self-assured, sure of yourself,
bold, fearless, unafraid
❷ *I am confident that we will win.*
• certain, sure, positive, convinced, optimistic, hopeful
OPPOSITE doubtful

confirm *VERB*
What he said confirmed my suspicions.
• to prove, to justify, to support, to back up,
to reinforce
OPPOSITE to disprove

confiscate *VERB*
*The teacher **confiscated** his ball.*
• to take away, to take possession of, to seize

conflict *(say* kon-flikt*) NOUN*
*There's a lot of **conflict** in their family.*
• disagreement, quarrelling, fighting, feuding,
hostility, trouble, unrest
conflict *(say* kun-flikt*) VERB*
➤ **to conflict with**
*The two accounts **conflict with** one another.*
• to disagree with, to differ from, to contradict,
to contrast with, to clash with

confront *VERB*
*I decided to **confront** her about the missing money.*
• to challenge, to stand up to, to face up to
➤ **to be confronted with**
*We are **confronted with** a difficult choice.*
• to face, to be faced with, to have to deal with

confuse *VERB*
❶ *The instructions **confused** me.*
• to puzzle, to bewilder, to mystify, to baffle, to perplex
❷ *You must be **confusing** me with someone else.*
• to mix up, to muddle, to get something confused

confused *ADJECTIVE*
❶ *I felt really **confused** at the end of the story.*
• puzzled, bewildered, baffled, mystified, perplexed
❷ *He gave a rather **confused** explanation.*
• muddled, jumbled, rambling, confusing, chaotic

confusion *NOUN*
❶ *I stared at them in **confusion**.*
• bewilderment, bafflement, puzzlement,
incomprehension
❷ *The room was in **confusion**.*
• disorder, chaos, uproar, a muddle, a jumble, a mess

congratulate *VERB*
*We **congratulated** the winners.*
• to applaud, to praise, to compliment

connect *VERB*
❶ *You have to **connect** the wires.*
• to join, to attach, to fasten, to link, to fix together
OPPOSITE to separate
❷ *What **connects** these two events?*
• to link, to relate, to associate,
to form a connection between

connection *NOUN*
*There is a close **connection** between our families.*
• a link, an association, a relationship, a bond

conquer *VERB*
❶ *He **conquered** his enemy.*
• to defeat, to beat, to overcome, to vanquish
❷ *Julius Caesar **conquered** Gaul.*
• to seize, to capture, to take, to win, to occupy
❸ *I **conquered** my fears.*
• to overcome, to control, to defeat, to get the
better of

conscientious *ADJECTIVE*
*He is a very **conscientious** pupil.*
• hard-working, careful, dependable, reliable,
responsible, dutiful, thorough
OPPOSITE careless

conscious *ADJECTIVE*
*The patient was **conscious** throughout the operation.*
• awake, aware, alert
OPPOSITE unconscious
➤ **to be conscious of**
*I was **conscious of** a strange smell.*
• to be aware of, to notice

consent *NOUN*
*His parents gave their **consent**.*
• agreement, permission, approval, authorisation
consent *VERB*
➤ **to consent to**
*The head has **consented to** our request.*
• to agree to, to grant, to approve of, to authorise
OPPOSITE to refuse

consequence *NOUN*
*He drank the potion without thinking of the
consequences.*
• effect, result, outcome

conservation *NOUN*
*Our group supports the **conservation** of wildlife.*
• preservation, protection, defence
OPPOSITE destruction

consider *VERB*
❶ *The detective **considered** the problem carefully.*
• to think about, to examine, to contemplate,
to ponder on, to reflect on, to study, to meditate on
❷ *I **consider** this to be my best work.*
• to believe, to judge, to reckon

considerable *ADJECTIVE*
*The cost of repairing the building will be **considerable**.*
• large, significant, substantial, major
OPPOSITES insignificant, minor

a
b
c
d
e
f
g
h
i
j
k
l
m
n
o
p
q
r
s
t
u
v
w
x
y
z

considerate ADJECTIVE
It was **considerate** of you to lend me your umbrella.
• kind, helpful, thoughtful, obliging, sympathetic, unselfish, caring
OPPOSITE selfish

consist VERB
➤ to consist of
The meal **consisted of** bread and cheese.
• to be made up of, to be composed of, to comprise, to contain, to include, to involve

consistent ADJECTIVE
These plants need to be kept at a **consistent** temperature.
• steady, constant, regular, stable, unchanging

console VERB
He tried to **console** me after I lost.
• to comfort, to cheer someone up, to soothe, to sympathise with, to support

conspicuous ADJECTIVE
The dirty mark very **conspicuous**.
• prominent, noticeable, obvious, visible, unmistakable

constant ADJECTIVE
There is a **constant** noise of traffic.
• continual, continuous, never-ending, non-stop, incessant, endless, everlasting, perpetual, unending, persistent, relentless
OPPOSITE occasional

constantly ADVERB
He is **constantly** complaining.
• always, continually, continuously, forever, incessantly, invariably, non-stop
He complains **non-stop**.
OPPOSITE occasionally

contact VERB
I'll **contact** you when I have some news.
• to make contact with, to get in touch with, to communicate with, to call, to speak to, to let someone know

contain VERB
This book **contains** a lot of information.
• to hold, to include, to have inside

container NOUN
Put the leftover sauce in a **container**.
• a box, a pot, a tub, a holder

WORD WEB

SOME TYPES OF CONTAINER:
• a bag, a barrel, a basket, a bin, a bottle, a bucket, a can, a carton, a cartridge, a case, a crate, a cup, a drum, a jar, a jug, a tank, a tin, a vat
» Look at **bag** and **drink**.

contaminate VERB
The river had been **contaminated** with chemicals.
• to pollute, to poison, to infect, to soil, to dirty
OPPOSITE to purify

contemplate VERB
❶ They **contemplated** what to do next.
• to consider, to ponder, to wonder, to reflect on, to think about
❷ She is **contemplating** moving to a new school.
• to consider, to plan, to think of, to have in mind
❸ We sat and **contemplated** the view.
• to look at, to view, to admire, to gaze at, to stare at

contempt NOUN
He looked at his enemy with **contempt**.
• scorn, hatred, loathing, disgust, dislike, derision
OPPOSITE admiration

content ADJECTIVE
I am **content** to sit reading a book.
• happy, contented, satisfied, pleased, willing, glad
OPPOSITE unwilling

contented ADJECTIVE
After her meal, the cat looked very **contented**.
• happy, pleased, content, satisfied, serene, tranquil, placid, peaceful, relaxed, comfortable, untroubled
OPPOSITE discontented

contest NOUN
The tennis final was an exciting **contest**.
• a competition, a game, a match, a battle, a challenge

contestant NOUN
There are twenty **contestants** in the spelling competition.
• a competitor, a participant, a player, a candidate

continual ADJECTIVE
I get sick of their **continual** arguing.
• constant, non-stop, incessant, endless, eternal, perpetual, unending, persistent, relentless
OPPOSITE occasional
» Look at **continuous**.

continue VERB
❶ *We continued our work until we had finished.*
• to keep up, to keep on with, to carry on with, to go on with, to proceed with, to persevere with
❷ *This rain can't continue for long.*
• to carry on, to go on, to last, to persist, to endure, to keep on
— Use **linger** for a smell or an impression that continues: *Her perfume lingered after she had gone.*

continuous ADJECTIVE
We had continuous rain all through our holiday.
• never-ending, non-stop, ceaseless, everlasting, incessant, unbroken, unceasing, uninterrupted
OPPOSITE intermittent
» *Look at* **continual**.

contract (say kon-trakt) NOUN
The player has signed a contract for a new club.
• an agreement, a deal, an undertaking
— An **alliance** or a **treaty** is a contract between countries.

contract (say kun-trakt) VERB
Metal contracts as it cools.
• to shrink, to tighten, to get smaller
OPPOSITE to expand

contradict VERB
I didn't dare to contradict the teacher.
• to challenge, to disagree with, to speak against

contrary (say kon-trair-i) ADJECTIVE
She can be very contrary sometimes.
• awkward, difficult, stubborn, obstinate, uncooperative, unhelpful, wilful
OPPOSITES cooperative, easy
➤ **contrary to** (say kon-tre-ri)
Contrary to popular belief, snakes are not slimy.
• in contrast to, as against, opposing, unlike, opposite to

contrast (say kun-trast) VERB
❶ *We were asked to contrast two poems.*
• to compare, to distinguish, to show the differences between
❷ *Her story contrasted with her friend's.*
• to clash
• to differ: *Her story differed from her friend's.*
contrast (say kon-trast) NOUN
There was a sharp contrast between their reactions.
• a difference, a distinction, an opposition
OPPOSITE a similarity

contribute VERB
❶ *Will you contribute to our school fund?*
• to donate, to give, to make a donation

❷ *She contributes a lot of ideas in class.*
• to add, to volunteer, to put forward, to suggest
➤ **to contribute to**
The wet weather contributed to the accident.
• to help cause, to be involved in

control NOUN
❶ *The captain has control over the crew.*
• authority, power, command
❷ *The pilot was at the controls.*
• the helm, the dashboard, the control panel
control VERB
❶ *The teacher controls what happens in the classroom.*
• to be in control of, to be in charge of, to manage, to run, to command, to direct, to lead, to guide, to regulate, to rule, to supervise
❷ *This switch controls the speed.*
• to regulate, to alter, to affect, to limit, to curb
— To **harness** something is to control and use it: *We can harness the power of the wind.*
❸ *I tried to control my anger.*
• to restrain, to suppress, to stifle, to subdue, to keep under control

convenient ADJECTIVE
❶ *Is Monday convenient for us to meet?*
• suitable, appropriate, possible
OPPOSITE inconvenient
❷ *The corner shop is in a very convenient location.*
• handy, useful, nearby, accessible
OPPOSITE inaccessible

conventional ADJECTIVE
❶ *It is conventional to send cards at Christmas.*
• customary, traditional, usual, accepted, common
OPPOSITE unconventional
❷ *Can an electric car go as fast as a conventional car?*
• normal, ordinary, standard, regular

conversation NOUN
We had a long conversation.
• a talk, a chat, a discussion
— A **gossip** is a conversation about other people.
— Use **dialogue** for conversation in a book, play or film.

convert VERB
We have converted our attic into a games room.
• to change, to adapt, to alter, to transform

convince VERB
The prisoner convinced them that he was innocent.
• to persuade, to satisfy, to make someone believe

convinced ADJECTIVE
I'm absolutely convinced that he's lying.
• positive, certain, sure, persuaded, confident

a
b
c
d
e
f
g
h
i
j
k
l
m
n
o
p
q
r
s
t
u
v
w
x
y
z

cook VERB

🕸 WORD WEB

SOME WAYS TO COOK FOOD:

• to bake, to barbecue, to boil, to casserole, to deep-fry, to fry, to grill, to microwave, to poach, to roast, to scramble, to simmer, to steam, to stew, to stir-fry, to toast

stew

blend

chop

OTHER WAYS TO PREPARE FOOD:

• to beat, to blend, to chop, to crush, to dice, to grate, to grind, to knead, to mince, to mix, to peel, to sieve, to sift, to slice, to stir, to whip, to whisk

» Look at **kitchen**.

fry

whisk

grate

😊 WRITING TIPS

Here are some useful words for writing about cooking:

SOME SOUNDS MADE BY COOKING:

• bubble, clank, clash, clatter, crackle, sizzle, hiss, pop, slosh, spatter, splash, splutter, sputter

The kitchen is full of steam and delicious cooking smells. Over the clatter of saucepans and crackle of the fire there is the chatter of excited and flustered voices as everyone works to prepare the meal.
—BETWEEN TWO SEAS, Marie-Louise Jensen

» *For ways to describe food look at* **food**.

cool ADJECTIVE

❶ *The weather is cool for the time of year.*
• chilly, cold
`OPPOSITE` warm

❷ *I had a lovely cool drink.*
• chilled, iced, refreshing
`OPPOSITE` hot

❸ *She stayed cool when everyone else panicked.*
• calm, relaxed, unflustered, serene
— A common simile is **as cool as a cucumber**.
`OPPOSITE` frantic

cool VERB

Let the cake cool before you ice it.
• to cool down, to get cool, to get cold
— To **chill** something is to make it cool.
— To **refrigerate** something is to cool it in a refrigerator.

cooperate VERB

They cooperated to build a shelter.
• to work together, to collaborate, to help each other, to support each other

cope VERB

Can you cope on your own?
• to manage, to get by, to continue, to survive
➤ **to cope with**
I can't cope with all this homework!
• to deal with, to handle, to manage
Lizards can cope with a lot of heat.
• to put up with, to tolerate, to bear, to withstand

copy NOUN

That isn't the original painting—it's a copy.
• a replica, a reproduction, a duplicate, an imitation, a likeness
— A **fake** or a **forgery** is a copy made to trick someone.
— A **clone** is a copy of a living thing.

copy VERB

❶ *I tried to copy the drawing.*
• to duplicate, to reproduce
— To **fake** or **forge** something is to copy it in order to trick someone.
— To **clone** a living thing is to produce a copy of it.
❷ *My parrot can copy my voice.*
• to imitate, to impersonate, to mimic

cord NOUN

The pilot pulled the cord to open his parachute.
• a string, a rope, a tape, a strap, a line
— A **cable** or a **flex** is an electrical cord.

core NOUN
It is very hot at the earth's core.
• the centre, the middle, the inside, the heart, the nucleus

corn NOUN
The farmer was growing corn in the field.
• grain, cereal, wheat

corner NOUN
I'll meet you at the corner of the road.
• a turn, a turning, a junction
— A corner formed by two lines is an **angle**.

correct ADJECTIVE
❶ *Your answers are all correct.*
• right, accurate, exact
OPPOSITE wrong
❷ *I hope he has given us correct information.*
• true, genuine, authentic, precise, reliable, factual
OPPOSITE false
❸ *Make sure you use the correct equipment.*
• proper, suitable, appropriate, acceptable
OPPOSITE wrong

correct VERB
❶ *I have to correct my spelling mistakes.*
• to alter, to rectify, to put right
❷ *Miss Nicol corrected our tests.*
• to mark, to grade

corrode VERB
This acid will corrode metal.
• to eat away, to wear away, to rust, to dissolve, to destroy, to erode

corrupt ADJECTIVE
Corrupt officials had accepted bribes.
• dishonest, criminal, untrustworthy, crooked *(informal)*
OPPOSITE honest

cost VERB costs, costing, cost
How much do these shoes cost?
• to be worth, to sell for, to go for

cost NOUN
The bill shows the total cost.
• the price, the charge, the fee, the payment, the amount
— The **fare** is the cost of travelling on public transport.

costume NOUN
The Irish dancers were wearing national costumes.
• an outfit, dress, clothing, clothes
— A **uniform** is a set of clothes worn by members of a school, army or organisation.

corn

— A costume you wear to look like someone else for a party is **fancy dress**.
» *Look at* **clothes**.

cosy ADJECTIVE
It was cold outside but I felt cosy in bed.
• snug, comfortable, warm, secure
OPPOSITE uncomfortable

count VERB
❶ *I counted the number of people on the bus.*
• to add up, to total, to tally up, to work out, to calculate, to compute
❷ *A goal scored by cheating doesn't count.*
• to matter, to be significant, to be important, to be valid
➤ **to count on**
You can count on me to support you.
• to depend on, to rely on, to trust

countless ADJECTIVE
I've seen that film countless times.
• numerous, innumerable, myriad, untold, infinite

country NOUN
❶ *Canada is a very big country.*
• a nation, a state, a land, a territory
— A **kingdom** or a **realm** is a country ruled by a king or queen.
❷ *We went for a picnic in the country.*
• the countryside, farmland
OPPOSITES town, city
— A word meaning 'to do with the country' is **rural**.
OPPOSITE urban

courage NOUN
The rescue dogs showed great courage.
• bravery, valour, heroism, fearlessness, boldness, daring, nerve
OPPOSITE cowardice

courageous ADJECTIVE
The warriors were courageous in battle.
• brave, heroic, valiant, fearless, daring, bold, gallant, intrepid, plucky
OPPOSITE cowardly

course NOUN
❶ *My mum is doing an art course.*
• classes, lessons
❷ *The hot-air balloon drifted off its course.*
• a direction, a path, a route, a way, a line
➤ **of course**
Of course you can come to my party.
• naturally, certainly, definitely, undoubtedly

a
b
c
d
e
f
g
h
i
j
k
l
m
n
o
p
q
r
s
t
u
v
w
x
y
z

courteous ADJECTIVE
*I received a **courteous** reply to my letter.*
• polite, respectful, well-mannered, civil
OPPOSITE rude

cover VERB
❶ *Clouds **covered** the sun.*
• to hide, to conceal, to obscure, to veil,
to blot out, to screen, to shroud, to wreathe
— Use to **engulf**, to **submerge** or to **swamp** when
liquid covers something.
❷ *I tried to **cover** the mark on the carpet.*
• to hide, to disguise, to camouflage, to mask,
to conceal
❸ *They **covered** hundreds of miles on their journey.*
• to travel, to go
❹ *The series **covers** a lot of historical events.*
• to deal with, to include, to contain

cover NOUN
❶ *I put some more **covers** on the bed.*
• a blanket, a quilt, a bedcover
❷ *The **cover** of the book was torn.*
• the wrapper, the jacket
❸ *On the bare hillside, there was no **cover** from
the storm.*
• shelter, protection, defence, shield,
refuge, sanctuary

cower VERB
*A frightened creature was
cowering in the corner.*
• to cringe, to shrink, to crouch,
to flinch, to quail

crack NOUN
❶ *There's a **crack** in this cup.*
• a break, a chip, a split, a fracture,
a flaw
❷ *The outlaw hid in a **crack** between
two rocks.*
• a gap, an opening, a crevice, a rift, a cranny
❸ *There was a loud **crack**.*
• a bang, a snap, a pop, an explosion

crack VERB
*You've **cracked** the plate.*
• to break, to fracture, to chip, to split
— Use **shatter** or **splinter** if something cracks into
many pieces.

crafty ADJECTIVE
*The fox was too **crafty** for them.*
• cunning, clever, shrewd, sly, sneaky, tricky, wily,
stealthy, sharp

cram VERB
*I can't **cram** any more into my suitcase.*
• to pack, to squeeze, to crush, to force, to jam

cramped ADJECTIVE
*The car was a bit **cramped**.*
• crowded, narrow, tight, uncomfortable
OPPOSITE roomy

crash NOUN
❶ *I heard a loud **crash** from the kitchen.*
• a bang, a smash
» *For other kinds of sound look at* **sound**.
❷ *We saw a nasty **crash** on the motorway.*
• an accident, a collision, a smash, a bump
— A **pile-up** is a crash involving a lot of vehicles.

crash VERB
❶ *She **crashed** her shopping trolley into me.*
• to smash, to bump, to knock, to ram, to barge
❷ *Two lorries **crashed** in the car park.*
• to collide, to have a crash, to have an accident
❸ *The computer **crashed** and I lost my work.*
• to freeze, to stop working, to go down

crater NOUN
*The surface of the moon is full of **craters**.*
• a pit, a hole, a hollow, a cavity

craters

crawl VERB
*I saw a caterpillar **crawling** along
a leaf.*
• to creep, to edge, to inch,
to slither, to wriggle

crazy ADJECTIVE
❶ *The dog went **crazy** when it was
stung by a wasp.*
• mad, insane, frantic, frenzied,
berserk, hysterical, wild
❷ *He has some **crazy** ideas!*
• absurd, ridiculous, ludicrous, bizarre, daft,
idiotic, senseless, silly, stupid
OPPOSITE sensible

creamy ADJECTIVE
*The sauce is lovely and **creamy**.*
• rich, smooth, thick, velvety

crease NOUN
*Can you iron the **creases** out of this shirt?*
• a wrinkle, a crinkle, a pucker, a fold, a furrow,
a groove, a line

crease VERB
*Pack the clothes carefully, so you don't **crease** them.*
• to crumple, to wrinkle, to crinkle, to crush, to pucker

create VERB
❶ *The cats were **creating** a racket outside.*
• to make, to cause, to produce
❷ *We have **created** a website for our chess club.*
• to set up, to start up, to bring about, to bring into existence, to originate
— You **write** a poem or story.
— You **compose** music.
— You **draw** or **paint** a picture.
— You **invent** or **think up** a new idea.
— You **design** a new product.
— You **devise** a plan.
— You **found** a new club or organisation.
— You **manufacture** or **produce** goods.
— You **generate** electricity.
— You **build** or **construct** a model or a building.
`OPPOSITE` to destroy

creation NOUN
❶ *This pizza recipe is my own **creation**.*
• a concept, an invention, an idea
❷ *The TV programme is about the **creation** of life on earth.*
• the beginning, the origin, the birth

creative ADJECTIVE
❶ *Katie is a very **creative** person.*
• artistic, imaginative, inventive, inspired
❷ *We came up with some **creative** ideas.*
• original, inventive, imaginative, novel, innovative, fresh
`OPPOSITE` unimaginative

creature NOUN
*A wild-looking **creature** emerged from the swamp.*
• an animal, a beast, a being
» *Look at* **animal**.

credit NOUN
*She deserves **credit** for trying.*
• praise, recognition, approval, honour
`OPPOSITES` criticism, disapproval

creep VERB creeps, creeping, crept
❶ *I **crept** out of bed without waking the others.*
• to slip, to sneak, to slink, to steal, to tiptoe
❷ *He **crept** along on his belly.*
• to crawl, to edge, to inch, to slither, to wriggle

creepy ADJECTIVE
*It's a bit **creepy** in the graveyard.*
• scary, frightening, eerie, ghostly, spooky, weird, sinister, uncanny, unearthly
» *Look at* **ghost**.

crew NOUN
» *For words for groups of people look at* **group**.

cricket NOUN

bail
stump

🕸 **WORD WEB**

SOME PEOPLE WHO PLAY CRICKET:

• a batsman, a bowler, a cricketer, a fielder, a wicketkeeper
— The **umpire** is the official who makes sure the rules are followed.

SOME OTHER TERMS USED IN CRICKET:

• bails, a bat, an innings, an over, a pitch, a run, stumps, a wicket

the wicket
(3 stumps)

crime NOUN
*Robbing a bank is a serious **crime**.*
• an offence, wrongdoing

criminal NOUN
*These men are dangerous **criminals**.*
• an offender, a wrongdoer, a villain, a rogue, a crook *(informal)*
— A **convict** is a criminal who has been sent to prison.

🕸 **WORD WEB**

SOME TYPES OF CRIMINAL:

• a bandit, a brigand, a burglar, a gangster, a highwayman, an outlaw, a pickpocket, a pirate, a poacher, a robber, a smuggler, a thief, a vandal

criminal ADJECTIVE
*The gang were involved in many **criminal** schemes.*
• illegal, unlawful, corrupt, dishonest, wrong, crooked *(informal)*
`OPPOSITE` honest

cringe VERB
*I **cringed** with embarrassment when my name was called.*
• to shrink, to flinch, to wince, to shudder

crisis NOUN
*The election result caused a **crisis** in the country.*
• an emergency, a problem, a difficulty, a predicament

crisp ADJECTIVE
❶ *Bake the biscuits until they are **crisp**.*
• crispy, crunchy, firm, brittle
`OPPOSITES` soft, soggy, limp
❷ *It was a **crisp** winter morning.*
• cold, fresh, frosty

critical ADJECTIVE
❶ *Some people made critical comments about my story.*
• negative, disapproving, unfavourable
OPPOSITE positive
❷ *The situation is critical.*
• serious, urgent
OPPOSITE unimportant
❸ *It is critical to get the right dose.*
• crucial, vital, essential
OPPOSITE unimportant

criticise VERB
She criticised us for being so careless.
• to blame, to condemn, to disapprove of, to find fault with, to reproach, to scold, to tell someone off
OPPOSITE to praise

criticism NOUN
I think his criticism of my singing was unfair.
• attack, disapproval, reproach
OPPOSITE praise

crockery NOUN
Please put the crockery away.
• china, dishes, plates

crooked ADJECTIVE
We sat down by an old crooked tree.
• bent, twisted, gnarled, warped
OPPOSITE straight

crop NOUN
❶ *The crop is growing in the fields.*
• grain, corn
❷ *We had a good crop of apples this year.*
• harvest, yield, produce

cross VERB
❶ *You can cross the river at the footbridge.*
• to go across, to pass over
— If a bridge **spans** a river, it goes across from one side to the other.
— To **ford** a river is to cross it by walking or riding through it.
❷ *Measure the angles where the lines cross.*
• to criss-cross, to intersect

cross ADJECTIVE
My mum will be cross if we're late.
• angry, annoyed, upset, vexed, irritated
— Use **irritable** or **grumpy** when someone is in a cross mood.
— Use **furious**, **livid** or **enraged** when someone is very cross.
OPPOSITE pleased
» Look at **angry**.

crouch VERB
The outlaws crouched silently in the bushes.
• to squat, to kneel, to stoop, to bend, to duck, to bob down, to hunch, to huddle

crowd NOUN
❶ *A crowd of people waited outside the theatre.*
• a gathering, a group, an assembly, a bunch, a cluster
— Use a **throng**, a **horde**, a **multitude**, a **crush** or a **swarm** to talk about a large crowd.
— Use a **mob** or a **gang** to talk about a noisy or violent crowd.
❷ *I was in the crowd for the final.*
• the audience, the spectators

crowd VERB
❶ *People crowded around to see what he was doing.*
• to gather, to collect, to assemble, to mass, to flock, to huddle
❷ *Hundreds of people crowded into the hall.*
• to push, to pile, to squeeze, to pack, to cram, to crush, to jam

crowded ADJECTIVE
The shops are always crowded on Saturdays.
• full, packed, teeming, swarming, overflowing, jammed
OPPOSITE empty

crucial ADJECTIVE
❶ *We are at a crucial point in the game.*
• important, critical, decisive, vital, significant
OPPOSITE insignificant
❷ *It is crucial to weigh the ingredients accurately.*
• vital, important, critical, essential, necessary
OPPOSITE unnecessary

crude ADJECTIVE
❶ *We made a crude shelter out of twigs.*
• rough, clumsy, basic, simple, makeshift, primitive
OPPOSITE skilful
❷ *The teacher told them to stop using crude language.*
• rude, vulgar, coarse, impolite, offensive, uncouth
OPPOSITE polite
❸ *The refinery processes crude oil.*
• raw, natural, unprocessed, unrefined
OPPOSITE refined

cruel ADJECTIVE
❶ *He was a cruel king.*
• heartless, pitiless, merciless, ruthless, brutal, savage, vicious, fierce, bloodthirsty
OPPOSITES kind, gentle
❷ *I think hunting is cruel.*
• barbaric, brutal, inhumane
OPPOSITE kind

crumb NOUN
*Wipe the **crumbs** off the table.*
• a bit, a fragment, a scrap, a morsel
» Look at **bit**.

crumble VERB
❶ *The walls of the castle were beginning to **crumble**.*
• to disintegrate, to break up, to collapse,
to fall apart, to decay, to decompose
❷ *We **crumbled** some bread to give to the ducks.*
• to crush, to grind, to pound

crunch VERB
*The dog was **crunching** on a bone.*
• to chew, to munch, to chomp, to grind
» Look at **eat** and **sound**.

crush VERB
❶ *Don't **crush** the flowers.*
• to squash, to flatten, to mangle, to trample
— To **crumple** or **screw up** paper or cloth is to crush
it so it wrinkles.
— To **grind** or **pound** something is to crush it into powder.
— To **mash** something is to crush it into a soft mass.
❷ *We **crushed** the other team.*
• to thrash, to hammer, to overwhelm, to beat
easily, to conquer, to vanquish

cry VERB
❶ *I was upset and started to **cry**.*
• to weep, to shed tears
— To **sob**, **wail**, **bawl** or **howl** is to cry loudly.
— To **whimper** is to cry quietly with a trembling sound.
— To **snivel** is to cry in an annoying way.
— To **lament** or to **mourn** is to cry or be sad about
something that has happened.
❷ *I heard someone **cry** for help.*
• to call, to shout, to yell, to exclaim
— To **scream**, **shriek** or to **screech** is to cry out
loudly in a high voice, often when you are afraid.
— To **roar**, to **bawl** or to **bellow** is to shout loudly,
often when you are angry.

cry NOUN
❶ *The wounded man let out a **cry** of pain.*
• a call, a shout, a yell, a yelp, an exclamation
— A **roar**, a **howl** or a **bellow** is a very loud cry.
— A **scream**, a **shriek** or a **screech** is a loud high cry,
usually of fear.
❷ *I heard the **cry** of a bird.*
• a squawk, a screech, a call, a squeak

cuddle VERB
*He **cuddled** his teddy bear.*
• to hug, to hold closely, to clasp, to embrace,
to snuggle with

cunning ADJECTIVE
*He had a **cunning** plan to escape.*
• clever, crafty, sly, devious, ingenious, wily, tricky,
sneaky, shrewd

cup NOUN

⬡ **WORD WEB**

— A **mug** is a large cup with
a handle, for hot drinks.
— A **beaker** or a **tumbler**
is a cup without a handle,
usually made of plastic or glass.
— A **goblet** is a decorative drinking cup with a
stem and a base.
— A **tankard** is a large heavy cup made of metal
or glass, usually for beer.
— A **trophy** is a metal cup given as a prize.

a cup

cupboard NOUN

⬡ **WORD WEB**

— A **cabinet** is a small cupboard.
— A **wardrobe** is a tall cupboard for hanging clothes.
— A **sideboard** is a piece of furniture with
cupboards, drawers and a flat top.
— A **dresser** is a sideboard with shelves on top.
— A **larder** or a **pantry** is a cupboard or small
room for storing food.
— A **locker** is a small cupboard with a key,
for example in a school or changing room.

cure VERB
*The doctors say they can **cure** his illness.*
• to heal, to treat, to make better, to relieve, to help

cure NOUN
*There is no **cure** for colds.*
• a remedy, a treatment, a medicine, a therapy
— An **antidote** is a cure for the effects of a poison.

curiosity NOUN
*Babies are full of **curiosity** about the world.*
• inquisitiveness, interest
— Use **nosiness**, **prying** or **snooping** to criticise
someone's curiosity about things that are not their
business.

curious ADJECTIVE
❶ *We were all very **curious** about the new teacher.*
• inquisitive, inquiring, interested, intrigued
— Use **nosy** when someone is curious about things
that are not their business.
OPPOSITES uninterested, indifferent

❷ *What is that **curious** smell?*
• odd, strange, peculiar, unusual, extraordinary, funny, mysterious, puzzling, weird

curl VERB
❶ *The snake **curled** itself around a branch.*
• to wind, to twist, to loop, to coil, to wrap, to curve, to turn, to twine
❷ *Steam **curled** upwards from the cauldron.*
• to coil, to spiral, to twirl, to swirl, to furl

curl NOUN
*The girl's hair was a mass of golden **curls**.*
• a wave, a ringlet, a coil, a loop, a twist, a roll, a spiral

curly ADJECTIVE
*My new doll has **curly** black hair.*
• curled, curling
— Use **wavy** for hair that is slightly curly.
— Use **frizzy** for hair that has small tight curls.
— Use **tousled** for hair that has untidy curls.
» *For more ways to describe hair look at* **hair.**
OPPOSITE straight

current NOUN
*The wooden raft drifted along with the **current**.*
• a flow
— The **tide** is the regular flow of sea water.
— A **draught** is a current of air.

current ADJECTIVE
❶ *Who is the **current** head teacher?*
• present, existing
OPPOSITES past, former
❷ *I try to find out about **current** events.*
• recent, modern, present-day, up-to-date
OPPOSITE past
❸ *Have you got a **current** passport?*
• valid, usable, up-to-date
OPPOSITES out-of-date, old

curve NOUN
❶ *There is a **curve** in the road.*
• a bend, a turn, a twist
❷ *I drew straight lines and **curves**.*
• a curl, a loop, an arc, a bulge, a swirl
— A **crescent** is a curve in the shape of a new moon.

curve VERB
*The road **curves** round to the right.*
• to bend, to wind, to turn, to twist, to meander, to loop

custom NOUN
*It is a **custom** to give presents at Christmas.*
• a tradition, a practice, a habit, a ritual

customary ADJECTIVE
*It is **customary** to leave the waiter a tip.*
• traditional, usual, normal, common, typical, conventional, expected
OPPOSITE unusual

customer NOUN
*There was a queue of **customers** at the checkout.*
• a buyer, a shopper, a client

cut VERB cuts, cutting, cut
❶ *The woodcutter was **cutting** logs.*
• to chop, to hack, to saw, to split
— To cut down a tree is to **fell** it.
— To cut parts off a bush or plant is to **prune** it.
— To shape something by cutting is to **carve** it.
❷ *The cook **cut** the apples into small pieces.*
• to chop, to slice, to dice
— To **mince** or to **shred** something is to cut it into very small pieces.
— To **grate** something is to cut it into small pieces by rubbing it on a grater.
— To cut something up so you can examine it is to **dissect** it.
❸ *Mum **cut** my hair.*
• to trim, to clip, to crop, to snip
— To **shave** hair is to remove it with a razor.
— To cut wool off a sheep is to **shear** it.
— To cut grass is to **mow** it.
— To cut corn is to **harvest** or to **reap** it.
❹ *Josh **cut** his foot on a sharp stone.*
• to gash, to wound, to slash, to stab, to pierce
❺ *The shop has **cut** its prices by 10%.*
• to lower, to reduce, to decrease

cut NOUN
*I've got a **cut** on my knee.*
• a wound, an injury
— A **gash** or a **slash** is a long deep cut.
— A **slit** is a long narrow cut.
— A **scrape** or a **scratch** is a shallow cut made by scraping.
— A **graze** is a wide shallow injury made by scraping.
— A **snip** is a cut made with scissors.
— A **notch** is a small V-shaped cut, usually in wood.

cute ADJECTIVE
*The kittens were so **cute**!*
• sweet, lovable, adorable, pretty, gorgeous

cute

A
B
C
D
E
F
G
H
I
J
K
L
M
N
O
P
Q
R
S
T
U
V
W
X
Y
Z

Dd

⚙ Can you think of 5 things a detective might look for?

⚙ Can you think of 3 verbs for things a detective might do?

⚙ Check the thesaurus to find answers!

damage VERB
*Many books were **damaged** in the fire.*
• to harm, to break, to spoil, to mar
— To damage something by using it a lot is to **wear it out**.
— To **cripple**, to **destroy**, to **ruin** or to **wreck** something is to damage it so badly that it will not work.
— To **sabotage** or to **vandalise** something is to damage it deliberately.

damage NOUN
*The storm has caused a lot of **damage**.*
• harm, destruction
— Use **devastation** for a lot of very serious damage.
— Use **injury** for damage to a person's body.
— Use **sabotage** for damage that has been caused deliberately.

damp ADJECTIVE
❶ *The room feels **damp**.*
• moist, clammy, dank, musty
❷ *I don't like this **damp** weather.*
• drizzly, foggy, misty, rainy, wet
— Use **humid** for weather that is damp and warm.
OPPOSITE dry

dance NOUN

 WORD WEB

SOME KINDS OF DANCE OR DANCING:

• ballet, ballroom dancing, breakdancing, country dancing, folk dancing, Irish dancing, a jig, line dancing, maypole dancing, a reel, salsa, Scottish country dancing, street dance, tap dancing, a tango, a waltz

dance VERB
*He **danced** for joy.*
• to jig about, to hop about, to jump about, to leap about, to prance, to skip, to frisk, to frolic
They brandished their swords and beat their shields with ringing blows and they pranced and leaped and were wilder than a storm.—THE HOUNDS OF THE MORRIGAN, Pat O'Shea

danger NOUN
❶ *Who knows what **dangers** lie ahead?*
• peril, trouble, hazard, menace, pitfall, threat, trap
❷ *There is a **danger** of storms.*
• a risk, a chance, a possibility

dangerous ADJECTIVE
❶ *We were in a **dangerous** situation.*
• hazardous, perilous, risky, precarious, treacherous, unsafe, alarming, menacing
❷ *The police arrested him for **dangerous** driving.*
• careless, reckless
❸ *These are **dangerous** chemicals.*
• harmful, poisonous, deadly, toxic
OPPOSITES harmless, safe

dangle VERB
*A bunch of keys **dangled** from the chain.*
• to hang, to swing, to sway, to droop, to wave, to flap

dare VERB
❶ *I didn't **dare** to speak.*
• to have the courage, to be brave enough, to have the nerve
❷ *They **dared** me to climb the tree.*
• to challenge, to defy

daring ADJECTIVE
*It was a very **daring** plan.*
• bold, brave, adventurous, courageous, fearless, intrepid, plucky, valiant
OPPOSITE timid

dark ADJECTIVE
❶ *The room was **dark**.*
• black, shadowy
— Use **pitch-black** if it is completely dark.
— Use **murky**, **gloomy** or **dingy** if a place is dark and unpleasant.
— Use **dim** if it is rather dark.
OPPOSITE bright
❷ *She wore a **dark** green coat.*
• deep
OPPOSITES pale, light

a b c d e f g h i j k l m n o p q r s t u v w x y z

dash VERB
We dashed home because it was raining.
• to run, to race, to hurry, to rush, to sprint, to bolt, to dart, to flee, to pelt
— To **scamper**, to **scurry** or to **scuttle** is to hurry somewhere with short steps.

dash NOUN
When the storm broke, we made a dash for shelter.
• a run, a rush, a race, a sprint

dawdle VERB
We're going to be late if you don't stop dawdling!
• to amble, to stroll, to wander, to linger, to loiter
— To **plod** or to **trudge** is to walk slowly with heavy steps.
— To **lag behind** or to **straggle** is to fail to keep up with others.

dawn NOUN
I was woken at dawn by the birds singing outside.
• daybreak, the break of day, the break of dawn, sunrise, first light
OPPOSITES dusk, sunset

day NOUN
❶ *Badgers sleep during the day.*
• daytime
OPPOSITE night
❷ *Things were different in my grandfather's day.*
• a time, an era, an age, a period

dazed ADJECTIVE
He had a dazed expression on his face.
• confused, bewildered, muddled, perplexed, stunned

dazzle VERB
I was dazzled by the bright lights.
• to daze, to blind
— To **glare** is to shine very brightly: *A white light glared out of the darkness.*
— A **glare** is a dazzling light: *She shielded her eyes against the sun's glare.*

dead ADJECTIVE
❶ *A dead fish floated near the river's edge.*
• lifeless, deceased
— You can use **late** to refer to a person who has recently died: *The widow talked about her late husband.*
OPPOSITE alive
❷ *The engine is dead.*
• not working, broken
— Use **flat** for a dead battery.

deadly ADJECTIVE
The snake's bite can be deadly.
• lethal, fatal, mortal
OPPOSITE harmless

deal VERB deals, dealing, dealt
Who is going to deal the cards?
• to give out, to hand out, to distribute, to share out
➤ **to deal with something**
I can deal with this problem.
• to cope with, to sort out, to attend to, to see to, to handle, to manage, to solve, to resolve

deal NOUN
I'll make a deal with you.
• an agreement, an arrangement, a bargain, a contract

dear ADJECTIVE
❶ *He was delighted to see his dear daughter again.*
• beloved, darling, precious, loved
❷ *I didn't buy the watch because it was too dear.*
• expensive, costly
OPPOSITE cheap

death NOUN
❶ *The Vikings mourned the death of their chief.*
• dying, end, passing
❷ *The accident resulted in several deaths.*
• fatality

debate NOUN
We had a debate about animal rights.
• a discussion, an argument, a dispute

debate VERB
We debated whether it is right to kill animals for food.
• to discuss, to argue about

debris NOUN
Debris from the crash was scattered over a large area.
• remains, wreckage, fragments, pieces

decay VERB
Dead leaves fall to the ground and decay.
• to decompose, to rot, to disintegrate, to break down
— To decay metal is to **corrode** it.

deceit NOUN
I saw through his deceit.
• deception, trickery, dishonesty, fraud, pretence, cheating, deceitfulness, lying
OPPOSITE honesty

deceive VERB
He had deceived them about who he really was.
• to fool, to trick, to cheat, to mislead, to lie to

decent ADJECTIVE
❶ *We know he is a decent man.*
• honest, honourable, good, noble, upright, worthy, respectable
❷ *I haven't had a decent meal for ages!*
• satisfactory, agreeable, good, acceptable
OPPOSITE bad

decide *VERB*
❶ *We **decided** to finish our work instead of going out to play.*
• to choose, to make a decision, to make up your mind, to opt, to resolve
❷ *That goal **decided** the whole tournament.*
• to settle, to determine, to influence

decision *NOUN*
❶ *Can you tell me what your **decision** is?*
• a choice, a preference
❷ *The judges announced their **decision**.*
• a conclusion, a judgement, a verdict, findings

decisive *ADJECTIVE*
❶ *A referee needs to be **decisive**.*
• firm, forceful, resolute, determined
`OPPOSITE` hesitant
❷ *It was a **decisive** victory.*
• convincing, definite, important, crucial

declare *VERB*
*He **declared** that we were the winners.*
• to announce, to state, to assert, to proclaim, to pronounce

decorate *VERB*
*We **decorated** the Christmas tree.*
• to trim, to festoon, to beautify, to prettify
— To decorate food is to **garnish** it.

decoration *NOUN*
*We put **decorations** around the room for the party.*
• an ornament, a trimming
— A decoration put on food is a **garnish**.

decorative *ADJECTIVE*
*The book had a **decorative** design on the cover.*
• ornamental, fancy, attractive, beautiful, colourful, pretty
`OPPOSITE` plain

decrease *VERB*
❶ *They have **decreased** their prices.*
• to reduce, to cut, to lower
❷ *Our enthusiasm **decreased** as the day went on.*
• to become less, to decline, to diminish, to lessen, to weaken, to dwindle, to wane, to shrink, to subside
`OPPOSITE` to increase

decrease *NOUN*
*There has been a **decrease** in the number of bees.*
• a decline, a drop, a fall, a cut, a reduction
`OPPOSITE` an increase

dedicate *VERB*
*He **dedicates** a lot of time to sport.*
• to devote, to commit

deduce *VERB*
*The detective **deduced** that the thief was very small.*
• to conclude, to work out, to infer, to reason, to gather

deed *NOUN*
*They thanked the rescue team for their heroic **deed**.*
• an act, an action, a feat, an exploit

deep *ADJECTIVE*
❶ *The pond is quite **deep** in the middle.*
`OPPOSITE` shallow
❷ *He felt **deep** regret about what happened.*
• intense, profound, earnest, genuine, sincere
❸ *She fell into a **deep** sleep.*
• heavy, sound
`OPPOSITE` light
❹ *The actor has a **deep** voice.*
• low, bass
`OPPOSITE` high

deer *NOUN*
— A male deer is a **buck** or a **stag**.
— A female deer is a **doe**.
— A young deer is a **fawn**.
— A **moose** or an **elk** is a very large kind of deer.
— A male deer's horns are called **antlers**.
— Meat from a deer is called **venison**.

a moose

defeat *VERB*
*The Greeks **defeated** the Trojans.*
• to beat, to conquer, to vanquish, to triumph over, to overcome
— To **crush** or to **thrash** someone is to defeat them easily.

defeat *NOUN*
*The team suffered a humiliating **defeat**.*
• a loss, a failure
`OPPOSITE` a victory

defence *NOUN*
❶ *The castle was built as a **defence** against attack.*
• a protection, a guard, a safeguard, a shield, a barrier, a barricade, a fortification
❷ *There is no possible **defence** for what he did.*
• an excuse, a justification, an explanation

defend *VERB*
❶ *They tried to **defend** themselves against the enemy.*
• to protect, to guard, to shield, to keep safe
`OPPOSITE` to attack
❷ *His friends tried to **defend** his actions.*
• to justify, to explain, to support, to stand up for

defiant ADJECTIVE
*The prisoner was **defiant** and refused to obey.*
• rebellious, insolent, challenging, disobedient, obstinate, stubborn, awkward, difficult, uncooperative
OPPOSITES obedient, cooperative

definite ADJECTIVE
❶ *Is it **definite** that we're going to move?*
• certain, sure, fixed, settled, decided
❷ *The doctor saw **definite** signs of improvement.*
• clear, distinct, noticeable, obvious, positive, unmistakable
OPPOSITE indefinite

definitely ADVERB
*I'll **definitely** phone you tomorrow.*
• certainly, for certain, unquestionably, without doubt, without fail
OPPOSITE perhaps

deflect VERB
*The goalkeeper was able to **deflect** the shot.*
• to divert, to turn aside, to intercept, to ward off

defy VERB
*The men **defied** their captain.*
• to disobey, to refuse to obey, to resist, to challenge, to stand up to, to confront
OPPOSITE to obey

degree NOUN
*The young gymnast showed a high **degree** of skill.*
• a standard, a level, a grade, an amount, an extent

delay VERB
❶ *The traffic **delayed** us.*
• to hold up, to detain, to hinder, to keep someone waiting, to make someone late
❷ *They **delayed** the race because of bad weather.*
• to postpone, to put off, to put back, to suspend
❸ *The situation is urgent so don't **delay**!*
• to hesitate, to linger, to pause, to wait, to dawdle, to loiter

delay NOUN
*There was a ten-minute **delay** before the game could start.*
• a hold-up, a wait, a pause

delete VERB
*I **deleted** your email by mistake.*
• to erase, to remove, to cut, to cut out, to cancel
— To **cross out** something is to delete it by drawing a line through it.

deliberate ADJECTIVE
❶ *That remark was a **deliberate** insult.*
• intentional, planned, calculated, conscious
OPPOSITES accidental, unintentional
❷ *He has a **deliberate** way of talking.*
• careful, steady, cautious, methodical, purposeful
OPPOSITES hasty, careless

deliberately VERB
*I would never **deliberately** upset anyone.*
• on purpose, intentionally, consciously, knowingly
OPPOSITES accidentally, unintentionally

delicate ADJECTIVE
❶ *The dress has **delicate** embroidery.*
• dainty, exquisite, intricate, fine
❷ *Take care not to damage the **delicate** material.*
• fragile, fine, flimsy, thin
❸ *The young plants are very **delicate**.*
• sensitive, tender, fragile
OPPOSITES tough, hardy
❹ *This is quite a **delicate** situation.*
• awkward, tricky, difficult

delicious ADJECTIVE
*The food at the banquet was **delicious**.*
• tasty, appetising, mouth-watering, luscious, succulent, scrumptious *(informal)*, yummy *(informal)*
» For other ways to describe food look at **food**.
OPPOSITES horrible, disgusting

delight NOUN
*She clapped her hands in **delight**.*
• happiness, joy, pleasure, glee

delight VERB
*The puppet show **delighted** the crowd.*
• to please, to charm, to entertain, to amuse, to divert, to enchant, to entrance, to fascinate, to thrill
OPPOSITE to dismay

delighted ADJECTIVE
*I was **delighted** with my present.*
• pleased, happy, thrilled, overjoyed, joyful, ecstatic, elated

delightful ADJECTIVE
*The poem she wrote was **delightful**.*
• lovely, pleasant, pleasing, charming, wonderful

deliver VERB
❶ *We can **deliver** the computer to your house.*
• to bring, to take, to transport, to ship, to supply
❷ *The head **delivered** a speech.*
• to give, to make, to read out

demand VERB
❶ She **demanded** an explanation.
• to insist on, to request, to require, to call for
— To demand something that belongs to you is to **claim** it.
❷ 'What do you want?' he **demanded**.
• to ask, to enquire

demand NOUN
❶ The king refused their **demands**.
• a request, a claim
❷ There is not much **demand** for ice lollies in winter.
• need, call

demolish VERB
They **demolished** the old block of flats.
• to destroy, to flatten, to knock down, to pull down, to tear down, to bulldoze
OPPOSITES to build, to construct

demonstrate VERB
❶ Lucy **demonstrated** how her model worked.
• to show, to illustrate, to display
❷ Campaigners were **demonstrating** in the street.
• to protest, to march

demonstration NOUN
❶ I watched a **demonstration** of the new computer game.
• a show, an exhibition, a display, a presentation
❷ There was a big **demonstration** against the war.
• a protest, a rally, a march

den NOUN
We built a **den** in the garden.
• a hideout, a shelter, a hiding place, a refuge
— A **lair** is the den of a wild animal.

dense ADJECTIVE
❶ The accident happened in **dense** fog.
• thick, heavy
❷ A **dense** crowd waited in the square.
• compact, packed, solid

dent NOUN
There was a large **dent** in the car door.
• a hollow, a knock, a bump, a dip

dent VERB
A football hit the car and **dented** it.
• to make a dent in, to knock, to push in

deny VERB
❶ The boy **denied** the accusation.
• to reject, to dispute, to disagree with, to contradict, to dismiss, to oppose
OPPOSITES to admit, to accept

❷ The school **denied** his request.
• to refuse, to say no to
OPPOSITE to agree to

depart VERB
What time is the train due to **depart**?
• to leave, to set off, to set out, to start
— Use to **take off** when an aircraft departs.
— Use to **sail** when a ship departs.
OPPOSITES to arrive, to get in

department NOUN
Mr Taylor works in the sales **department**.
• a section, a division, an office

depend VERB
➤ **to depend on someone**
The chicks **depend on** their mother.
• to rely on, to be dependent on, to need, to count on
➤ **to depend on something**
My success will **depend on** good luck.
• to be decided by, to be determined by, to be influenced by

dependable ADJECTIVE
My friend is very **dependable**.
• reliable, trustworthy, loyal, faithful, trusty, steady
OPPOSITE unreliable

depressed ADJECTIVE
He felt a bit **depressed** after he lost.
• dejected, desolate, discouraged, downcast, downhearted, forlorn, gloomy, glum, hopeless, melancholy, miserable, mournful, sad, unhappy
OPPOSITE cheerful

depression NOUN
❶ She sank into a state of **depression**.
• despair, dejection, desolation, gloom, glumness, hopelessness, melancholy, misery, sadness, unhappiness
OPPOSITE cheerfulness
❷ The rain had collected in a **depression** in the ground.
• a hollow, a dip, a pit, a dent, a hole, a rut

derelict ADJECTIVE
They plan to pull down those **derelict** buildings.
• crumbling, neglected, deserted, abandoned, ruined, dilapidated

descend VERB
He slowly **descended** the ladder.
• to climb down, to clamber down, to come down, to go down, to move down
— To descend through the air is to **drop** or to **fall**.
— To descend through water is to **sink**.
OPPOSITE to ascend

a
b
c
d
e
f
g
h
i
n
o
p
q
r
s
t
u
v
w
x
y
z

descendant NOUN
He claimed to be a **descendant** of William the Conqueror.
- successor, heir

OPPOSITE ancestor

describe VERB
❶ An eyewitness **described** the accident.
- to report, to recount, to give an account of, to explain

— To **outline** something is to describe it briefly.
❷ How would you **describe** your house?
- to represent, to characterise

— To **depict** or to **portray** something is to describe it in a story or show it in a picture or film.

description NOUN
❶ I wrote a **description** of our day at the seaside.
- a report, an account, a story

❷ Write a **description** of your favourite character in the play.
- a portrait, a representation, a sketch, a profile

desert NOUN

⚙ WORD WEB

THINGS YOU MIGHT SEE IN A DESERT:

- a cactus, a mirage, an oasis, a sand dune, a sandstorm

— A **caravan** is a group of people travelling across a desert.

SOME ANIMALS WHICH LIVE IN DESERTS:

- an armadillo, a camel, a chameleon, a gerbil, a lizard, a rattlesnake, a scorpion, a vulture

The lions were easily found. There were only two of them, of course, and they were lying close together, each on its tawny side on the sandy desert at the edge of the oasis.—THE MAGIC CITY, E. Nesbit

desert VERB
He **deserted** his friends when they needed him.
- to abandon, to leave, to forsake, to betray

— To **maroon** or **strand** someone somewhere is to desert them in a place they can't get away from.

deserve VERB
You **deserve** a treat after all your hard work.
- to be worthy of, to be entitled to, to have earned, to merit

design NOUN
❶ This is the winning **design** for the new library.
- a plan, a drawing, an outline, a sketch

— A **prototype** or a **model** is a first example of something, used for making others.

❷ Do you like the **design** of this wallpaper?
- a pattern, a style, a decoration

design VERB
They **designed** a new type of engine.
- to create, to develop, to invent, to devise, to conceive of, to think up

despair NOUN
I felt **despair** when I saw how bad the damage was.
- depression, desperation, gloom, hopelessness, misery, anguish, dejection, melancholy, pessimism

OPPOSITE hope

desperate ADJECTIVE
❶ The shipwrecked crew were in a **desperate** situation.
- hopeless, grave, serious, severe, critical, drastic, dire, urgent

❷ I was **desperate** to go home.
- longing, anxious, frantic

despicable ADJECTIVE
The pirates were known for **despicable** acts of cruelty.
- disgraceful, hateful, shameful, loathsome, vile

despite PREPOSITION
We went for a walk **despite** the rain.
- in spite of, regardless of, notwithstanding

OPPOSITE because of

dessert NOUN
For **dessert**, there's an ice-cream sundae.
- pudding, sweet

destroy VERB
❶ An avalanche **destroyed** the village.
- to devastate, to crush, to smash, to wreck

— To **demolish**, to **flatten** or to **knock down** a building is to destroy it.

— To **annihilate** something or to **wipe it out** is to destroy it completely so it no longer exists.

❷ He tried to **destroy** his rival's reputation.
- to ruin, to wreck, to sabotage

destruction NOUN
❶ The hurricane caused **destruction** all along the coast.
- devastation, damage, demolition, ruin

OPPOSITE creation

❷ Global warming may cause the **destruction** of many animal species.
- annihilation, extermination, extinction, elimination, wiping out

OPPOSITE conservation

detail NOUN

Her account was accurate in every detail.

• a fact, a feature, an aspect, a point, an item, a respect

detailed ADJECTIVE

It was a very detailed description.

• precise, exact, specific, full, thorough, elaborate, comprehensive

OPPOSITES rough, vague

detect VERB

I detected the smell of gas.

• to notice, to identify, to recognise

— Use **to observe** or **to spot** when you detect something with your eyes.

detective NOUN

 WRITING TIPS

Here are some words you could use when writing about a **detective**:

THINGS A DETECTIVE MIGHT LOOK FOR:

• an alibi, a bloodstain, clues, evidence, an eyewitness, fingerprints, footprints, a murder weapon, proof, tracks, a crook, a culprit, a suspect

That stain should have been the final proof that Sir Henry had bumped off his wife in one of the most gruesome murders any detective would have to solve.

—MASTER DETECTIVE, Astrid Lindgren

THINGS A DETECTIVE MIGHT DO:

• to analyse, to investigate, to observe, to deduce, to make a deduction, to detect something, to follow a hunch, to watch someone, to pursue someone, to shadow someone, to tail someone, to trace someone, to track someone down, to interrogate someone, to question someone, to search a place, to solve a case

WORDS TO DESCRIBE A DETECTIVE:

• famous, clever, smart, tough

— A **plain-clothes** detective is a police detective who dresses in normal clothes, not a uniform.

— A **private** detective is one who does not work for the police but is paid by someone to solve a case.

— An **amateur** detective is one who solves cases as a hobby.

deteriorate VERB

The weather started to deteriorate.

• to worsen, to decline, to get worse

OPPOSITE to improve

determination NOUN

With strong determination you will succeed.

• commitment, will, courage, dedication, persistence, resolution

determined ADJECTIVE

❶ *The queen was a very determined woman.*

• resolute, decisive, firm, strong-willed, persistent, single-minded

❷ *I'm determined to finish the race.*

• committed, resolved

detour NOUN

I wasted time by taking a detour.

• a diversion, an indirect route

develop VERB

❶ *He developed a new type of camera.*

• to invent, to create, to come up with, to devise

❷ *A friendship developed between them.*

• to grow, to evolve, to advance

development NOUN

❶ *Were there any developments while I was away?*

• an event, a happening, an incident, an occurrence, a change

❷ *We are pleased with the development of our website.*

• growth, advance, expansion, progress

device NOUN

This device controls the temperature.

• a tool, an implement, an instrument, an appliance, an apparatus, a gadget, a contraption

devious ADJECTIVE

They found out about his devious plan to trick them.

• cunning, deceitful, dishonest, furtive, sly, sneaky, treacherous, wily

devote VERB

She devotes all her free time to sport.

• to dedicate, to commit, to assign, to allocate

devoted ADJECTIVE

He's a devoted supporter of our team.

• loyal, faithful, dedicated, enthusiastic, committed

OPPOSITES fickle, unenthusiastic

diagram NOUN

We drew a diagram of the life cycle of a frog.

• a chart, a plan, a drawing, a sketch

dialogue NOUN

There is a lot of dialogue in the play.

• conversation, talk, talking, discussion, chat

a
b
c
d
e
f
g
h
i
j
k
l
m
n
o
p
q
r
s
t
u
v
w
x
y
z

diary NOUN

I wrote all about the party in my diary.

• a journal, a record

— A **log** is a record of what happens every day on a journey.

— A **blog** is a website on which you write regularly about something.

— A **vlog** is a website on which you regularly post short videos about something.

did *(past tense of do)*

die VERB

❶ *It's sad when a pet dies.*

• to pass away

❷ *Thankfully nobody died in the fire.*

• to perish, to be killed

— To **starve** is to die from lack of food.

— To **suffocate** is to die from lack of oxygen.

❸ *The flowers will die if they don't have water.*

• to wither, to wilt, to droop, to fade

➤ **to die down**

The flames will die down eventually.

• to become less, to decline, to decrease, to subside, to weaken, to dwindle, to wane

➤ **to die out**

When did the dinosaurs die out?

• to become extinct, to cease to exist, to come to an end, to disappear, to vanish

differ VERB

❶ *Opinions differ about why this happens.*

• to be different, to vary, to contrast, to conflict

❷ *We differ on this issue.*

• to disagree, to clash, to be in conflict, to oppose someone

difference NOUN

❶ *Can you see any difference between these two pictures?*

• a contrast, a distinction

OPPOSITE a similarity

❷ *This money will make a difference to their lives.*

• a change, an alteration, a modification, a variation

different ADJECTIVE

❶ *The two brothers are completely different.*

• dissimilar, contrasting

• unlike: *The two brothers are completely unlike one another.*

❷ *We have different opinions about some things.*

• differing, contradictory, opposite, clashing, conflicting

❸ *The packet contains sweets of different flavours.*

• various, assorted, mixed, several, diverse, numerous

❹ *Let's go somewhere different on holiday this year.*

• new, original, fresh, unusual, exciting

❺ *Everyone's handwriting is different.*

• distinct, distinctive, individual, special, unique

OPPOSITES identical, similar

difficult ADJECTIVE

❶ *We were faced with a difficult problem.*

• hard, challenging, complicated, complex, tricky, tough, puzzling, baffling, perplexing

— **Obscure** means difficult to understand: *There were some really obscure words that I had to look up in the dictionary.*

OPPOSITES simple, easy

— Some words for a **difficult** situation:

• a dilemma, a predicament, a plight, a puzzle, a struggle

❷ *It is a difficult climb to the top of the hill.*

• challenging, hard, tough, strenuous, formidable, tiring, exhausting

OPPOSITE easy

❸ *She can be difficult when she doesn't get what she wants.*

• awkward, fussy, demanding, contrary, troublesome, obstinate, stubborn, uncooperative, unhelpful

OPPOSITE cooperative

difficulty NOUN

❶ *The explorers were used to facing difficulty.*

• trouble, challenges, struggles, hardship, ordeals

❷ *I had a few difficulties with the work.*

• a problem, a complication, an obstacle, a hindrance, a hitch, a snag

dig VERB **digs, digging, dug**

❶ *They dug a path through the snow.*

• to excavate, to gouge out, to hollow out, to scoop out, to shovel

— To dig coal, metal or a precious stone out of the ground is to **mine** it.

— To dig stone or slate out of the ground is to **quarry** it.

❷ *Rabbits had dug under the fence.*

• to tunnel, to burrow

dignified ADJECTIVE

Even though they were rude, the old lady remained very dignified.

• refined, polite, calm, grave, serious, noble, respectable, distinguished

OPPOSITE undignified

dignity NOUN

❶ *Their laughter spoilt the **dignity** of the occasion.*
• formality, seriousness, solemnity
❷ *She handled the problem with **dignity**.*
• calmness, poise, self-control, politeness

dim ADJECTIVE

❶ *I could see the **dim** outline of a figure in the mist.*
• indistinct, obscure, faint, blurred, fuzzy, hazy, shadowy, vague
OPPOSITE clear
❷ *The light in the cave was rather **dim**.*
• dark, dull, dingy, murky, gloomy
OPPOSITE bright

dinosaur NOUN

 WORD WEB

SOME TYPES OF DINOSAUR:

• a brachiosaurus, a brontosaurus, a diplodocus, an iguanodon, a megalosaurus, a pterodactyl, a stegosaurus, a triceratops, a T-rex or tyrannosaurus rex, a velociraptor

I could see at my very feet the glade of the iguanodons, and farther off was a round opening in the trees which marked the swamp of the pterodactyls.—THE LOST WORLD, Arthur Conan Doyle
— A person who studies dinosaurs and fossils is a **palaeontologist**.

 WRITING TIPS

Here are some words you could use for writing about **dinosaurs**:

SOME WAYS A DINOSAUR MIGHT MOVE:

• to crash, to thunder, to stamp, to stalk, to lunge, to hurtle, to spring, to flap its wings, to thrash its tail, to tear with its teeth

SOME WAYS TO DESCRIBE A DINOSAUR'S BODY:

• vast, huge, massive, scaly, horned, frilled, winged, two-legged

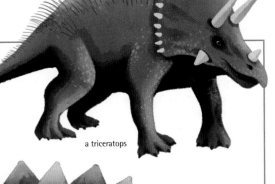

a triceratops

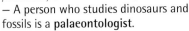
a stegosaurus

a tyrannosaurus rex

a brontosaurus

a
b
c
d
e
f
g
h
i
j
k
l
m
n
o
p
q
r
s
t
u
v
w
x
y
z

dip VERB
❶ *I **dipped** my hand in the water.*
• to immerse, to lower, to plunge, to submerge, to dunk
❷ *The road **dips** down into the valley.*
• to descend, to go down, to slope down

dip NOUN
*There was a **dip** in the road ahead.*
• a hollow, a hole, a depression, a slope

direct ADJECTIVE
❶ *It would be quicker to take the **direct** route.*
• straight, shortest
OPPOSITE indirect
❷ *Please give me a **direct** answer.*
• straightforward, frank, honest, sincere, blunt, plain, unambiguous
OPPOSITES ambiguous, vague

direct VERB
*Can you **direct** me to the station?*
• to guide, to point, to show the way, to give directions

direction NOUN
*Which **direction** did they go in?*
• way, route, course, path
➤ **directions**
*I read the **directions** for building the model.*
• instructions, guidance, guidelines, information

dirt NOUN
❶ *The floor was covered in **dirt**.*
• filth, grime, mess, muck, mud, dust
❷ *Chickens scratched in the **dirt**.*
• earth, soil, ground, mud

dirty ADJECTIVE
❶ *Those **dirty** clothes need to be washed.*
• filthy, grimy, grubby, mucky, messy, soiled, stained
— Bedraggled means wet and dirty.
OPPOSITE clean
❷ *The water is too **dirty** to drink.*
• polluted, contaminated, murky, impure, unhygienic
OPPOSITE pure

disadvantage NOUN
*One **disadvantage** of going by train is the cost.*
• a drawback, an inconvenience, a hindrance, a snag, a problem

directions

disagree VERB
*My sister and I often **disagree** about music.*
• to argue, to differ, to clash, to quarrel, to squabble, to fight, to fall out
OPPOSITE to agree
➤ **to disagree with**
*He **disagrees with** everything I say.*
• to argue with, to contradict, to oppose, to object to

disagreement NOUN
*We had a **disagreement** over who was to blame.*
• an argument, a dispute, a debate, a quarrel, a row, a clash, a squabble, a conflict
OPPOSITE an agreement

disappear VERB
❶ *He **disappeared** into the darkness.*
• to vanish, to become invisible, to melt, to flee
OPPOSITE to appear
❷ *My worries all **disappeared**.*
• to vanish, to fade, to dissolve, to evaporate

disappoint VERB
*She didn't want to **disappoint** her friends by cancelling the party.*
• to let down, to upset
OPPOSITES to please, to satisfy

disappointed ADJECTIVE
*I felt **disappointed** with my picture.*
• unhappy, sad, let down, dissatisfied, discontented
OPPOSITES pleased, satisfied

disapprove VERB
➤ **to disapprove of**
*My mum **disapproves** of mobile phones at the table.*
• to object to, to dislike, to condemn, to criticise
OPPOSITE to approve of

disaster NOUN
*The fire was a terrible **disaster**.*
• a catastrophe, a calamity, a tragedy

✦ WORD WEB

SOME TYPES OF NATURAL DISASTER:
• an avalanche, an earthquake, an epidemic, a famine, a fire, a flood, a hurricane, a landslide, a plague, a tornado, a tsunami, a volcanic eruption

disastrous ADJECTIVE
*The flood was **disastrous** for the town.*
• catastrophic, devastating, destructive, dire, dreadful, terrible, tragic

discomfort NOUN
His injury still causes him some discomfort.
• trouble, pain, soreness, distress
OPPOSITES ease, comfort

disconnect VERB
We need to disconnect the cooker before we can move it.
• to detach, to unplug, to unhook
— You can use to **cut off** for disconnecting a phone.
OPPOSITE to connect

discourage VERB
❶ *Don't let her criticism discourage you.*
• to demoralise, to depress
• to get down: *Don't let it get you down.*
OPPOSITES to motivate, to encourage
❷ *The burglar alarm will discourage thieves.*
• to deter, to put off, to dissuade, to prevent, to stop
OPPOSITE to encourage

discover VERB
❶ *We discovered an old map in the attic.*
• to find, to come across, to spot, to locate, to unearth, to uncover
❷ *I discovered that he had a twin sister.*
• to find out, to learn, to become aware, to realise
— To **notice** or to **observe** something is to discover it because you see it.

discovery NOUN
Scientists have made an exciting new discovery.
• a find, a breakthrough
— The **findings** of an experiment are the things you discover by doing it.

discreet ADJECTIVE
Not many people know about her illness, so please be discreet.
• tactful, sensitive, delicate, careful, diplomatic
OPPOSITE tactless

discuss VERB
I discussed the idea with my parents.
• to talk about, to debate

discussion NOUN
We had a discussion about pocket money.
• a talk, a conversation, a debate

disease NOUN
There is no cure for the disease.
• an illness, a sickness, a complaint, a condition
— An **infection**, a **virus** or a **bug** *(informal)* is a disease caused by a tiny organism.
» *Look at illness.*

disgrace NOUN
❶ *His crimes brought disgrace on his family.*
• humiliation, shame, embarrassment, dishonour
❷ *The way he treats them is a disgrace!*
• an outrage, a scandal, a shame

disguise VERB
I tried to disguise my feelings.
• to conceal, to hide, to cover up, to mask, to camouflage
➤ **to disguise yourself as**
The spy disguised himself as a hotel porter.
• to dress up as, to pretend to be

disgust NOUN
I felt disgust at their cruelty.
• horror, dislike, loathing, contempt, repulsion
— Use **nausea** if something makes you feel physically sick.
OPPOSITE liking

disgust VERB
The smell of rotting food disgusted us.
• to repel, to revolt, to sicken, to horrify, to shock, to offend, to distress
OPPOSITE to please

disgusting ADJECTIVE
The stew in the cauldron looked disgusting.
• repulsive, revolting, sickening, appalling, offensive, horrible, nasty, loathsome, gross *(informal)*
OPPOSITES delightful, pleasing

dish NOUN
❶ *Mum served the pudding in a glass dish.*
• a bowl, a basin, a plate, a platter
❷ *This is a traditional Iranian dish.*
• a recipe, a meal, food, a speciality

dishonest ADJECTIVE
❶ *They were fooled by a dishonest salesman.*
• deceitful, lying, sneaky, tricky, cheating, devious, untrustworthy
OPPOSITE honest
❷ *The guards were dishonest and had been bribed.*
• corrupt, immoral, crooked *(informal)*
OPPOSITE honest

disguise

❸ *What he said was **dishonest**.*
• false, misleading, untrue, untruthful
OPPOSITE truthful

dislike VERB
❶ *I **dislike** cold weather.*
• to hate, to detest, to loathe
OPPOSITES to like, to appreciate
❷ *She **dislikes** violent video games.*
• to object to, to disapprove of, to condemn, to disagree with
OPPOSITES to like, to approve of

dislike NOUN
*She was filled with **dislike** for him.*
• hatred, loathing, disapproval, disgust, revulsion
OPPOSITE liking

disloyal ADJECTIVE
*He was **disloyal** to his friends.*
• unfaithful, treacherous, fickle, false, unreliable, untrustworthy
OPPOSITE loyal

dismiss VERB
❶ *The teacher **dismissed** the class.*
• to send away, to discharge, to let go
❷ *She was **dismissed** from her job.*
• to sack, to fire *(informal)*, to give someone the sack
❸ *They **dismissed** all my ideas.*
• to reject, to discard, to disregard, to ignore

disobedient ADJECTIVE
*The children were very **disobedient**.*
• naughty, badly behaved, unruly, uncooperative, rebellious, insolent, defiant, contrary, difficult
OPPOSITE obedient

disobey VERB
❶ *The referee makes sure no one **disobeys** the rules.*
• to break, to ignore, to disregard, to defy
❷ *Soldiers are trained never to **disobey**.*
• to be disobedient, to rebel, to revolt, to mutiny, to defy orders
OPPOSITE to obey

disorder NOUN
*There was complete **disorder** in the room.*
• chaos, confusion, uproar, upheaval, turmoil, tumult, a disturbance, a commotion
OPPOSITE order

display VERB
*We will **display** the pictures in the hall.*
• to exhibit, to show, to put on show, to set out
— To display something in a boastful way is to **flaunt** it or to **show it off**.

display NOUN
*We set out a **display** of our artwork.*
• an exhibition, a show, a presentation

dispose VERB
➤ **to dispose of something**
*It's important to **dispose of** your rubbish correctly.*
• to get rid of, to discard, to throw away

disrupt VERB
*Bad weather **disrupted** the tennis tournament.*
• to interfere with, to cause problems with, to upset, to interrupt, to disturb

dissatisfied ADJECTIVE
*I was **dissatisfied** with my piano playing.*
• displeased, disappointed, discontented, frustrated, annoyed, unhappy
OPPOSITE satisfied

dissolve VERB
*The pill **dissolves** in water.*
• to melt, to disperse, to disintegrate

distance NOUN
*What is the **distance** from earth to the sun?*
• the measurement, the space, the extent
— The distance across something is its **width** or **breadth**.
— The distance along something is its **length**.
— The distance between two points is a **gap** or an **interval**.

distant ADJECTIVE
*I'd love to travel to **distant** countries.*
• faraway, far, remote, isolated
— A distant place is an **outpost**: *This was the furthest **outpost** of the Roman Empire.*
OPPOSITE close

distinct ADJECTIVE
❶ *I saw a **distinct** improvement in his writing.*
• clear, definite, noticeable, unmistakable, evident, obvious, visible, distinguishable
OPPOSITE indistinct
❷ *The word has two **distinct** meanings.*
• different, separate, distinctive, individual

distinction NOUN
❶ There's a clear **distinction** between the real diamond and the fake.
• a difference, a contrast
❷ She is a musician of **distinction**.
• honour, glory, merit, excellence

distinguish VERB
❶ It was impossible to **distinguish** one twin from the other.
• to tell apart, to pick out, to tell the difference between, to make a distinction between
❷ What **distinguishes** humans from other animals?
• to set apart, to be the difference between, to be a distinction between
❸ I **distinguished** a shape in the fog.
• to make out, to identify, to perceive, to recognise

distort VERB
The mirror **distorts** your image.
• to warp, to contort, to bend, to twist

distract VERB
Don't **distract** the bus driver.
• to divert the attention of, to disturb, to put off

distress NOUN
❶ The trapped animal was clearly in **distress**.
• suffering, torment, pain
❷ This worrying incident caused a lot of **distress** to parents.
• anxiety, anguish, worry, dismay, grief, sorrow

distress VERB
We could see that the news **distressed** her.
• to upset, to disturb, to trouble, to worry, to alarm, to dismay
OPPOSITE to comfort

distribute VERB
The coach **distributed** water to the players at half-time.
• to give out, to hand round, to dispense, to issue, to share out

distrust VERB
I **distrusted** the professor from the moment I met him.
• to mistrust, to suspect, to doubt, to question, to be suspicious of, to be wary of, to be unsure about
OPPOSITE to trust

distrust NOUN
There was a lot of **distrust** between them.
• mistrust, suspicion, suspiciousness, doubt, wariness, caution
OPPOSITE trust

disturb VERB
❶ Sorry to **disturb** you when you're working.
• to bother, to interrupt, to annoy, to pester, to trouble, to disrupt
❷ The news **disturbed** them.
• to distress, to trouble, to upset, to worry, to concern, to alarm

disused ADJECTIVE
They made the **disused** railway line into a cycle track.
• abandoned, unused, closed down

ditch NOUN
We dug a **ditch** to drain away the water.
• a trench, a channel, a drain, a gully, a furrow

dive VERB
❶ The mermaid **dived** into the water.
• to plunge, to jump, to leap
❷ The eagle **dived** towards its prey.
• to swoop, to plummet

divide VERB
❶ We **divided** the class into two groups.
• to separate, to split, to break up
OPPOSITE to combine
❷ I **divided** the cake between my friends.
• to distribute, to share, to split, to cut up

divine ADJECTIVE
❶ The temple is used for **divine** worship.
• holy, religious, sacred, spiritual
❷ The Greeks believed **divine** beings lived on Mount Olympus.
• godlike, immortal, heavenly

division NOUN
❶ The **division** of a pizza into seven equal pieces is not easy.
• dividing, splitting, separation, sharing
❷ They work in different **divisions** of the same company.
• a department, a section, a unit

dive

dizzy ADJECTIVE
After I went on the ride I felt **dizzy**.
• giddy, dazed, faint, unsteady, light-headed

a b c d e f g h i j k l m n o p q r s t u v w x y z

do VERB does, doing, did, done

😮 OVERUSED WORD

Try to use a more interesting word instead of **do**. Here are some ideas and examples:

WHEN DO MEANS 'ACT':

*We have to **do** something about this.*
• to act, to take action

FOR DOING TASKS:

*I have a lot of jobs to **do** this morning.*
• to carry out, to perform, to accomplish, to complete, to attend to, to get on with, to handle, to undertake

'Could we get on with this? I really do have some urgent business to attend to,' said Loki.—OLAF THE VIKING, Martin Conway.

FOR DOING SCHOOLWORK:

*I can't **do** the last question.*
• to answer, to solve, to work out, to puzzle out, to fathom

FOR DOING AN EXPERIMENT OR OPERATION:

*They **did** some tests on the substance they found.*
• to carry out, to conduct, to perform

WHEN DO MEANS 'CAUSE':

*The fire **did** a lot of damage.*
• to cause, to bring about, to produce, to result in, to inflict

WHEN DO MEANS 'BE GOOD ENOUGH':

*If you don't have card, paper will **do**.*
• to be acceptable, to be satisfactory, to be sufficient

VERBS USED INSTEAD OF DO WITH CERTAIN NOUNS:

— to **make** a mistake or an attempt
— to **give** a performance or a speech
— to **commit** a crime
— to **conduct** a survey, an interview or an enquiry
— to **practise** medicine, law or dentistry

dock NOUN
*A boat was waiting for us at the end of the **dock**.*
• a harbour, a quay, a jetty, a wharf, a pier, a port

doctor NOUN
*She is a fully qualified **doctor**.*
• a physician

✳ WORD WEB

SOME TYPES OF DOCTOR:

— A **GP** or a **general practitioner** is a doctor who treats all kinds of illness and sends people to a specialist if necessary.
— A **specialist** is a doctor who knows a lot about one type of illness.
— A **consultant** is a senior doctor in a hospital.
— A **surgeon** is a doctor who performs operations.
— An **anaesthetist** is a doctor who puts people to sleep during operations.
— A **paediatrician** is a doctor who specialises in children's health.
— A **psychiatrist** is a doctor who specialises in mental illness.

document NOUN
*The library contains many old **documents**.*
• a paper, a record
— A **file** is a computer document.
— A **certificate** is an official document that records and proves something.

— A **licence** or a **permit** is an official document showing that someone is allowed to do something.
— A **deed** is a legal document showing who owns something.

dodge VERB
*I managed to **dodge** the snowball.*
• to avoid, to evade, to side-step

dog NOUN

 WORD WEB

— A female dog is a **bitch**.
— A young dog is a **puppy** or **pup**.
— A **hound** is a dog used for hunting or racing.
— A **stray** is a dog that does not have a home.
— A **pedigree** dog is one with a single pure breed.
— A **mongrel** is a dog of mixed breeds.
— A **jackal** is a wild animal similar to a dog.
— A word meaning 'to do with dogs' is **canine**.

SOME BREEDS OF DOG:

• an Alsatian, a beagle, a bloodhound, a boxer, a bulldog, a collie, a corgi, a dachshund, a Dalmatian, a greyhound, a husky, a Labrador, a Pekinese or Pekingese, a pointer, a poodle, a pug, a spaniel, a terrier

SOME WORKING DOGS:

• a guide dog, a guard dog, a police dog, a sheepdog, a sniffer dog
» *Look at* **animal**.

WRITING TIPS

Here are some useful words for writing about **dogs**:

SOUNDS MADE BY DOGS:

• bark, growl, howl, snap, snarl, whine, woof, yap, yelp

SOME THINGS DOGS DO:

• to bound, to leap, to spring, to trot, to race, to chase, to dash, to lick, to pant, to slobber, to sniff, to chew, to gnaw, to wag its tail
Her mother was crying and laughing all at once, and Diggy Bert was lick-slobbering her hands and her face . . . while the other dogs leapt and yapped.
—HAZEL, Julie Hearn

WAYS TO DESCRIBE DOGS:

• loyal, faithful, trusty, affectionate, shaggy, hairy, yappy, barking, snarling, aggressive, fierce, ferocious

done *(past participle of **do**)*

doomed ADJECTIVE
*The expedition was **doomed** from the start.*
• cursed, condemned, ill-fated, jinxed

door NOUN

WORD WEB

— A **hatch** or a **trapdoor** is a door in a wall, floor or ceiling.
— The **doorway** is the opening into which a door fits.
— The **doorstep** is the step or piece of ground outside a door.
— A **porch** is a small enclosed area with a roof outside a door.

dot NOUN
*There were some little **dots** of paint on the carpet.*
• a spot, a speck, a fleck, a mark
— A full **stop** is the dot you put at the end of a sentence.

doubt NOUN
*I have no **doubt** about his honesty.*
• uncertainty, hesitation, reservation, concern, suspicion
OPPOSITES confidence, certainty

doubt VERB
❶ *I **doubt** that we will finish on time.*
• to question, to be uncertain, to be unsure,
• to suspect not: *I **suspect** that we will **not** finish on time.*
OPPOSITES to be sure, to be certain
❷ *They **doubted** his story.*
• to suspect, to be suspicious about, to mistrust, to be wary of, to be unsure of, to be uncertain of
OPPOSITES to trust, to believe

doubtful ADJECTIVE
❶ *He looked **doubtful** but agreed to let us go.*
• dubious, unsure, uncertain, unconvinced, hesitant, distrustful, suspicious
OPPOSITES certain, confident
❷ *Victory is **doubtful**.*
• questionable, unlikely, uncertain
OPPOSITE certain

downfall NOUN
*His pride caused his **downfall**.*
• ruin, collapse, fall, failure

a
b
c
d
e
f
g
h
i
j
k
l
m
n
o
p
q
r
s
t
u
v
w
x
y
z

draft NOUN
*I wrote a **draft** of my story.*
• an outline, a plan, a sketch, a rough version
draft VERB
*I began to **draft** my story.*
• to outline, to plan, to prepare, to sketch out

drag VERB
❶ *The tractor **dragged** the car out of the ditch.*
• to pull, to tow, to tug, to draw, to haul, to heave, to lug
`OPPOSITE` to push
❷ *Don't **drag** your feet when you walk!*
• to shuffle, to scrape
`OPPOSITE` to pick up

dragon NOUN

WRITING TIPS

Here are some useful words for writing about dragons:

SOME WAYS TO DESCRIBE A DRAGON:

• fearsome, fierce, ferocious, fiery, fire-breathing, mighty, monstrous, scaly, spiked, winged

THINGS A DRAGON MIGHT DO:

• to breathe fire, to furl or unfurl its wings, to puff smoke, to roar, to snort, to soar, to swoop, to thrash its tail
And there was the Horntail . . . crouched low over her clutch of eggs, her wings half furled, her evil, yellow eyes upon him, a monstrous, scaly black lizard, thrashing her spiked tail.–HARRY POTTER AND THE GOBLET OF FIRE, J. K. Rowling

PLACES WHERE A DRAGON MIGHT LIVE:

• a cave, a den, a lair

drain NOUN
*The water runs away along a **drain**.*
• a ditch, a pipe, a channel, a drainpipe
– A **gutter** is a drain along a roof or street, for taking away rainwater.
– A **sewer** is an underground drain for taking away dirty water from toilets.

drank (past tense of **drink**)

draught NOUN
*I felt a **draught** of air from the open window.*
• a breeze, a current, a movement, a puff

draw VERB draws, drawing, drew, drawn
❶ *I have **drawn** a picture for you.*
• to sketch, to trace
– To **doodle** is to draw pictures while you are thinking about something else.
❷ *I **drew** the princess sitting on a horse.*
• to depict, to portray, to represent
❸ *We **drew** 1-1.*
• to tie, to finish equal
❹ *She **drew** the curtains.*
• to close, to open, to pull back
➤ **to draw near**
*As the creature **drew near**, I began to get nervous.*
• to approach, to advance, to come near

drawing NOUN

WORD WEB

SOME TYPES OF DRAWING:

• a cartoon, a design, a doodle, an illustration, a sketch

drawn (past participle of **draw**)

dreadful *ADJECTIVE*
❶ *There was a dreadful accident.*
• horrible, terrible, appalling, horrendous, distressing, shocking, tragic, serious
OPPOSITE minor
❷ *The weather was dreadful.*
• awful, terrible, abysmal, abominable, foul, vile
OPPOSITES good, pleasant

dream *NOUN*
❶ *I had a strange dream last night.*
– A **nightmare** or a **bad dream** is a frightening dream.
– A **daydream** or a **fantasy** is a kind of dream you have when you are awake.
❷ *It's her dream to become a vet.*
• an ambition, a fantasy, a wish, a goal

dress *NOUN*
❶ *She wore a long dress.*
• a frock, a gown, a robe
❷ *They are wearing traditional dress.*
• clothes, clothing, an outfit, a costume, garments
» *Look at* **clothes**.

dress *VERB*
❶ *I helped to dress the baby.*
• to clothe, to put clothes on
OPPOSITE to undress
❷ *A nurse dressed my wound.*
• to bandage, to put a dressing on, to bind up

drew *(past tense of* **draw***)*

drink *NOUN*

✦ **WORD WEB**

SOME HOT DRINKS:
• cocoa, hot chocolate, coffee, tea

SOME COLD DRINKS:
• cordial, lemonade, juice, milk, a milkshake, a smoothie, squash, water
– **Pop** is another word for fizzy drinks.

SOME ALCOHOLIC DRINKS:
• beer, brandy, cider, rum, whisky, wine
– *Spirits* are very strong alcoholic drinks.

drink *VERB* **drinks, drinking, drank, drunk**
He picked up the glass of milk and drank it.
– To **sip** something is to drink it slowly, taking small amounts.

– To **gulp** or to **swig** is to drink quickly, taking large amounts.
– To **guzzle** or to **slurp** is to drink noisily.
– To **lap** is to drink something with the tongue, like a cat.

drip *VERB*
Rain water dripped down from the leaves.
• to drop, to dribble, to splash, to trickle

drip *NOUN*
Dad was worried by the drips of oil underneath the car.
• a drop, a spot, a dribble, a splash, a trickle

drive *VERB* **drives, driving, drove, driven**
❶ *She drives her new car very carefully.*
• to steer, to manoeuvre, to control, to operate
❷ *We drove along listening to music.*
• to travel, to ride
– To **zoom** or to **speed** along is to go very fast.
– To **crawl** or to **creep** along is to go very slowly.
❸ *The dog drove the sheep through the gate.*
• to direct, to guide, to herd, to steer

drive *NOUN*
We went for a drive in the country.
• a ride, a trip, a journey, an outing, an excursion

driven *(past participle of* **drive***)*

droop *VERB*
Plants tend to droop in dry weather.
• to sag, to wilt, to wither, to bend, to flop, to be limp

droop

drop *NOUN*
❶ *Large drops of rain began to fall.*
• a drip, a droplet, a spot, a bead, a blob
❷ *There's been a drop in temperature.*
• a decrease, a fall, a reduction

drop *VERB*
❶ *I dropped a cup and it broke.*
• to let go of, to let fall, to let slip
❷ *He dropped onto the sofa exhausted.*
• to fall, to collapse, to flop, to slump
❸ *Rubble dropped onto us from above.*
• to fall, to rain down, to shower, to cascade, to pour down
❹ *Membership of the club has dropped.*
• to fall, to decrease, to reduce

drove *(past tense of* **drive***)*

drug NOUN
A new **drug** has been discovered for back pain.
• a medicine, a remedy, a treatment

drunk (past participle of **drink**)

dry ADJECTIVE
❶ Nothing will grow in this **dry** soil.
• arid, parched, barren
OPPOSITE wet
❷ I hope the weather stays **dry**.
• fair, fine
— A **drought** is a long period of dry weather.
OPPOSITE wet

duck NOUN
— A male duck is a **drake**.
— A young duck is a **duckling**.

a drake (male)   a duck (female)

duck VERB
❶ Oliver **ducked** to avoid the snowball.
• to bend, to bob down, to crouch, to stoop
❷ My friends threatened to **duck** me in the pool.
• to dip, to immerse, to plunge, to submerge

due ADJECTIVE
❶ The train is **due** in five minutes.
• expected, anticipated
❷ Your homework is **due** tomorrow.
• owed, owing

dug (past tense of **dig**)

dull ADJECTIVE
❶ The play was so **dull** that I fell asleep.
• boring, monotonous, tedious, tiresome, uninteresting, unexciting
OPPOSITE interesting

❷ I don't like the **dull** colours in this room.
• dim, dingy, drab, dreary, dismal, faded, gloomy, sombre
OPPOSITE bright, colourful
❸ The sky was **dull** that day.
• cloudy, overcast, grey, sunless, murky
OPPOSITE clear

dumb ADJECTIVE
The spectators were struck **dumb** with amazement.
• speechless, mute, silent

dump VERB
❶ I decided to **dump** some of my old toys.
• to get rid of, to throw away, to throw out, to discard, to dispose of, to scrap
❷ She **dumped** her bags in the hall.
• to put down, to drop, to leave, to throw, to fling, to sling

dusk NOUN
Bats begin to emerge at **dusk**.
• twilight, nightfall, sunset, sundown
OPPOSITE dawn

dusty ADJECTIVE
The books we found in the attic were very **dusty**.
• dirty, grimy
OPPOSITE clean

duty NOUN
❶ I have a **duty** to help my parents.
• a responsibility, an obligation
❷ I carried out my **duties** conscientiously.
• a job, a task, an assignment, a chore

Ee

⚙ Can you think of
3 different ways
to say 'excited'?

⚙ Do you know
a word for an
exciting ending
to a story?
C _ _ _ _ H _ _ G _ R

⚙ Check the thesaurus to find answers!

eager ADJECTIVE
He is always **eager** to help.
• keen, enthusiastic, willing, avid, anxious, impatient
OPPOSITE unenthusiastic

early ADJECTIVE
❶ The bus was **early** today.
• ahead of time, ahead of schedule
— Use **punctual** or **on time** when something arrives
at exactly the right time.
OPPOSITE late
❷ His **early** attempts were not successful.
• first, initial, original
OPPOSITES recent, latest

earn VERB
❶ Sahil **earns** extra pocket money washing cars.
• to receive, to get, to make, to be paid, to obtain
❷ She worked hard and **earned** her success.
• to deserve, to merit

earth NOUN
❶ This is the largest lake on **earth**.
• the globe, the planet,
• the world: This is the largest lake in the **world**.
❷ The **earth** was so dry that many plants died.
• the ground, the soil, the land

earthquake NOUN
The **earthquake** did not do much damage.
• a tremor, a shock, a quake

easy ADJECTIVE
The game is very **easy** to play.
• straightforward, simple, uncomplicated,
basic, obvious
OPPOSITES difficult, complicated

eat VERB eats, eating, ate, eaten
Have you **eaten** anything today?
• to consume, to have (something) to eat
— To **breakfast** is to eat breakfast.
— To **lunch** is to eat lunch.
— To **dine** is to eat dinner.
— Use **feed on** to say what an animal eats: They **feed**
mostly on insects.

😲 **OVERUSED WORD**

Here are some more interesting words you can use
when you want to say **eat**:

TO EAT GREEDILY OR QUICKLY:

• to guzzle, to gobble, to devour, to gulp, to bolt
down, to polish off, to wolf down
She **wolfed down** the entire pizza.

TO EAT NOISILY:

• to munch, to chomp, to crunch, to gnash,
to gnaw
— Use **slurp** for a liquid food or a drink: Tom was
slurping his soup.

TO EAT WITH ENJOYMENT:

• to relish, to savour, to dig into, to tuck into
The campers **tucked into** their breakfast.

TO EAT IN SMALL AMOUNTS:

• to nibble, to taste, to peck at, to pick at
I wasn't very hungry and **picked at** my food.
Giant skeletons set upon his shattered car, splitting
it apart as if it were a metal nut, digging in with
knife-fork fingers, chomping off bumpers . . . biting
the robot chauffeur to bits, and fighting over the
choicest morsels . . . , guzzling the oily sauce
from the engine.—LYDIA'S TIN LID DRUM,
Neale Osborne
» For various things
to eat look at **food**.

a
b
c
d
e
f
g
h
i
j
k
l
m
n
o
p
q
r
s
t
u
v
w
x
y
z

eaten (past participle of **eat**)

eccentric ADJECTIVE
Uncle Otto has always been a little **eccentric**.
• odd, peculiar, strange, weird, unusual, unconventional
OPPOSITE conventional

echo VERB
The sound **echoed** across the valley.
• to resound, to reverberate

edge NOUN
❶ There was a fence around the **edge** of the field.
• the border, the perimeter, the boundary, the margin
— The **circumference** is the edge of a circle.
— The **kerb** or the **verge** is the edge of a road.
❷ The **edge** of the plate is chipped.
• the rim, the border
— The **brim** is the edge of a cup or container.
❸ Leave a space at the **edges** of the page.
• the margin, the border
❹ Don't go too close to the **edge** of the cliff.
• the brink, the end, the verge
❺ We live on the **edge** of town.
• the outskirts, the suburbs
❻ The knife has a sharp **edge**.
• a side, a blade

edit VERB
The letters were **edited** before they were published.
• to revise, to correct, to adapt

edition NOUN
We're preparing the summer **edition** of our magazine.
• a copy, an issue, a number, a version

educate VERB
The job of a school is to **educate** young people.
• to teach, to train, to inform, to instruct

education NOUN
This school is for the **education** of young witches and wizards.
• schooling, teaching, training, instruction

effect NOUN
❶ One **effect** of global warming is that the ice caps are melting.
• a result, a consequence, an outcome

❷ The magic potion was beginning to have an **effect**.
• an impact, an influence

effective ADJECTIVE
The medicine was very **effective**.
• successful, efficient

efficient ADJECTIVE
An **efficient** worker can do the job in an hour.
• effective, competent, able, capable, proficient
OPPOSITE inefficient

effort NOUN
❶ A lot of **effort** went into my juggling act.
• work, energy, trouble, labour, toil
❷ This was my first **effort**.
• an attempt, a try, an endeavour, a go

elaborate ADJECTIVE
The plot of the book is so **elaborate** that I got lost.
• complicated, complex, detailed, intricate, involved
OPPOSITE simple

elderly ADJECTIVE
I helped an **elderly** man to cross the road.
• aged, ageing, old
OPPOSITE young

elect VERB
We **elected** a new captain.
• to vote for, to appoint, to choose, to pick

elegant ADJECTIVE
She always wears **elegant** clothes.
• smart, attractive, stylish, tasteful, sophisticated
OPPOSITE inelegant

embarrass VERB
Will it **embarrass** you if I tell people our secret?
• to humiliate, to make (someone) uncomfortable, to upset

embarrassed ADJECTIVE
Don't feel **embarrassed**—everyone makes mistakes!
• awkward, uncomfortable, ashamed, humiliated, bashful, flustered, self-conscious, shy

emerge *VERB*
*A ship **emerged** from the fog.*
• to appear, to come out
— Use to **loom** if something appears as very large, tall and rather frightening: *A dark tower **loomed** out of the fog.*

emergency *NOUN*
*Try to keep calm in an **emergency**.*
• a crisis, a serious situation, an urgent situation

emotion *NOUN*
*His voice was full of **emotion**.*
• feeling, passion, sentiment

emphasis *NOUN*
❶ *In the word 'tiger' the **emphasis** is on the first syllable.*
• the stress, the accent, the weight, the beat
❷ *We give a lot of **emphasis** to teamwork.*
• importance, stress, focus, priority

emphasise *VERB*
*She **emphasised** the important points.*
• to highlight, to stress, to focus on, to underline

employ *VERB*
*The factory plans to **employ** more workers.*
• to hire, to engage, to give work to, to take on

employment *NOUN*
*He's looking for **employment**.*
• work, a job, an occupation, a profession, a trade
» *For various kinds of employment look at* **job**.

empty *ADJECTIVE*
❶ *Please put the **empty** milk bottles outside the door.*
OPPOSITE full
— A **vacuum** or a **void** is a completely empty space, with nothing in it including air.
❷ *The house next to ours has been **empty** for weeks.*
• unoccupied, uninhabited, vacant, deserted
OPPOSITE occupied
❸ *There is still some **empty** space on the wall.*
• blank, bare, clear, unused

empty *VERB*
*She **emptied** her bag on to the table.*
• to tip, to tip out, to pour out, to turn out
— To empty water from a place is to **drain** it.
OPPOSITE to fill

encounter *VERB*
❶ *He **encountered** her outside the station.*
• to meet, to come across, to run into, to bump into, to come face-to-face with
❷ *We **encountered** some problems.*
• to experience, to come upon, to confront, to be faced with

encourage *VERB*
❶ *We went to the match to **encourage** our team.*
• to inspire, to support, to motivate, to cheer, to spur on
OPPOSITE to discourage
❷ *I **encouraged** my friend to audition for the play.*
• to urge, to persuade, to prompt
OPPOSITE to discourage

end *NOUN*
❶ *We walked to the **end** of the lane.*
• the limit, the bottom, the boundary
❷ *Please go to the **end** of the queue.*
• the back, the rear, the tail
❸ *The stick has a bell on the **end**.*
• the tip, the point
❹ *The **end** of the film was the most exciting part.*
• the ending, the finish, the close, the conclusion

end *VERB*
❶ *I thought the journey would never **end**.*
• to finish, to stop, to cease, to conclude, to be over
❷ *She wants to **end** the use of animals in experiments.*
• to stop, to ban, to abolish, to eliminate, to put an end to, to put a stop to

A
B
C
D
E
F
G
H
I
J
K
L
M
N
O
P
Q
R
S
T
U
V
W
X
Y
Z

endanger *VERB*
*Plastic pollution **endangers** marine life.*
• to put at risk, to threaten, to put in danger
OPPOSITE to protect

ending *NOUN*
*The **ending** of the film was the most exciting part.*
• the end, the finish, the close, the conclusion

endless *ADJECTIVE*
❶ *I'm tired of this **endless** rain.*
• constant, continuous, continual, incessant,
non-stop, perpetual, relentless
❷ *Teachers need **endless** patience.*
• limitless, infinite, unending, unlimited,
everlasting

enemy *NOUN*
*They used to be friends but now they are bitter
enemies.*
• an opponent, a foe, a rival
— If someone is your enemy, you can say they are
hostile to you.
OPPOSITES a friend, an ally

energetic *ADJECTIVE*
❶ *She's a very **energetic** person.*
• enthusiastic, animated, active, lively
— Use **sprightly** for an energetic older person.
OPPOSITE inactive
❷ *They did some **energetic** dancing.*
• lively, vigorous, strenuous, tiring, brisk, fast
OPPOSITE slow

energy *NOUN*
❶ *Wind is a renewable source of **energy**.*
• power, fuel
❷ *The dancers had a lot of **energy**.*
• liveliness, life, vigour, enthusiasm, spirit, stamina

engine *NOUN*
*The lawnmower needs a new **engine**.*
• a motor, a mechanism, a turbine
— A railway engine is a **locomotive**.

enjoy *VERB*
*The children **enjoyed** the film.*
• to like, to love, to get pleasure from,
to be pleased by, to admire, to appreciate
— To **relish** something is to enjoy it a lot.

enjoyable *ADJECTIVE*
*It was an **enjoyable** trip.*
• pleasant,
pleasurable,
agreeable,
delightful,
entertaining, amusing
OPPOSITE unpleasant

enlarge *VERB*
*The school is going to **enlarge**
the playground.*
• to expand, to extend, to develop,
to make bigger
— To make something wider is to **widen**
or to **broaden** it.
— To make something longer is to **extend**
or to **lengthen** it.
— To make something seem larger is to
magnify it.
OPPOSITE to reduce

enormous *ADJECTIVE*
***Enormous** waves battered the ship.*
• huge, massive, colossal, vast, gigantic,
immense, great, tremendous, terrific,
mammoth, humungous *(informal)*,
ginormous *(informal)*
— Use **towering** for something that is
extremely tall or high: *They were at
the foot of a **towering** cliff.*
OPPOSITE small

enough
DETERMINER
*Is there **enough**
food for us all?*
• sufficient, plenty of
— Ways to say 'not
enough' or 'barely enough':
• insufficient, lacking,
meagre, scarce, scanty
• short: *In the winter, food is
short.*

enough *ADVERB*
*The table is big **enough** for all
of us.*
• sufficiently: *The table is
sufficiently big for all of us.*

renewable energy (wind turbines)

enquiry *NOUN*
❶ *We had some* **enquiries** *about the school.*
• a question, a query, a request
❷ *There was an official* **enquiry** *into the accident.*
• an investigation, a study, an examination

ensure *VERB*
Please **ensure** *that you lock the door.*
• to make certain, to make sure, to confirm, to see

enter *VERB*
❶ *Silence fell as I* **entered** *the room.*
• to come in, to walk in
— To **barge in** is to enter a place suddenly, without permission or without warning.
OPPOSITE to leave
❷ **Enter** *your password.*
• to insert, to put in, to type, to write, to record
❸ *Our class decided to* **enter** *the competition.*
• to take part in, to enrol in, to sign up for, to go in for, to join in, to participate in
OPPOSITE to withdraw from

entertain *VERB*
The storyteller **entertained** *us with funny stories.*
• to amuse, to divert, to please, to keep (someone) amused, to make (someone) laugh
OPPOSITE to bore

enthusiasm *NOUN*
The children showed a lot of **enthusiasm.**
• interest, keenness, eagerness, energy, commitment

enthusiastic *ADJECTIVE*
She is very **enthusiastic** *about science.*
• passionate, excited, avid, eager, devoted
• keen: *She's very* **keen** *on science.*
• interested: *She's very* **interested** *in science.*
• committed: *She's very* **committed** *to science.*
— An enthusiastic supporter of something is a **fan.**

entire *ADJECTIVE*
Donald spent the **entire** *evening watching television.*
• complete, whole, total, full

entitle *VERB*
The voucher **entitles** *you to claim a discount.*
• to permit, to allow, to enable, to authorise

entrance *(say en-transs) NOUN*
❶ *Please pay at the* **entrance**
• the entry, the way in, the access, the door, the gate
OPPOSITE the exit
❷ *They stood at the cave* **entrance.**
• the mouth, the opening
❸ *They were surprised by his sudden* **entrance.**
• an arrival
OPPOSITE an exit

entrance *(say in-trahnss) VERB*
The crowd were **entranced** *by the fireworks display.*
• to charm, to delight, to please, to enchant

entry *NOUN*
❶ *A van was blocking the* **entry** *to the school.*
• the way in, the entrance, the access, the gate, the doorway
❷ *Every evening I write an* **entry** *in my diary.*
• an item, a note

envious *ADJECTIVE*
He was **envious** *of his brother's success.*
• jealous, resentful

environment *NOUN*
Animals should live in their natural **environment.**
• habitat, surroundings, setting, conditions, situation
➤ **the environment**
We must do all we can to protect **the environment.**
• the natural world, nature, the earth, the world

✳ **WORD WEB**

SOME ENVIRONMENTAL PROBLEMS:

• pollution, plastic pollution, climate change, global warming, endangered animals, deforestation

PROTECTING THE ENVIRONMENT:

• eco-friendly, recycling, renewable energy, clean air, conservation, wildlife, rainforest

envy NOUN
He was full of envy when he saw his friend's bike.
• jealousy, resentment, bitterness

envy VERB
I don't envy his success at all.
• to be jealous of, to resent
• to grudge: *I don't grudge him his success.*

equal ADJECTIVE
❶ *Give everyone an equal amount.*
• equivalent, identical, matching, similar, fair
❷ *The scores were equal at half-time.*
• even, level, the same, square
— To make the scores equal is to **equalise**.

equipment NOUN
The shed is full of gardening equipment.
• apparatus, gear, kit, implements, instruments, tools, materials, machinery

era NOUN
Shakespeare lived in the Elizabethan era.
• an age, a period, a time, days

erase VERB
I erased the writing on the board.
• to delete, to remove, to rub out, to wipe out, to get rid of

erode VERB
The floodwater eroded the riverbank.
• to wear away, to eat away, to destroy

errand NOUN
I went on an errand to the corner shop.
• a job, a task, an assignment
— A **mission** is an important or dangerous errand that someone is sent to do.

erratic ADJECTIVE
The team's performance has been erratic this season.
• inconsistent, irregular, uneven, unreliable, changeable, unpredictable
OPPOSITE consistent

error NOUN
❶ *The accident was the result of an error by the driver.*
• a mistake, a fault, a lapse, a blunder
❷ *I think there is an error in your calculation.*
• an inaccuracy, a mistake, a flaw

escape VERB
❶ *Why did you let him escape?*
• to get away, to run away, to make your escape, to bolt, to flee, to get out, to break free, to break out
— To **evade**, **elude** or **escape** capture is to avoid being caught.
— To **avoid** or **elude** someone is to avoid being caught by them.
❷ *I managed to escape the washing-up.*
• to avoid, to get out of, to dodge, to evade

especially ADVERB
I love fruit, especially strawberries.
• above all, most of all, particularly

essential ADJECTIVE
Vegetables are an essential part of our diet.
• important, necessary, basic, vital, principal, chief, crucial

establish VERB
❶ *The club was established in 1901.*
• to set up, to start, to begin, to create, to found
❷ *We must establish what really happened.*
• to prove, to show, to confirm, to find out

estimate NOUN
What is your estimate of how much it will cost?
• an assessment, a calculation, a guess, a judgement, an opinion

estimate VERB
Can you estimate the area of this room?
• to judge, to gauge, to calculate, to assess, to work out, to guess

even ADJECTIVE
❶ *Work on an even surface.*
• level, flat, smooth, straight
OPPOSITE uneven
❷ *The scores were even at half-time.*
• equal, level, matching, identical, the same, square
OPPOSITE different
❸ *The numbers 2, 4 and 6 are even.*
OPPOSITE odd

evening NOUN
We should be there by evening.
• dusk, nightfall, sundown, sunset, twilight

event NOUN
❶ *Her autobiography describes the main events of her life.*
• a happening, an incident, an occurrence, an episode
— A **phenomenon** is a strange or unusual event.

❷ *There was an event to mark the launch of the new film.*
• a function, an occasion, a party, a reception, a ceremony, an entertainment

eventually ADVERB
The journey took ages, but eventually we arrived.
• finally, at last, in the end, ultimately

everyday ADJECTIVE
Don't dress up—just wear your everyday clothes.
• normal, ordinary, usual, regular, customary

evidence NOUN
This piece of paper is evidence that he is lying.
• proof, confirmation
— An **alibi** is evidence that someone was not in a place when a crime was committed there.

evil ADJECTIVE
❶ *Who would do such an evil deed?*
• wicked, immoral, wrong, sinful, cruel, foul, hateful, vile
OPPOSITE good
❷ *The charm was used to keep away evil spirits.*
• malevolent, diabolical

evil NOUN
The good witch tried to fight against evil.
• wickedness, badness, wrongdoing, sin, immorality, villainy, malevolence
OPPOSITES good, goodness

exact ADJECTIVE
❶ *Can you tell me the exact amount?*
• accurate, precise, correct, true, actual
OPPOSITES approximate, rough
❷ *This model is an exact copy of the building.*
• identical, perfect, faithful, detailed

exactly ADVERB
At what time exactly did you leave the house?
• precisely, specifically, accurately, correctly, strictly
OPPOSITES approximately, roughly

exaggerate VERB
He tends to exaggerate his problems.
• to magnify, to overstate, to overdo
OPPOSITE to understate

examination NOUN
❶ *They have to pass an examination to qualify.*
• an exam, a test, an assessment
❷ *They carried out an examination of the evidence.*
• an analysis, an inspection, an investigation, a study, a survey

❸ *He was sent to hospital for an examination.*
• a check-up
— A **scan** is an examination using light beams or X-rays.

examine VERB
❶ *We examined the water samples.*
• to analyse, to inspect, to study, to investigate, to scrutinise, to review
❷ *The doctor examined my ears.*
• to check, to test, to look at

example NOUN
❶ *Give me an example of what you mean.*
• an instance, an illustration, a case
— A **sample** or a **specimen** is a small amount of something that gives an example of what it is like.
❷ *She's an example to us all.*
• a model, a role model, an ideal

exceed VERB
Its speed can exceed 100 miles per hour.
• to surpass, to go over, to pass, to beat

excel VERB
She excels at sprinting.
• to stand out, to be exceptional, to shine

excellent ADJECTIVE
That's an excellent idea!
• brilliant, outstanding, exceptional, first-class, extraordinary, fantastic, remarkable, tremendous, terrific, wonderful, superb, great, marvellous
» *For other ways to describe something good look at* **good**.
OPPOSITES bad, awful, second-rate

except PREPOSITION
Everyone got a prize except me.
• apart from, but, with the exception of, excluding

exceptional ADJECTIVE
❶ *Her performance was exceptional.*
• outstanding, extraordinary, remarkable, first-rate, amazing, stunning
OPPOSITE average
❷ *Such cold weather in June is exceptional.*
• unusual, extraordinary, uncommon, unexpected, rare, strange, surprising
OPPOSITES normal, usual

excessive ADJECTIVE
The prices they charge are excessive.
• too much, extreme, unreasonable, unjustified, ridiculous, extravagant
OPPOSITES reasonable, moderate

a
b
c
d
e
f
g
h
i
j
k
l
m
n
o
p
q
r
s
t
u
v
w
x
y
z

exchange VERB
I exchanged the jeans for a bigger size.
• to change, to swap, to trade
• to replace: *I replaced the jeans with a bigger size.*

excite VERB
The thought of going on a trip excited the class.
• to thrill, to stimulate, to stir up
— To **electrify** someone is to suddenly excite them very much.
OPPOSITE to calm

excited ADJECTIVE
Everyone got very excited at the party.
• lively, animated, eager, enthusiastic
— Use **feverish**, **frantic** or **frenzied** to mean wildly excited.
— Use **hysterical** to mean excited and emotional in a way that is out of control.
— Use **agitated** to mean excited and worried.
— Use **thrilled** or **elated** to mean excited and pleased.
OPPOSITE calm

excitement NOUN
❶ *I could hardly bear the excitement!*
• thrill
— Use **suspense** or **tension** for excitement that comes from not knowing what is going to happen.
❷ *The news caused great excitement.*
• drama, a sensation, a stir

exciting ADJECTIVE
❶ *The last few minutes of the match were so exciting!*
• dramatic, eventful, thrilling, gripping, sensational, electrifying, tense, spectacular
— A **cliffhanger** is an exciting ending to a story or situation, when you do not know what will happen next.
— The **climax** of a story or event is the most exciting part.
❷ *The story was about their exciting adventures.*
• exotic, epic, adventurous, unusual, romantic, glamorous, thrilling
OPPOSITES dull, boring

exclaim VERB
'It's amazing!' she exclaimed.
• to cry, to call out, to shout, to yell, to burst out, to declare
» *For other ways to say something look at* **say**.

exclamation NOUN
Holmes gave an exclamation of surprise.
• a cry, a shout, a yell
— An **oath** is an exclamation that is a swear word.

WRITING TIPS

SOMEONE WHO IS ANGRY OR DISAPPOINTED MIGHT EXCLAIM:
• blast!, bother!, drat!, alas!, oh dear!

SOMEONE WHO IS HAPPY OR RELIEVED MIGHT EXCLAIM:
• hooray or hurray!, hoorah or hurrah!, yippee!, phew!, thank goodness!

SOMEONE WHO IS DISGUSTED MIGHT EXCLAIM:
• ugh!, ew!, yuck!

SOMEONE WHO IS SURPRISED OR ALARMED MIGHT EXCLAIM:
• goodness me!, good gracious!, good grief!, good heavens!, my goodness!
'My goodness!' said Commander Pott anxiously. 'Now we've had it!'—CHITTY CHITTY BANG BANG, Ian Fleming

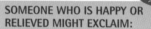

exclude VERB
They excluded me from their game.
• to leave (someone) out, to keep (someone) out, to reject, to banish, to ban, to bar

excuse (say iks-kewss) NOUN
What is your excuse for being so late?
• a reason, an explanation, a justification, a defence

excuse (say iks-kewz) VERB
I can't excuse his bad behaviour.
• to forgive, to pardon, to overlook
OPPOSITE to punish

exercise NOUN
❶ *Exercise helps to keep you fit.*
• sport, physical activity, working out, training
❷ *We did a training exercise.*
• a practice, a drill

exercise VERB
If you exercise regularly, you will keep fit.
• to train, to work out, to take exercise

exhaust VERB
❶ *The steep climb up the hill exhausted me.*
• to tire, to wear out

❷ *We had exhausted our supply of food.*
• to finish, to go through, to use up, to consume

exhaust NOUN
The exhaust from cars damages the environment.
• fumes, smoke, emissions, gases

exhausted ADJECTIVE
After a hard race, we lay exhausted on the grass.
• tired out, worn out, fatigued, shattered
— Use **breathless**, **gasping** or **panting** if someone is very tired and out of breath.

exhibit VERB
Her paintings were exhibited in galleries all over Europe and America.
• to display, to show, to present, to put up

exhibition NOUN
We went to see an exhibition of paintings by Picasso.
• a display, a show

exist VERB
❶ *Do fairies really exist?*
• to be real, to occur, to be found
❷ *We can't exist without water.*
• to live, to remain alive, to survive, to continue, to last

exit NOUN
❶ *I'll wait for you by the exit.*
• the door, the way out, the doorway, the gate, the barrier
OPPOSITE the entrance
❷ *The robbers made a hurried exit.*
• a departure
OPPOSITE an entrance

exit VERB
He exited the room quickly.
• to leave, to depart from, to go out of, to withdraw from
OPPOSITE to enter

expand VERB
Their business is expanding rapidly.
• to grow, to increase, to develop, to enlarge
OPPOSITE to contract, to shrink

expect VERB
❶ *I didn't expect that it was going to rain.*
• to think, to believe, to imagine, to anticipate, to predict, to foresee, to forecast
❷ *The teacher expects our full attention.*
• to require, to want, to demand, to insist on

expel VERB
❶ *A fan expels the stale air.*
• to send out, to force out, to get rid of
❷ *He was expelled from school.*
• to dismiss, to exclude, to ban, to remove, to throw out, to send away
— To **eject** someone from a building is to make them leave it.
— To **exile** or **banish** someone is to make them leave their country as a punishment.

expense NOUN
She was worried about the expense of the holiday.
• cost, charges

expensive ADJECTIVE
❶ *The jacket was too expensive for me.*
• dear, costly
OPPOSITE cheap
❷ *They stayed in an expensive hotel.*
• luxury, lavish, extravagant, posh (informal)
OPPOSITE

experience NOUN
❶ *I had a strange experience.*
• an event, a happening, an occurrence, an incident, an episode
— An **adventure** is an exciting experience.
— An **ordeal** is a very unpleasant experience.
❷ *Have you had any experience of working in a shop?*
• practice, involvement

experience VERB
He told us about what he had experienced during the war.
• to undergo, to go through, to live through
— To **endure**, to **suffer** or to be **subjected to** something is to experience something bad.

experiment NOUN
We carried out a scientific experiment.
• a test, a trial
— A series of experiments is **research**, an **investigation** or a **study**.

expert NOUN
He's a computer expert.
• a specialist, a genius, a master, a geek (informal)

expert ADJECTIVE
Only an expert sailor could cross the ocean.
• brilliant, capable, competent, experienced, knowledgeable, skilful, skilled, highly trained
OPPOSITE beginner

a b c d e f g h i j k l m n o p q r s t u v w x y z

explain VERB

❶ *She explained the plot of the film to me.*
• to describe, to help (someone) understand, to interpret
❷ *What could explain these strange events?*
• to account for, to be the reason for, to be an explanation for
— To **justify** or **excuse** bad behaviour is to explain it.

explanation NOUN

❶ *He gave a brief explanation of how his invention worked.*
• an account, a description, a demonstration
❷ *They could find no explanation for the accident.*
• a reason, an excuse, a justification

explode VERB

The firework exploded with a bang.
• to blow up, to go off, to detonate, to burst, to go bang

explore VERB

They explored the island.
• to search, to survey, to travel around, to look round, to investigate, to examine

explorer NOUN

The explorers were looking for the legendary Lost City.
• an adventurer, a traveller, a voyager, a discoverer, a navigator

😊 WRITING TIPS

Here are some useful words or writing about **explorers**:

WORDS TO DESCRIBE AN EXPLORER:
• adventurous, bold, brave, daring, dashing, intrepid

TYPES OF EXPLORER:
• Arctic, polar, tropical, jungle, planetary, space, deep-sea, underwater
*The shipwreck was found by a team of **underwater** explorers.*

THINGS AN EXPLORER MIGHT FIND:
• a cave, a cavern, an inscription, a labyrinth, a maze, a mummy, a parchment, a riddle, a secret chamber, a secret passage, a skeleton, a temple, a tomb, a treasure chest, a tunnel

THINGS AN EXPLORER MIGHT USE:
• binoculars, a chart, a compass, a map, rope, a telescope, a torch
Stella checked and re-checked her pockets and her explorer's bag . . . to make sure she had her telescope, compass, magnifying glass, pocket map, emergency mint cake, matches and ball of string.—THE POLAR BEAR EXPLORERS' CLUB, Alex Bell

explosion NOUN

The explosion rattled the windows.
• a blast, a bang
— An **eruption** is an explosion from a volcano.
— An **outburst** is an explosion of laughter or shouting.

express VERB

You will all get a chance to express your opinion.
• to communicate, to voice, to convey, to put into words

expression NOUN

❶ *She had a puzzled expression.*
• a look, an appearance, a face
❷ *What does the expression 'on the loose' mean?*
• a phrase, a saying, a term
— A **cliché** is an expression people use too much.
❸ *Oscar plays the piano with a lot of expression.*
• feeling, emotion, passion

extend VERB

❶ *We decided to extend our stay.*
• to lengthen, to prolong, to make longer
OPPOSITE to shorten
❷ *She extended one arm.*
• to stretch out, to hold out, to put out, to reach out, to stick out

extra ADJECTIVE

❶ *There is an extra charge for taking your bike on the train.*
• additional, further, added
❷ *I brought extra food in case we need it.*
• more, spare, excess

extract (say eks-trakt) NOUN

I read an extract from her new book.
• a passage, a quotation
— A **clip** is an extract from a film.

extract (say iks-trakt) VERB

The dentist had to extract a tooth.
• to pull out, to remove, to take out

extraordinary ADJECTIVE

The astronauts saw many extraordinary sights.
• amazing, astonishing, remarkable, outstanding,

A B C D E F G H I J K L M N O P Q R S T U V W X Y Z

exceptional, incredible, fantastic, marvellous, rare, special, strange, curious, surprising, unusual, weird, wonderful
OPPOSITE ordinary

extreme *ADJECTIVE*
❶ *He was in extreme danger.*
• great, intense, severe, acute
❷ *She lives on the extreme edge of the town.*
• farthest, furthest

extremely *ADVERB*
The mission was extremely dangerous.
• seriously, intensely, acutely, enormously, terribly

eye *NOUN*

 WORD WEB

PARTS OF THE EYE:

• eyeball, eyelash, eyelid, iris, lens, pupil, retina
— A word meaning 'to do with eyes' is **optical**.

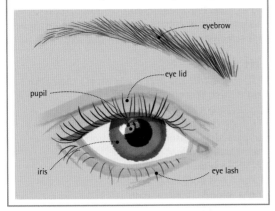

eyebrow

eye lid

pupil

iris

eye lash

 WRITING TIPS

You can use these words to describe **eyes**:
• bright, shining, glittering, twinkling, gleaming, sharp, bulging, puffy, bloodshot, fishy, downcast
— **Beady** eyes are small and bright.
— **Glassy** or **glazed** eyes are without expression.
— **Piercing** eyes seem to look right through you.
— **Steely** eyes look at you in a tough and determined way.
— **Bleary** eyes are tired and do not see well.
— **Misty**, **moist**, **tearful** or **watery** eyes have tears in them.
Mr Wonka's bright twinkling blue eyes rested for a moment on Charlie's face.—CHARLIE AND THE CHOCOLATE FACTORY, Roald Dahl

⚙ Can you think of 5 different words for 'frightened'?

⚙ Lots of phrases connected with fear use the idea of cold. Can you think of any?

⚙ Check the thesaurus to find answers!

fabulous *ADJECTIVE*
❶ *We had a fabulous time at the party.*
• excellent, wonderful, brilliant, fantastic, marvellous, superb, tremendous, amazing
❷ *Dragons are fabulous creatures.*
• mythical, legendary, imaginary, fanciful
OPPOSITE real

face *NOUN*
❶ *I saw his shocked face.*
• an expression, features, a look
❷ *A cube has six faces.*
• a side, a surface

 WRITING TIPS

Here are some useful words for describing a **face**:

TO DESCRIBE ITS SHAPE:

• long, flat, oval, round, rounded, chubby, puffy
— Someone's **complexion** is the type of skin on their face.
» *For parts of a face look at eye and nose.*

TO DESCRIBE A THIN FACE:

• thin, gaunt, haggard, delicate, fine

TO DESCRIBE A PALE FACE:

• ashen, pale, pallid, pasty, sickly

TO DESCRIBE A WRINKLED FACE:

• wrinkled, wrinkly, shrivelled, wizened, weather-beaten
Doc Spencer . . . was a tiny man with tiny hands and feet and a tiny round face. The face was as brown and

a
b
c
d
e
f
g
h
i
j
k
l
m
n
o
p
q
r
s
t
u
v
w
x
y
z

wrinkled as a shrivelled apple.—DANNY THE CHAMPION OF THE WORLD, Roald Dahl

TO DESCRIBE A FACE THAT LOOKS HEALTHY:
• ruddy, tanned, glowing, fresh, flushed, rosy

TO DESCRIBE A FACE THAT LOOKS HAPPY:
• radiant, sunny, cheerful, beaming

TO DESCRIBE A FACE THAT HAS NO EXPRESSION:
• blank, dead, expressionless, emotionless, vacant

face VERB
❶ *Stand and face your partner.*
• to turn towards, to look towards
❷ *The astronauts had to face many dangers.*
• to confront, to cope with, to deal with, to face up to, to stand up to, to encounter
OPPOSITE to avoid

fact NOUN
❶ *It is a fact that dodos are now extinct.*
• a reality, a truth, a certainty
OPPOSITE fiction
❷ *She explained the facts of the case.*
• the details
— Facts which help to prove something are **evidence** or **proof**.

fade VERB
❶ *Sunlight has faded the colours of the curtains.*
• to make paler, to bleach, to whiten, to dim
OPPOSITE to brighten
❷ *Their enthusiasm started to fade.*
• to wane, to decrease, to weaken, to disappear, to vanish, to dwindle, to fail, to diminish
OPPOSITES to increase, to grow
❸ *The sound of their voices gradually faded as they walked away.*
• to grow faint, to get quieter, to die away, to die down, to disappear, to vanish
OPPOSITE to grow louder

fail VERB
❶ *Their attempts to reach the summit failed.*
• to be unsuccessful, to go wrong, to fall through, to be a failure, to be in vain
OPPOSITE to succeed
❷ *One of the engines failed.*
• to break down, to cut out, to give up, to stop working
❸ *The professor failed to warn us of the danger.*
• to neglect, to forget, to omit
OPPOSITE to remember

failure NOUN
❶ *The experiment was a failure.*
• a disaster, a fiasco, a disappointment
OPPOSITE a success
❷ *The storm caused a power failure.*
• a breakdown, a fault

faint ADJECTIVE
❶ *We heard a faint cry for help.*
• weak, low, quiet, soft, muffled, hushed
OPPOSITE loud
❷ *The image is faint and hard to see.*
• faded, dim, unclear, indistinct, vague, blurred, hazy, pale
OPPOSITES clear, distinct
❸ *There was a faint smell of burning in the air.*
• delicate, slight
OPPOSITE strong
❹ *He was so hungry that he felt faint.*
• dizzy, giddy, light-headed, unsteady, weak

faint VERB
The explorers nearly fainted from exhaustion.
• to pass out, to collapse, to become unconscious, to lose consciousness, to swoon (old use)

fair ADJECTIVE
❶ *It's not fair if she gets more sweets than I do.*
• right, just, reasonable, proper
OPPOSITE unfair
❷ *I think the referee was very fair.*
• impartial, unbiased, objective, honourable, honest, independent
OPPOSITE biased
❸ *The twins both have fair hair.*
• light, blonde, golden, pale
OPPOSITE dark
❹ *We have a fair chance of winning.*
• reasonable, moderate, average, acceptable, satisfactory, respectable
❺ *They set sail under fair weather.*
• fine, dry, bright, sunny, clear, cloudless, pleasant

fair NOUN
My sister won a teddy bear at the fair.
• a fairground, a fete, a festival, a carnival, a gala

fairly ADVERB
❶ *The competition will be judged fairly.*
• honestly, properly, justly, impartially, objectively
❷ *I did fairly well in the race.*
• quite, moderately, pretty (informal), reasonably

88

fairy NOUN

 WRITING TIPS

Here are some useful words you could use when writing about **fairies**:
• feathery, fluttering, glittering, glowing, golden, iridescent, shimmering, silvery, sparkling, translucent, twinkling
To Anne's amazement there was a flash of light and, in place of the ancient crone, there stood a shimmering fairy.—SHORT AND SPOOKY, Louise Cooper

faithful ADJECTIVE

My dog, Scruffy, is my faithful friend.
• loyal, devoted, reliable, trustworthy, dependable, firm, staunch
OPPOSITES disloyal, unfaithful

fake NOUN

That's not a real Roman coin—it's a fake.
• a copy, an imitation, a reproduction, a replica, a forgery, a sham
— A **hoax** is a fake event in which people are made to believe something that is not true.
— An **impostor** is a person who makes people believe they are someone else.

fake ADJECTIVE

He was using a fake passport.
• false, sham
— Use **counterfeit** or **forged** for money or a document.
— Use **imitation** for a material: *They are imitation diamonds, not real.*

fake VERB

The photographs had been faked.
• to copy, to imitate, to forge

fall VERB falls, falling, fell, fallen

❶ *I fell and hurt my knee.*
• to tumble, to slip, to lose your balance
— To **trip** or to **stumble** is to fall over something.
❷ *A tree had fallen across the path.*
• to crash, to topple, to come down
— To **plunge** or to **plummet** is to suddenly fall a long way: *The car plunged off a cliff.*
❸ *Snow was beginning to fall.*
• to drop, to come down, to descend
— If something **rains down**, **showers down** or **pours down**, it falls from above in large quantities: *Arrows rained down on them.*

❹ *The temperature fell to zero.*
• to go down, to become lower, to decrease, to decline, to lessen, to diminish, to dwindle
➤ **to fall apart**
My bag is falling apart.
• to disintegrate, to break up, to come to pieces
➤ **to fall behind**
His feet hurt and he fell behind.
• to lag, to trail, to dawdle, to straggle
➤ **to fall for something**
I can't believe you fell for that story.
• to believe, to swallow, to be taken in by, to be tricked by
➤ **to fall in**
The roof of the cabin fell in.
• to cave in, to collapse, to give way
➤ **to fall out**
She fell out with her friend.
• to argue, to disagree, to quarrel, to squabble, to bicker

fall NOUN

❶ *Ellen had a fall and cut her knee.*
• a tumble, a slip
❷ *We noticed a sharp fall in the temperature.*
• a drop, a decrease, a lowering
OPPOSITES a rise, an increase

fallen (past participle of **fall**)

false ADJECTIVE

❶ *The information they gave us was false.*
• wrong, incorrect, untrue, inaccurate, mistaken, misleading, faulty
OPPOSITE correct
❷ *The spy was travelling with a false passport.*
• fake, sham
— Use **counterfeit** or **forged** for money or a document.
— Use **artificial** or **imitation** for a material: *They are imitation diamonds, not real.*
OPPOSITES genuine, real
❸ *He turned out to be a false friend.*
• disloyal, unfaithful, unreliable, untrustworthy, treacherous
OPPOSITES loyal, true

fame NOUN

Her Olympic medal brought her international fame.
• celebrity, glory, honour, reputation, prominence
— Fame that you get for doing something bad is **notoriety**.

familiar *ADJECTIVE*
Seagulls are a familiar sight on the beach.
• common, commonplace, everyday, normal, ordinary, usual, regular, customary, frequent, routine
OPPOSITE rare

family *NOUN*
❶ *Some of my family live in New Zealand.*
• relations, relatives
— Someone's **ancestors** are members of their family who lived before them.
— Someone's **descendants** are members of their family who live after them.
❷ *She comes from a family of farmers.*
• background
— A **clan** is a group of related families, especially in Scotland.
— A **tribe** is a group of families living together, ruled by a chief.
— A **dynasty** is a group of people from the same powerful family: *The country was ruled by the same dynasty for hundreds of years.*

famous *ADJECTIVE*
He was a famous football player.
• well-known, celebrated, renowned, notable, prominent, distinguished, illustrious, legendary
— Use **notorious** or **infamous** if someone is famous for something bad.
OPPOSITE unknown, obscure

fan *NOUN*
I'm a big fan of science fiction.
• an enthusiast, an admirer, a follower, a supporter
— A **fanatic** is an extreme fan: *I like football, but I'm not a football fanatic.*

fancy *ADJECTIVE*
Mum bought a fancy hat for my cousin's wedding.
• elaborate, decorative, ornamental, ornate, special
OPPOSITE plain

fantastic *ADJECTIVE*
❶ *We had a fantastic time at camp.*
• excellent, wonderful, brilliant, fabulous, marvellous, superb, tremendous, amazing
❷ *The story is full of fantastic creatures.*
• imaginary, incredible, fanciful, extraordinary, strange, odd, weird, bizarre
OPPOSITE realistic

far *ADJECTIVE*
❶ *The castle stood in the far north of the country.*
• distant, faraway, remote
OPPOSITE nearby

❷ *The ferry took us to the far side of the river.*
• opposite, other
OPPOSITE near

farm *NOUN*

 WORD WEB

SOME TYPES OF FARM:

• a dairy farm, a fruit farm, a poultry farm
— An **arable farm** is one that grows crops.
— A **ranch** is a large cattle farm in North America or Australia.
— A **smallholding** is a small farm.
— A **vineyard** is a farm growing grapes.

SOME PLACES AND THINGS ON A FARM:

• a barn, a dairy, a farmhouse, a farmyard, a haystack, a meadow, a pigsty, a plough, a shed, a stable, a tractor
— A **paddock** is a field for keeping horses.
— **Pasture** is land with grass for cows or other animals to eat.

SOME FARM ANIMALS:

• a bull, a bullock, a chicken, a cow, a duck, a goat, a hen, a goose, a horse, a pig, a rooster, a sheep, a sheepdog, a turkey
— Birds kept on a farm are **poultry**.
— Cows kept for milk or beef are **cattle**.
— Farm animals in general are **livestock**.

farm *VERB*
The MacDonalds had farmed the land for centuries.
• to cultivate, to work, to till, to plough

fashion *NOUN*
Those boots are the latest fashion.
• a trend, a craze, a style, a look

fashionable *ADJECTIVE*
❶ *She wears fashionable clothes.*
• trendy, stylish, cool, up-to-date
OPPOSITES unfashionable, out-of-date
❷ *Vegan food is very fashionable right now.*
• popular, in fashion
OPPOSITE unfashionable

fast *ADJECTIVE*
They were going at a fast pace.
• quick, rapid, speedy, swift, brisk, smart, hurried, hasty
— A **breakneck** pace is very fast and dangerous.
— A fast train is an **express** train.
OPPOSITE slow

fast ADVERB
❶ *She was riding her bike very* **fast**.
• quickly, speedily, swiftly, rapidly, briskly
— To go **headlong** somewhere is to go very fast without taking care.
❷ *The lid was stuck* **fast**.
• firmly, securely, tightly
❸ *Shh! The baby is* **fast** *asleep*.
• deeply, sound, soundly, completely

fasten VERB
❶ *They* **fastened** *their ropes to the rock face.*
• to tie, to fix, to attach, to connect, to join, to link, to bind, to knot
— To **buckle** something is to fasten it with a buckle.
— To **button** something is to fasten it with a button.
— To **clip** something is to fasten it with a clip.
— To **nail** something is to fasten it with a nail.
— To **pin** something is to fasten it with a pin.
❷ *They* **fastened** *the gate with a heavy chain.*
• to lock, to secure, to seal
— To **bolt** something is to fasten it with a bolt.

fat ADJECTIVE
Your cat will get **fat** *if you overfeed her.*
• overweight, obese, chubby, podgy, pudgy, plump, flabby, stout

fatal ADJECTIVE
He delivered a **fatal** *blow with his sword.*
• deadly, lethal, mortal

fate NOUN
❶ *It was* **fate** *that we met.*
• destiny, fortune, chance, luck
❷ *The villain met a nasty* **fate**.
• destiny, end, death

fault NOUN
❶ *It was my* **fault** *that we missed our bus.*
• responsibility
— If something is your fault, you are **to blame**.
❷ *There is one major* **fault** *with this plan.*
• a defect, a flaw, a snag, a problem, a weakness

favour NOUN
❶ *I asked my friend to do me a* **favour**.
• a good deed, a good turn, a kindness, a service
❷ *The captain's plan found* **favour** *with most of the crew.*
• approval, support, liking
➤ **to be in favour of something**
We're all **in favour of** *longer holidays.*
• to approve of, to support, to agree with, to favour

favourite ADJECTIVE
What is your **favourite** *book?*
• preferred, best-loved, number-one, top

fear NOUN
❶ *When he saw the monster, he shook with* **fear**.
• fright, dread, alarm
— Use **terror** for very strong fear.
— Use **horror** for strong fear and disgust.
— Use **panic** for sudden strong fear when you do not know what to do.
❷ *He has a* **fear** *of high places.*
• a phobia, a dread
fear VERB
There is nothing to **fear**.
• to be frightened of, to be afraid of, to be scared of, to be alarmed about, to dread

fearful ADJECTIVE
❶ *The young warrior had a* **fearful** *look in his eyes.*
• frightened, scared, afraid, nervous, anxious
— Use **terrified** or **petrified** to mean very fearful.
— Use **panicky** to mean not knowing what to do because of fear.
OPPOSITE fearless
❷ *The erupting volcano was a* **fearful** *sight.*
• frightening, terrifying, shocking, fearsome, appalling, ghastly, dreadful, terrible, formidable

feast NOUN
The king held a great **feast** *to celebrate his birthday.*
• a banquet, a dinner

feather NOUN
— A **plume** is a large feather.
— A **quill** is a feather used as a pen.
— All the feathers on a bird are its **plumage**.
— Soft fluffy feathers are down.

a quill

feature NOUN
❶ *The building has some unusual* **features**.
• a characteristic, a detail, a point, an aspect, a quality, a peculiarity
❷ *There was a* **feature** *about our school in the newspaper.*
• an article, a report, a story, an item, a piece

feed VERB feeds, feeding, fed
The recipe makes enough to **feed** *six people.*
• to provide for, to give food to, to nourish

feel VERB feels, feeling, felt
❶ *I* **felt** *the rabbit's silky ears.*
• to touch, to caress, to stroke
❷ *We had to* **feel** *our way out of the cave.*
• to grope, to fumble

— To **rummage** is to feel inside something: *She rummaged in the drawer for some scissors.*
❸ *It feels colder today.*
• to appear, to seem
❹ *I feel we should help them.*
• to think, to believe, to consider
➤ **to feel like**
Do you feel like a walk?
• to want, to be in the mood for, to wish for *(formal)*, to desire *(formal)*, to fancy *(informal)*

feeling NOUN
❶ *I had a strange feeling.*
• a sensation, a sense
❷ *Try to think about other people's feelings.*
• an emotion, a sentiment

feeling

WORD WEB

SOME WORDS FOR FEELINGS:

• alarm, amusement, anger, anticipation, anxiety, bitterness, boredom, comfort, confusion, contempt, desire, discomfort, disgust, dislike, dismay, doubt, elation, embarrassment, enthusiasm, envy, excitement, exhaustion, fear, frustration, fury, glee, gloom, gratitude, guilt, happiness, hate, hatred, hope, horror, jealousy, joy, love, mistrust, nervousness, nostalgia, optimism, pain, passion, pessimism, pity, pleasure, pride, rage, regret, relief, sadness, satisfaction, scorn, shame, surprise, suspicion, sympathy, tiredness, triumph, unhappiness, weariness, wonder, worry

There were so many feelings and passions and there was so much sudden happiness swirling around in the air it made his head spin.—CHARLIE AND THE GREAT GLASS ELEVATOR, Roald Dahl

fell *(past tense of* **fall***)*

fence NOUN
The mansion was surrounded by a tall fence.
• a barrier, a railing
— A **palisade** is a fence around a camp to defend it, made of wooden posts or railings.
— A **stockade** is a fence made of large stakes, as a defence or to hold in animals.

festival NOUN
The town holds a festival every summer.
• a carnival, a fete, a gala, a fair, a celebration
— A **jubilee** is a festival to celebrate a special anniversary.

festive ADJECTIVE
Chinese New Year is a festive occasion.
• joyful, joyous, cheerful, happy, merry, jolly
OPPOSITES gloomy, sombre

fetch VERB
I fetched the shopping from the car.
• to get, to bring, to carry, to collect, to transport, to convey, to pick up, to retrieve

fibre NOUN
Rope is made by twisting fibres together.
• a thread, a strand, a filament

fiction NOUN
» *For various kinds of literature look at* **writing***.*

fidget VERB
The children were bored and started to fidget.
• to be restless, to fiddle about, to shuffle about, to play about, to mess about

field NOUN
❶ *Cattle were grazing in the field.*
• the meadow, the pasture
— A **paddock** is a small field for horses.
— A **pitch** or a **ground** is a field for playing sport.
❷ *Electronics is not my field.*
• an area, a speciality, an interest

fierce ADJECTIVE
They had to run from a fierce tiger.
• vicious, ferocious, savage, brutal, violent, wild

fiery ADJECTIVE
❶ *They sheltered from the fiery heat of the desert sun.*
• blazing, burning, hot, intense, fierce, raging, flaming
❷ *She has a fiery temper.*
• violent, hot, passionate, excitable

fight NOUN
❶ *There was a fight between two gangs.*
• a battle, a clash, a confrontation, a struggle, a scrap *(informal)*
— A **brawl** or a **punch-up** is a fight without weapons.
— A **scuffle** is a fight that is not serious.
— A **bout** is a fight in boxing or wrestling.
— A **duel** is a fight, usually with weapons, arranged between two people.
— **Combat** is fighting between soldiers.
❷ *We support the fight to save the rainforest.*
• a campaign, a struggle, a battle

fight VERB fights, fighting, fought
❶ *Two boys were fighting in the playground.*
• to have a fight, to struggle, to wrestle, to grapple, to scuffle, to clash
— To **spar** is to box or fight without trying to hurt each other.
— To **confront** or to **challenge** someone is to try to get them to fight you.
❷ *We will fight the decision to close our local library.*
• to oppose, to battle, to resist, to campaign against, to protest against
— To **combat** something is to fight and try to end it: *The superhero combats crime.*

fighter NOUN

WORD WEB

PEOPLE WHO FIGHT IN A WAR OR CONFLICT:

• a warrior, a soldier
— A **knight** was a nobleman and fighter in medieval times.
— A **gladiator** was a fighter who fought as entertainment in Roman times.
— A **samurai** was a warrior in ancient Japan.

PEOPLE WHO FIGHT AS A SPORT:

• a boxer, a wrestler, a martial artist

a samurai

figure NOUN
❶ *Please write the figure '8' on the board.*
• a number, a numeral, a digit
❷ *Two figures could be seen outside.*
• a shape, a form, a person

fill VERB
❶ *Dad filled the trolley with shopping.*
• to load, to pack, to stuff, to cram
— To fill something with air is to **inflate** it or **blow** it **up**.
OPPOSITE empty
❷ *What can I use to fill this hole?*
• to close up, to plug, to seal, to block, to stop up
❸ *Tourists filled the square.*
• to crowd, to crowd into, to occupy, to cram into, to jam into, to swamp
— Use to **flood** if light or a feeling fills a place: *Sunlight flooded the room.*

filling NOUN
The pie had a creamy filling.
• stuffing, insides, contents

film NOUN
We watched a funny film.

 WORD WEB

SOME TYPES OF FILM:

• an action film, an adventure film, a comedy, a horror film, a superhero film, a thriller
— An **animation**, an **animated film** or a **cartoon** is a film made from drawings or computer images that appear to move.
— A **documentary** is a film that gives information about real events.
— A **western** is a film about cowboys.
— A **classic** is a film that is well-known and thought to be very good.

OTHER WORDS RELATING TO FILMS:

— **Cinema** means films in general.
— **Dialogue** is conversation between people in a film.
— The **plot** of a film is the story.
— A **screenplay** or a **script** is the story and words of a film written down.
— The **credits** are the names listed at the end or beginning of a film, showing who helped to make it.
— A **premiere** is the first public showing of a film.
— A **sequel** is a film that continues the story of another one.

filthy ADJECTIVE
Those trainers are filthy!
• dirty, mucky, messy, grimy, grubby, muddy, soiled, stained
OPPOSITE clean

final ADJECTIVE
❶ *The final moments of the match were very tense.*
• last, closing, concluding
OPPOSITE opening
❷ *What was the final result?*
• eventual, ultimate

finally ADVERB
I finally finished the book.
• eventually, at last, in the end

find VERB finds, finding, found
❶ *Did you find any fossils on the beach?*
• to come across, to discover, to see, to spot, to locate, to encounter
— To find something buried or hidden is to **unearth** it.

a b c d e **f** g h i j k l m n o p q r s t u v w x y z

❷ *I **found** my missing shoe under the bed.*
• to track down, to locate, to retrieve, to recover, to trace
OPPOSITE to lose
❸ *Did the doctor **find** what was wrong?*
• to find out, to detect, to identify, to diagnose
❹ *I **found** that digging was hard work.*
• to find out, to become aware, to realise, to learn, to observe

fine *ADJECTIVE*
❶ *Don't worry—I'm **fine**.*
• well, healthy, OK, unhurt, unharmed
❷ *It's **fine** if you want to bring a friend.*
• acceptable, satisfactory, OK, all right, allowed, permitted
OPPOSITE unacceptable
❸ *Spiders spin very **fine** thread.*
• delicate, fragile, thin, flimsy, slender, slim
OPPOSITE thick
❹ *The dunes were made of **fine** sand.*
• dusty, powdery, thin
OPPOSITE coarse
❺ *As the weather was **fine**, we took a picnic.*
• dry, fair, sunny, bright, clear, cloudless, pleasant
OPPOSITE dull
❻ *The town hall is a very **fine** building.*
• splendid, magnificent, beautiful, impressive

finger *NOUN*
— Your short fat finger is your **thumb**.
— The finger next to your thumb is your **index finger**.
— The next finger is your **middle finger**.
— The next finger is your **ring finger** or **third finger**.
— Your small thin finger is your **little finger**.
— The joints in your fingers are your **knuckles**.

middle finger
ring finger (or third finger)
index finger
thumb
little finger

finish *VERB*
❶ *I've **finished** my book.*
• to complete, to reach the end of
OPPOSITE to start
❷ *The concert should **finish** around nine o'clock.*
• to end, to stop, to conclude, to terminate
OPPOSITE to start
❸ *We've **finished** all the biscuits.*
• to eat, to eat up, to consume, to use up, to polish off

finish *NOUN*
*We stayed to watch the parade until the **finish**.*
• the end, the close, the conclusion
OPPOSITE the start

fire *NOUN*
*The campers toasted marshmallows in the **fire**.*
• a blaze, flames
— A **bonfire** is a fire outside.
— A **beacon** is a large fire used as a signal.
— An **inferno** is a large fierce destructive fire.
— **Embers** are small pieces of glowing coal or wood after a fire has gone out.
➤ **on fire**
*The whole forest seemed to be **on fire**.*
• alight, ablaze, burning, blazing, lit, ignited, in flames

☺ **WRITING TIPS**

Here are some useful words for writing about **fire**:

THINGS A FIRE DOES:

• to blaze, to crackle, to spit, to glow, to leap, to flare up, to dance, to break out, to erupt, to spread, to rage, to consume something, to devour something, to die down
The rain was driven noisily against the windows; the fire crackled and glowed.—BILLY TOPSAIL AND COMPANY, Norman Duncan

WORDS TO DESCRIBE A FIRE:

• blazing, roaring, bright, cheerful, glowing, warm, fierce, raging, dying

fire *VERB*
*The soldier **fired** his gun twice.*
• to shoot, to discharge
— To fire a missile is to **launch** it.

firm *ADJECTIVE*
❶ *The ground here is **firm**.*
• hard, solid, rigid, compact
OPPOSITE soft
❷ *Make sure the ladder is **firm**.*
• steady, stable, secure, fixed, strong, sturdy
OPPOSITE unsteady
❸ *Mum is a **firm** believer in eating your vegetables.*
• strong, staunch, definite, determined, resolute
OPPOSITE unsure

firm *NOUN*
*She runs a small **firm**.*
• a company, a business, an organisation, an enterprise

first ADJECTIVE

❶ The **first** person to finish was Ayesha.

• earliest, fastest, quickest

❷ My **first** impression was not very good.

• original, initial, earliest

➤ **at first**

At **first**, we thought it was going to be easy.

• at the beginning, to start with, initially, originally

fish NOUN

🕸 **WORD WEB**

SOME TYPES OF FISH:

• carp, cod, eel, haddock, hake, halibut, herring, mackerel, minnow, perch,

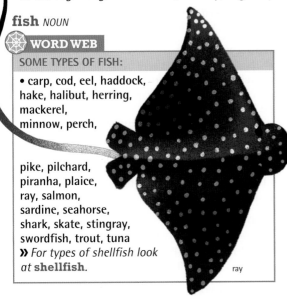

pike, pilchard, piranha, plaice, ray, salmon, sardine, seahorse, shark, skate, stingray, swordfish, trout, tuna

» For types of shellfish look at **shellfish**.

ray

fit ADJECTIVE

❶ I walk to school every day to keep **fit**.

• healthy, well, strong, robust, athletic

— A common simile is **as fit as a fiddle**.

OPPOSITE unhealthy

❷ The food was not **fit** to eat.

• suitable, appropriate, good enough, right, worthy

OPPOSITE unsuitable

fit VERB

❶ The lid doesn't **fit** the box.

• to go with, to match, to be the right size for

❷ The music **fits** the film perfectly.

• to be suitable for, to be appropriate to, to suit, to match

❸ We need to **fit** a new lock on the door.

• to install, to put in place, to place

fit NOUN

My friend and I had a **fit** of the giggles.

• an attack, an outburst

fix VERB

❶ We **fixed** a rope to the rock.

• to fasten, to attach, to connect, to join, to link, to secure

❷ Let's **fix** a time for the party.

• to decide on, to agree on, to set, to arrange, to settle, to determine

❸ Dad says he can **fix** my bike.

• to repair, to mend

fizz VERB

The lemonade **fizzed** when I opened the bottle.

• to hiss, to bubble, to foam, to froth

fizzy ADJECTIVE

Could I have a bottle of **fizzy** water, please?

• sparkling, bubbly, gassy, foaming

OPPOSITE still

flag NOUN

The street was decorated with **flags** for the carnival.

• a banner, a streamer

flap VERB

❶ The sail **flapped** in the wind.

• to flutter, to sway, to swing, to wave

❷ The huge bird **flapped** its wings.

• to beat

flash VERB

We saw a light **flash** from an upstairs window.

• to shine, to beam, to blaze, to flare, to glare, to gleam, to glint, to glimmer, to glitter, to wink

— To **sparkle** or **twinkle** is to flash many times or with many small lights.

flash NOUN

There was a **flash** of light in the sky.

• a flare, a beam, a blaze, a gleam, a glint, a ray, a burst, a flicker, a glimmer, a sparkle

flat ADJECTIVE

❶ You need a **flat** surface to write on.

• even, level, smooth

— A common simile is **as flat as a pancake**.

OPPOSITE uneven

❷ Lie **flat** on the ground.

• horizontal, outstretched

— To be lying flat with your face down is to be **prone**.

OPPOSITE upright

❸ The front tyre of my bike was **flat**.

• deflated, punctured

OPPOSITE inflated

❹ My phone battery is **flat**.

• dead

OPPOSITE fully charged

flaunt VERB

He was **flaunting** his expensive watch.

• to show off, to display, to exhibit

flavour NOUN

❶ *I don't like the flavour of the sauce.*
• a taste, a tang
❷ *Which flavour of ice cream do you like best?*
• a kind, a sort, a variety

😊 WRITING TIPS

Here are some words you could
use to describe **flavours**:
• acidic, bitter, bland,
chocolatey, delicate, fiery,
fresh, fruity, garlicky, hot,
lemony, mellow, mild, minty,
peppery, pungent, salty,
savoury, sharp, sour, spicy,
subtle, sweet, tangy, tart, tasty

*The chocolate was melty, tasty
with hints of fruity flavour too.*
—LYDIA'S TIN LID DRUM, Neale Osborne

fiery

lemony

chocolatey

flavour VERB

The sauce was flavoured with garlic and herbs.
• to season, to spice

flaw NOUN

There was a major flaw in their escape plan.
• a problem, a hitch, a snag, a weakness, a fault,
a defect

flee VERB flees, fleeing, fled

When they heard the alarm, the robbers fled.
• to run away, to bolt, to fly, to escape, to get
away, to take off

flew (past tense of fly)

flexible ADJECTIVE

The soles are made from flexible material.
• bendy, supple, elastic, springy
OPPOSITES rigid, inflexible

flicker VERB

The candlelight flickered in the draught.
• to glimmer, to waver, to flutter, to twinkle,
to blink, to shimmer

flinch VERB

He flinched as an arrow flew past his head.
• to wince, to recoil, to cringe, to shrink back,
to start, to jump

fling VERB flings, flinging, flung

I flung a stone into the pond.
• to throw, to cast, to sling, to toss, to hurl,
to pitch, to chuck (informal)

float VERB

We watched the twigs float gently down the river.
• to sail, to drift, to glide, to slip, to slide
— To **waft** or to **hover** is to float on air.

flock NOUN

» *For groups of animals look at* **group**.

flock VERB

People flocked round to see what was happening.
• to crowd, to gather, to collect, to herd

flood NOUN

❶ *The flood of water swept away the bridge.*
• a deluge, a rush, a torrent, a tide
❷ *The restaurant has received a flood of complaints.*
• a barrage, a succession
— You can also say that someone is **flooded with**
complaints or calls.

flood VERB

The river burst its banks and flooded the valley.
• to drown, to swamp, to submerge, to engulf,
to immerse

floppy ADJECTIVE

The dog had long floppy ears.
• droopy, limp, saggy, soft
OPPOSITES stiff, rigid

flourish VERB

He flourished at his new school.
• to thrive, to be successful, to do well, to progress,
to prosper

flow VERB

The rainwater flowed along the gutter.
• to run, to stream
— To **drip**, **dribble** or **trickle** is to flow slowly.
— To **seep** or **leak** is to flow very slowly and gradually.
— Use to **ooze** for a thick liquid that flows slowly.
— To **gush**, **pour**, **rush** or **flood** is to flow fast in large
amounts.
— To **cascade** is to flow fast in a downward direction.
— To **gurgle**, **babble** or **burble** is to flow noisily over
stones.
*They followed a narrow path for a while until they came to a
place where a small stream cascaded down through a rocky
V-shaped gully.*—SHARK ISLAND, David Miller

flow NOUN

❶ *There was a steady flow of water into the pond.*
• a stream
— Use a **flood**, a **torrent**, a **rush** or a **gush** for a large
fast flow.
— Use a **cascade** for a fast downward flow.
❷ *It's hard work rowing against the flow.*
• the current, the tide

flower NOUN
*We admired the **flowers** in her garden.*
• a bloom, a blossom

WORD WEB

SOME WILD FLOWERS:

• bluebell, buttercup, catkin, clover, cornflower, cowslip, daisy, dandelion, forget-me-not, foxglove, heather, orchid, poppy, primrose

SOME GARDEN FLOWERS:

• anemone, carnation, chrysanthemum, crocus, dahlia, daffodil, geranium, hibiscus, honeysuckle, fuchsia, hyacinth, iris, jasmine, lavender, lilac, lily, lupin, marigold, narcissus, nasturtium, pansy, peony, petunia, rose, snowdrop, sunflower, sweet pea, tulip, violet, wallflower

a tulip
a rose
an iris

flower VERB
*Most plants **flower** in the summer.*
• to bloom, to blossom, to bud

flown (past participle of **fly**)

fluffy ADJECTIVE
*Four **fluffy** ducklings were swimming in the pond.*
• feathery, furry, fuzzy, downy, soft

flush VERB
*Rory **flushed** with embarrassment.*
• to blush, to go red, to colour, to redden

flustered ADJECTIVE
*I get **flustered** when I have to read in assembly.*
• agitated, embarrassed, uncomfortable, bothered, unsettled, upset, confused
OPPOSITE calm

flutter VERB
❶ *A moth **fluttered** about the light bulb.*
• to flit, to flap, to fly, to flicker, to quiver
❷ *Flags **fluttered** in the breeze.*
• to flap, to wave, to sway

fly NOUN
» *For various insects look at* **insect.**

fly

fly VERB flies, flying, flew, flown
❶ *Two swallows were **flying** high in the sky.*
• to glide, to hover, to float
— To **flit**, to **flutter** or to **dart** is to fly around quickly.
— To **swoop** or to **dive** is to fly downwards quickly.
❷ *Suddenly the eagle **flew** into the air.*
• to rise, to soar, to mount, to take off, to take flight

foam NOUN
*The bath water was covered with **foam.***
• bubbles, froth, lather

foam VERB
*The mixture in the cauldron **foamed** and gurgled.*
• to froth, to bubble, to fizz, to boil, to seethe

focus VERB
*She **focused** the binoculars on the bird.*
• to adjust, to target, to zoom in on
➤ **to focus on**
*This morning we are **focusing on** spelling.*
• to concentrate on, to emphasise, to think about

focus NOUN
➤ **in focus**
*I can't get the image **in focus.***
• clear, sharp, distinct
➤ **out of focus**
*My photos were a bit **out of focus.***
• blurry, blurred, fuzzy, indistinct, unclear, hazy

fog NOUN
*I couldn't see very far in the **fog.***
— Use **mist** or **haze** for thin fog.
— **Smog** is a thick mixture of smoke and fog.

fold VERB
***Fold** the paper along the dotted line.*
• to bend, to double over, to crease

fold NOUN
*Cut along the **fold.***
• a crease, a bend

follow VERB

❶ *I followed my friend down the street.*
• to go after, to go behind
— To **chase**, to **pursue** or to **run after** someone is to try to catch them.
— To **shadow**, to **trail** or to **stalk** someone is to follow them secretly.
— To **trail** or to **track** a person or an animal is to follow the tracks they have left.
❷ *Why does thunder always follow lightning?*
• to come after, to succeed
OPPOSITE to precede
❸ *Follow this path until you reach the river.*
• to go along, to keep to, to take
❹ *I followed the instructions on the packet.*
• to carry out, to comply with, to obey, to observe
❺ *We found it hard to follow the story.*
• to understand, to comprehend, to grasp, to keep up with

follower NOUN

He had many loyal followers.
• a supporter, a disciple, a fan

food NOUN

We need to buy some food.
• something to eat, refreshments, nourishment, provisions, grub *(informal)*
— **Fodder** or **feed** is food for farm animals.

✳ WORD WEB

SOME TYPES OF FOOD:

• butter, cereal, cheese, chocolate, crisps, custard, eggs, flour, gravy, honey, ice cream, jam, jelly, ketchup, macaroni, marzipan, mayonnaise, mustard, noodles, oil, pasta, pastry, popcorn, rice, spaghetti, sugar, vinegar

BREAD AND CAKES:

• bagel, biscuit, bread, bun, cake, cookie, cracker, crumpet, cupcake, gateau, gingerbread, muffin, poppadom, sandwich, scone, sponge, toast, wafer, wrap

SOME PREPARED DISHES:

• barbecue, chips, curry, haggis, lasagne, omelette, pancake, pie, pizza, porridge, soup, stew, tart, trifle
» Look at **drink**, **fish**, **fruit**, **herb**, **meat**, **spice** and **vegetable**.
» For ways to cook and prepare food look at **cook**.
» For ways of eating look at **eat**.
» For types of meals look at **meal**.

😊 WRITING TIPS

You can use these words to describe **food**.

TO DESCRIBE HOW FOOD LOOKS OR FEELS:

• chewy, creamy, crispy, crumbly, crunchy, dry, flaky, gooey, greasy, juicy, lumpy, milky, mushy, rubbery, runny, sloppy, smooth, soggy, sticky, stodgy, syrupy, watery
» For words to describe flavours look at **flavour**.
» For words to describe smells look at **smell**.

TO DESCRIBE FOOD YOU LIKE:

• appetising, delicious, luscious, mouth-watering, tasty, tempting, scrummy *(informal)*, yummy *(informal)*

TO DESCRIBE FOOD YOU DON'T LIKE:

• disgusting, revolting, indigestible, inedible, nauseating, stomach-turning, tasteless, flavourless, unappetising, yucky *(informal)*, overcooked, undercooked

Measle didn't think the food was very good. The stew was watery and tasteless and the vegetables were soggy and overcooked.—MEASLE AND THE DOOMPIT, Ian Ogilvy

fool VERB

The spy fooled everyone with his disguise.
• to deceive, to trick, to mislead, to hoax, to con *(informal)*

fool NOUN

Only a fool would believe that ridiculous story.
• an idiot, an imbecile

foolish ADJECTIVE

It would be foolish to stand too close to the lions.
• stupid, silly, idiotic, senseless, ridiculous, unwise, absurd, crazy, mad, daft *(informal)*
OPPOSITE sensible

foot NOUN

❶ *Rhona walked on the sand in her bare feet.*
— A **paw** is the foot of a cat, dog or bear.
— A **hoof** is the foot of a horse, cow or deer.
— A **trotter** is a pig's foot.
❷ *We set up camp at the foot of the mountain.*
• the base, the bottom

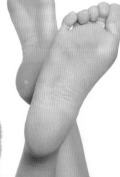
feet

a cat paw

a dog paw

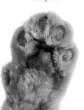

football NOUN

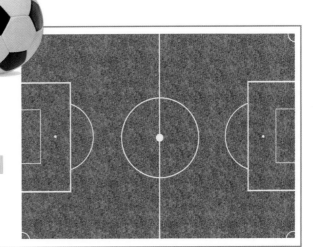

SOME PEOPLE WHO PLAY FOOTBALL:

- a footballer, a goalkeeper,
a defender, a forward, a striker,
a midfielder, a winger
— The **referee** is the official in charge of making
sure the rules are followed.
— A **linesman** is one of the officials who stands
at the side and helps the referee.

SOME OTHER TERMS USED IN FOOTBALL:

- kick-off, the pitch, the goal, the goalposts,
the crossbar, a shot, a header, a tackle, offside,
a corner, a throw-in, a free kick, a penalty,
a red card, a yellow card

forbidden ADJECTIVE

*Skateboarding is forbidden
in the playground.*
- banned, barred,
prohibited

OPPOSITE allowed

force NOUN

❶ *The firefighters had to use force to open
the door.*
- strength, power, violence, might, effort, energy
❷ *The force of the explosion broke all the windows.*
- an impact, an effect, a shock
❸ *The soldiers are part of a peacekeeping force.*
- a group, a unit, a team, a corps

force VERB

❶ *They were forced to hand over their money.*
- to compel, to make, to oblige, to order
❷ *They forced tough new rules on the children.*
- to impose, to inflict, to subject to
They subjected the children to tough new rules.
❸ *We had to force the door open.*
- to break, to wrench, to prise, to lever

forecast NOUN

The weather forecast is for snow tomorrow.
- an outlook, a prediction

forecast VERB forecasts, forecasting,
forecast, forecasted

Snow has been forecast for Tuesday.
- to predict, to foresee, to foretell

foreign ADJECTIVE

❶ *Lots of foreign tourists visit Oxford in the
summer.*
- overseas, international
❷ *I like travelling to foreign countries.*
- overseas, distant, faraway, exotic, remote, far-off

foresee VERB foresees, foreseeing, foresaw,
foreseen

Do you foresee any problems with our plan?
- to anticipate, to expect, to predict, to forecast,
to prophesy, to foretell

forest NOUN

They got lost in the forest.
- a wood
— A **rainforest** or a **jungle** is a tropical forest.

forget VERB forgets, forgetting, forgot,
forgotten

❶ *I forgot my swimming things.*
- to leave behind, to leave out, to overlook
❷ *Don't forget to turn off the lights.*
- to omit, to neglect, to fail
OPPOSITE to remember

forgetful ADJECTIVE

*As the professor grew older, he became more
forgetful.*
- absent-minded, careless, vague, distracted

forgive VERB forgives, forgiving, forgave,
forgiven

Please forgive me for being late.
- to excuse, to pardon

form NOUN
❶ *I made out the form of a man through the mist.*
• a shape, a figure, an outline, a silhouette
❷ *Ice is a form of water.*
• a kind, a sort, a type, a variety
❸ *Tasha and I are in the same form.*
• a class, a set
❹ *If you want to come on the trip, fill in this form.*
• a document, a paper, a sheet, a questionnaire

form VERB
❶ *The sculptor formed the clay into the shape of a bird.*
• to shape, to mould, to model, to make
❷ *My friends and I formed a club.*
• to set up, to establish, to found, to create, to start
❸ *Icicles had formed on the roof of the cave.*
• to appear, to develop, to grow

formal ADJECTIVE
❶ *It was a formal occasion.*
• official, ceremonial, serious, important
OPPOSITES casual, informal
❷ *The letter was written in a formal style.*
• correct, proper, polite
OPPOSITE informal

former ADJECTIVE
In former times, the castle was surrounded by a moat.
• earlier, previous, past

fort NOUN
A few soldiers were left to defend the fort.
• a fortress, a stronghold, a castle
» Look at **castle**.

fortunate ADJECTIVE
We were fortunate to have good weather.
• lucky, in luck, blessed
OPPOSITE unfortunate, unlucky

fortune NOUN
❶ *It was good fortune that I arrived at that moment.*
• chance, luck, an accident
❷ *The witch offered to tell his fortune.*
• future, destiny, fate
❸ *She dreamed of fame and fortune.*
• wealth, riches, possessions

fossil NOUN
I found a fossil on the beach.
— An **ammonite** is a fossil with a spiral shape.
— A **trilobite** is a fossil of a creature whose body had three parts.
— **Amber** is fossilised tree sap.
— A person who studies fossils is a **palaeontologist**.

a trilobite

amber

an ammonite

fought (past tense of **fight**)

foul ADJECTIVE
There was a foul smell in the cave.
• disgusting, revolting, repulsive, nasty, offensive, rotten, horrible, vile, nauseating
OPPOSITE pleasant

found (past tense of **find**)

found VERB
The school was founded a hundred years ago.
• to establish, to set up, to start, to begin, to create

foundation NOUN
❶ *The house was built on shaky foundations.*
• ground, a base
❷ *She started a charitable foundation.*
• an organisation, an institute, an institution
❸ *There are lots of myths about the foundation of Rome.*
• the founding, the beginning, the setting up, the establishment, the origins

fountain NOUN
A fountain of water shot into the air.
• a jet, a spout, a spray, a spring, a spurt

fox NOUN

 WORD WEB

- A male fox is a **dog**.
- A female fox is a **vixen**.
- A young fox is a **cub**.
- A fox lives in an **earth**.

fragile ADJECTIVE
The old paper is very **fragile**.
• breakable, delicate, brittle, easily damaged, frail, weak
OPPOSITE strong

frame NOUN
The **frame** of the house is made of timber.
• the framework, the structure, the shell, the skeleton

frank ADJECTIVE
He gave me his **frank** opinion of the story.
• honest, sincere, genuine, direct, blunt, straightforward, truthful
OPPOSITE insincere

frantic ADJECTIVE
❶ I was **frantic** with worry when our kitten got lost.
• desperate, hysterical, crazy, in a frenzy
❷ There was **frantic** activity on the day of the wedding.
• excited, frenzied, feverish, wild, mad
OPPOSITE calm

frayed ADJECTIVE
The old woman wore a **frayed** cloak.
• tattered, ragged, worn, shabby, threadbare

free ADJECTIVE
❶ You are **free** to wander anywhere in the park.
• able, allowed, permitted
OPPOSITE restricted
❷ After two years in captivity, the hostages were **free** at last.
• freed, liberated, released, let go
OPPOSITE imprisoned
❸ I got a **free** drink with my sandwich.
• complimentary, free of charge
❹ The bathroom is **free** now.
• available, unoccupied, vacant, empty
OPPOSITE occupied, busy

free VERB
The soldiers **freed** the prisoners.
• to release, to liberate, to set free, to untie, to unchain
OPPOSITE to imprison

freedom NOUN
The animals have a lot of **freedom** in the safari park.
• liberty, independence

freezing ADJECTIVE
It's **freezing** outside today.
• chilly, frosty, icy, wintry, raw, bitter

frequent ADJECTIVE
❶ My friend sends me **frequent** messages.
• numerous, constant, continual, repeated, countless
OPPOSITE infrequent
❷ Robins are **frequent** visitors to the garden.
• regular, habitual, common, familiar
OPPOSITE rare

fresh ADJECTIVE
❶ The shop bakes **fresh** bread every day.
• new
OPPOSITE old, stale
❷ I put **fresh** sheets on the bed.
• new, clean, different
OPPOSITE dirty, used
❸ Eat lots of **fresh** fruit.
• natural, raw, unprocessed
OPPOSITE preserved, processed
❹ Sally went outside to get some **fresh** air.
• clean, cool, crisp, refreshing, bracing
OPPOSITE stuffy
❺ I felt nice and **fresh** after my swim.
• refreshed, revived, restored, invigorated, energetic

friend NOUN
She went to the park with her **friends**.
• a companion, a pal (informal), a mate (informal)
- A **playmate** is a friend you play with.
- A **partner** is someone you work or do something with.
- An **acquaintance** is someone you know but not very well.
- An **ally** is someone who helps you in a fight or disagreement.
OPPOSITE enemy

friendly ADJECTIVE
❶ Our neighbour is very **friendly**.
• kind, pleasant, good-natured, likeable, warm, affectionate, loving, cordial, sociable
❷ Are you **friendly** with Tom?
• close, familiar, pally (informal), matey (informal)
❸ It's a very **friendly** club.
• welcoming, hospitable, warm
OPPOSITE unfriendly, hostile

a b c d e f g h i j k l m n o p q r s t u v w x y z

friendship NOUN
Their friendship has lasted for many years.
- **closeness, affection, fondness, familiarity, attachment**
— An **alliance** is a formal friendship between countries or political groups.
OPPOSITE hostility

fright NOUN
❶ *He gasped in fright.*
- **fear, terror, alarm, horror, panic, dread**
❷ *The noise gave me a fright.*
- **a scare, a shock, a surprise, a start**

frighten VERB
Sorry—I didn't mean to frighten you.
- **to scare, to alarm**
— To **terrify** or to **petrify** someone is to frighten them very much.
— To **startle** or to **shock** someone is to frighten them by being unexpected.
— To **panic** someone is to frighten them so that they do not know what to do.

frightened ADJECTIVE
I felt very frightened when the lights went out.
- **afraid, scared, alarmed, fearful**
— Use **terrified** or **petrified** to mean very frightened.
— Use **startled** or **shocked** to mean frightened by something unexpected.
— Use **panicky** when someone is frightened and does not know what to do.

😊 **WRITING TIPS**

Here are some things someone might do if they feel **frightened**:
- **to go** or **turn pale, to cower, to cringe, to flinch, to shrink, to jump, to start, to gulp, to swallow hard, to shudder, to quake** or **shake in your boots, to tremble** or **shake like a leaf, to freeze, to be frozen** or **paralysed with fear**
— You could say that something **sends shivers down your spine** or **chills your blood.**
— You could also say that your **blood freezes.**
The glimpse I caught before father pulled me away made my blood freeze in horror: I could see black-clad men on horseback around the house.–SIGRUN'S SECRET, Marie-Louise Jensen

frightening ADJECTIVE
Some of the children found the film frightening.
- **alarming, scary, chilling**
— Use **terrifying, horrifying** or **petrifying** if something is very frightening.
— Use **creepy, spooky, eerie** or **uncanny** for something that is strange and slightly frightening.

— Use **sinister** or **menacing** if something is frightening because it seems evil or harmful.
— Use **startling** for something that makes you jump.

frill NOUN
My party dress has a frill round the hem.
- **a ruffle, a ruff, a flounce, a fringe**

frisky ADJECTIVE
The new lion cubs in the zoo are very frisky.
- **playful, lively, high-spirited, sprightly**

frog NOUN
— A young frog is a **tadpole.**
— Frogs' eggs are **frogspawn.**
— The sound a frog makes is a **croak.**

front NOUN
At last we got to the front of the queue.
- **the head, the start, the beginning**
OPPOSITES the back, the rear
— The front of a ship is the **bow** or **prow.**
— The front of a plane is the **nose.**
— The front of a picture is the **foreground.**

front ADJECTIVE
The horse had injured one of its front legs.
- **fore**
OPPOSITE back, rear, hind

frontier NOUN
We crossed the frontier between France and Italy.
- **the border, the boundary**

froth NOUN
I like a lot of froth on my hot chocolate.
- **foam, bubbles**
— **Lather** is soapy froth.
— **Scum** is dirty froth.

frown VERB
She frowned at me and told me to stop talking.
- **to scowl, to glare, to glower**
— To **grimace** is to frown because you are in pain or embarrassed.
— To **sulk** or to **pout** is to frown because you did not get what you wanted.

frown NOUN
From his frown I could tell something was wrong.
- **a scowl, a glare, a glower**
— A **grimace** is a frown of pain or embarrassment.
— A **pout** is a frown because you did not get what you wanted.
Now her eyes were dark with anger, there was a deep, frowning crease in the middle of her forehead, her lips were pressed together in a thin line, and her mouth was drawn down at the corners in a scowl.–MEASLE: THE PITS OF PERIL! Ian Ogilvy

fruit NOUN

WORD WEB

SOME TYPES OF FRUIT:

• an apple, an apricot, an avocado, a banana, blackberries, blueberries, cherries, a coconut, cranberries, elderberries, a fig, gooseberries, grapes, a guava, a kiwi fruit, lychees, a mango, a melon, mulberries, a nectarine, a papaya, a peach, a pear, a pineapple, a plum, raspberries, strawberries, a tomato, a watermelon

SOME CITRUS FRUITS:

• a grapefruit, a lemon, a lime, an orange, a satsuma, a tangerine

DRIED FRUITS:

• currants, dates, prunes, raisins, sultanas

an apple

a pear

a peach

an orange

grapes

a lime

a nectarine

a tangerine

an apricot

a blackberry

a banana

gooseberries

a tomato

rhubarb

cherries

raisins

a papaya

star fruit

a kiwi fruit

a raspberry

a plum

a coconut

a passion fruit

a strawberry

dates

a grapefruit

a lemon

an avocado

cranberries

a pineapple

a mango

a watermelon

fry VERB
» For ways to cook things look at **cook**.

fugitive NOUN
Police searched everywhere for the **fugitives**.
• a runaway, an outlaw
— A **refugee** is someone running away from war or cruel treatment.

fulfil VERB
She **fulfilled** her ambition to play tennis at Wimbledon.
• to achieve, to realise, to accomplish, to carry out, to complete, to succeed in

full ADJECTIVE
❶ My suitcase is completely **full**.
• filled, loaded, overflowing
OPPOSITE empty
❷ The school hall was **full** for the concert.
• packed, crowded, jammed, crammed, busy
OPPOSITE empty
❸ I want to hear the **full** story.
• complete, detailed, comprehensive, thorough
OPPOSITE incomplete
❹ The horses were galloping at **full** speed.
• top, maximum, greatest, highest
OPPOSITE minimum

fun NOUN
We had some **fun** at the beach.
• enjoyment, amusement, pleasure, play, entertainment, diversion, recreation
➤ **to make fun of someone**
It was cruel to **make fun of** her when she fell over.
• to mock, to jeer at, to laugh at, to ridicule, to taunt, to tease

fun ADJECTIVE
We did some **fun** activities at the end of the lesson.
• enjoyable, playful, light-hearted, amusing, frivolous
OPPOSITE serious

function NOUN
What is the **function** of this tool?
• the purpose, the job, the task, the use, the role

function VERB
This camera doesn't **function** properly.
• to work, to operate, to go, to run, to perform

funny ADJECTIVE
❶ There are some very **funny** jokes in the film.
• amusing, humorous, comic, comical, entertaining, diverting
— Use **hilarious** or **hysterical** to mean very funny.
— Use **witty** to mean funny and clever.
OPPOSITE serious
❷ There's a **funny** smell in here.
• strange, odd, peculiar, curious, weird, bizarre

fur NOUN
Arctic foxes have thick white **fur** in the winter.
• hair, a coat, a pelt

furious ADJECTIVE
The manager was **furious** when his team lost.
• angry, mad, enraged, infuriated, incensed, livid, outraged, fuming, raging, seething

furniture NOUN
» For some types of furniture look at **cupboard** and **seat**.

furry ADJECTIVE
A small **furry** creature was curled inside the box.
• fluffy, hairy, woolly, fuzzy, fleecy

fury NOUN
She threw the box across the room in **fury**.
• anger, rage, outrage, wrath (old use)
— An outburst of fury is a **tantrum** or a **fit of rage**.

fuss NOUN
There was a lot of **fuss** about moving the chairs.
• commotion, bother, upheaval, trouble, excitement

fuss VERB
Please don't **fuss**!
• to fret, to worry, to make a fuss

fussy ADJECTIVE
He is very **fussy** about what he eats.
• hard to please, particular, awkward, picky (informal)

Gg

⚙ Can you think of 5 different words meaning 'very good'?

⚙ Can you think of 3 different ways to say 'quite good, but not very'?

⚙ Check the thesaurus to find answers!

gadget NOUN
This is a gadget for opening cans.
• a tool, an instrument, an implement, a device, a contraption

gain VERB
She gained some useful experience.
• to get, to acquire, to obtain, to earn, to win
OPPOSITE to lose

game NOUN
❶ *My favourite game is hide-and-seek.*
• an amusement, a pastime, a sport, an activity, a recreation
❷ *We are going to a football game on Saturday.*
• a match, a contest, a competition, a tournament

✸ WORD WEB

SOME GAMES:

• bingo, a board game, bowling, cards, charades, chess, conkers, darts, dominoes, patience, poker, pool, snooker
» For more games look at **sport**.

chess

a console

darts

gang NOUN
❶ *They were attacked by a gang of bandits.*
• a pack, a band, a mob, a group
❷ *She went out with a gang of friends.*
• a group, a bunch, a crowd

gap NOUN
The animals escaped through a gap in the fence.
• an opening, a space, a hole, a break, a crack

garden NOUN

✸ WORD WEB

TYPES OF GARDEN:

— An **allotment** is a rented garden for growing vegetables.
— A **yard** is an outdoor area with a hard surface such as concrete.
— An **orchard** is a garden planted with fruit trees.

THINGS YOU MIGHT FIND IN A GARDEN:

• a hedge, a lawn, a flower bed, a vegetable patch, a patio, a terrace, a bench, a greenhouse, a pond, a fountain
The house he lived in, on the edge of the town, was quite small; but his garden was very large and had a wide lawn and stone seats and weeping-willows hanging over.–DOCTOR DOLITTLE, Hugh Lofting
» For garden flowers look at **flower**.
» For garden tools look at **tool**.

gas NOUN
The mixture gave off a nasty-smelling gas.
• vapour, fumes

gasp VERB
At the end of the race we lay gasping for breath.
• to pant, to puff, to gulp

gather VERB
❶ *A crowd gathered to listen.*
• to assemble, to collect, to come together, to converge, to flock, to huddle
OPPOSITE to disperse
❷ *We gathered blackberries from the hedges.*
• to pick, to pluck, to collect, to harvest
❸ *I need to gather some information for my project.*
• to collect, to get together, to find

gave (past tense of **give**)

gaze VERB
He gazed at his reflection in the mirror.
• to stare, to look

a b c d e f g h i j k l m n o p q r s t u v w x y z

— To **gape** at something is to stare at it in a surprised way, with your mouth open.

— To **glare** at someone is to stare at them angrily.

— To **scan** something is to move your eyes across it looking for something: *She scanned the horizon, hoping to see a ship.*

gear NOUN
We put our fishing gear in the back of the car.
• equipment, stuff, things, tackle

general ADJECTIVE
❶ *The general opinion is we get too much homework.*
• widespread, popular, overall, common, usual
❷ *I've only got a general idea of where we are.*
• rough, approximate, vague, indefinite
OPPOSITES accurate, specific, detailed

generally ADVERB
I generally travel to school by bus.
• usually, normally, as a rule, chiefly, mostly, mainly

generous ADJECTIVE
❶ *It was generous of you to give me your seat.*
• kind, unselfish, noble, good
OPPOSITE selfish
❷ *We each got a generous helping of ice cream.*
• ample, large, lavish, plentiful
OPPOSITE meagre

genius NOUN
Tara is a genius at maths.
• an expert, a master, a mastermind, a wizard
— If someone is a genius you can say that they are gifted or brilliant: *Tara is brilliant at maths.*

gentle ADJECTIVE
❶ *Be gentle with the baby.*
• kind, tender, careful, loving, good-tempered
OPPOSITE rough
❷ *There was a gentle breeze.*
• light, slight, mild, soft
OPPOSITE strong

genuine ADJECTIVE
❶ *Is that a genuine diamond?*
• real, actual, authentic
OPPOSITE fake
❷ *She seems like a very genuine person.*
• honest, sincere, frank, earnest, straightforward
OPPOSITE false

gesture NOUN
She opened her arms in a gesture of welcome.
• a sign, a signal, a motion, a movement

get VERB gets, getting, got

😮 OVERUSED WORD

Try to use a more interesting word when you want to say **get**. Here are some ideas:
❶ *We're getting a rabbit.*
• to acquire, to buy, to purchase, to obtain
❷ *We can get medicine from plants.*
• to derive, to obtain, to extract
❸ *Can you get me another blanket, please?*
• to bring, to fetch, to find
❹ *Cory got a medal for swimming.*
• to receive, to gain, to earn, to win, to achieve, to be awarded
— To get points or goals is to **score** them.
❺ *What time did you get to the bus stop?*
• to arrive at, to reach, to come to
OPPOSITE to leave
❻ *It was starting to get dark.*
• to grow, to become, to turn
❼ *I got a stomach bug on holiday last year.*
• to catch, to develop, to pick up, to come down with
❽ *You'll never get Oscar to eat celery.*
• to persuade, to urge, to influence, to coax, to tempt

ghost NOUN
He thought he had seen a ghost.
• a spirit, a spectre, a spook, a phantom, a ghoul, an apparition

😊 WRITING TIPS

Here are some ideas for writing about **ghosts**:

THINGS A GHOST MIGHT DO:

• to appear, to cackle, to clang, to clank its chains, to flit, to float, to glide, to haunt somewhere, to howl, to hover, to moan, to pass through walls, to screech, to vanish
The air was filled with phantoms, wandering hither and thither in restless haste, and moaning as they went.—A CHRISTMAS CAROL, Charles Dickens

SOME SPOOKY PLACES:

• a castle, a cavern, a cellar, a cemetery, a chamber, a crypt, a dungeon, a graveyard, a haunted house, a sunken ship, a tomb, a tunnel, a vault

giant ADJECTIVE
A giant tree towered above us.
• gigantic, huge, enormous, massive, immense, mammoth, colossal, vast
OPPOSITE tiny

❾ *I didn't **get** the joke.*
• to understand, to see, to follow, to comprehend, to grasp
➤ **to get off**
— To get off a train or a bus is to **leave** it.
— To get off a ship or a plane is to **disembark**.
— To get on a bicycle or horse is to **dismount**.
➤ **to get on** or **along**
*How are you **getting on** with playing the guitar?*
• to manage, to cope, to progress, to succeed
— To **thrive** or to **prosper** is to get on well.
➤ **to get on** or **into**
— To get on a ship or in a plane is to **embark**.
— To get on a bicycle or horse is to **mount** it.
➤ **to get out of**
*My sister **got out of** doing the washing-up.*
• to avoid, to evade, to shirk

gift NOUN
❶ *These flowers would make a nice **gift**.*
• a present
❷ *Elsa has a **gift** for music.*
• a talent, an ability, a flair, a genius

giggle VERB
*Ailsa and I couldn't stop **giggling**.*
• to snigger, to titter, to chuckle, to chortle

girl NOUN
• a lass, a child, a kid *(informal)*, a youngster, a teenager, a teen
— A **maid** or a **maiden** is an old-fashioned word for a girl.

give VERB gives, giving, gave, given

😃 **OVERUSED WORD**

Try to use a more interesting word when you want to say **give**. Here are some ideas:
❶ *Will you **give** me that piece of paper?*
• to hand, to pass
❷ *My parents **gave** me a new bike.*
• to buy, to present
*My parents **presented** me with a new bike.*

❸ *She **gave** a copy of the book to each child.*
• to issue, to distribute, to provide, to supply, to deal out
❹ *The judges **gave** first prize to our team.*
• to award, to present
❺ *Will you **give** something to our charity collection?*
• to contribute, to donate, to offer
❻ *He **gave** a loud laugh.*
• to utter, to emit, to let out, to produce
❼ *We are **giving** a concert at the end of term.*
• to present, to put on, to lay on, to organise, to arrange
➤ **to give in**
*Eventually I **gave in** and admitted I'd lost.*
• to surrender, to yield, to submit, to quit, to relent
➤ **to give out**
*The torch **gave out** a faint light.*
• to emit, to produce, to generate, to send out, to radiate, to discharge
*The teacher **gave out** pencils.*
• to hand out, to pass round, to distribute, to dispense
➤ **to give up**
*He **gave up** eating biscuits to try to lose weight.*
• to stop, to cease, to quit, to refrain from, to sacrifice

given *(past participle of **give**)*

glad ADJECTIVE
❶ *I'm **glad** to hear that you're feeling better.*
• pleased, happy, delighted, thrilled
OPPOSITE sad
❷ *He'll be **glad** to help you.*
• willing, ready, pleased, delighted
OPPOSITE reluctant

glamorous ADJECTIVE
*The actress looked very **glamorous**.*
• beautiful, attractive, gorgeous, elegant, stylish, fashionable

glance VERB
*The bus driver **glanced** quickly at his watch.*
• to look quickly, to peek, to peep
— To **glimpse** something is to see it for a very short time.

glare VERB
*The troll **glared** at us from under his bushy eyebrows.*
• to scowl, to glower, to frown, to stare
glare NOUN
*Miss Frump silenced the children with an angry **glare**.*
• a scowl, a glower, a frown, a stare

a b c d e f g h i j k l m n o p q r s t u v w x y z

glasses NOUN

WORD WEB

SOME GLASSES

• spectacles, microscope, binoculars, telescope, magnifying glass
She put on her glasses to read the letter.

a magnifying glass

binoculars

spectacles

a microscope

a telescope

gleam NOUN
I saw a gleam of moonlight between the clouds.
• a glimmer, a glint, a flash, a ray, a shaft

gleam VERB
The lights gleamed on the water.
• to glimmer, to glint, to glisten, to shimmer, to shine

glimpse VERB
I glimpsed a deer running through the forest.
• to catch sight of, to spot, to spy

glimpse NOUN
We caught a glimpse of a dolphin's tail.
• a peek, a peep, a flash

glitter VERB
The jewels glittered under the bright lights.
• to sparkle, to twinkle, to shimmer, to glimmer, to glint, to glisten, to flash, to shine, to wink

global ADJECTIVE
The Internet is a global network of computers.
• worldwide, international, universal

gloom NOUN
❶ *We could hardly see in the gloom of the cave.*
• darkness, dimness, shade, shadow
— Use **dusk** or **twilight** for the gloomy light in the evening when the sun sets.
❷ *There was an air of gloom after the match.*
• depression, sadness, unhappiness, melancholy, misery, despair

gloomy ADJECTIVE
❶ *It was cold and gloomy in the cellar.*
• dark, dingy, dim, dismal, dreary, sombre, murky, shadowy
OPPOSITE bright
❷ *Eeyore was feeling gloomy again.*
• glum, miserable, depressed, sad, unhappy, melancholy, low, downcast, dejected
OPPOSITE cheerful

glow NOUN
The soft glow of burning candles lit the room.
• brightness, shine, gleam, radiance

glow VERB
The embers of the bonfire were still glowing.
• to shine, to gleam, to burn
— Use **luminous** or **fluorescent** for something that glows in the dark.

glue NOUN
Put a blob of glue on each corner of the paper.
• adhesive, paste, gum

glue VERB
Glue the edges of the box together.
• to stick, to paste, to bond, to seal

glum ADJECTIVE
Why are you looking so glum?
• gloomy, miserable, depressed, sad, unhappy, melancholy, low, downcast, dejected
OPPOSITE cheerful

go VERB goes, going, went, gone

OVERUSED WORD

Try to use a more interesting word when you want to say **go**. Here are some ideas and examples:
❶ *A carriage was going slowly along the road.*
• to move, to progress, to proceed
» Look at **move** and **walk**.
❷ *My granny has always wanted to go to China.*
• to travel to, to journey to, to visit
— Use **to voyage** for a long journey by ship or spacecraft: *They dreamed of voyaging to other planets.*
❸ *Some of the guests had already gone.*
• to leave, to depart, to set out
❹ *By morning, the snow had all gone.*
• to disappear, to vanish

⑤ *This path **goes** to the village.*
• to lead, to run, to take someone
*This path **takes** you to the village.*

⑥ *Her hair **went** down to her waist.*
• to reach, to extend, to stretch

⑦ *The mountaineer's face **went** blue with cold.*
• to become, to turn, to grow

⑧ *My watch won't **go**.*
• to function, to operate, to work, to run

⑨ *Cups and saucers **go** on the bottom shelf.*
• to belong, to be kept, to be placed

⑩ *Time **goes** slowly when you're bored.*
• to pass, to go by, to elapse

➤ to go back
*I had to **go back** because I forgot my bag.*
• to return, to retreat, to retrace your steps

➤ to go down
*She **went down** the ladder carefully.*
• to descend, to climb down

➤ to go off
❶ *A bomb **went off** nearby.*
• to explode, to blow up, to detonate
❷ *The milk will **go off** if it's not in the fridge.*
• to go bad
— Use to **turn sour** for milk or cream.
— Use to **rot** for vegetables, fruit, meat or fish.
— Use to **go mouldy** for bread.

➤ to go on
❶ *What's **going on** over there?*
• to happen, to occur, to take place
❷ *Please **go on** with your story.*
• to carry on, to continue, to keep going, to proceed

➤ to go up
*We **went up** the stairs to bed.*
• to mount, to climb, to ascend

➤ to go with
*Do these shoes **go with** my dress?*
• to match, to suit, to complement, to blend with

go NOUN
*Would you like to have a **go** with my new game?*
• a try, an attempt, a turn, a chance, an opportunity

goal NOUN
*Our **goal** is to protect wildlife.*
• an aim, an ambition, an intention, an object,
an objective, a purpose, a target

god or **goddess** NOUN
*Zeus was one of the **gods** of ancient Greece.*
• a deity, an idol
— A word meaning 'to do with a god or goddess'
is **divine**.

gone *(past participle of **go**)*

good ADJECTIVE

 OVERUSED WORD

Try to use a more interesting word when you want
to say **good**. Here are some ideas and examples:

WORDS FOR VERY GOOD:

• excellent, fine, lovely, wonderful, fantastic,
fabulous, terrific, tremendous, sensational,
splendid, great, cool *(informal)*, outstanding,
exceptional
*That is a **wonderful** idea!*
OPPOSITES terrible, awful

WAYS TO SAY QUITE GOOD, BUT NOT VERY:

• fair, decent, all right, satisfactory, acceptable,
average
— Use **mediocre** to mean not very good, but not
terrible.
*It's a **decent** film, but I preferred the book.*

FOR A GOOD PERSON OR GOOD CREATURE:

• honest, moral, decent, noble, honourable,
generous, kind, kindly, merciful, worthy, righteous
*There was once a **kindly** old wizard who used his
magic generously and wisely for the benefit of his
neighbours.*—THE TALES OF BEEDLE THE BARD, J. K. Rowling
OPPOSITES evil, wicked

FOR GOOD BEHAVIOUR:

• well-behaved, obedient, polite
*Michael is a **well-behaved** boy.*
— A common simile is **as good as gold**.
OPPOSITES naughty, disobedient

FOR A GOOD FRIEND:

• true, loyal, reliable, dependable, trusty, trustworthy
*My dog, Rusty, is a **loyal** companion.*

FOR A GOOD FEELING OR GOOD MOOD:

• happy, cheerful, light-hearted, positive, contented
*Mr Fox was in a **cheerful** mood after his tea.*

FOR A GOOD EXPERIENCE OR GOOD NEWS:

• pleasant, enjoyable, delightful, agreeable,
pleasing
*The trip was very **enjoyable**.*
OPPOSITES unpleasant, disagreeable

FOR A GOOD BOOK OR GOOD FILM:

• interesting, exciting, gripping, thrilling,
fascinating
*It was a **gripping** story.*
OPPOSITES dull, tedious

a
b
c
d
e
f
g
h
i
j
k
l
m
n
o
p
q
r
s
t
u
v
w
x
y
z

A B C D E F G H I J K L M N O P Q R S T U V W X Y Z

FOR A GOOD DESCRIPTION OR GOOD EXPLANATION:

• clear, vivid, precise, accurate
*She gave us very **precise** instructions.*

FOR A GOOD PERFORMER OR GOOD WORK:

• skilful, skilled, talented, gifted, able, capable, competent, strong
*My friend Chris is a **talented** dancer.*
OPPOSITES poor, awful

FOR GOOD FOOD:

• delicious, tasty, well-cooked
– Use healthy, nutritious or wholesome for food that is good for you.
– Use hearty or substantial for a large meal.
*We ate a **hearty** breakfast before we set off.*
OPPOSITES bad, inedible

FOR A GOOD EXCUSE OR GOOD REASON:

• acceptable, valid, proper, satisfactory, legitimate
*I hope you have a **valid** excuse for being late.*
OPPOSITES poor, unacceptable

FOR GOOD TIMING:

• convenient, suitable, appropriate
*Is this a **convenient** time to talk?*
OPPOSITES inconvenient, unsuitable

FOR GOOD WEATHER:

• fine, favourable, fair, dry, warm, sunny
*We are hoping for **fine** weather tomorrow.*
OPPOSITES poor, unfavourable

---

goodbye NOUN
➤ to say goodbye
*It's time for me to **say goodbye**.*
• to say farewell, to bid someone farewell, to take your leave
*It's time for me to **take my leave**.*

good-looking ADJECTIVE
*Do you think he is **good-looking**?*
• attractive, handsome, nice-looking
OPPOSITE ugly

goods PLURAL NOUN
*They sell all sorts of household **goods**.*
• items, merchandise, wares

gorgeous ADJECTIVE
*The gardens look **gorgeous** in the summer.*
• beautiful, glorious, dazzling, stunning, splendid, superb, glamorous, handsome

gossip VERB
*I was **gossiping** on the phone with my friend.*
• to chat, to chatter

gossip NOUN
*Don't believe all the **gossip** you hear.*
• talk, rumours, scandal

govern VERB
*The ancient Romans **governed** a vast empire.*
• to rule, to run, to lead, to command, to direct, to manage, to be in charge of

grab VERB
*The thief **grabbed** the bag and ran away.*
• to seize, to grasp, to snatch, to pluck, to clutch, to grip, to get hold of

graceful ADJECTIVE
*The dancer's movements are so **graceful**.*
• agile, nimble, smooth, flowing, beautiful, elegant
OPPOSITES clumsy, graceless

grade NOUN
*He got the top **grade** in his exam.*
• a mark, a level, a standard, a class

grade VERB
*Eggs are **graded** according to size.*
• to group, to classify, to sort, to rank

gradual ADJECTIVE
*There has been a **gradual** improvement.*
• steady, slow, regular
OPPOSITE sudden

grain NOUN
❶ *The **grain** will be harvested soon.*
• cereals, corn
❷ *Some **grains** of sand stuck to my toes.*
• a particle, a speck, a bit

grand ADJECTIVE
*The emperor lived in a **grand** palace.*
• magnificent, splendid, great, impressive, imposing, majestic

grass NOUN
*People were told not to walk on the **grass**.*
• lawn, turf
– Pasture is grass growing for farm animals to eat.
– A meadow is a field of grass.

grateful ADJECTIVE
*I'm **grateful** for your help.*
• thankful, appreciative, obliged
OPPOSITE ungrateful

gratitude NOUN
We sent some flowers to show our gratitude.
• thanks, appreciation

graveyard NOUN
He was buried in the local graveyard.
• a burial ground, a cemetery, a churchyard

greasy ADJECTIVE
These chips are too greasy.
• fatty, oily

great ADJECTIVE
❶ *Their voices echoed round the great hall.*
• huge, large, enormous, vast, immense
OPPOSITE small
❷ *Mozart was a great composer.*
• notable, famous, important, distinguished, outstanding, brilliant, major, leading
OPPOSITE minor
❸ *That is a great idea!*
• excellent, marvellous, brilliant, fantastic, outstanding, superb, tremendous, terrific, wonderful
OPPOSITES bad, awful

greedy ADJECTIVE
Don't be so greedy—you'll never eat all that.
• selfish, gluttonous, piggish *(informal)*
— A common simile is as greedy as a pig.

green ADJECTIVE, NOUN

 WORD WEB

SOME SHADES OF GREEN:

• bottle green, emerald, jade, khaki, lime green, olive green, pea green

greet VERB
My aunt greeted us with a friendly wave.
• to welcome, to hail, to salute, to receive

grew *(past tense of **grow**)*

grey ADJECTIVE
❶ *The old wizard had a bushy grey beard.*
• silver, silvery, grizzled, whitish
❷ *The day began cold and grey.*
• dull, cloudy, overcast, gloomy, murky

 WORD WEB

SOME SHADES OF GREY:

• ash, charcoal grey, dove grey, silver, slate grey

grief NOUN
They were full of grief at their friend's death.
• sorrow, sadness, unhappiness, distress, anguish
OPPOSITE joy

grieve VERB
After the old lady died, the family needed time to grieve.
• to mourn, to lament, to weep
— If someone is grieving a loved one's death, you can say that they are **bereaved** or **in mourning**.
OPPOSITE to rejoice

grim ADJECTIVE
❶ *The judge had a grim expression.*
• stern, severe, harsh, sombre
OPPOSITE cheerful
❷ *The detective made a grim discovery.*
• unpleasant, horrible, dreadful, terrible, hideous, shocking, gruesome, grisly
OPPOSITE pleasant

grin NOUN
My brother had a grin on his face.
• a beam, a broad smile

grin VERB
She grinned at me and put her thumb up.
• to beam, to smile broadly

grind VERB grinds, grinding, ground
❶ *Grind the spices into a fine paste.*
• to crush, to pound, to mash, to mill
— To **trample** something is to grind it under your feet.
❷ *The ship ground against the rocks.*
• to scrape, to rub

grip VERB
❶ *She gripped my arm.*
• to grasp, to seize, to clutch, to clasp, to hold
— To **clench** is to close your hand or teeth tightly around something: *His fists clenched the steering wheel.*
❷ *The audience was gripped by the film.*
• to fascinate, to engross, to absorb, to rivet

groan VERB
The wounded soldier groaned with pain.
• to cry out, to moan, to sigh, to protest

groove NOUN
Thick grooves had been carved in the stone wall.
• a channel, a furrow, a rut, a cut, a scratch
— A **notch** is a V-shaped groove.

ground *(past tense of **grind**)*

A
B
C
D
E
F
G
H
I
J
K
L
M
N
O
P
Q
R
S
T
U
V
W
X
Y
Z

ground NOUN
❶ *I planted some seeds in the **ground**.*
• the earth, the soil, the land
❷ *The sports **ground** was too wet to play on.*
• a field, a pitch, a park

group NOUN
❶ *There was a large **group** waiting at the bus stop.*
• a crowd, a gathering, a throng, a troop
— Use a **mob** for a large angry group.
❷ *There was a **group** of trees growing close together.*
• a cluster, a clump, a bunch, a set
❸ *We sorted the fossils into different **groups**.*
• a category, a class, a type, a kind, a sort
❹ *The book **group** meets once a month.*
• a club, a society, an association

group VERB
*They were all **grouped** around the table.*
• to cluster, to gather, to collect, to crowd
*We **grouped** the objects according to colour.*
• to arrange, to classify, to sort, to order, to organise

grow VERB grows, growing, grew, grown
❶ *The sunflowers have **grown** quickly.*
• to develop, to get bigger, to get taller, to shoot up
— Use to **germinate** or to **sprout** when a seed first starts to grow.
— Use to **flourish** or to **thrive** to mean something is growing well and is healthy: *Our tomato plants are flourishing.*
❷ *My mum **grows** herbs in the garden.*
• to cultivate, to plant, to produce
❸ *The number of children in the school is **growing**.*
• to increase, to rise, to go up
OPPOSITES to decrease, to fall

grown (past participle of grow)

grown-up NOUN
*Ask a **grown-up** if you need help.*
• an adult
OPPOSITES a child, a young person

✸ WORD WEB

WORDS FOR GROUPS OF PEOPLE:
— a **battalion** or **brigade** or **regiment** of soldiers
— a **class** of pupils
— a **crew** of sailors or workers
— a **gang** of criminals
— a **horde** of attackers or invaders
— a **party** of tourists
— a **team** of players or competitors

GROUPS OF MUSICIANS:
— A **band** is a group that plays pop music or brass instruments.
— An **orchestra** is a large group of people with different instruments, usually playing classical music.
— A **choir** is a group of singers, especially in a church.
— A **chorus** is a large choir.
— A **duo** is a group of two musicians or singers.
— A **trio** is a group of three musicians or singers.
— A **quartet** is a group of four musicians or singers.
— A **quintet** is a group of five musicians or singers.

WORDS FOR GROUPS OF ANIMALS:
— an **army** or a **colony** of ants
— a **brood** of chicks
— a **colony** of seals
— a **flock** of sheep, goats or birds
— a **herd** of cattle
— a **litter** of puppies, piglets or kittens
— a **pack** of wolves or dogs
— a **pride** of lions

— a **school** of fish, whales or dolphins
— a **shoal** of fish
— a **swarm** of insects

WORDS FOR GROUPS OF THINGS:
— a **batch** of cakes, biscuits or bread
— a **bunch** or a **bouquet** of flowers
— a **constellation** of stars
— a **convoy** of ships or vehicles
— a **flight** of stairs
— a **grove** of fruit trees
— a **pack** of cards

a bunch or bouquet of flowers

a batch of cakes

a pack of cards

a pack of wolves

grown-up ADJECTIVE
*You are **grown-up** enough to walk to school by yourself now.*
• mature, responsible, sensible
OPPOSITES immature, childish

growth NOUN
❶ *We measured the **growth** of the plants.*
• development, increase
❷ *She was pleased with the **growth** of her business.*
• development, expansion, enlargement, increase, rise

grub NOUN
*I found a **grub** on the cabbage leaf.*
• a larva, a maggot, a caterpillar

grudge NOUN
*He wanted me to lose because he had a **grudge** against me.*
• a grievance, bitterness, resentment
• spite: *He wanted me to lose out of **spite**.*

a grub

gruesome ADJECTIVE
*She told a **gruesome** tale.*
• grisly, gory, ghastly, hideous, monstrous, revolting, sickening, appalling, dreadful, shocking

grumble VERB
*You're always **grumbling** about your homework!*
• to complain, to moan, to groan, to protest, to whine, to whinge

grumpy ADJECTIVE
*Why are you so **grumpy** today?*
• bad-tempered, cross, irritable, moody, sulky
— Use **gruff** for a grumpy voice or manner.
OPPOSITE good-humoured

guarantee VERB
*I **guarantee** that you will enjoy the show.*
• to promise, to assure, to pledge, to undertake

guarantee NOUN
*He gave me a **guarantee** that his method would work.*
• a promise, an assurance, a pledge, an undertaking

guard VERB
*The cave was **guarded** by a one-eyed giant.*
• to protect, to defend, to stand guard over, to patrol, to watch over

guard NOUN
*A **guard** was on duty at the gate.*
• a sentry, a lookout, a watchman

guardian NOUN
*The **guardian** of the treasure was a fierce dragon.*
• a defender, a protector, a guard, a keeper

guess VERB
*There was a prize for **guessing** the weight of the cake.*
• to estimate, to judge, to work out, to gauge, to predict, to reckon, to infer

guess NOUN
*My **guess** is that it will rain tomorrow.*
• an estimate, a prediction, a feeling, a hunch

guest NOUN
*They had **guests** at their house.*
• a visitor, a caller

guide VERB
*He **guided** us through the forest.*
• to lead, to steer, to conduct, to escort, to accompany, to direct, to show the way

guilt NOUN
❶ *The prisoner admitted his **guilt**.*
• responsibility, blame, wrongdoing
OPPOSITE innocence
❷ *You could see the look of **guilt** on her face.*
• shame, remorse, regret, repentance

guilty ADJECTIVE
❶ *The accused man was found **guilty**.*
• responsible, to blame, at fault, in the wrong
OPPOSITE innocent
❷ *I feel really **guilty** about leaving her to tidy up on her own.*
• ashamed, bad, sorry, remorseful, repentant, sheepish
OPPOSITE unrepentant

gun NOUN
» *For various weapons look at **weapon**.*

gush NOUN
*There was a **gush** of water from the tap.*
• a rush, a stream, a torrent, a cascade, a flood, a jet, a spout, a spurt

gush VERB
*Water **gushed** from the broken pipe.*
• to rush, to stream, to flow, to pour, to flood, to spout, to spurt, to squirt

gust NOUN
*A **gust** of wind whipped up the leaves.*
• a blast, a rush, a puff, a squall, a flurry

a b c d e f g h i j k l m n o p q r s t u v w x y z

 Can you think of 5 different words to describe a happy person?

 What word could you use to mean 'happy because you have won'?

 Check the thesaurus to find answers!

habit NOUN
*She has a **habit** of playing with her hair.*
• a custom, a practice, a routine, a way

had (past tense of **have**)

hair NOUN
*Rapunzel's **hair** reached down to the ground.*
• locks, tresses
— A **strand** of hair is a single piece.
— A **lock** of hair is a small bunch or curl.
— A **hank** of hair is a thick bunch or curl.

⊕ WORD WEB

HAIR ON AN ANIMAL:

• bristles, a coat, fur, a mane, whiskers
— **Down** is short soft feathers, for example on a duckling.
— **Fleece** is wool on a sheep.
— A **pelt** is an animal skin with fur or hairs on it.

☺ WRITING TIPS

You can use these words to describe **hair**:

SOME HAIRSTYLES:

• a braid, a bun, bunches, cornrows, curls, a fringe, a pigtail, a plait, a ponytail, ringlets, a topknot
Brigit's forehead glistened and her hair was curling in little damp ringlets at her temples.—THE HOUNDS OF THE MORRIGAN, Pat O'Shea

TO DESCRIBE LIGHT-COLOURED HAIR:

• blonde, fair, golden, grey, mousy, platinum blonde, silver, strawberry blonde, white

TO DESCRIBE DARK HAIR:

• black, dark, ebony, jet black, raven

TO DESCRIBE BROWN OR RED HAIR:

• auburn, brown, chestnut, fiery, ginger, red, sandy, strawberry blonde

TO DESCRIBE CURLY, THICK OR MESSY HAIR:

• bushy, coarse, curly, dishevelled, frizzy, matted, shaggy, spiky, straggly, tangled, tousled, unkempt, wavy, windswept, wiry
An old man sat inside, a gaunt, pitiful little old man with tousled grey hair.—MIO'S KINGDOM, Astrid Lindgren

TO DESCRIBE THIN, FLAT OR STRAIGHT HAIR:

• fine, floppy, flowing, glossy, greasy, lank, limp, shiny, silky, wispy

TO DESCRIBE SHORT HAIR:

• bristly, cropped, shaved, short, tufty
» *For ways to describe animal hair look at* **animal**.

hairy ADJECTIVE
*Mammoths were like elephants with thick **hairy** coats.*
• shaggy, bushy, bristly, woolly, fleecy, furry, fuzzy

handle NOUN
*The door **handle** is broken.*
• the grip, the knob
— The **hilt** is the handle of a sword or dagger.

handle VERB
❶ *Please don't **handle** the exhibits.*
• to touch, to feel, to hold, to stroke, to fondle

❷ *I thought you **handled** the situation very well.*
• to manage, to deal with, to cope with, to tackle

handsome ADJECTIVE
*He looked **handsome** in his suit.*
• attractive, good-looking, nice-looking, gorgeous
OPPOSITES ugly, unattractive

handy ADJECTIVE
❶ *This gadget is **handy** for getting lids off jars.*
• useful, helpful, practical
OPPOSITE awkward
❷ *The corner shop is very **handy**.*
• convenient, accessible, close at hand, nearby
OPPOSITE inaccessible

hang VERB hangs, hanging, hung
❶ *I **hung** the picture on the wall.*
• to fasten, to fix, to attach, to suspend
❷ *A sloth was **hanging** from the branch.*
• to dangle, to be suspended, to swing, to sway
❸ *His hair **hung** down over his eyes.*
• to droop, to drop, to flop
➤ **to hang about** or **around**
Some boys were hanging around on the street corner.
• to linger, to loiter, to dawdle
➤ **to hang on to something**
Hang on to the rope.
• to cling on to, to hold on to, to grip, to grasp, to clutch, to clasp
Hang on to your ticket.
• to keep, to retain (formal), to save

happen VERB
*Did anything interesting **happen** today?*
• to take place, to occur, to arise, to come about, to crop up

happiness NOUN
*The birthday girl's face glowed with **happiness**.*
• joy, delight, glee, pleasure, contentment, gladness, merriment
— Use **ecstasy** or **bliss** for very great happiness and pleasure.
OPPOSITE sorrow

happy ADJECTIVE

  OVERUSED WORD

Try to use a more interesting word when you want to say **happy**. Here are some ideas and examples:

TO DESCRIBE A HAPPY MOOD OR HAPPY PERSON:
• cheerful, cheery, joyful, jolly, merry, bright, light-hearted, contented
*Laura is always **cheerful** and **bright**.*
OPPOSITES gloomy, sad

WORDS MEANING VERY HAPPY:
• thrilled, ecstatic, elated, overjoyed
*Dax found himself giggling, **elated** and fizzy with excitement, as if someone had, indeed, given him a new puppy.*—SHAPESHIFTER 5: STIRRING THE STORM, Ali Sparkes

FOR HAPPY ABOUT A SUCCESS OR VICTORY:
• triumphant, jubilant, gleeful, delighted
*The team came back **jubilant** after the match.*
OPPOSITES disappointed, devastated

FOR A HAPPY TIME OR HAPPY EXPERIENCE:
• enjoyable, joyous, glorious, blissful, heavenly
*They spent a **glorious** summer on the island.*
OPPOSITE miserable

TO BE HAPPY TO DO SOMETHING:
• pleased, glad, willing, delighted
*I would be **glad** to help organise the party.*
OPPOSITE unwilling

harbour NOUN
*Several yachts were tied up in the **harbour**.*
• a port, a dock, a mooring, a quay, a pier, a wharf

hard ADJECTIVE

  OVERUSED WORD

Try to use a more interesting word when you want to say **hard**. Here are some ideas and examples:

FOR HARD GROUND OR A HARD SURFACE:
• solid, firm, compact, rigid, stiff
*The ground was **solid** with frost.*
— A common simile is **as hard as a rock**.
OPPOSITE soft

FOR A HARD PULL OR HARD HIT:
• strong, forceful, mighty, heavy, powerful, sharp
— Use **vicious** or **savage** for a hard hit or kick intended to hurt someone.
OPPOSITE light

a b c d e f g **h** i j k l m n o p q r s t u v w x y z

FOR HARD WORK:

- tough, strenuous, tiring, exhausting

*Digging the tunnel was **strenuous** work.*

OPPOSITE easy

FOR A HARD PROBLEM OR HARD QUESTION:

- difficult, challenging, complicated, complex, tricky, tough, puzzling, baffling, perplexing

Did she know him or didn't she know him? It was a perplexing puzzle, and occupied him a long time . . .
—THE PRINCE AND THE PAUPER, Mark Twain

OPPOSITE simple

hard *ADVERB*

❶ *We practised **hard** all morning.*

- energetically, keenly

❷ *He kicked the ball as **hard** as he could.*

- firmly, forcefully, powerfully, heavily, strongly, sharply

harden *VERB*

*We left the cement to **harden**.*

- to set, to solidify, to stiffen

OPPOSITE to soften

hardly *ADVERB*

*I could **hardly** see in the fog.*

- barely, scarcely, only just

hardship *NOUN*

*They suffered years of **hardship** during the war.*

- suffering, trouble, difficulty, distress, misery, misfortune, need

harm *VERB*

❶ *His captors didn't **harm** him.*

- to hurt, to injure, to wound

❷ *Plastic is **harming** the environment.*

- to damage, to spoil, to ruin, to wreck

harm *NOUN*

*Drinking water won't do you any **harm**.*

- damage, hurt, injury

OPPOSITE benefit

harmful *ADJECTIVE*

*Too much sun can be **harmful**.*

- damaging, dangerous, destructive, unhealthy

OPPOSITES harmless, beneficial

harmless *ADJECTIVE*

❶ *The snake is **harmless**.*

- safe

— Use **non-toxic** for a substance that is not poisonous.

OPPOSITES harmful, dangerous

❷ *It was just a **harmless** joke.*

- innocent, inoffensive

OPPOSITES malicious, offensive

harsh *ADJECTIVE*

❶ *The machine made a **harsh** sound.*

- rough, grating

— Use **shrill** or **piercing** for a high and harsh sound.

OPPOSITE soft

❷ *We blinked in the **harsh** light.*

- bright, brilliant, dazzling, glaring

OPPOSITES soft, subdued

❸ *These animals can survive in a **harsh** climate.*

- severe, extreme, hard, bleak

OPPOSITE mild

❹ *I think the punishment was a little **harsh**.*

- hard, cruel, severe, strict, extreme, strong, unkind

OPPOSITE lenient

harvest *NOUN*

*There was a good **harvest** of apples this year.*

- a crop, a yield

— **Produce** is things grown on a farm: *They sell their **produce** at the market.*

haste *NOUN*

*We worked with great **haste**.*

- hurry, speed, urgency

hasty *ADJECTIVE*

❶ *The robbers made a **hasty** exit.*

- fast, hurried, quick, sudden, swift, rapid, speedy

OPPOSITE slow

❷ *I regretted my **hasty** decision.*

- rash, impulsive, rushed, hurried, reckless, impatient, thoughtless

OPPOSITES careful, thoughtful

hat *NOUN*

🕸 **WORD WEB**

SOME KINDS OF HAT:

- a baseball cap, a beanie, a beret, a boater, a bonnet, a bowler hat, a cap, a deerstalker, a helmet, a fez, a flat cap, a panama, a skullcap, a sombrero, a straw hat, a top hat, a woolly hat

a top hat

a baseball hat

a woolly hat

hate *VERB*
I hate rainy days!
• to dislike, to detest, to despise, to loathe
− You can also say that you **can't stand** or **can't bear** something.

hatred *NOUN*
The evil wizard stared with hatred in his eyes.
• hate, loathing, dislike, hostility, contempt
OPPOSITE love

have *VERB* **has, having, had**
❶ *I have my own phone now.*
• to own, to possess
❷ *The book has ten chapters.*
• to consist of, to comprise, to include
❸ *The school has had lots of emails.*
• to receive, to get, to be given, to be sent
❹ *We had a few problems.*
• to experience, to encounter, to go through, to meet with, to run into, to face, to suffer
❺ *Have you had breakfast?*
• to eat, to take, to consume
❻ *I am having a party at the weekend.*
• to hold, to organise, to host, to throw
➤ **have to** (also **have got to**)
I have to go soon.
• must, need to, ought to, should

hazard *NOUN*
The road through the mountains is full of hazards.
• a danger, a peril, a pitfall, a risk, a threat, a trap

haze *NOUN*
I could hardly see through the haze.
• fog, mist, cloud, steam, vapour

a fez

OTHER THINGS YOU WEAR ON YOUR HEAD:

• a headscarf, a hijab, a turban

PARTS OF A HAT:

− The edge of a hat is the **brim**.
− The part that sticks out at the front of a cap is the **peak**.
− A large feather in a hat is a **plume**.

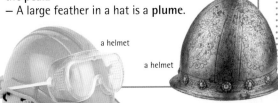
a helmet

a helmet

head *NOUN*
❶ *I bumped my head.*
− Your **skull** is the bone in your head.
❷ *Can you do the sum in your head?*
• your mind, your brain
❸ *There is a new head of the music department.*
• a leader, a manager, a chief, a director, a boss
❹ *They got to the head of the queue.*
• the front, the top
OPPOSITES the back, the rear, the end

head *VERB*
❶ *The professor was chosen to head the expedition.*
• to lead, to be in charge of, to direct, to command, to manage
❷ *Where were they heading?*
• to aim for, to make for, to go towards

heading *NOUN*
Each chapter had a different heading.
• a title
− A **caption** is the words printed with a picture to describe it.
− A **headline** is the title of a newspaper story.

head teacher *NOUN*
The head teacher runs the school.
• the head, the principal, the headmaster or headmistress

heal *VERB*
❶ *It took two months for my leg to heal properly.*
• to mend, to recover, to get better
❷ *Part of a vet's job is to heal sick animals.*
• to cure, to treat, to make better

health *NOUN*
❶ *Exercise is good for your health.*
• fitness, well-being, strength
❷ *The puppies are in excellent health.*
• condition, shape
» *Look at **medicine**.*

healthy *ADJECTIVE*
❶ *The children all look healthy and well fed.*
• well, fit, strong, sturdy, in good shape
OPPOSITE ill, sickly
❷ *Porridge makes a very healthy breakfast.*
• wholesome, nutritious, nourishing, good for you
OPPOSITE unhealthy

heap *NOUN*
There was an untidy heap of clothes on the floor.
• a mound, a pile, a stack, a mass, a mountain

heap *VERB*
We heaped up all the rubbish in the corner.
• to pile, to stack, to collect

hear VERB hears, hearing, heard
❶ *Did you hear what she said?*
• to catch, to listen to, to pick up
— To **overhear** something is to hear it by accident or without the speaker knowing.
— To **make out** or to **distinguish** something is to manage to hear it when it is not clear: *I distinguished a few words of English in what they said.*
— Your **hearing** is your ability to hear.
— A sound that is **audible** can be heard.
— A sound that is **inaudible** cannot be heard.
— A sound that is **in earshot** is close enough to be heard.
❷ *Have you heard the news?*
• to be told, to discover, to find out, to learn

heart NOUN
❶ *My grandma has a special place in my heart.*
• feelings, emotions, affections, love
❷ *The hotel is in the heart of the city.*
• the centre, the middle

heat NOUN
We could feel the heat of the sun.
• warmth

😊 **WRITING TIPS**

Here are some useful words for writing about **heat**:

WORDS TO DESCRIBE HEAT:

• baking, blazing, blistering, boiling, burning, fiery, flaming, intense, intolerable, raging, roasting, scalding, scorching, steamy, stifling, sweltering, tropical

WORDS FOR A VERY HOT PLACE:

• a furnace, an inferno
The Gog stopped just as he reached the fire's edge. Half a dozen guards spread out behind him. They shielded their faces from the blistering heat and smoke and waited for orders.—THE MYSTIFYING MEDICINE SHOW, J. C. Bemis

heat VERB
A stove heats the house.
• to warm, to warm up

heavy ADJECTIVE
❶ *The box was too heavy for me to lift.*
• hefty, bulky, solid, substantial, massive
❷ *Heavy rain was falling.*
• extreme, torrential, severe
❸ *He gave the box a heavy shove.*
• forceful, powerful, strong, mighty

height NOUN
❶ *The plane was flying at its normal height.*
• altitude
❷ *His height is an advantage in basketball.*
• tallness, size

coriander

held (past tense of **hold**)

help NOUN
❶ *Thank you for your help.*
• assistance, aid, support, cooperation, advice
❷ *Would a torch be of any help to you?*
• use, benefit
help VERB
❶ *Could you please help me with my luggage?*
• to assist, to aid, to lend a hand, to give someone a hand
❷ *Friends should help one another.*
• to support, to back, to be helpful to, to cooperate with, to stand by
❸ *I can't help coughing.*
• to avoid, to stop yourself, to prevent yourself, to refrain from

helpful ADJECTIVE
❶ *The staff were friendly and helpful.*
• obliging, cooperative, kind, considerate, thoughtful, sympathetic
OPPOSITE unhelpful
❷ *The teacher gave us some helpful advice.*
• useful, valuable, worthwhile, beneficial
OPPOSITE worthless

helping NOUN
I had a second helping of ice cream.
• a serving, a portion, a share, a ration

helpless ADJECTIVE
Kittens are born blind and helpless.
• powerless, weak, feeble, dependent, vulnerable
OPPOSITES independent, strong

hem NOUN
The hem of my skirt needs sewing up.
• the border, the edge
hem VERB
➤ to hem someone in
The bus was hemmed in by some parked cars.
• to shut in, to box in, to encircle, to enclose, to surround

mint

rosemary

herb NOUN

parsley

SOME COMMON HERBS:

• basil, chives, coriander, mint, oregano, parsley, rosemary, sage, thyme

The garden was full of sunshine and the scent of lavender, thyme and rosemary, mixed with the smell of the sea.—THE FLIP-FLOP CLUB: CHARMED SUMMER, Ellen Richardson

» *Look at* **spice**.

basil

herd NOUN

» *For groups of animals look at* **group**.

heroic ADJECTIVE

*The firefighters made a **heroic** effort to put out the blaze.*

• bold, brave, courageous, daring, fearless, noble, selfless, valiant

OPPOSITE cowardly

» *For writing about superheroes look at* **superhero**.

hesitant ADJECTIVE

*I was **hesitant** about asking a question.*

• uncertain, unsure, doubtful, cautious, timid, shy, wary

OPPOSITE confident

hesitate VERB

*I **hesitated** for a moment before ringing the doorbell.*

• to pause, to delay, to wait, to hold back, to dither, to falter, to waver

hide VERB hides, hiding, hid, hidden

❶ *Quick! Someone's coming—we'd better **hide**.*

• to take cover, to keep out of sight

— To go into **hiding** is to hide for a long time.

❷ *I **hid** the letter in a drawer.*

• to conceal, to hide away, to bury

OPPOSITE to uncover, to reveal

❸ *The clouds **hid** the sun.*

• to blot out, to cover, to screen, to shroud, to veil, to mask, to obscure

OPPOSITE to uncover

❹ *I tried to **hide** my feelings.*

• to disguise, to conceal, to keep secret, to suppress, to mask

OPPOSITE to show

high ADJECTIVE

❶ *The castle was surrounded by a **high** wall.*

• tall, towering, lofty, elevated

OPPOSITE low

❷ *The pixie spoke in a **high** voice.*

• high-pitched, squeaky, sharp

— Use **shrill** or **piercing** to mean unpleasantly high and loud.

OPPOSITE deep

chives

❸ *Some shops charge very **high** prices.*

• inflated, exorbitant, excessive

— Something with a high price is **expensive** or **costly**.

OPPOSITE low

highlight NOUN

*The **highlight** of the holiday was seeing a dolphin.*

• the high point, the climax

highlight VERB

*The teacher **highlighted** some important points to remember.*

• to emphasise, to draw attention to, to underline, to pick out

highly ADVERB

*It is **highly** unusual to see badgers during the day.*

• extremely, exceedingly, exceptionally, immensely, decidedly

hill NOUN

❶ *From the top of this **hill** you can see for miles.*

• a mount, a peak, a ridge

— A **mound** is a small hill.

❷ *Jenny pushed her bike up the steep **hill**.*

• a slope, a rise, an incline, an ascent, a gradient

hint NOUN

❶ *I don't know the answer—can you give me a **hint**?*

• a clue, an indication, a sign, a suggestion, an inkling

❷ *The website has some useful spelling **hints**.*

• a tip, a suggestion, advice

hint VERB

*She **hinted** that she would like to come too.*

• to give a hint, to suggest, to imply, to indicate

historic ADJECTIVE

*The first landing on the moon was a **historic** event.*

• famous, notable, important, renowned, significant, major

OPPOSITE insignificant

hit VERB hits, hitting, hit

❶ *Auntie Flo **hit** the burglar on the head with her umbrella.*

• to strike, to knock, to bang, to bash, to crack, to rap, to whack, to wallop *(informal)*

— To **tap** someone or something is to hit them lightly.

— To **punch** or **thump** someone is to hit them with a closed fist.

thyme

— To **smack** or **slap** someone is to hit them with an open hand.

— To **swipe** is to hit something with a quick sideways movement.

— To **cuff** someone is to hit them with your hand.

— To **beat** or **thrash** someone is to hit them many times with a stick.

❷ *I hit my knee on the corner of the desk.*

• to bump, to knock, to strike, to bash, to whack

— To **batter** or to **pound** something is to hit it repeatedly and hard: *He battered his fists on the door.*

❸ *The car went out of control and hit a tree.*

• to bump into, to run into, to crash into, to smash into, to collide with

❹ *The drought has hit many farms in the area.*

• to affect, to damage, to harm, to hurt

hit *NOUN*

❶ *Matt got a nasty hit on the head.*

• a bump, a blow, a bang, a knock, a whack

— A **punch** is a hit with a fist.

— A **slap** or a **smack** is a hit with an open hand.

❷ *Her new record is a big hit.*

• a success, a triumph, a bestseller

hoarse *ADJECTIVE*

The referee's voice was hoarse from shouting.

• rough, harsh, husky, gruff, croaky

hobby *NOUN*

My favourite hobby is reading.

• a pastime, a pursuit, an interest, an activity, a recreation

hold *VERB* **holds, holding, held**

❶ *Make sure you hold the handrail.*

• to clasp, to grasp, to grip, to clutch, to grab, to seize, to cling to, to hang on to

❷ *Can I hold the baby?*

• to carry, to cuddle, to hug, to embrace, to cradle

❸ *One of the boys was holding a stick.*

• to brandish, to wield

❹ *The jug holds two litres.*

• to take, to contain, to fit, to carry, to have space for

❺ *We held a party to celebrate their win.*

• to throw, to host, to have, to organise

❻ *She holds the world record.*

• to have, to possess

❼ *The police held him in a cell.*

• to detain, to confine, to keep

➤ **to hold someone up**

We were held up by the traffic.

• to delay, to hinder, to slow down, to keep back

hold *NOUN*

The vet took a firm hold of the dog's collar.

• a grip, a grasp, a clutch, a clasp

hole *NOUN*

❶ *The meteor created a massive hole in the ground.*

• a pit, a hollow, a crater, a dent, a depression, a cavity

— A **pothole** is a hole in a road surface, or a deep natural hole in the ground.

— A **chasm** or an **abyss** is a very deep opening in the ground.

— A **shaft** is a deep narrow hole in a mine or building.

❷ *The rabbit disappeared into its hole.*

• a burrow, a tunnel, a den

— An **earth** is a hole where a fox or badger lives.

— A **warren** is an area with a lot of rabbit holes.

❸ *The money fell through a hole in my pocket.*

• an opening, a gap, a break, a slit, a split, a tear, a vent

— A **puncture** is a small hole in a tyre.

— A **leak** is a hole through which liquid or gas escapes.

holiday *NOUN*

We spent our summer holiday in Ireland.

• a vacation, a break, time off

hollow *ADJECTIVE*

Tennis balls are hollow.

• empty, unfilled

OPPOSITE solid

hollow *NOUN*

The ball rolled into a hollow in the ground.

• a dip, a dent, a depression, a hole, a pit, a crater, a cavity

holy *ADJECTIVE*

❶ *The Greeks considered this a holy place.*

• sacred, blessed

❷ *The pilgrims were holy people.*

• religious, spiritual, devout, pious, godly, saintly

home NOUN
*The hurricane forced people to flee their **homes**.*
• a house, a residence, a dwelling
— A **den** is a wild animal's home.
— A bird's or animal's **habitat** is the type of place where it lives.

WORD WEB

SOME HOMES:

• an apartment, a bungalow, a caravan, a castle, a chalet, a cottage, a farmhouse, a flat, a hut, an igloo, a lodge, a manor, a mansion, a mobile home, a palace, a shack, a shanty, a tent, a tepee, a terraced house, a villa

After a few more steps, they saw, at the end of a long road near a clump of trees, a tiny cottage built of straw. 'Someone must live in that little hut,' said Pinocchio. 'Let us see for ourselves.'–THE ADVENTURES OF PINOCCHIO, Carlo Collodi

honest ADJECTIVE
❶ *He's an **honest** boy, so he gave the money back.*
• good, honourable, moral, trustworthy
OPPOSITE dishonest
❷ *Please give me your **honest** opinion.*
• sincere, genuine, truthful, frank
OPPOSITE insincere

honour NOUN
❶ *Her success brought **honour** to the school.*
• credit, praise, respect, a good reputation
❷ *It's an **honour** to meet you.*
• a privilege

honour VERB
*There was a special ceremony to **honour** the winners.*
• to celebrate, to praise, to pay tribute to

honourable ADJECTIVE
*The knight was an **honourable** man.*
• noble, good, honest, principled, moral, righteous, trustworthy, worthy, decent

hop VERB
*The goblins **hopped** about in excitement.*
• to jump, to leap, to skip, to spring, to prance, to bound, to dance
» *For ways that animals move look at **animal**.*

hope VERB
*I **hope** to get a bike for my birthday.*
• would like
— Use to **wish** for something you want but is unlikely or impossible: *I **wish** it was my birthday tomorrow.*

hope NOUN
❶ *My **hope** is to win.*
• an ambition, a dream, a desire, a wish
❷ *There's **hope** of better weather tomorrow.*
• a prospect, a possibility, a likelihood

hopeful ADJECTIVE
❶ *I am feeling **hopeful** about the football match.*
• optimistic, confident, positive, expectant
OPPOSITE pessimistic
❷ *The future is beginning to look more **hopeful**.*
• promising, encouraging, favourable, reassuring
OPPOSITE discouraging

hopeless ADJECTIVE
❶ *The shipwrecked crew were in a **hopeless** situation.*
• desperate, impossible, bleak, wretched
OPPOSITE hopeful
❷ *I'm **hopeless** at ice skating.*
• bad, terrible, incompetent, useless
OPPOSITE good, competent

horizontal ADJECTIVE
*Lay the pole on the ground in a **horizontal** position.*
• flat, level
OPPOSITE vertical

a horizontal spirit level

horrible ADJECTIVE
*What a **horrible** smell!*
• awful, terrible, horrid, dreadful, appalling, unpleasant, disagreeable, offensive, disgusting, revolting, repulsive, hideous, nasty, ghastly, vile, loathsome, gross *(informal)*
OPPOSITE pleasant

horrific ADJECTIVE
*They were faced with a **horrific** sight.*
• horrifying, terrifying, shocking, gruesome, dreadful, appalling, ghastly, hideous, grisly, sickening

horrify VERB
*The sight of the ugly monster **horrified** them.*
• to appal, to shock, to terrify, to alarm, to sicken, to disgust

horror NOUN
*The sight of the beast filled me with **horror**.*
• terror, fear, dread, fright, alarm, disgust

horse NOUN

WORD WEB

— A male horse is a **stallion** and a female is a **mare**.
— A young horse is a **foal**, **colt** (male) or **filly** (female).
— A **charger** is a horse ridden by a knight.
— A **steed** is an old or poetic word for a horse.
— A **mule** is a cross between a donkey and a horse.

SOME TYPES OF HORSE:

• a carthorse, a pony, a racehorse, a Shetland pony, a shire horse

COLOURS OF HORSES:

• black, chestnut, dapple grey, white
— A **bay** is reddish brown.
— A **palomino** has a gold coat with a white mane.
— A **piebald** horse has patches of different colours.
— A **roan** is brown or black, with some white hairs.

THINGS USED FOR RIDING A HORSE:

• a rein, a saddle, stirrups

— A **harness** is the set of straps put around a horse's head and neck to control it.
— A **bridle** is the part of a harness that fits over a horse's head.
— A **bit** is the part of a horse's bridle put into its mouth.
— A **halter** is a strap put around a horse's head so it can be led.
— A **girth** is a band fastened around a horse's belly to keep the saddle on.

WRITING TIPS

Here are some useful words for writing about **horses**:

NOISES A HORSE MAKES:

• to neigh, to whinny, to snort
In the eerie silence of no man's land all that could be heard was the jingle of the harness and the snorting of the horses.–WAR HORSE, Michael Morpurgo

WAYS A HORSE MOVES:

• to buck, to canter, to charge, to flick its tail, to gallop, to nuzzle, to rear, to toss its mane, to trot

THINGS A RIDER DOES:

• to mount, to dismount, to saddle, to harness, to tether, to tie up, to spur, to drive, to urge
Swinging up to a secure seat in the saddle, he urged the horse forward and galloped up the mountain road.—DRAGONFLY, Julia Golding

hot ADJECTIVE

❶ *The weather has been **hot** this summer.*
• warm
— Use **balmy** to describe pleasantly warm weather.
— Use **blazing**, **boiling**, **blistering**, **roasting** or **scorching** to mean extremely hot.
— Use **sweltering** or **stifling** to describe weather that is unpleasantly hot with no wind.
OPPOSITES cold, cool

» *For some tips on writing about heat look at* **heat**.
❷ *Be careful with that **hot** pan.*
• red hot, burning hot, boiling hot, sizzling, steaming
— Use **scalding** for liquid that is hot enough to burn your skin.
— Use **piping hot** for food or drink that is nice and hot.
OPPOSITES cold, cool
❸ *These chillies are very **hot**.*
• spicy, peppery, fiery
OPPOSITE mild

house (say howss) NOUN

*It was a small village with just a few **houses**.*
• a dwelling, a residence, a home, a building
» *For types of building look at* **building**.
» *For types of home look at* **home**.
» *For rooms in a house look at* **room**.

house (say howz) VERB

*The farm animals are **housed** indoors during the winter.*
• to accommodate, to lodge, to shelter

however ADVERB

❶ *I couldn't lift the stone, **however** hard I tried.*
• no matter how
❷ *Spiders' silk is thin; **however**, it is also strong.*
• nevertheless, nonetheless, yet, but, still, even so

howl VERB

*The wind **howled**.*
• to shriek, to scream, to wail, to yowl

hug VERB
*Ellie was **hugging** her teddy bear.*
• to cuddle, to clasp, to embrace, to hold, to cling to, to squeeze

huge ADJECTIVE
*Elephants are **huge** animals.*
• enormous, massive, colossal, vast, gigantic, immense, great, mammoth, humungous *(informal)*, ginormous *(informal)*
— Use **towering** for something that is extremely tall or high: *They were at the foot of a **towering** cliff.*
OPPOSITE tiny

hum VERB
*We heard insects **humming** in the air.*
• to buzz, to drone, to murmur, to whirr
» *Look at* **sound**.

humble ADJECTIVE
❶ *He was very **humble** despite his success.*
• modest, meek, polite, respectful
OPPOSITES proud, boastful
❷ *Hansel and Gretel lived in a **humble** cottage.*
• simple, modest, plain, ordinary
OPPOSITE grand

humid ADJECTIVE
*I don't like this **humid** weather.*
• clammy, sticky, steamy, sweaty, damp
OPPOSITE fresh

humiliate VERB
*He was **humiliated** by his failure.*
• to embarrass, to shame
— If someone feels humiliated you can say that they feel **ashamed** or **foolish**.

humorous ADJECTIVE
*It is meant to be a **humorous** story.*
• amusing, funny, comic, entertaining, jovial, light-hearted
— Use **witty** to mean humorous and clever.
OPPOSITE serious

humour NOUN
*I liked the **humour** in the film.*
• comedy, jokes
— Use **wit** to mean clever humour.

hump NOUN
*Camels have **humps** on their backs.*
• a bump, a lump, a bulge, a swelling

hung *(past tense of* **hang***)*

hunger NOUN
*By dinner time I was faint with **hunger**.*
• lack of food
— Use **starvation** or **famine** for hunger that is bad enough to make someone ill or die.

hungry ADJECTIVE
*I'm **hungry**! What's for lunch?*
• starving, famished, ravenous, peckish *(informal)*

hunt VERB
❶ *Lions **hunt** deer.*
• to chase, to pursue, to track
❷ *I **hunted** in the attic for our old photos.*
• to search, to seek, to look, to rummage

hunt NOUN
❶ *Some of the king's men joined the **hunt**.*
• a pursuit, a chase
❷ *The detective was on a **hunt** for clues.*
• a search, a quest

hurry VERB
❶ *If you want to catch the bus, you'd better **hurry**.*
• to be quick, to make haste *(formal)*, to get a move on *(informal)*
OPPOSITE to dawdle
❷ *Alice saw the White Rabbit **hurrying** past.*
• to rush, to dash, to fly, to speed, to scurry, to scamper, to scuttle
OPPOSITES to amble, to stroll

hurry NOUN
*In our **hurry**, we forgot the tickets.*
• rush, haste, speed, urgency

hurt VERB
❶ *Be careful not to **hurt** yourself with the scissors.*
• to harm, to injure, to wound
❷ *I fell and **hurt** my knee.*
• to injure, to cut, to graze, to scrape, to bruise, to sprain, to twist
❸ *My head **hurts**.*
• to ache, to be sore, to be painful
— Use **throb** or **to pound** to describe a banging pain.
— Use **to sting** or **to smart** for a sharp pain.
❹ *It **hurt** me when they laughed at my picture.*
• to upset, to distress, to offend, to sadden, to wound

hut NOUN
*The children came across a **hut** in the forest.*
• a shed, a shack, a cabin, a shelter, a shanty

hysterical ADJECTIVE
*There was a lot of **hysterical** screaming at the spider.*
• crazy, frenzied, frantic, mad, wild, uncontrollable

a
b
c
d
e
f
g
h
i
j
k
l
m
n
o
p
q
r
s
t
u
v
w
x
y
z

 How many different types of insect can you think of?

 Can you think of 3 different words for how an insect might move?

 Check the thesaurus to find answers!

ice NOUN

WORD WEB

SOME FORMS OF ICE:

• frost, a glacier, an iceberg, an icicle

WRITING TIPS

Here are some ideas for words you could use when writing about **ice**:

WAYS TO DESCRIBE ICE:

• brittle, cracked, frozen solid, glassy, glittering, hard, packed, slippery, smooth, treacherous

PIECES OF ICE:

• a block, a cake, a chunk, a cube, a layer, a lump, a mass, a sheet, a splinter, a sliver, a shard

ice cubes

THINGS ICE DOES:

• to break, to crack, to form, to melt, to splinter, to cover, to cling

And still the ice clung grey and curdled along the shore, and under the frozen snow the ground was hard as iron.—THE EAGLE OF THE NINTH, Rosemary Sutcliff

icy ADJECTIVE

❶ *You need to dress warmly in icy weather.*
• freezing, frosty, wintry, bitter, biting
❷ *Careful—the pavements are icy.*
• frozen, slippery, treacherous

idea NOUN

❶ *I've got a great idea!*
• a plan, a suggestion, a proposal, a thought
— A **brainwave** is a good idea that you suddenly think of.
❷ *She has some funny ideas about life.*
• a belief, a notion, an opinion, a view, a theory
❸ *The film gave us an idea of life during wartime.*
• an impression, a picture, a hint

ideal ADJECTIVE

It's ideal weather for a picnic.
• perfect, excellent

identical ADJECTIVE

The twins are identical.
• matching, exactly alike
— If two things are identical you can say they are duplicates.
OPPOSITE different

identify VERB

The police asked if I could identify the thief.
• to recognise, to name, to distinguish, to pick out

idol NOUN

The singer is an idol to millions.
• a hero, a heroine, a role model, a star, a celebrity

ignorant ADJECTIVE

I felt very ignorant for not knowing the answer.
• uneducated, simple, stupid
» *For ways to say you do not know something look at* **know**.

ignore VERB

I ignored his silly comments.
• to take no notice of, to pay no attention to, to disregard
— To **overlook** something is not to notice it.

ill ADJECTIVE
1 *I felt too ill to go to school.*
• sick, unwell, poorly
— Use **nauseous** or **queasy** if you feel as if you are going to vomit.
— Use **sickly** or **unhealthy** if someone is often ill.
» *For common illnesses look at* **illness.**
OPPOSITES healthy, well
2 *He drank the potion, but fortunately there were no ill effects.*
• bad, harmful, adverse, damaging
OPPOSITE good

illegal ADJECTIVE
It is illegal to park here.
• unlawful, against the law, banned, prohibited, forbidden
OPPOSITE legal

illegible ADJECTIVE
The signature on the letter was illegible.
• unreadable, unclear, indistinct, incomprehensible
OPPOSITES legible, readable

illness NOUN
What kind of illness is he suffering from?
• an ailment, a complaint, a condition, a disease, a disorder, a sickness
— An **infection** or a **bug** *(informal)* is an illness caused by germs.
— An **attack** or a **fit** is a sudden illness: *She had an attack of coughing.*
— An **outbreak** of an illness is when it suddenly affects a number of people in an area.
— An **epidemic** is an illness that spreads quickly to a large number of people.

 WORD WEB

SOME COMMON ILLNESSES AND CONDITIONS:
• acne, an allergy, anorexia, appendicitis, arthritis, asthma, bronchitis, cancer, chickenpox, a cold, a cough, depression, diabetes, diarrhoea, eczema, epilepsy, a fever, flu or influenza *(formal)*, hay fever, a headache, indigestion, leukaemia, malaria, measles, mumps, pneumonia, rheumatism, smallpox, a sore throat, tonsillitis
— **Scurvy** is a disease caused by lack of fresh fruit and vegetables, that used to be suffered by sailors on long voyages.
» *For ways to treat illness look at* **medicine.**

illustrate VERB
1 *Are you going to illustrate your story?*
• to put pictures in
2 *Let me illustrate what I mean.*
• to show, to demonstrate, to make clear, to explain, to give an example of

illustration NOUN
1 *I like books with lots of illustrations.*
• a picture, a photograph, a drawing
— A **diagram** is an illustration showing the parts of something or how it works.
2 *I'll give you an illustration of what I mean.*
• an example, an instance, a demonstration

image NOUN
1 *What do you think of the image on the front of the book?*
• a picture, a photograph, a representation
— An **icon** is a small image used to represent something on a computer screen.
2 *You can see your image in the mirror.*
• a reflection, a likeness
3 *He is very concerned about his image.*
• a reputation, a name
— Your image of someone is your **impression** or **opinion** of them.

imaginary ADJECTIVE
The story takes place in an imaginary universe.
• imagined, non-existent, unreal, made-up, pretend, invented, fictional, false, fabulous, mythical, legendary
OPPOSITE real

imagination NOUN
The children showed so much imagination in their designs.
• creativity, inventiveness, inspiration, initiative, originality, vision

imaginative ADJECTIVE
Roald Dahl wrote highly imaginative stories.
• creative, inventive, inspired, original, novel, ingenious, fresh
OPPOSITES unimaginative, dull

imagine VERB
Imagine that you are in a spaceship heading for Mars.
• to picture, to pretend, to visualise, to form a mental picture

a b c d e f g h i j k l m n o p q r s t u v w x y z

imitate *VERB*
Parrots can **imitate** the human voice.
• to copy, to reproduce, to mimic, to echo, to impersonate

immature *ADJECTIVE*
My brother is so **immature** sometimes.
• childish, babyish, juvenile
OPPOSITE mature

immediate *ADJECTIVE*
My email got an **immediate** reply.
• instant, prompt, speedy, swift
OPPOSITE slow

immediately *ADVERB*
You must fetch a doctor **immediately**!
• at once, now, straight away, this minute, instantly

immoral *ADJECTIVE*
It would be **immoral** to steal the money.
• wrong, wicked, bad, sinful, dishonest, corrupt
OPPOSITES moral, right

immortal *ADJECTIVE*
The ancient Greeks believed their gods were **immortal**.
• undying, eternal, everlasting
OPPOSITE mortal

impact *NOUN*
❶ The crater was caused by the **impact** of a meteor.
• a crash, a collision, a smash, a blow, a strike
❷ The Internet has had a big **impact** on our lives.
• an effect, an influence
• an impression: The Internet has made a big **impression** on our lives.

impatient *ADJECTIVE*
❶ He got **impatient** when I still didn't understand.
• frustrated, irritated, infuriated, agitated, annoyed
OPPOSITE patient

❷ The crowd were **impatient** for the show to begin.
• anxious, restless, eager, keen, in a hurry

imply *VERB*
Are you **implying** that I am a liar?
• to suggest, to hint, to indicate

impolite *ADJECTIVE*
It would be **impolite** to refuse the invitation.
• rude, bad-mannered, ill-mannered, disrespectful, discourteous, insulting, offensive
— Use **cheeky** to mean rude or disrespectful without being nasty.
— Use **impertinent**, **impudent** or **insolent** when someone does not show enough respect for someone important or in authority.
OPPOSITE polite

important *ADJECTIVE*
❶ The World Cup is an **important** sporting event.
• major, significant, big, momentous, outstanding, historic
OPPOSITES minor, insignificant
❷ This is a very **important** decision.
• serious, major, key, grave, vital, essential, crucial
OPPOSITES minor, insignificant
❸ The prime minister is an **important** person.
• prominent, powerful, influential, notable, distinguished
OPPOSITE unimportant

impossible *ADJECTIVE*
We used to think that space travel was **impossible**.
• unthinkable, unrealistic, impractical, unachievable
OPPOSITE possible

impress *VERB*
She **impressed** the crowd with her football skills.
• to delight, to please, to astound, to excite, to inspire

impression *NOUN*
❶ I had the **impression** that something was wrong.
• a feeling, an idea, a sense, a notion, a suspicion, a hunch
❷ The film made a big **impression** on them.
• an effect, an impact
• an influence: The film had a big **influence** on them.
❸ This is my **impression** of an elephant.
• an imitation, an impersonation

impressive *ADJECTIVE*
The graphics in the game are very **impressive**.
• striking, spectacular, remarkable, astounding, admirable, exciting, inspiring
OPPOSITE unimpressive

imprison *VERB*
*The thief was **imprisoned** for two years.*
• to jail, to lock up, to confine, to detain
OPPOSITE to liberate

improve *VERB*
❶ *Your maths is **improving** every week.*
• to get better, to progress, to advance, to develop, to come on
OPPOSITE to deteriorate
❷ *How can I **improve** this story?*
• to make better, to enhance, to refine

incident *NOUN*
*There was an amusing **incident** at school this morning.*
• an event, an occurrence, a happening, an episode

include *VERB*
*The book **includes** lots of pictures and maps.*
• to contain, to incorporate, to comprise, to involve
OPPOSITE to exclude

income *NOUN*
*His monthly **income** was very small.*
• pay, salary, wages, earnings

incomplete *ADJECTIVE*
❶ *The new football stadium is still **incomplete**.*
• unfinished, uncompleted, not ready
OPPOSITE complete
❷ *I heard an **incomplete** version of the story.*
• partial, limited, imperfect
OPPOSITE full

inconvenient *ADJECTIVE*
*The guests arrived at an **inconvenient** time.*
• awkward, difficult, unsuitable, inappropriate, unfortunate
OPPOSITE convenient

incorrect *ADJECTIVE*
*That answer is **incorrect**.*
• wrong, mistaken, inaccurate, false
OPPOSITE correct

increase *VERB*
❶ *The amount of traffic has **increased**.*
• to grow, to go up, to build up, to rise, to climb, to mount, to multiply
— To **soar** or to **surge** is to suddenly increase a lot.
— To **double** is to become twice as much.
❷ *He **increased** his speed.*
• to raise, to put up, to boost, to intensify, to turn up
— To **enlarge** or **expand** something is to increase its size.
— To **extend** or **lengthen** something is to increase its length.

— To **widen** or **broaden** something is to increase its width.
— To **prolong** something is to increase the time it takes.
» *For opposites look at **decrease**.*

incredible *ADJECTIVE*
❶ *It seems **incredible** that someone could survive for so long in the desert.*
• unbelievable, extraordinary, unlikely, unimaginable, improbable, far-fetched, absurd
OPPOSITE likely
❷ *This is an **incredible** book!*
• extraordinary, amazing, astounding, magnificent, marvellous, spectacular, brilliant, fantastic

independent *ADJECTIVE*
❶ *My granny is a very **independent** person.*
• self-sufficient, self-reliant, free
OPPOSITE dependent
❷ *We need an **independent** opinion.*
• impartial, neutral, objective, unbiased
OPPOSITE biased

indulge *VERB*
*They **indulged** their children too much.*
• to spoil, to pamper
➤ **to indulge in**
*I **indulged in** a nice hot bath.*
• to enjoy, to relish, to treat yourself to

infamous *ADJECTIVE*
*Dick Turpin was an **infamous** highwayman.*
• notorious

infect *VERB*
*A virus may have **infected** the water supply.*
• to contaminate, to pollute, to poison

infection *NOUN*
*The **infection** spread rapidly.*
• a disease, a virus, a contamination

infectious *ADJECTIVE*
*Chickenpox is highly **infectious**.*
• contagious, catching

inferior *ADJECTIVE*
❶ *The clothes were of **inferior** quality.*
• poor, bad, cheap, mediocre
OPPOSITES superior, best
❷ *Officers can give orders to those of **inferior** rank.*
• lesser, lower, junior
OPPOSITES superior, higher

a virus

a bee

infinite ADJECTIVE
*Teachers need **infinite** patience.*
• limitless, endless, unending, unlimited, everlasting
OPPOSITE finite

influence NOUN
*Your parents have a big **influence** on your life.*
• an effect, an impact

influence VERB
*Money did not **influence** my decision.*
• to affect, to have an effect on, to direct, to guide, to control, to motivate

influential ADJECTIVE
*She was a very **influential** writer.*
• important, significant, powerful, leading, major
OPPOSITE unimportant

inform VERB
*Please **inform** us if you move house.*
• to tell, to notify, to let someone know

informal ADJECTIVE
❶ *The party will be a very **informal** event.*
• casual, relaxed, easy-going, friendly
OPPOSITES formal, ceremonial
❷ *Emails are usually written in an **informal** style.*
• familiar, chatty, colloquial, personal
OPPOSITES formal, correct

information NOUN
*There is more **information** on our website.*
• details, facts, data, material
— **Directions** are information about how to get somewhere.
— **Instructions** are information about how to do or use something.
— **Input** is information put into a computer.

ingenious ADJECTIVE
*The professor came up with an **ingenious** plan.*
• clever, brilliant, inspired, inventive, imaginative, original, crafty, cunning

inhabit VERB
*People **inhabited** the caves thousands of years ago.*
• to live in, to occupy, to dwell in, to settle in

inhabitant NOUN
*The island has fewer than thirty **inhabitants**.*
• a resident, a native, an occupant
— A **citizen** is an inhabitant of a particular city or country.
— The **population** of a place is all its inhabitants.

inherit VERB
*She **inherited** the farm from her uncle.*
• to be left, to come into
— Someone who inherits is an **heir**.

injure VERB
*Was anyone **injured** in the accident?*
• to hurt, to harm, to wound
— Some verbs meaning **injure**:
• to **bruise**, **cut** or **graze** skin
• to **break** or **fracture** a bone
• to **sprain** a wrist or ankle
• to **twist** an ankle
• to **dislocate** a shoulder, elbow or other joint

injury NOUN
*She escaped without any serious **injury**.*
• a wound, harm, hurt

⊛ WORD WEB

SOME TYPES OF INJURY:

• a bite, a bruise, a burn, a cut, a fracture, a gash, a graze, a scald, a scratch, a sprain, a sting, a strain

inner ADJECTIVE
*A passageway led to the **inner** chamber.*
• central, inside, interior, internal, middle
OPPOSITES outer, exterior

innocent ADJECTIVE
❶ *The jury found the man **innocent**.*
• guiltless, blameless, free from blame
OPPOSITE guilty
❷ *He was just an **innocent** child.*
• harmless, pure, naive
OPPOSITE wicked

inquiry NOUN
» *Look at enquiry.*

insane ADJECTIVE
❶ *It was rumoured that the king had gone **insane**.*
• mad, crazy, disturbed, mentally ill
OPPOSITE sane
❷ *It would be **insane** to swim in the sea in January!*
• crazy, mad, daft, senseless, stupid, foolish, idiotic
OPPOSITES sensible, wise

inscription NOUN
*The professor read the **inscription** on the tomb.*
• engraving, carving, writing

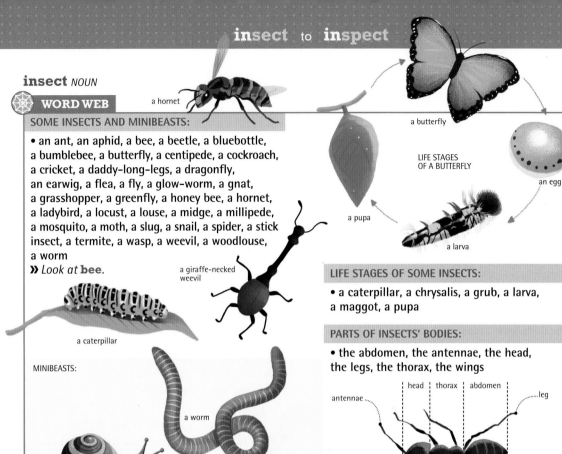

insect NOUN

🕸 WORD WEB

SOME INSECTS AND MINIBEASTS:

• an ant, an aphid, a bee, a beetle, a bluebottle, a bumblebee, a butterfly, a centipede, a cockroach, a cricket, a daddy-long-legs, a dragonfly, an earwig, a flea, a fly, a glow-worm, a gnat, a grasshopper, a greenfly, a honey bee, a hornet, a ladybird, a locust, a louse, a midge, a millipede, a mosquito, a moth, a slug, a snail, a spider, a stick insect, a termite, a wasp, a weevil, a woodlouse, a worm

» *Look at* **bee**.

a hornet

a butterfly

LIFE STAGES OF A BUTTERFLY

an egg

a pupa

a larva

a giraffe-necked weevil

a caterpillar

MINIBEASTS:

a worm

a snail

LIFE STAGES OF SOME INSECTS:

• a caterpillar, a chrysalis, a grub, a larva, a maggot, a pupa

PARTS OF INSECTS' BODIES:

• the abdomen, the antennae, the head, the legs, the thorax, the wings

antennae .... head | thorax | abdomen .... leg

😊 WRITING TIPS

Here are some words you could use when writing about **insects**:

THINGS INSECTS DO:

• to bite, to burrow, to buzz, to hum, to crawl, to flit, to flutter, to fly, to scurry, to scuttle, to swarm

GROUPS OF INSECTS:

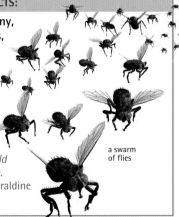

• a cloud, a colony, a swarm, a mass, a plague, a procession

Hercules could see a thundercloud of flies hanging beyond the mountain. He could hear their buzzing.
—GREEK HEROES, Geraldine McCaughrean

a swarm of flies

insert VERB
*He **inserted** a flower into his buttonhole.*
• to place, to push, to tuck, to put

inside ADJECTIVE
*The **inside** doors are all painted green.*
• indoor, inner, interior, internal
OPPOSITE outside

inside NOUN
*The **inside** of the nest was lined with feathers.*
• interior, inner surface, centre, core, heart, middle
OPPOSITE outside

insist VERB
*She **insisted** that the bag belonged to her.*
• to declare, to state, to maintain, to stress, to emphasise, to swear, to claim
➤ to insist on
*The magician **insisted on** silence before he began.*
• to demand, to require

inspect VERB
*They **inspected** the damage done by the storm.*
• to check, to examine, to investigate, to study, to survey, to scrutinise, to review

inspiration NOUN
❶ *What was the **inspiration** behind your story?*
• an impulse, a motivation
❷ *The scientist had a sudden **inspiration**.*
• an idea, a thought

inspire VERB
*The book **inspired** me to write my own story.*
• to motivate, to prompt, to stimulate,
to encourage, to spur on

install VERB
*We have **installed** a new computer in the classroom.*
• to put in, to set up, to place
OPPOSITE to remove

instant ADJECTIVE
*His idea was an **instant** success.*
• immediate, quick, rapid, fast, prompt, swift

instant NOUN
*The shooting star was gone in an **instant**.*
• a moment, a second, a flash

instinct NOUN
❶ *An animal's natural **instinct** is to care for
its young.*
• an urge, an inclination, an impulse
❷ *My **instincts** told me he was lying.*
• intuition, a hunch, a feeling

instruct VERB
❶ *All the staff are **instructed** in first aid.*
• to teach, to train, to coach, to tutor
❷ *The police officer **instructed** the cars to wait.*
• to tell, to order, to direct, to command

instructions NOUN
*Please follow the **instructions** carefully.*
• directions, guidelines, orders, information

instrument NOUN
*Doctors use a special **instrument** to test your blood
pressure.*
• a tool, an implement, a utensil, an appliance,
a device, a gadget
— A **contraption** is a strange-looking or clumsy device.
» *For musical instruments look at* **music**.

insufficient ADJECTIVE
» *For ways to say 'not enough' look at* **enough**.

insult VERB
❶ *He was **insulted** not to be invited to the wedding.*
• to offend, to upset, to hurt, to outrage, to shock
❷ *She said they had **insulted** her and called her names.*
• to be rude to, to be offensive to, to jeer at

insult NOUN
*It is considered an **insult** to refuse a gift.*
• rudeness, an offence, a snub

intact ADJECTIVE
*Despite the storm our tent was still **intact**.*
• whole, in one piece, undamaged, unbroken

intelligence NOUN
❶ *It takes **intelligence** to work out the answer.*
• cleverness, brains (informal), understanding,
comprehension, reason, sense, wisdom, wit
— **Brilliance** or **genius** is very great intelligence.
OPPOSITE stupidity
❷ *The spy was sent to gather secret **intelligence**.*
• information, knowledge, data, facts

intelligent ADJECTIVE
*The aliens from Planet Zog are highly **intelligent**.*
• clever, bright, brainy (informal), smart, quick,
sharp, perceptive, shrewd, able
— **Brilliant** means highly intelligent.
OPPOSITES unintelligent, stupid

intend VERB
❶ *What do you **intend** to do?*
• to plan, to aim, to mean, to have in mind,
to propose
❷ *The class is **intended** for non-swimmers.*
• to design, to set up, to aim
*The class is **aimed** at non-swimmers.*

intense ADJECTIVE
❶ *The pain in my leg was **intense**.*
• extreme, acute, severe, sharp, great, strong,
violent
OPPOSITES slight, mild
❷ *He felt **intense** anger.*
• deep, passionate, powerful, strong, profound
OPPOSITE mild

intention NOUN
*It wasn't my **intention** to hurt your feelings.*
• an aim, an objective, an intent, a plan, a goal

intentional ADJECTIVE
*That was an **intentional** foul.*
• deliberate, conscious, calculated, planned,
intended, wilful
OPPOSITE accidental

interest VERB
*Her story really **interested** me.*
• to appeal to, to attract, to intrigue, to excite,
to fascinate
OPPOSITE to bore

interest NOUN
❶ *The things I brought in to show the class created a lot of interest.*
• curiosity, enthusiasm, excitement
❷ *The information was of no interest to me.*
• importance, significance, consequence, value
❸ *My interests include judo and playing the trombone.*
• a hobby, a pastime, a pursuit, an activity

interested ADJECTIVE
I was really interested by what she had to say.
• fascinated, intrigued, absorbed, engrossed, riveted, gripped
— Ways to say **not interested**:
• bored, detached, indifferent, unconcerned, uninterested

interesting ADJECTIVE
This is a really interesting book.
• fascinating, absorbing, intriguing, engrossing, riveting, gripping, stimulating, entertaining
OPPOSITES boring, dull

interfere VERB
This is my project so please don't interfere.
• to intervene, to get involved, to intrude, to meddle
— Use to **pry** or to **snoop** when someone tries to find out about something that is none of their business.

international ADJECTIVE
They took part in an international tournament.
• global, worldwide

interpret VERB
Can you interpret these symbols?
• to decode, to translate, to understand, to explain, to make sense of

interrupt VERB
❶ *Please don't interrupt while I am speaking.*
• to intervene, to break in
— To **barge in** is to interrupt by coming into a room unexpectedly.
❷ *Heavy rain interrupted the tennis match.*
• to stop, to suspend, to disrupt

interval NOUN
❶ *There will be a short interval in the middle of the play.*
• a break, a pause, a rest, an interlude
— An **intermission** is a break in a play or film.
— **Half-time** is a break in the middle of a sports game.
❷ *There were posts at regular intervals along the road.*
• a space, a gap, a distance

interview VERB
He interviewed the author about her new book.
• to question, to talk to
— To **interrogate** someone is to question them closely, especially when you think they have done something wrong.

introduce VERB
❶ *Let me introduce you to my friend.*
• to present
❷ *They have introduced a new school uniform.*
• to bring in,
to establish,
to create, to initiate,
to start, to begin

introduction NOUN
Did you read the introduction to the book?
• a preface
— A **prologue** is an introduction to a poem, play or long story.

invade VERB
The Vikings invaded many parts of Europe.
• to attack, to enter,
to occupy,
to overrun,
to raid

invalid ADJECTIVE
❶ *The ticket is invalid because it is out of date.*
• unacceptable, unusable, worthless
❷ *That is an invalid argument.*
• false, unsound, unreasonable, illogical, irrational
OPPOSITE valid

invent VERB
Who invented the computer?
• to create, to devise, to think up, to come up with, to conceive, to design, to develop

invention NOUN
His latest invention was a kind of lie detector.
• a creation, a design, a concept

investigate VERB
Police are investigating the cause of the accident.
• to examine, to explore, to enquire into, to look into, to study, to probe, to research, to scrutinise

a
b
c
d
e
f
g
h
i
j
k
q
r
s
t
u
v
w
x
y
z

investigation NOUN
An **investigation** showed how the accident happened.
• an examination, an enquiry, an analysis, a study, a review, a survey

invisible ADJECTIVE
When he wore the magic cloak he was **invisible**.
• unseen, hidden, concealed, camouflaged, undetectable
OPPOSITE visible

invite VERB
Our neighbours **invited** us to a party.
• to ask
— To **summon** someone is to order them to come.

investigation

involve VERB
❶ Her job **involves** a lot of travel.
• to include, to comprise, to require, to demand, to mean
❷ The argument did not **involve** me.
• to concern, to affect, to include
— To be involved in something is to **take part** or **participate** in it.

irregular ADJECTIVE
❶ The wall was made of stones of **irregular** sizes.
• uneven, varying, various
OPPOSITES regular, even
❷ They eat at **irregular** times.
• varying, erratic, unpredictable, random
OPPOSITES regular, steady
❸ The word 'child' has an **irregular** plural.
• unusual, exceptional
OPPOSITE regular

irregular

irrelevant ADJECTIVE
❶ I ignored his **irrelevant** comments.
• pointless, unrelated, unconnected, unnecessary, inappropriate
OPPOSITE relevant
❷ It is **irrelevant** whether the story was written by a boy or a girl.
• unimportant, insignificant, beside the point
OPPOSITE relevant

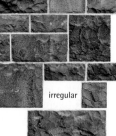

irresistible ADJECTIVE
I had an **irresistible** urge to laugh.
• overwhelming, overpowering, uncontrollable, powerful

irresponsible ADJECTIVE
It's **irresponsible** to leave the tap running.
• reckless, thoughtless, inconsiderate, uncaring, unthinking
OPPOSITE responsible

irritable ADJECTIVE
Why are you so **irritable** today?
• bad-tempered, grumpy, moody, quarrelsome, cross, impatient
OPPOSITES good-humoured, cheerful

irritate VERB
The noise began to **irritate** me.
• to annoy, to bother, to infuriate, to anger, to provoke, to vex, to madden, to get on someone's nerves *(informal)*, to drive someone mad *(informal)*

isolated ADJECTIVE
❶ They came to an **isolated** cottage.
• remote, inaccessible, lonely, secluded, out of the way, cut off
OPPOSITE accessible
❷ There have been a few **isolated** cases of cheating.
• single, uncommon, unusual, abnormal, exceptional, unique
OPPOSITE common

issue VERB
❶ They **issued** pens and paper to everyone.
• to give out, to distribute, to supply, to circulate
❷ Fire **issued** from the dragon's mouth.
• to come out, to emerge, to appear, to flow, to gush, to erupt

issue NOUN
We care about environmental **issues**.
• a matter, a topic, a concern, a question, a problem

itch VERB
My nose **itches**.
• to tickle, to tingle, to prickle

itch NOUN
I had an annoying **itch** on my foot.
• a tickle, a tingling, a prickle

item NOUN
How many **items** did you buy?
• a thing, an object, an article

Jj

⚙ How many different types of jewel can you think of?

⚙ Can you think of 3 words to describe jewels?

⚙ Check the thesaurus to find answers!

jagged *ADJECTIVE*
The ship hit a jagged rock.
• spiky, sharp, rough, uneven
OPPOSITE smooth

jail *NOUN*
He had been in jail for five years.
• prison
— A **cell** is a prisoner's room in a jail.
— A **dungeon** is an underground prison.

jail *VERB*
They were jailed for robbery.
• to imprison, to lock up, to confine, to hold

jam *VERB*
❶ *The window has jammed and I can't open it.*
• to stick, to get stuck
❷ *The roads are jammed at rush hour.*
• to block, to clog, to obstruct
❸ *I jammed my things into a backpack.*
• to cram, to pack, to stuff, to squeeze, to squash, to crush

jealous *ADJECTIVE*
I think they are jealous of my success.
• envious, resentful, grudging

jerk *VERB*
❶ *She jerked her hand away.*
• to pull, to tug, to yank, to pluck, to wrench
❷ *The train jerked forward.*
• to jolt, to jump, to leap, to bounce, to bump, to shudder, to twitch

jet *NOUN*
A jet of water shot high in the air.
• a spout, a spurt, a squirt, a gush, a stream, a fountain

jewel *NOUN*
Her crown glittered with jewels.
• a gem, a gemstone, a precious stone

🕸 WORD WEB

SOME TYPES OF JEWEL:

• amber, a diamond, an emerald, jade, jet, an opal, a pearl, a ruby, a sapphire, a turquoise

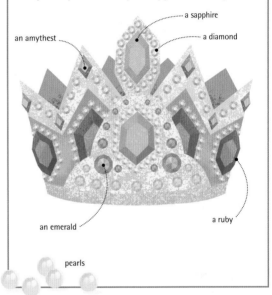

an amythest · · · · · · · ·
a sapphire · · · · · · · · ·
a diamond · · · · · · · · ·
an emerald · · · · · · · · ·
a ruby · · · · · · · · · ·
pearls

😊 WRITING TIPS

Here are some words you could use for writing about **jewels**:

WORDS TO DESCRIBE JEWELS:

• bright, brilliant, costly, dazzling, flashing, glimmering, glistening, glittering, magnificent, precious, priceless, sparkling, twinkling

WORDS FOR DECORATED WITH JEWELS:

• adorned with, covered with, encrusted with, glittering with, set with, sprinkled with, studded with

The soldier wore a handsome green and gold uniform, with a tall hat in which was a waving plume, and he had a belt thickly encrusted with jewels.
—THE PATCHWORK GIRL OF OZ, L. Frank Baum

a
b
c
d
e
f
g
h
i
j
k
l
m
n
o
p
q
r
s
t
u
v
w
x
y
z

jewellery NOUN

SOME ITEMS OF JEWELLERY:

• a bangle, a bracelet, a brooch, a chain, a crown, earrings, a locket, a necklace, a pendant, a ring, a tiara

a locket

jingle VERB
Some coins *jingled* in his back pocket.
• to jangle, to chink, to clink, to tinkle

job NOUN
❶ *Being a vet sounds like an interesting job.*
• an occupation, a profession, a career, work, employment
❷ *Mum gave me some jobs to do.*
• a task, a chore, an errand

 WORD WEB

SOME JOBS:

• an accountant, an actor, an architect, an artist, an astronaut, an author, a barber, a blacksmith, a builder, a bus driver, a carer, a chauffeur, a chef, a cleaner, a coach, a coastguard, a cook, a courier, a critic, a dancer, a dentist, a detective, a doctor, a dressmaker, a dustman, an editor, an electrician, an engineer, an estate agent, a farmer, a firefighter, a fisherman, a gardener, a hairdresser, a journalist, a lawyer, a lecturer, a librarian, a manager, a mechanic, a midwife, a musician, a nanny, a nurse, an office worker, an optician, a pharmacist, a photographer, a pilot, a plumber, a police officer, a politician, a postman or postwoman, a programmer, a reporter, a sailor, a scientist, a secretary, a security guard, a shepherd, a shop assistant, a shopkeeper, a steward, a taxi driver, a teacher, a technician, a train driver, a traffic warden, a vet, a waiter or waitress, a web designer, a writer, a zookeeper

join VERB
❶ *Join the two ends of the rope together.*
• to connect, to fasten, to attach, to link, to fix
OPPOSITE to detach
❷ *This is where the roads join.*
• to meet, to merge, to converge
OPPOSITES to divide, to split

❸ *I have joined the drama club.*
• to become a member of, to enrol in, to sign up for
— To **enlist** is to join the armed forces.
OPPOSITE to leave

join NOUN
If you look hard, you can still see the join.
• a joint, a connection, a link
— A **seam** is the join where two pieces of cloth are sewn together.

joint ADJECTIVE
Preparing the meal was a joint effort.
• combined, shared, common, communal, cooperative, united, mutual
OPPOSITE individual

joke NOUN
❶ *Do you know any good jokes?*
• a funny story, a witticism
— A **pun** is a joke made by using a word that sounds the same as another word.
— A **riddle** is a puzzling question told as a joke.
❷ *It was just meant to be a joke.*
• a trick, a tease, a laugh, a giggle (informal), fun
— A **prank** is a trick played as a joke.

joke VERB
❶ *Those two are always laughing and joking.*
• to tell jokes, to make jokes, to have a laugh
❷ *I was only joking.*
• to tease, to kid (informal), to make a joke
OPPOSITE to be serious

jolt VERB
The car jolted over the bumps in the road.
• to jerk, to jog, to jar, to bump, to bounce, to shake, to shudder

journalist NOUN
She works as a journalist.
• a reporter, a correspondent, a writer

journey NOUN
On their journey, they will see the pyramids.
• a trip, travels, a route
— An **expedition** is a long journey to do something.
— An **excursion** is a journey for pleasure.
— A **voyage** is a journey in a ship or spaceship.
— A **crossing** is a journey across water or the desert.
— A **drive** is a journey in a car.
— A **ride** is a journey in a vehicle, or on a bike or horse.

— A **flight** is a journey in an aircraft or spacecraft.
— A **pilgrimage** is a journey to a holy place.
— A **tour** is a journey around several places.
— A **trek** is a long journey, especially on foot.

joy NOUN
I felt sheer joy when I scored.
• delight, glee, happiness, joyfulness, gladness, jubilation
OPPOSITE **sorrow**

joyful ADJECTIVE
❶ *The wedding was a joyful occasion.*
• happy, merry, joyous, jolly
OPPOSITE **sad**
❷ *We felt joyful at the news.*
• happy, delighted, joyous, elated, jubilant, triumphant
OPPOSITE **sad**

judge VERB
❶ *I judged that the best thing to do was leave.*
• to decide, to consider, to reckon, to calculate, to estimate
❷ *Who's judging the poetry competition?*
• to be the judge for, to decide on, to assess

judgement NOUN
❶ *In your judgement, what should we do?*
• an opinion, a view, a belief, an assessment
❷ *They have to respect the court's judgement.*
• a decision, a finding, a ruling, a verdict
❸ *His comments show a lack of judgement.*
• wisdom, sense, understanding

jumble NOUN
There was a jumble of clothes on the floor.
• a mess, a muddle, a clutter, a confusion
jumble VERB
Please don't jumble up the pages.
• to muddle, to mix up, to mess up, to shuffle
OPPOSITE **to order**

jump VERB
❶ *Suddenly a rabbit jumped in front of us.*
• to leap, to spring, to bound, to bounce, to hop

jump

— To **pounce** is to jump like a cat attacking something.
— To **lunge** is to suddenly jump forwards.
❷ *I jumped into the water.*
• to leap, to dive, to plunge

❸ *All the horses jumped the fence.*
• to leap over, to vault, to clear
❹ *The children were jumping around excitedly.*
• to prance, to dance, to frolic, to skip, to bounce
❺ *The loud bang made them all jump.*
• to start, to flinch, to wince, to jolt, to jerk, to twitch
jump NOUN
With a jump, the grasshopper landed on the leaf.
• a leap, a spring, a bound, a hop

jungle NOUN
Thousands of insect species are found in the jungle.
• a rainforest, a tropical forest

⬡ **WORD WEB**   orchids

SOME TYPES OF PLANTS IN THE JUNGLE:

• an acacia tree, bamboo, a baobab tree, the canopy, a creeper, foliage, mango tree, an orchid, a palm tree, swamp, the undergrowth

SOME ANIMALS FOUND IN THE JUNGLE:

• a crocodile, a gecko, a gorilla, a jaguar, a hummingbird, a lizard, a macaw, a monkey, a mosquito, an orangutan, a parrot, a piranha, a snake, a tapir, a tarantula, a tiger, a toucan, a tree frog
This tiger . . . lived in a wild stretch of country criss-crossed with ravines and covered in dense jungle.—TOM SCATTERHORN: THE MUSEUM'S SECRET, Henry Chancellor

junk NOUN
The garage is full of old junk.
• rubbish, clutter, jumble, trash, scrap

just ADVERB
❶ *It's just what I wanted.*
• exactly, precisely
❷ *I was just trying to help.*
• only, simply, merely
❸ *We just made it in time.*
• only just, barely, hardly, scarcely
❹ *He has just left.*
• recently, a moment ago

justice NOUN
All we want is justice.
• fairness, right, impartiality
OPPOSITE **injustice**

justify VERB
How can you justify spending so much money?
• to defend, to excuse, to account for, to explain, to support

a
b
c
d
e
f
g
h
i
j
k
l
m
n
o
p
q
r
s
t
u
v
w
y
z

A
B
C
D
E
F
G
H
I
J
K
L
M
N
O
P
Q
R
S
T
U
V

⚙ Can you think of 3 different things a knight might use or carry?

⚙ Do you know a word for a knight's horse?

⚙ Check the thesaurus to find answers!

keen ADJECTIVE
❶ *She is a keen member of the team.*
• enthusiastic, eager, fervent, avid, devoted, committed, motivated
OPPOSITE unenthusiastic
❷ *I was keen to get started.*
• eager, anxious, impatient
OPPOSITE reluctant
❸ *Owls have keen eyesight.*
• sharp, acute, piercing
OPPOSITE poor

keep VERB keeps, keeping, kept
❶ *Let's keep the rest of the cake for later.*
• to save, to conserve, to preserve, to retain, to hold on to, to set aside
❷ *We keep the key in this drawer.*
• to store, to put, to stow, to shut
❸ *He keeps his room tidy.*
• to maintain
❹ *Please keep still.*
• to stay, to remain
❺ *A man in the audience kept coughing.*
• to persist in, to go on, to carry on, to continue
— If someone keeps doing something, you can say that they do it **continually**.
❻ *They keep rabbits.*
• to raise, to support, to care for

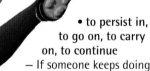

kick

kick VERB
The goalkeeper kicked the ball into the air.
• to strike, to boot *(informal)*, to hit, to drive, to send, to shoot
» *For other ways to hit something look at* **hit**.

kidnap VERB
In the story, a boy is kidnapped by pirates.
• to capture, to seize, to carry off, to snatch

kill VERB
Several people were killed in the explosion.
— To **die** is to be killed: *Several people died in the explosion.*
— To **slay** is an old word meaning 'to kill'. *The knight slayed the dragon.*
— To **murder** someone is to kill them deliberately and illegally.
— To **assassinate** someone is to kill a ruler or leader.
— To **execute** someone is to kill them as a punishment.
— To **massacre** or **slaughter** people is to kill a large number of them.
— To **slaughter** an animal is to kill it for food.
— To **sacrifice** an animal or person is to kill them as a gift to a god.
— To **exterminate** a group of animals or people is to kill them all.
— To **poison** someone is to kill them with poison.
— To **electrocute** someone is to kill them with electricity.
— To **strangle** or **throttle** someone is to kill them by squeezing their throat.

kind NOUN
❶ *What kind of music do you like to play?*
• a sort, a type, a variety, a style
— A **breed** of dog is a kind of dog.
— A **species** of animal is a kind of animal.
❷ *What kind of car is that?*
• a make, a brand

kind ADJECTIVE
❶ *He's a very kind boy.*
• kind-hearted, caring, good-natured, kindly, affectionate, warm, loving, friendly, sweet, sympathetic, compassionate, considerate
❷ *It was kind of you to give me your seat.*
• generous, good, thoughtful, obliging, considerate, understanding, unselfish, gracious, noble
OPPOSITE unkind

king NOUN
He was crowned as the new king.
• a monarch, a sovereign, a ruler

kingdom NOUN
He ruled over a vast kingdom.
• a realm, a monarchy

kit NOUN

I've forgotten my games kit.

• gear, equipment, things, an outfit

kitchen NOUN

» *For cooking look at* **cook**.

» *For rooms look at* **room**.

knew (past tense of **know**)

knife NOUN

WORD WEB

SOME KINDS OF KNIFE:

• a bread knife, a butter knife, a carving knife, a dagger, a penknife

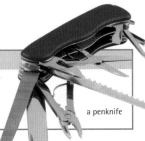

a penknife

knight NOUN

 WRITING TIPS

Here are some words you could use for writing about a **knight**:

THINGS A MEDIEVAL KNIGHT MIGHT HAVE:

• chain mail, a coat of arms, a falcon, a gauntlet, a helmet, a lance, a pennant, a shield, a spear, a suit of armour, a sword, a tunic
— A **charger** or a **steed** was a knight's horse.
— A **squire** or a **page** was a young man who served a knight.

WAYS TO DESCRIBE A KNIGHT:

• bold, brave, chivalrous, faithful, gallant, handsome, loyal, noble, true, valiant, worthy, wounded

SOME THINGS A KNIGHT MIGHT DO:

• to battle, to fight, to gallop, to go on a quest, to joust, to ride, to slay a dragon

Trumpets blared, horses neighed and the knights clashed together in combat. Some were unhorsed, tumbling noisily from their sweating steeds, and many a lance shivered in pieces.
—TALES OF GODS AND MEN, John Bailey

a helmet
a shield
armour
a gauntlet
a lance

knob NOUN

❶ *The knob had fallen off the door.*

• a handle

❷ *She started fiddling with the knobs on the machine.*

• a switch, a button, a control

knock VERB

❶ *Someone knocked on the door.*

• to tap, to rap
— To **bang**, to **hammer** or to **pound** is to knock very loudly.

❷ *I knocked my head as I got out of the car.*

• to bump, to bang, to hit, to strike, to bash (informal)

know VERB knows, knowing, knew, known

❶ *Do you know how to print a document?*

• to understand, to be aware, to remember, to comprehend
— Ways to say you do not **know** something:

• to have no idea, to be unaware, to have no knowledge of, to have no clue (informal)
— You can also say that you **haven't the faintest idea** or **haven't the foggiest idea** (informal): *I haven't the faintest idea how to print a document.*

❷ *As soon as I saw the present, I knew what it was.*

• to recognise, to realise, to identify, to be aware of

❸ *Do you know Oliver?*

• to be acquainted with, to have met, to be a friend of

knowledge NOUN

❶ *She has a good knowledge of computers.*

• an understanding, a grasp
• familiarity: *She has a lot of familiarity with computers.*

❷ *An encyclopedia contains a lot of knowledge.*

• information, data, facts, learning, wisdom

known (past participle of **know**)

a
b
c
d
e
f
g
h
i
j
k
l
m
n
o
p
q
r
s
t
u
v
w
x
y
z

A B C D E F G H I J K L M N O P Q R S T U V W X Y Z

⚙ Can you think of 3 different words or phrases meaning 'to laugh'?

⚙ Do you know a word that means 'to laugh in an unkind way'?

⚙ Check the thesaurus to find answers!

label NOUN
The washing instructions are on the **label**.
• a tag, a ticket, a sticker

label VERB
I've **labelled** all the boxes, so we'll know what's in them.
• to tag, to mark, to identify, to put a label on

lack NOUN
They were forced to give up because of a **lack** of money.
• a shortage, an absence, a want, a need
— **Famine** is a lack of food.
— **Drought** is a lack of water.
OPPOSITE an abundance

lack VERB
The game **lacked** excitement.
• to be short of, to be without, to need, to want, to be missing, to not have enough

lag VERB
One runner was **lagging** behind the others.
• to straggle, to trail, to fall, to dawdle, to linger, to loiter

laid (past tense of **lay**)

lake NOUN
We rowed across the **lake**.
• a pond, a pool
— A **lagoon** is a saltwater lake.
— A **loch** is a lake in Scotland.
— A **reservoir** is a lake used to supply water.

lame ADJECTIVE
❶ The horse was **lame** and could not run.
• crippled, limping
❷ What a **lame** excuse!
• feeble, weak, unconvincing, poor

land NOUN
❶ This **land** is good for growing crops.
• ground, soil, earth
❷ The baron owned a lot of **land**.
• property, grounds
• an estate: The baron owned a large **estate**.
❸ China is a **land** with an ancient history.
• a country, a nation, a state, a territory, a region

land VERB
❶ The plane **landed** exactly on time.
• to touch down, to arrive
OPPOSITE to take off
❷ The ship will **land** at Dover.
• to dock, to berth, to come ashore
OPPOSITES to sail, to set sail
❸ The bird **landed** on a small branch.
• to alight, to come to rest, to settle, to perch
— If a bird **roosts** somewhere, it sits and sleeps there.

landscape NOUN
We sat on the hill and admired the **landscape**.
• the countryside, the scenery, the view, the scene, the outlook, the prospect

ancient languages on the Rosetta Stone

lane NOUN
》 Look at **road**

language NOUN
❶ The scroll was written in an ancient **language**.
• a tongue
— A **dialect** is a form of a language used by people in one part of a country.
❷ The author uses very poetic **language**.
• wording, phrasing, style, vocabulary, expressions

large ADJECTIVE
❶ Elephants are **large** animals.
• big, huge, enormous, colossal, giant, gigantic, immense, great, massive, mighty, ginormous (informal)
— Use **bulky** or **hefty** for something that is large and heavy.
— Use **towering** for something that is very tall or high.

❷ *The cook gave me a **large** helping of pudding.*
• generous, abundant, lavish, hearty
❸ *Is this room **large** enough for dancing in?*
• spacious, roomy, sizeable
❹ *The storms caused damage over a **large** area.*
• wide, broad, extensive, widespread, vast
» *For more ideas on how to say large look at **big**.*

last ADJECTIVE
❶ *Z is the **last** letter of the alphabet.*
• final, closing, concluding, terminating, ultimate
OPPOSITE first
❷ *Did you see his **last** film?*
• latest, most recent
OPPOSITE next

last NOUN
➤ **at last**
*We reached our destination **at last**.*
• finally, eventually, in the end

last VERB
❶ *The show **lasts** for two hours.*
• to continue, to carry on, to go on, keep on
❷ *Most plants cannot **last** long without water.*
• to hold out, to remain, to keep going, to live, to survive

late ADJECTIVE
*The bus is **late**.*
• delayed, overdue
OPPOSITES early, on time

later ADVERB
*I'll phone you **later**.*
• afterwards, in a while, in due course, subsequently

laugh VERB
*The clown did a trick and all the children **laughed**.*
• to chuckle, to chortle, to giggle
— To **snigger** is to laugh quietly in an unkind way.
— To **titter** is to laugh in a silly way.
— To **cackle** is to give a harsh laugh.
— To **roar with laughter** or **shriek with laughter** is to laugh a lot loudly.
— To **burst out laughing** is to suddenly start to laugh.
➤ **to laugh at**
*They **laughed at** his clothes.*
• to mock, to make fun of, to ridicule, to scoff at, to jeer at, to sneer at

laughter NOUN
*We heard bursts of **laughter** coming from the kitchen.*
• laughing, amusement, hilarity, mirth

launch VERB
*They **launched** a rocket to the moon.*
• to send off, to fire, to blast off, to set off

law NOUN
*Everyone must obey the **laws**.*
— A **rule** or **regulation** is a law, especially in a game or organisation.
— A **bill** is a plan for a new law in parliament.
— An **act** is a new law that a government makes.

lay (past tense of lie)
lay VERB lays, laying, laid
❶ ***Lay** the map out on the table.*
• to put down, to set down, to place, to spread
❷ *Please **lay** the table for dinner.*
• to set, to arrange

layer NOUN
❶ *The walls needed two **layers** of paint.*
• a coat, a coating, a covering
❷ *The pond was covered in a **layer** of ice.*
• a sheet, a film, a skin

lazy ADJECTIVE
*My **lazy** little brother stayed in bed all day!*
• idle, inactive, indolent

lead VERB leads, leading, led
❶ *The rescuers **led** the climbers to safety.*
• to guide, to conduct, to escort, to steer
OPPOSITE to follow
❷ *This path **leads** to the village.*
• to go, to run, to take someone

a b c d e f g h i j k l m n o p q r s t u v w x y z

❸ *Dr Martez will **lead** the expedition.*
• to be in charge of, to direct, to head,
to command, to run, to control, to supervise
➤ **to lead to**
*What has **led** to this situation?*
• to cause, to produce, to bring about, to trigger,
to give rise to, to result in

lead NOUN
❶ *The team followed the captain's **lead**.*
• example, guidance, leadership, direction
❷ *Keep the dog on a **lead**.*
• a leash, a strap, a chain
❸ *Don't trip over the **lead**.*
• a cable, a flex, a wire, a cord
➤ **in the lead**
*The British cyclist is **in the lead**.*
• leading, winning, ahead, in first place, in front

leader NOUN
*The **leader** of the pirates was Captain Cutlass.*
• the head, the chief, the commander, the captain,
the boss *(informal)*

leak NOUN
*The plumber mended a **leak** in the water tank.*
• a crack, a hole, an opening, a drip
— A **puncture** is a leak in a tyre.

leak VERB
*The juice had **leaked** all over my school bag.*
• to drip, to dribble, to seep, to trickle, to escape
— Use to **ooze** for thick liquid that leaks slowly.

lean VERB leans, leaning, leaned or leant
❶ *She **leant** across to look at my book.*
• to bend, to incline, to stretch, to bow
❷ *The old building **leans** to one side.*
• to slant, to slope, to tilt, to tip
❸ *I **leaned** against the wall.*
• to recline, to rest, to prop yourself,
to support yourself
— To **loll** or to **lounge** is to lean in a relaxed lazy way.

leap VERB leaps, leaping, leapt or leaped
*The dog **leaped** in the air to catch the ball.*
• to jump, to spring, to bound
》 *For more ways of jumping look at **jump**.*

learn VERB learns, learning, learnt or learned
❶ *We **learned** about Rosa Parks today.*
• to discover, to find out
❷ *I've **learned** how to make porridge.*
• to pick up, to master, to gather, to grasp
❸ *I've got to **learn** the words of this song.*
• to learn by heart, to memorise

leave VERB leaves, leaving, left
❶ *Do you have to **leave** now?*
• to go, to go away, to depart, to take your leave,
to set off
— When a ship leaves, it **sails** or **sets sail**.
— When a plane leaves, it **takes off**.
OPPOSITE to arrive
❷ *He **left** the room quickly.*
• to exit, to go out of
OPPOSITE to enter
❸ *Don't **leave** me here on my own!*
• to abandon, to desert, to forsake
❹ *My mum didn't like her job so she **left**.*
• to quit, to resign
— To **retire** is to leave because you have reached an
age where you do not need to work any more.
❺ *Leave your shoes here.*
• to place, to put down, to set down, to deposit
➤ **to leave someone** or **something out**
*You've **left** my name **out**.*
• to miss out, to omit, to exclude, to forget

leave NOUN
*The guard had left his post without **leave**.*
• permission, authorisation, approval

led *(past tense of **lead**)*

left *(past tense of **leave**)*

legal ADJECTIVE
*Is it **legal** to park here?*
• lawful, allowed, permitted, legitimate,
permissible
OPPOSITE illegal

legend NOUN
*I like reading **legends**
about ancient heroes.*
• a myth, a story,
a folk tale, a fairy
tale, a fable
》 *Look at **myth**.*

a centaur,
a mythical beast

load NOUN
Camels can carry heavy loads.
• a burden, a weight, a cargo

load VERB
❶ *We loaded the suitcases into the car.*
• to pack, to pile, to heap, to stack
❷ *He was loaded with shopping bags.*
• to weigh down, to burden

local ADJECTIVE
Our local shop delivers newspapers.
• neighbourhood, nearby

location NOUN
The pilot made a note of his location.
• a position, a situation, whereabouts, a spot, a site

lock NOUN
There was a heavy lock on the lid of the chest.
• a fastening, a clasp, a padlock, a bolt, a latch

lock VERB
Make sure you lock the door when you go out.
• to fasten, to secure, to bolt

➤ **to lock someone up**
The witch locked him up in an attic.
• to imprison, to confine, to detain, to chain

logical ADJECTIVE
We need to think about the problem in a logical way.
• rational, reasonable, sensible, valid, intelligent, clear, methodical
OPPOSITE illogical

lonely ADJECTIVE
❶ *Cara felt lonely while her friends were away.*
• alone, friendless, solitary, abandoned, neglected, forlorn, forsaken
❷ *The climbers sheltered in a lonely hut.*
• remote, isolated, inaccessible, secluded, solitary, out of the way

long ADJECTIVE
It was a very long wait.
• lengthy, prolonged
— Use **endless** or **never-ending** if something is too long.
OPPOSITE short

long VERB
➤ **to long for something**
I longed for a drink.
• to yearn for, to crave, to wish for, to pine for

145

look VERB
❶ *If you look carefully, you'll see an owl in the tree.*
• to watch, to observe, to study
❷ *She looks tired.*
• to appear, to seem
➤ **to look after someone** or **something**
We looked after their pets when they went on holiday.
• to take care of, to care for, to mind, to tend, to watch, to watch over, to protect, to guard
➤ **to look for something**
He was looking for his keys.
• to hunt for, to search for, to seek
➤ **to look out**
Look out, or you'll get wet.
• to beware, to pay attention, to take care, to watch out, to be careful

😮 OVERUSED WORD

Try to use a more interesting word when you want to say **look**. Here are some ideas and examples:

TO LOOK QUICKLY:

• to glance, to glimpse, to peek, to peep
The sermon seems to be taking forever. I glance at Hannah and she grimaces at me.—BETWEEN TWO SEAS, Marie-Louise Jensen

TO LOOK CAREFULLY OR FOR A LONG TIME:

• to stare, to eye, to peer, to study, to scrutinise, to regard, to examine, to inspect, to gaze
He gazed at his reflection in the mirror.
— To **gape** is to stare with a surprised expression.
— To **scan** or to **survey** a wide area is to look over it.
I scanned the horizon looking for a sail.

TO LOOK ANGRILY:

• to glare, to glower, to frown, to scowl
'The next time you mimic me I'll rip your ears off,' she promised, glowering at them, her dark blue eyes sparkling with indignation.—SHAPESHIFTER 5: STIRRING THE STORM, Ali Sparkes

look NOUN
❶ *Did you get a look at what she was wearing?*
• a glance, a glimpse, a peep, a view
❷ *The guard had an unfriendly look.*
• an appearance, an expression, a face, a manner, an air, a bearing

loop NOUN
Make a loop in the string and then tie a knot.
• a coil, a hoop, a circle, a ring, a bend, a curl

loop VERB
The cowboy looped the reins round a fence post.
• to coil, to wind, to curl, to twist

loose ADJECTIVE
❶ *My tooth is loose.*
• wobbly, insecure, shaky
OPPOSITES firm, secure
❷ *These jeans are loose around the waist.*
• slack, baggy, roomy, big
OPPOSITE tight
❸ *The dog was loose.*
• free, out, at large, at liberty, untied
OPPOSITES tied up, shut in

loosen VERB
Can you loosen these knots?
• to undo, to unfasten, to untie, to slacken, to release
OPPOSITE to tighten

lorry NOUN
» *For types of vehicle look at* **transport**.

lose VERB loses, losing, lost
❶ *Debbie has lost one of her gloves.*
• to mislay, to misplace, to be unable to find
OPPOSITE to find
❷ *Unfortunately, our team lost.*
• to be defeated, to get beaten, to suffer a defeat
OPPOSITE to win

loss NOUN
❶ *She reported the loss of her phone.*
• disappearance, mislaying
❷ *I had a loss of confidence.*
• a failure, a decline, a decrease

lot NOUN
We are having another lot of visitors this weekend.
• a group, a batch, a set
➤ **a lot of** (or **lots of**)
❶ *We are going to need a lot of help.*
• a large amount of, a good or great deal of, plenty of, loads of (informal)
❷ *There are a lot of people waiting.*
• many, numerous, a large or great number of

loud ADJECTIVE
The whole house was kept awake by the loud music.
• noisy, blaring, booming, deafening, rowdy, resounding, thunderous
— A **piercing** or **shrill** sound is loud and high.
— A **racket** is a loud noise.
— A **cacophony** is a loud unpleasant noise.
OPPOSITES quiet, soft

lounge VERB
They lounged in the garden all day.
• to relax, to laze, to loll, to sprawl, to lie around, to be lazy, to idle, to take it easy
» *For rooms look at* **room**.

A B C D E F G H I J K L M N O P Q R S T U V W X Y Z

love NOUN
❶ *She was full of love for her sister.*
• affection, tenderness, devotion, fondness, adoration
❷ *We both had a love for the outdoors.*
• a liking, a passion, an enthusiasm, a fondness

love VERB
❶ *They love each other and want to get married.*
• to be in love with, to be devoted to, to care for, to adore, to cherish, to idolise
❷ *I love pizza.*
• to adore, to be partial to, to enjoy, to be fond of

lovely ADJECTIVE

😮 OVERUSED WORD

Try to use a more interesting word when you want to say **lovely**. Here are some ideas and examples:

FOR A LOVELY PERSON:

• charming, delightful, lovable, likeable, sweet, enchanting
'I told you they loved singing!' cried Mr Wonka. 'Aren't they delightful? Aren't they charming? But you mustn't believe a word they said. It's all nonsense, every bit of it!'—CHARLIE AND THE CHOCOLATE FACTORY, Roald Dahl

FOR A LOVELY EXPERIENCE:

• pleasant, pleasing, enjoyable, fantastic, marvellous, wonderful, delightful, entertaining, amusing
We had a fantastic time on the school trip.

FOR SOMETHING THAT LOOKS LOVELY:

• beautiful, gorgeous, stunning, appealing, attractive, pretty, spectacular
Soon the cave was filled with hundreds of beautifully coloured bubbles, all drifting gently through the air. It was truly a wonderful sight.—THE BFG, Roald Dahl

FOR A LOVELY DAY:

• fine, glorious, wonderful, beautiful, sunny
It's a glorious day for a bicycle trip.
OPPOSITES nasty, horrible
» *For lovely food look at* **food**.
» *For a lovely smell look at* **smell**.

loving ADJECTIVE
Mum gave me a loving hug.
• affectionate, kind, warm, tender, fond, devoted

low ADJECTIVE
❶ *The garden is surrounded by a low wall.*
• short, small
❷ *Cook the stew at a low temperature.*
• cool, moderate
❸ *They were soldiers of low rank.*
• junior, inferior, modest, humble
❹ *The tuba plays low notes.*
• deep, bass
OPPOSITE high
❺ *We spoke in low voices.*
• quiet, soft, subdued, muffled
OPPOSITE loud

lower VERB
❶ *The supermarket lowered its prices.*
• to reduce, to cut, to bring down, to decrease, to lessen
❷ *Please lower the volume.*
• to turn down, to decrease
❸ *He lowered the blinds.*
• to let down, to pull down
OPPOSITE to raise

loyal ADJECTIVE
He was a loyal friend.
• true, faithful, reliable, dependable, trustworthy, devoted, firm, staunch
OPPOSITE disloyal

luck NOUN
❶ *It was sheer luck that we met.*
• accident, chance, coincidence, fluke, fate, destiny
❷ *With a bit of luck we could win.*
• fortune, good fortune

lucky ADJECTIVE
❶ *I got the right answer by a lucky guess.*
• accidental, chance, unintentional, unplanned
❷ *Some lucky person won a million pounds.*
• fortunate, happy

lump NOUN
❶ *Lumps of sticky clay stuck to his boots.*
• a chunk, a clump, a wad, a mass, a hunk, a ball
— A lump of gold is a **nugget**.
— A lump of cheese is a **wedge**.
❷ *I could feel a lump on my head.*
• a bump, a swelling, a bulge

lurk VERB
The jaguar lurked in wait for its prey.
• to loiter, to prowl, to crouch, to hide, to lie in wait

luxury NOUN
❶ *Sometimes I buy myself a little luxury like a chocolate bar.*
• a treat, an indulgence
OPPOSITE a necessity
❷ *The millionaire lived a life of luxury.*
• wealth, affluence, expense, comfort
OPPOSITE poverty

a b c d e f g h i j k l m n o p q r s t u v w x y z

A
B
C
D
E
F
G
H
I
J
K
L
M
N
O
P
Q
R
S
T
U
V
W
X
Y
Z

⚙ Can you think of 3 words to describe the moon?

⚙ Do you know a word that means 'to do with the moon'?

⚙ Check the thesaurus to find answers!

machine NOUN
Do you know how this machine works?
• an apparatus, an appliance, a device, a contraption

a printer

a Tardis

mad ADJECTIVE
❶ *You must be mad to go out on a day like this.*
• crazy, daft, insane, stupid, silly, foolish, idiotic
OPPOSITES sensible, wise
❷ *The crowd went mad when the singer appeared.*
• crazy, frantic, frenzied, berserk, hysterical
❸ *(informal) Olivia is mad about horses.*
• enthusiastic, fanatical, passionate

made (past tense of **make**)

magazine NOUN
I bought a magazine to read on the train.
• a journal, a paper, a comic

magic NOUN
❶ *Do you believe in magic?*
• sorcery, witchcraft, wizardry, spells, charms, enchantments
❷ *There was a clown at the party who did magic.*
• conjuring, tricks

magic ADJECTIVE
There seemed to be something magic about the book.
• magical, supernatural

✸ **WORD WEB**

SOME MAGICAL CREATURES:
• a dragon, a dwarf, an elf, a fairy, a genie, a giant, a gnome, a goblin, an imp, a leprechaun, a mermaid, an ogre, a pixie, a sprite, a troll, a unicorn, a vampire, a werewolf

MAGICAL ACTIONS:
• to become invisible, to bewitch someone, to brew a potion, to enchant someone, to cast a spell, to conjure something up, to transform something, to vanish

THINGS CONNECTED WITH MAGIC:
• a broomstick, a cauldron, a charm, an elixir, a magic potion, a phial, a spell, a spellbook, a wand
Neville had somehow managed to melt Seamus's cauldron into a twisted blob and their potion was seeping across the stone floor, burning holes in people's shoes.—HARRY POTTER AND THE PHILOSOPHER'S STONE, J. K. Rowling
» *Look at* **fairy** *and* **myth.**

a dragon

magician NOUN
❶ *The magician pulled a scarf out of his hat.*
• a conjuror
❷ *A magician turned him into a frog.*
• a sorcerer, a witch, a wizard

magnificent ADJECTIVE
❶ *The mountain scenery was magnificent.*
• beautiful, glorious, splendid, spectacular, impressive
❷ *The queen lived in a magnificent palace.*
• grand, imposing, majestic
Lloyd was expecting a big, imposing film studio with a huge sign across the front and glass doors opening into a glittering foyer.—FACING THE DEMON HEADMASTER, Gillian Cross

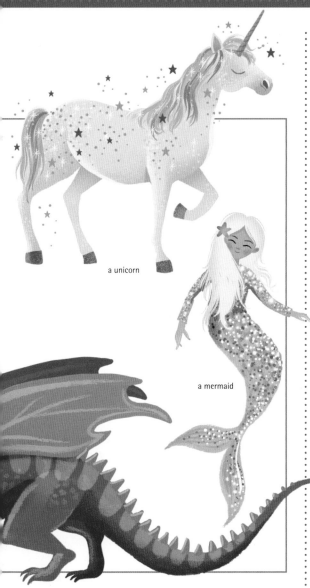

a unicorn

a mermaid

main ADJECTIVE
❶ *What was the **main** point of the story?*
• central, chief, most important, basic, essential, fundamental, primary
❷ *Their **main** food is fish.*
• principal, major, usual, staple, basic
❸ *They live near a **main** road.*
• major, large, big, busy, important
OPPOSITES minor, unimportant

mainly ADVERB
*Chimpanzees eat **mainly** fruit and vegetables.*
• largely, mostly, chiefly, principally, primarily

major ADJECTIVE
❶ *There are delays on all the **major** roads into the city.*
• main, principal, primary, big, important
❷ *There has been a **major** accident.*
• serious, severe, significant
❸ *Winning the cup was a **major** achievement.*
• big, great, considerable, significant, important
OPPOSITES minor, unimportant

majority NOUN
➤ **the majority of**
*The **majority of** children walk to school.*
• the greater number of, the bulk of, most
OPPOSITE the minority

make VERB makes, making, made
❶ *We **made** a shelter out of leaves and branches.*
• to build, to construct, to create, to assemble, to put together, to produce, to manufacture
❷ *They've **made** the attic into a games room.*
• to change, to turn, to convert, to modify, to transform, to alter
❸ *Those two are always **making** trouble.*
• to cause, to create, to bring about, to give rise to, to provoke
❹ *The noise **made** him jump.*
• to cause
*The noise **caused** him to jump.*
❺ *We can't **make** her go if she doesn't want to.*
• to force, to compel, to order
• to oblige: *We can't **oblige** her to go if she doesn't want to.*
❻ *They tried to **make** me admit I was wrong.*
• to persuade, to induce, to get
*They tried to **get** me to admit I was wrong.*
❼ *He **made** some money washing cars.*
• to earn, to gain, to get, to obtain, to acquire, to receive
❽ *Can I **make** a suggestion?*
• to offer, to propose, to put forward
❾ *2 and 2 **make** 4.*
• to add up to, to come to, to total
➤ **to be made up of**
*An insect's body is **made up of** three main parts.*
• to consist of, to comprise, to be composed of, to contain, to include
➤ **to make something up**
*I **made up** a funny song.*
• to create, to invent, to think up, to come up with

make NOUN
*What **make** of computer do you have?*
• a brand, a model, a label

a
b
c
d
e
f
g
h
i
j
k
l
m
n
o
p
q
r
s
t
u
v
w
x
y
z

man NOUN
*I'll ask the **man** in the ticket office.*
• a bloke (informal), a guy (informal),
a chap (informal)
– A **gentleman** is a polite word for a man.
– A **husband** is a married man.
– A **father** is a man who has children.
– A **bachelor** is an unmarried man.
– A **fiancé** is a man who is engaged to be married.
– A **bridegroom** is a man on his wedding day.
– A **widower** is a man whose wife or husband has died.

manage VERB
❶ *I can't **manage** all this work on my own.*
• to cope with, to deal with, to take on, to carry out
❷ *We'll have to **manage** without a phone.*
• to cope, to make do, to get along, to get by
❸ *She **manages** a restaurant.*
• to be in charge of, to run, to direct, to supervise,
to lead

manager NOUN
*If you have a problem, talk to the **manager**.*
• the director, the supervisor, the chief, the head,
the boss (informal)

manner NOUN
❶ *He waved the stick around in a dangerous
manner.*
• a way, a fashion
❷ *Her **manner** was pleasant.*
• behaviour, an air, a look, a bearing, an expression
➤ **manners**
*Trolls have no **manners**!*
• politeness, courtesy
➤ **bad manners**
*It's **bad manners** to interrupt.*
• rude, impolite, discourteous

many DETERMINER
*I've been on an aeroplane **many** times.*
• a lot of, lots of, plenty of, numerous, frequent,
countless, myriad, untold
OPPOSITE few

map NOUN
*We downloaded a **map** of Paris.*
• a plan, a chart, a diagram
– An **atlas** is a book of maps.

march VERB
*The soldiers **marched** in a
long line.*
• to parade, to file, to troop,
to stride, to pace

mark NOUN
❶ *There were dirty **marks** all over the wall.*
• a spot, a stain, a smear, a smudge, a streak
– A **speck** is a tiny mark.
– A **blot** is a mark left by a blob of ink.
❷ *They followed the **marks** left by the animal in
the snow.*
• tracks, a trail, footprints
❸ *What **mark** did you get in the spelling test?*
• a score, a grade

mark VERB
❶ *Your shoes have **marked** the carpet.*
• to stain, to smudge, to damage, to dirty
❷ *The teacher **marked** our maths tests.*
• to correct, to grade, to assess

market NOUN
» *Look at **shop**.*

marry VERB
*In what year did your grandparents **marry**?*
• to get married, to wed
» *Look at **wedding**.*

marsh NOUN
*He felt himself sinking into the **marsh**.*
• a swamp, a bog

marvellous ADJECTIVE
❶ *The professor showed us his **marvellous** inventions.*
• amazing, remarkable, extraordinary, incredible,
miraculous, astonishing
OPPOSITE ordinary
❷ *We had a **marvellous** time at the beach.*
• excellent, superb, tremendous, wonderful,
fantastic, splendid, terrific, brilliant
OPPOSITES bad, awful

mash VERB
*The dinosaur **mashed** the leaves under its feet.*
• to crush, to smash, to pound, to grind, to squash

mass NOUN
❶ *There was a **mass** of rubbish to clear away.*
• a heap, a pile, a mound, a stack
❷ *There was a **mass** of people in front of the stage.*
• a crowd, a group, a horde, a throng

march

massive ADJECTIVE
» Look at **huge**.

match NOUN
The semi-final was a really exciting **match**.
• a game, a contest

match VERB
Your top **matches** your eyes.
• to go with, to complement, to suit, to blend in with, to tone with
OPPOSITE to contrast with

material NOUN
❶ Leggings are made of stretchy **material**.
• cloth, fabric
» For types of cloth look at **cloth**.
❷ The cleaning **materials** are in the cupboard.
• stuff, things, substances

matter NOUN
❶ This is a serious **matter**.
• an issue, a subject, a topic, an affair, a concern, a business, a situation
❷ Soil is made partly of plant **matter**.
• material, stuff, substance
❸ What's the **matter** with the car?
• trouble, a problem, a difficulty, a worry

matter VERB
It doesn't **matter** if you're a bit late.
• to be important, to make a difference

mature ADJECTIVE
❶ The zoo has two **mature** gorillas.
• adult, fully grown
OPPOSITE young
❷ He is very **mature** for his age.
• grown-up, responsible, sensible
OPPOSITES immature, childish

maximum NOUN
❶ The heat is at its **maximum** at midday.
• highest point, peak, upper limit
OPPOSITE minimum
❷ The **maximum** we could invite is 25.
• most, greatest number
OPPOSITE minimum

maximum ADJECTIVE
What is the **maximum** speed of the rocket?
• greatest, top, highest, largest
OPPOSITE minimum

maybe ADVERB
Maybe they missed the bus.
• perhaps, possibly
OPPOSITE definitely

maze NOUN
We were lost in a **maze** of underground tunnels.
• a labyrinth, a network, a web, a warren

meal NOUN

✸ WORD WEB

SOME TYPES OF MEAL:

• breakfast, brunch, dinner, lunch, tea, supper
— A **feast** or a **banquet** is a large and special meal for a lot of people.
— A **snack** is a small quick meal.
— A **picnic** is a meal eaten outside.
— A **barbecue** is a meal cooked outside.
— A **buffet** is a meal where people help themselves to food.
— A **takeaway** is a meal you buy ready cooked.
» Look at **food**.

skewers for a barbecue

mean VERB means, meaning, meant
❶ A red light **means** 'stop'.
• to indicate, to signify, to imply, to convey, to communicate, to stand for, to symbolise
❷ I **meant** to tell him, but I forgot.
• to intend, to plan, to aim, to want

mean ADJECTIVE
❶ Scrooge was too **mean** to buy any presents.
• selfish, miserly, stingy (informal)
OPPOSITE generous
❷ That was a **mean** trick.
• unkind, unpleasant, nasty, spiteful, cruel, malicious
OPPOSITE kind

meaning NOUN
What is the **meaning** of this symbol?
• the significance, the sense, the explanation, the interpretation, the definition

measure VERB
Measure the height of the wall.
• to calculate, to gauge, to assess
— To measure the weight of something is to **weigh** it.

measurement NOUN
What are the **measurements** of this room?
• the dimensions, the size, the extent, the proportions

meat NOUN

 WORD WEB

SOME KINDS OF MEAT:

• bacon, beef, chicken, duck, goose, ham, lamb, pork, turkey
— **Mutton** is meat from an adult sheep.
— **Veal** is meat from a calf.
— **Venison** is meat from a deer.
— **Game** is meat from a wild animal or bird that is hunted.

PIECES AND FORMS OF MEAT:

• a burger, a chop, a fillet, a leg, a joint, mince, a sausage, a rib, a steak
— A **rasher** is a piece of bacon.

My mother had cooked really scrummy lamb chops, roasted to a crisp in a hot oven, with vegetables that had been rolled around in the lamb fat and browned.
—THE KISSING CLUB, Julia Clarke

medicine NOUN
❶ *This medicine is for coughs.*
• a drug, a medication, a treatment, a remedy
— An amount of medicine taken at one time is a **dose**.
— Medicine which a doctor gives you is a **prescription**.
❷ *Herbs have been used in medicine for thousands of years.*
• healing, treatment, therapy

 WORD WEB

SOME TYPES OF MEDICINE:

• an anaesthetic, an antibiotic, an antidote, an antiseptic, a painkiller, a tonic

FORMS IN WHICH YOU TAKE MEDICINE:

• a capsule, an inhaler, an injection, a lotion, a lozenge, an ointment, a pill, a tablet, a vaccine
» For types of doctor look at **doctor**.

In cabinets and shelves, filling crates and hanging from pegs in the ceiling were the supplies for the medicine show's tonics. Coils of dried snake skins . . . Strings of fragrant herbs. Jars of bleached bones. Powders and liquids in a rainbow of colours.
—THE MYSTIFYING MEDICINE SHOW, J. C. Bemis

medium ADJECTIVE
The man was of medium height.
• average, middle, standard, moderate, normal
medium NOUN
The Internet is an important medium of communication.
• a means, a mode, a method, a way, a channel

meet VERB meets, meeting, met
❶ *We're meeting outside the cinema at eight.*
• to gather, to meet up, to assemble, to collect
❷ *My parents met me at the station.*
• to pick up, to fetch, to greet, to welcome
❸ *While I was out shopping I met someone I knew.*
• to come across, to encounter, to run into, to bump into, to see
❹ *Have you met Sally?*
• to be introduced to, to know
Do you know Sally?
❺ *This is where the two rivers meet.*
• to come together, to merge, to converge, to join, to connect

meeting NOUN
There was a meeting at school about the trip.
• a gathering, a discussion
— A **conference** is a large meeting or set of meetings where people discuss a topic.
— A **rendezvous** is a time when you have arranged to meet someone.

melt VERB
The ice began to melt in the sun.
• to thaw, to soften, to unfreeze
— To melt frozen food is to **defrost** it.
— **Molten** rock or metal has melted because of great heat.
OPPOSITE to freeze

member NOUN
➤ to be a member of something
Are you a member of the book club?
• to belong to, to have joined

memorable ADJECTIVE
It was a very memorable holiday.
• unforgettable, notable, impressive, remarkable, outstanding
OPPOSITE ordinary

memorise VERB
I have to memorise my words for the play.
• to learn, to learn by heart, to remember
OPPOSITE to forget

memory NOUN
❶ *She has happy memories of her childhood.*
• a recollection, an impression
❷ *I will keep this in my memory for ever.*
• mind, remembrance

melt

mend VERB
❶ *Can you mend my bike?*
• to fix, to repair
❷ *They had to mend their old clothes.*
• to patch, to sew up
— To **darn** socks or knitted clothes is to mend them.

mention VERB
❶ *Nobody mentioned the stolen money.*
• to refer to, to speak about, to talk about
❷ *She mentioned that she liked cats.*
• to say, to remark, to reveal, to disclose, to let out

mercy NOUN
The evil queen showed no mercy.
• compassion, pity, sympathy, kindness
OPPOSITE cruelty

merit NOUN
The idea has a lot of merit.
• quality, value, worth, excellence

merit VERB
His claim merits consideration.
• to deserve, to be entitled to, to be worth,

merry ADJECTIVE
The postman was whistling a merry tune.
• cheerful, happy, jolly, bright, joyful, lively
OPPOSITE gloomy

mess NOUN
Who's going to clear up this mess?
• clutter, muddle, untidiness, disorder, chaos, confusion, jumble, litter

mess VERB
➤ **to mess about**
We spent the day messing about on the beach.
• to play about, to fool around, to muck about *(informal)*
— To **lie about**, **lounge about** or **loll about** is to lie or sit in a relaxed way not doing anything.

message NOUN
Did you get my message?
• a note, a letter, a text, an email, a communication
— A **post** is a message you put on a website.

messy ADJECTIVE
My bedroom is really messy!
• untidy, muddled, cluttered, disorderly, disorganised, chaotic, dirty
OPPOSITE neat

met *(past tense of* **meet***)*

metal NOUN

WORD WEB

brass

SOME COMMON METALS:

• aluminium, brass, bronze, chrome, copper, gold, iron, lead, magnesium, mercury, pewter, platinum, silver, steel, tin, zinc
— An **alloy** is a metal made from a mixture of other metals.
— **Ore** is rock with metal in it.
— Something that looks or sounds like metal is **metallic**.

ore

mercury

method NOUN
My granny has a secret method for making jam.
• a technique, a way, a procedure, a process

middle NOUN
A scarecrow stood in the middle of the field.
• the centre, the midpoint
》 *Look at* **centre**.

middle ADJECTIVE
He drove along the middle lane.
• central

might NOUN
I banged at the door with all my might.
• strength, power, energy, force, vigour

mild ADJECTIVE
❶ *He's a mild person who never gets angry.*
• gentle, kind, placid, good-tempered
OPPOSITES difficult, bad-tempered
❷ *The weather was quite mild.*
• pleasant, warm, temperate
OPPOSITE severe
❸ *The soup had a mild flavour.*
• delicate, subtle, bland
OPPOSITE strong
❹ *It was only a mild illness.*
• slight
OPPOSITE serious

mind NOUN
❶ *Her mind was very sharp.*
• brain, intelligence, understanding, wit, judgement, reasoning
❷ *I had an image of him in my mind.*
• brain, head, imagination, memory
➤ **to change your mind**
I've changed my mind—I will come with you after all.
• to reconsider, to rethink, to have second thoughts

mind VERB
❶ *They won't mind if I'm late.*
• to bother, to care, to worry, to be upset, to be annoyed, to object, to disapprove
❷ *Mind the step!*
• to look out for, to watch out for, to beware of, to be careful of

minimum NOUN
❶ *The minimum we could charge is 50 pence.*
• the smallest amount, the least
OPPOSITE maximum
❷ *This line shows where the water reached its minimum.*
• lowest level, lowest point
OPPOSITE maximum
➤ **a minimum of**
You need a minimum of four players.
• at least

minimum ADJECTIVE
Set the oven to the minimum temperature.
• least, smallest, lowest
OPPOSITE maximum

minor ADJECTIVE
❶ *I only had a minor part in the play.*
• small, unimportant, insignificant
OPPOSITE major
❷ *It was only a minor problem.*
• slight, insignificant, unimportant, mild, petty
OPPOSITE severe

miraculous ADJECTIVE
The patient made a miraculous recovery.
• amazing, astonishing, astounding, extraordinary, incredible, marvellous, unbelievable, wonderful, mysterious, inexplicable

misbehave VERB
My puppy has been misbehaving again!
• to behave badly, to be naughty, to be disobedient, to be cheeky
OPPOSITE to behave

mischief NOUN
The twins are always getting up to mischief.
• naughtiness, bad behaviour, disobedience, cheekiness

miserable ADJECTIVE
❶ *You look miserable—what's the matter?*
• sad, unhappy, gloomy, glum, depressed, dejected, melancholy, mournful, tearful
OPPOSITES cheerful, happy
❷ *The weather was cold and miserable.*
• dismal, dreary, depressing, unpleasant
OPPOSITE pleasant

misery NOUN
He felt such misery when he had to leave.
• sadness, sorrow, unhappiness, grief, distress, despair, anguish, torment, heartache
OPPOSITE happiness

misfortune NOUN
They had suffered a lot of misfortune.
• bad luck, trouble, hardship

miss VERB
❶ *The arrow missed the target.*
• to fall short of, to go wide of
OPPOSITE to hit
❷ *I missed my home when I was away.*
• to long for, to yearn for, to pine for, to mourn, to grieve for
❸ *If we leave now, we should miss the traffic.*
• to avoid

missing ADJECTIVE
She found the missing keys in a drawer.
• lost, mislaid, misplaced, absent

mission NOUN
She was sent on a secret mission.
• an expedition, a journey, a voyage, a quest, a venture, an adventure, an operation

mist NOUN
❶ *We drove slowly through the mist.*
• fog, haze, cloud, drizzle
❷ *I couldn't see because of the mist on my glasses.*
• condensation, steam

mistake NOUN
This piece of writing is full of mistakes.
• an error, a blunder, a slip, a lapse
— A **misspelling** is a spelling mistake.
— A **misprint** is a mistake in a printed book.

mistake VERB mistakes, mistaking, mistook, mistaken
➤ **to mistake someone for someone**
She mistook me for my brother.
• to get someone mixed up with, to confuse someone with, to get someone confused with, to get someone muddled up with, to muddle someone up with

misunderstand VERB misunderstands, misunderstanding, misunderstood
I think you misunderstood what I said.
• to mistake, to get wrong, to miss the point of
OPPOSITE to understand

mix VERB
❶ *If you mix red and white you get pink.*
• to combine, to blend, to put together, to mingle

2 *Put all the ingredients in a bowl and mix them.*
• to stir, to blend, to beat, to whisk
➤ **to mix something up**
Please don't mix up my papers.
• to muddle, to jumble, to confuse
— To mix up playing cards is to **shuffle** them.

mixed *ADJECTIVE*
The pudding was made with mixed berries.
• assorted, various, varied, different

mixture *NOUN*
1 *Sleet is a mixture of rain and snow.*
• a blend, a combination
2 *Pour the pancake mixture into a pan.*
• mix, batter
3 *There's an odd mixture of things in the drawer.*
• an assortment, a variety, a collection, a jumble

moan *VERB*
1 *The wounded warrior moaned in pain.*
• to groan, to cry out, to wail, to howl
— To **wail** or to **howl** is to give a long loud high cry.
— To **whimper** is to give a soft trembling cry.
2 *Stop moaning about the food.*
• to complain, to grumble, to grouse, to whine

mobile *ADJECTIVE*
A mobile library visits once a fortnight.
• movable, travelling
— Use **portable** for something that you can carry around.
OPPOSITE stationary

mock *VERB*
They mocked his clothes.
• to make fun of, to laugh at, to ridicule, to scoff at, to jeer at, to sneer at

model *NOUN*
1 *I'm building a model of a space rocket.*
• a copy, a replica, a toy
2 *Your phone is like mine, but a newer model.*
• a version, a design, a type

model *ADJECTIVE*
1 *I built a model aeroplane.*
• miniature, toy
2 *She's a model pupil.*
• ideal, perfect

model *VERB*
The artist models figures in clay.
• make, mould, shape, construct, fashion

moderate *ADJECTIVE*
Her first book was a moderate success.
• average, fair, modest, medium, reasonable
OPPOSITE exceptional

modern *ADJECTIVE*
1 *All the equipment in their kitchen was modern.*
• new, up-to-date, advanced, high-tech, the latest
OPPOSITE out-of-date
2 *She has a very modern haircut.*
• fashionable, stylish, trendy
OPPOSITE old-fashioned

modest *ADJECTIVE*
1 *He's very modest about his success.*
• humble, quiet, reserved, shy, bashful
OPPOSITE conceited
2 *Although they were rich, they lived in a modest house.*
• ordinary, normal, average
OPPOSITE showy

moisture *NOUN*
There is a lot of moisture in the air.
• damp, water, liquid, wetness, humidity

moment *NOUN*
1 *Could you please wait a moment?*
• a minute, a second, an instant
2 *At that moment, all the lights went out.*
• a point, an instant, a time

money *NOUN*
How much money do you have with you?
• cash, currency, funds, finance
— A large amount of money is **riches**, **wealth** or a **fortune**: *His invention brought him great wealth.*

monster *NOUN*
A sea monster reared its head above the waves.
• a beast, a creature, a brute

 WORD WEB

SOME TYPES OF MONSTER:
• a dragon, a giant, an ogre, a troll, a vampire, a werewolf

 WRITING TIPS

Here are some useful words for writing about a monster:

WAYS TO DESCRIBE A MONSTER:
• fearsome, terrifying, terrible, hideous, horrible, mythical, legendary, prehistoric, cruel, vicious, fierce, ferocious, winged, scaly, slimy, hairy
Towering over them, with glittering black eyes and sharp yellow teeth, was a huge brown hairy monster.
—SWITCH 1: SPIDER STAMPEDE, Ali Sparkes

mood NOUN
*What sort of **mood** is he in today?*
• a temper, a humour, a state of mind, a disposition

moody ADJECTIVE
*Why are you so **moody** today?*
• sulky, sullen, grumpy, bad-tempered, irritable
OPPOSITE cheerful

moon NOUN

 WRITING TIPS

Here are some useful words for writing about the **moon**:

THINGS THE MOON DOES:

• to shine, to gleam, to glow, to beam, to cast a light, to rise, to appear, to break through the clouds, to peep through the clouds, to ride in the sky, to hang over the horizon
— When the moon **wanes**, the bright part you can see gets smaller.
— When the moon **waxes**, it gets fuller.

WORDS FOR DESCRIBING THE MOON:

• crescent, full, new, three-quarter, waning, waxing, pale, bright, gleaming, plump, round
— Lunar means 'to do with the moon'.
Gradually it grew darker and darker, and then a pale three-quarter moon came up over the tops of the clouds and cast an eerie light over the whole scene.
—JAMES AND THE GIANT PEACH, Roald Dahl

moor NOUN
*The tower stood on a windswept **moor**.*
• moorland, heath

moral ADJECTIVE
*She was a very **moral** person.*
• good, honest, truthful, decent, honourable, righteous
OPPOSITE immoral

moral NOUN
*The **moral** of this story is that crime doesn't pay.*
• lesson, message, meaning

more DETERMINER
*The soup needs **more** pepper.*
• extra, further, added, additional
OPPOSITE less

morning NOUN
➤ **in the morning**
*The expedition set off early **in the morning**.*
• at daybreak, at dawn, at first light, at sunrise

mosque NOUN
»» *For places of worship look at **building**.*

mostly ADVERB
*I spend my money **mostly** on books.*
• mainly, largely, chiefly, generally, typically

motion NOUN
*He summoned the waiter with a **motion** of his hand.*
• a gesture, a movement

motive NOUN
*The police can find no **motive** for the crime.*
• a cause, a reason, a purpose, grounds

mound NOUN
❶ *Her desk was covered with **mounds** of paper.*
• a heap, a pile, a stack, a mass
❷ *There used to be a castle on top of that **mound**.*
• a hill, a rise, a hump
— A **barrow** is an ancient mound of earth over a grave.

mount VERB
❶ *She **mounted** the pony and rode off.*
• to get on, to jump onto
❷ *The butler slowly **mounted** the stairs.*
• to go up, to climb, to ascend
❸ *The gallery is **mounting** a new exhibition.*
• to put up, to set up, to display

mountain NOUN
*We climbed to the top of the **mountain**.*
• a peak, a hill
— The **summit** of a mountain is the top.
— A **mountain range** is a group or line of mountains.
— A **mountainous** area has many mountains.

 WRITING TIPS

Here are some useful words for writing about **mountains**:

SOME WORDS TO DESCRIBE A MOUNTAIN:

• barren, craggy, icy, jagged, lofty, looming, massive, misty, rocky, rugged, shrouded in mist, snow-capped, snowy, soaring, towering

THINGS YOU MIGHT SEE ON OR NEAR A MOUNTAIN:

• an avalanche, a boulder, a crag, a glacier, a glen, a gorge, a ledge, a mountain pass, a mountain stream, a precipice, a ridge, a torrent, rocks, a valley
Around them sat jagged snow-covered mountains, the peaks of many smothered by thick cloud.—VILLAIN.
NET 2: DARK HUNTER, Andy Briggs

mourn VERB
He was still mourning the loss of his friend.
• to grieve for, to lament for

mouth NOUN
❶ *The crocodile slept with its mouth wide open.*
• jaws
— A dog's muzzle is its nose and mouth.
❷ *They lived in a village at the mouth of the river.*
• an outlet
— An estuary or a firth (Scottish) is a wide river mouth.
❸ *The mouth of the cave was hidden by trees.*
• the entrance, the opening

move VERB

move NOUN
❶ *Don't make a move!*
• a movement, a motion, a gesture
❷ *The spy was watching their every move.*
• an action, a step, a deed, a manoeuvre
❸ *Is it my move next?*
• a turn, a go, a chance, an opportunity

movement NOUN
The robot made a sudden jerky movement.
• a motion, a move, an action, a gesture

moving ADJECTIVE
The story was so moving that I started to cry.
• emotional, touching, affecting, sad

OVERUSED WORD

Try to use a more interesting word when you want to say **move**. Here are some ideas and examples:

TO MOVE SOMETHING FROM ONE PLACE TO ANOTHER:
• to carry, to push, to pull, to drag, to transport, to transfer, to shift
They shifted the piano into the front room.

TO MOVE FROM A POSITION:
• to go, to leave, to depart, to budge
The camel stared and refused to budge.

TO MOVE QUICKLY:
• to hurry, to dash, to dart, to race, to run, to rush, to hurtle, to speed, to sprint, to streak, to scramble, to scurry, to whizz
» *Look at run.*
They hurtled back through the overgrown weeds, shoving Piddle under the fence and scrambling after him as fast as they could go.—SWITCH 1: SPIDER STAMPEDE, Ali Sparkes

TO MOVE SLOWLY:
• to amble, to crawl, to dawdle, to saunter, to slouch, to stroll
Yawning and grumbling, the Weasleys slouched outside with Harry behind them.—HARRY POTTER AND THE CHAMBER OF SECRETS, J. K. Rowling

TO MOVE TOWARDS SOMETHING:
• to advance, to approach, to come, to proceed, to progress
The lookout saw a pirate ship approaching.

TO MOVE AWAY:
• to back, to retreat, to reverse, to withdraw
The serpent retreated, hissing, into its lair.

TO MOVE DOWNWARDS:
• to drop, to descend, to fall, to sink, to swoop
A pair of vultures swooped down from the sky.

TO MOVE UPWARDS:
• to rise, to ascend, to climb, to mount, to soar
A hot-air balloon soared into the sky.

TO MOVE GRACEFULLY:
• to flow, to glide, to slide, to drift
Some swans glided gently across the pond.

TO MOVE CLUMSILY:
• to stumble, to stagger, to flounder, to lurch, to lumber, to shuffle, to totter, to trundle
The ogre stumbled up the narrow steps.

TO MOVE STEALTHILY:
• to creep, to crawl, to edge, to inch, to slink, to slip, to sneak, to steal, to tiptoe
The secret agent edged carefully along the wall.
» *To describe how an animal or bird moves look at* **animal** *and* **bird**.

descend and slither

sprint

amble

a
b
c
d
e
f
g
h
i
j
k
l
m
n
o
p
u
x
y
z

mud NOUN

The tractor left a trail of **mud** on the road.

• dirt, muck, soil, earth, sludge

muddle VERB

❶ Who **muddled** the papers on my desk?

• to mix up, to mess up, to jumble up, to shuffle

OPPOSITE to tidy

❷ They got **muddled** and took the wrong turning.

• to confuse, to bewilder, to puzzle, to perplex

muddle NOUN

Her clothes were all in a **muddle** on the floor.

• a jumble, a mess, a tangle, confusion

muddy ADJECTIVE

❶ Take off your **muddy** shoes.

• dirty, messy, mucky, filthy

OPPOSITE clean

❷ The ground was too **muddy** to play.

• boggy, marshy, waterlogged, wet, swampy

OPPOSITES dry, firm

mumble VERB

We couldn't hear the actor as he was **mumbling**.

• to mutter, to talk indistinctly

murmur VERB

We heard voices **murmuring** in the room above.

• to mutter, to mumble, to whisper

museum NOUN

 WORD WEB

THINGS YOU MIGHT SEE IN A MUSEUM:

• an amphora, an artefact, a Canopic jar, a crown, a fossil, a frieze, hieroglyphics, a mask, a mosaic, a mummy, a papyrus, a relic, a sceptre, a skeleton, a statue

PEOPLE WHO WORK AT A MUSEUM:

— A **curator** is someone who looks after the objects in a museum.

— An **archaeologist** is someone who studies ancient civilisations from the remains of buildings and objects.

— An **Egyptologist** is someone who studies the civilisation of ancient Egypt.

— A **palaeontologist** is someone who studies prehistoric fossils.

» Look at **dinosaur**.

music NOUN

They heard beautiful **music** coming from the garden.

• a tune, a melody, a song

 **WORD WEB**

VARIOUS KINDS OF MUSIC:

• blues, classical music, country and western, dance music, disco music, folk music, gospel, hiphop, jazz, opera, pop music, punk, rap, reggae, rock, soul

FAMILIES OF MUSICAL INSTRUMENTS:

• brass, keyboard, percussion, strings, woodwind

SOME STRINGED INSTRUMENTS:

• a banjo, a cello, a double bass, a guitar, a harp, a lute, a sitar, a ukulele, a viola, a violin

SOME BRASS INSTRUMENTS:

• a bugle, a cornet, a French horn, a horn, a trombone, a trumpet, a tuba

SOME OTHER INSTRUMENTS PLAYED BY BLOWING:

• bagpipes, a bassoon, a clarinet, a flute, an oboe, a pipe, a recorder, a saxophone

a tambourine

cymbals

a drum kit

a harp

a clarinet

SOME KEYBOARD INSTRUMENTS:

• an accordion, a keyboard, an organ, a piano, a synthesiser

SOME PERCUSSION INSTRUMENTS:

• cymbals, a drum, a tambourine, a triangle, a xylophone

PEOPLE WHO PLAY INSTRUMENTS:

• a bugler, a cellist, a clarinettist, a drummer, a flautist, a guitarist, a harpist, an oboist, an organist, a pianist, a piper, a trombonist, a trumpeter, a violinist

The sweet music, so haunting and compelling, seemed to rise up among the trees, floating mysteriously to and fro, now loud, now faint, but all the time dwindling and dying, until it was heard no more . . .
—THE LITTLE GREY MEN, B.B.

a trumpet

an accordion

a sitar

mutual ADJECTIVE
*It is in our **mutual** interest to work together.*
• joint, common, shared

mysterious ADJECTIVE
*They uncovered a **mysterious** sign on the wall.*
• strange, puzzling, baffling, mystifying, perplexing, curious, weird

mystery NOUN
*What really happened was a **mystery**.*
• a puzzle, a riddle, a secret, an enigma

mystify VERB
*The strange message **mystified** us.*
• to puzzle, to baffle, to bewilder, to perplex

myth NOUN

✸ WORD WEB

CREATURES FOUND IN MYTHS AND LEGENDS:

• the Abominable Snowman, a banshee, a basilisk, a centaur, a Cyclops, a dragon, a dwarf, an elf, a fairy, a genie, a giant, a gnome, a goblin, an imp, a kraken, a leprechaun, a mermaid, the Minotaur, a nymph, an ogre, a phoenix, a pixie, a serpent, a siren, a sprite, a troll, a unicorn, a vampire, a werewolf, a yeti

First came an animal that Connie recognized immediately as a unicorn . . . [A] gilded horn rose majestically from the centre of its forehead, and a silver mane foamed down its neck, scintillating with reflected flame.—COMPANIONS 1: SECRET OF THE SIRENS, Julia Golding

» *Look at* **dragon** *and* **fairy**.

mythical ADJECTIVE
*The unicorn is a **mythical** beast.*
• fabulous, fanciful, imaginary, invented, fictional, legendary, mythological
OPPOSITE real

a b c d e f g h i j k l **m** n o p q r s t u v w x y z

A B C D E F G H I J K L M N O P Q R S T U V W X Y Z

⚙ Can you think of 5 different words to describe a nice person?

⚙ Can you think of a word to describe
a) a nice smell
b) nice food
c) nice weather?

⚙ Check the thesaurus to find answers!

nag *VERB*
*He was always **nagging** her to work harder.*
• to badger, to pester, to scold

naked *ADJECTIVE*
*The baby lay **naked** on the mat.*
• bare, nude, undressed
OPPOSITE clothed

name *NOUN*
❶ *I don't know her brother's **name**.*
• a first name, a forename
— A **surname** or a **family name** is the name shared by members of a family.
— A **Christian name** is a name given to a Christian when he or she is baptised.
— A **nickname** is something people call you instead of your real name.
❷ *What is the **name** used for this device?*
• a term

name *VERB*
❶ *We **named** the puppy Buster.*
• to call
❷ *Can you **name** the city in this picture?*
• to identify, to recognise
❸ *The team has **named** a new coach.*
• to nominate, to choose, to select, to appoint

narrow *ADJECTIVE*
*The rabbit squeezed through a **narrow** opening in the fence.*
• thin, slender, slim
OPPOSITE wide

nasty *ADJECTIVE*
❶ *Don't be **nasty** to your brother.*
• unkind, unpleasant, mean, malicious, spiteful, cruel, unfriendly, disagreeable
❷ *There was a **nasty** smell coming from the bin.*
• unpleasant, offensive, disgusting, repulsive, revolting, horrible, foul, rotten
OPPOSITES agreeable, pleasant
» *Look at* **bad**.

nation *NOUN*
*People from many **nations** compete in the Olympic Games.*
• a country, a state, a land

natural *ADJECTIVE*
❶ *This jumper is made of **natural** wool.*
• real, genuine, pure
OPPOSITE artificial
❷ *It's only **natural** to be nervous before an exam.*
• normal, common, understandable, reasonable, usual
OPPOSITE unnatural

nature *NOUN*
❶ *I like TV programmes about **nature**.*
• natural history, wildlife
❷ *She has a very kind **nature**.*
• a character, a disposition, a personality

naughty ADJECTIVE
The children were being quite naughty.
• bad, badly behaved, disobedient, mischievous, unruly, rude, cheeky, troublesome
OPPOSITE well–behaved

near PREPOSITION
Our house is near the school.
• close to, not far from, nearby, handy for, convenient for, accessible from, round the corner from

nearly ADVERB
Thank goodness, it's nearly lunchtime!
• almost, practically, virtually, just about, approaching

neat ADJECTIVE
❶ *Please leave the room as neat as possible.*
• clean, orderly, tidy, trim
❷ *Her handwriting is very neat.*
• precise, skilful, tidy
OPPOSITE untidy

necessary ADJECTIVE
It is necessary to water plants in dry weather.
• essential, required, important, vital, crucial, needed
OPPOSITE unnecessary

need VERB
❶ *I need a pound coin for the locker.*
• to require, to want, to be short of, to lack
❷ *The charity needs our support.*
• to depend on, to rely on
need NOUN
There's a need for more shops in our area.
• a call, a demand, a requirement

negative ADJECTIVE
Tourism does have some negative effects.
• bad, harmful, damaging, undesirable, destructive
OPPOSITE positive
negative NOUN
We listed the negatives and positives of the plan.
• a disadvantage, a drawback, an inconvenience, a problem
OPPOSITE positive

neglect VERB
She's been neglecting her work.
• to forget, to ignore, to overlook, to disregard, to pay no attention to

negotiate VERB
I negotiated with dad over my pocket money.
• to bargain, to haggle, to deal, to discuss

neighbourhood NOUN
They live in a very nice neighbourhood.
• an area, a district, a community

nervous ADJECTIVE
I felt nervous before I went on stage.
• anxious, worried, apprehensive, jumpy, tense, agitated, uneasy, restless
OPPOSITE calm

neutral ADJECTIVE
A referee has to be neutral.
• impartial, fair, unbiased
OPPOSITE biased

new ADJECTIVE
❶ *Start on a new sheet of paper.*
• clean, fresh, unused
— Something new and unused is **in mint condition.**
❷ *The hospital has very new equipment.*
• modern, current, up-to-date, high-tech, latest, recent
❸ *See if you can think of some new ideas.*
• fresh, original, novel, innovative, creative, different
OPPOSITE old

news NOUN
Have you got any news about Tom?
• information, a report
— A **bulletin** is a short news announcement.

next ADJECTIVE
❶ *He lives in the house next to the chip shop.*
• adjacent, closest, nearest
OPPOSITE distant
❷ *If you miss the bus, you can catch the next one.*
• following, subsequent
OPPOSITE previous

nice ADJECTIVE

 OVERUSED WORD

Try to use a more interesting word when you want to say **nice**. Here are some ideas and examples:

FOR A NICE PERSON:

• good, kind, helpful, thoughtful, generous, caring, likeable, charming, friendly, pleasant, warm
[He] no longer trusted Janey. It was hard because she was still so likeable, so warm and bright and caring.
—SHAPESHIFTER 5: STIRRING THE STORM, Ali Sparkes

FOR A NICE EXPERIENCE:

• delightful, enjoyable, wonderful, marvellous, splendid, fantastic
We had an enjoyable time on holiday.

FOR SOMETHING THAT LOOKS NICE:

• beautiful, attractive, pleasing, lovely, pretty
— Use **gorgeous** or **stunning** for something that looks very nice.
The view from the top of the hill is stunning.

FOR A NICE SMELL:

• fragrant, sweet-smelling, scented, perfumed

FOR NICE FOOD:

• delicious, tasty, appetising, mouth-watering
The fruit was so daintily colored and so fragrant, and looked so appetizing and delicious that Dorothy stopped and exclaimed: 'What is it, do you s'pose?'
—DOROTHY AND THE WIZARD OF OZ, L. Frank Baum

FOR NICE WEATHER:

• fine, fair, beautiful, sunny, warm
— Use **glorious** for very nice weather.
It was a glorious day for our picnic.
» For other ways to describe something you like look at **good**.

night NOUN
Badgers usually come out at night.
• night-time, dark
— Animals which are active at night are **nocturnal** animals.

noise NOUN
❶ *There is too much noise in here.*
• a din, a racket, a row, an uproar, a commotion, a tumult, a cacophony, pandemonium
❷ *I heard a strange noise outside.*
• a sound
» For various noises look at **sound**.

noisy ADJECTIVE
❶ *The people next door were playing noisy music.*
• loud, blaring, booming, deafening, thunderous
❷ *The children are very noisy this morning.*
• rowdy, boisterous, talkative
OPPOSITE quiet

nonsense NOUN
Stop talking nonsense!
• rubbish, drivel, gibberish, gobbledegook

normal ADJECTIVE
❶ *It was just a normal day.*
• ordinary, average, standard, typical, usual, routine
❷ *It's normal to feel tired at the end of the day.*
• natural, common, usual, reasonable, understandable
OPPOSITE abnormal

nose NOUN
❶ *He stuck his nose into the flower.*
— A **muzzle** or a **snout** is an animal's nose.
— To **nuzzle** something is to rub it with your nose.
❷ *I sat in the nose of the boat hoping to spot a dolphin.*
• the front, the bow, the prow

a bottlenose dolphin

nosy *ADJECTIVE (informal)*
*Stop being so **nosy** and asking all these questions!*
• curious, prying, snooping
– **Inquisitive** is a positive way to say 'nosy'.
– If someone tries to find things out in a nosy way, you can say that they **pry** or **snoop**.

note *NOUN*
*I found a **note** saying that he would be home for tea.*
• a message, a letter, a reminder, a communication

note *VERB*
❶ *They **noted** landmarks along the way.*
• to notice, to spot, to take note of, to pay attention to, to heed, to observe
❷ *The detective **noted** the address on a scrap of paper.*
• to jot down, to make a note of, to write down, to record, to scribble

nothing *NOUN*
*Four minus four equals **nothing**.*
• nought, zero, nil

notice *NOUN*
*Someone put up a **notice** about the meeting.*
• a sign, a poster, an advertisement
➤ **to take notice of something**
*They **took** no **notice of** the warning.*
• to heed, to pay attention to, to attend to, to note

notice *VERB*
❶ *Did you **notice** what he was wearing?*
• to note, to spot, to take note of, to pay attention to, to heed, to observe
❷ *I **noticed** a funny smell in the room.*
• to become aware of, to detect, to note, to sense

noticeable *ADJECTIVE*
❶ *There has been a **noticeable** improvement in the weather.*
• definite, distinct, notable, significant
❷ *The tower is **noticeable** for miles around.*
• visible, conspicuous, prominent

notorious *ADJECTIVE*
*He was a **notorious** liar as well as a thief.*
• infamous, well-known, disgraceful, scandalous

now *ADVERB*
❶ *My cousins are **now** living in Melbourne.*
• at present, at the moment, currently, nowadays
❷ *I'll phone her **now**.*
• immediately, at once, straight away, without delay, instantly

I will be home for tea!
Pete
x x x

a note

nuisance *NOUN*
*The traffic noise is a real **nuisance**.*
• an annoyance, an irritation, an inconvenience, a bother, a problem, a drawback, a pest

number *NOUN*
❶ *Add the **numbers** together to get the answer.*
• a figure
– A **numeral** is a symbol that represents a number.
– A **digit** is any of the numerals from 0 to 9.
❷ *A large **number** of people applied for the job.*
• an amount, a quantity, a group, a bunch *(informal)*
– A **handful** is a small number of things or people.
– A **host** or a **multitude** of things or people is a large number of them.

numerous *ADJECTIVE*
*There are **numerous** spelling mistakes on this page.*
• many, a lot of, lots of, plenty of, countless, myriad, untold
OPPOSITE few

nut *NOUN*

🕸 **WORD WEB**

SOME KINDS OF NUT:

• an acorn, an almond, a cashew, a chestnut, a coconut, a conker, a hazelnut, a macadamia, a peanut, a pistachio, a walnut

a coconut

walnuts

pistachios

peanuts

almonds

macadamias

hazelnuts

⚙ Can you think of 3 different words for 'old'?

⚙ Can you think of 3 words to describe something that is 'old and in bad condition'?

⚙ Check the thesaurus to find answers!

obedient *ADJECTIVE*
The dog seems very **obedient**.
• good, well-behaved, disciplined, manageable
OPPOSITE disobedient

obey *VERB*
We have to **obey** the rules.
• to follow, to abide by, to carry out, to keep to, to respect
OPPOSITE to disobey

object *NOUN*
❶ What is that strange **object**?
• an article, an item, a thing
❷ The **object** of the game is to match all the cards.
• the aim, the point, the purpose, the goal, the intention, the objective

object *VERB*
➤ to object to something
Several people **objected** to the plan.
• to oppose, to complain about, to disapprove of, to disagree with, to protest against
OPPOSITES to accept, to support

objection *NOUN*
The lawyer made an **objection**.
• a protest, a complaint, opposition, disapproval, disagreement

objective *NOUN*
Their **objective** was to reach the top of the hill.
• an aim, a goal, an intention, a target, an ambition, an object, a purpose

observant *ADJECTIVE*
If you're **observant**, you might see a fox.
• alert, sharp-eyed, watchful
OPPOSITE unobservant

observe *VERB*
❶ We **observed** the birds in their natural habitat.
• to watch, to study, to look at, to view
❷ I **observed** footprints in the snow.
• to notice, to note, to see, to detect, to spot, to perceive

obsession *NOUN*
Football is Frank's **obsession**.
• a passion, an addiction

obstacle *NOUN*
❶ There was an **obstacle** in the road.
• an obstruction, a barrier, a blockage, a block
❷ His shyness was an **obstacle** to making friends.
• a problem, a difficulty, a hindrance, a hurdle, a hitch, a snag

obstinate *ADJECTIVE*
The **obstinate** camel refused to budge.
• stubborn, wilful, determined, uncooperative
OPPOSITE cooperative

obtain *VERB*
You must **obtain** your parents' consent.
• to get, to acquire, to be given

obvious *ADJECTIVE*
❶ He told some **obvious** lies.
• glaring, evident, blatant, unmistakable, clear, apparent
❷ The tower is **obvious** from miles around.
• conspicuous, notable, noticeable, prominent, visible
OPPOSITE inconspicuous

obviously *ADVERB*
❶ She was **obviously** upset.
• clearly, evidently, unmistakably, undeniably, visibly
❷ **Obviously**, you need to know the password.
• of course, naturally, clearly

occasion *NOUN*
❶ The wedding was a happy **occasion**.
• an event, a happening, an incident, an occurrence
❷ I've been to London on several **occasions**.
• a time, a moment, an instance

occasional ADJECTIVE
*We have **occasional** disagreements.*
• odd, irregular, infrequent
OPPOSITES frequent, regular

occasionally ADVERB
*I see my cousins **occasionally**, but not often.*
• sometimes, now and again, from time to time, once in a while, every so often
OPPOSITES frequently, often

occupation NOUN
❶ *Being a teacher sounds like an interesting occupation.*
• a job, a profession, a career, work, employment
» *For various occupations look at* **job**.
❷ *Vivek's favourite **occupation** is reading.*
• an activity, a hobby, a pastime, a pursuit

occupy VERB
❶ *He found someone already **occupying** his chair.*
• to use, to fill, to take, to sit in
— To occupy a home is to **live in**, **dwell in** or **inhabit** it.
❷ *We must find something to **occupy** the children.*
• to keep busy, to amuse, to divert

occur VERB
*She told us what had **occurred**.*
• to happen, to take place, to come about, to arise
➤ **to occur to someone**
*An idea **occurred** to me.*
• to strike, to dawn on, to hit, to come to

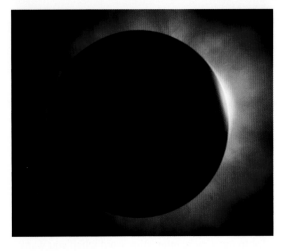

occurrence NOUN
*An eclipse of the sun is an unusual **occurrence**.*
• an event, a happening, an incident, a phenomenon

odd ADJECTIVE
❶ *Her behaviour seemed **odd**.*
• strange, unusual, peculiar, curious, bizarre, puzzling, funny, weird, eccentric
OPPOSITE normal
❷ *He could only find two **odd** socks.*
• single, spare, unmatching
OPPOSITE matching

offend VERB
*I hope my joke didn't **offend** you.*
• to upset, to annoy, to give or cause offence to, to insult, to hurt someone's feelings, to anger, to displease, to annoy

offensive ADJECTIVE
❶ *He apologised for his **offensive** remarks.*
• insulting, rude, upsetting, impolite
❷ *The gas has an **offensive** smell.*
• unpleasant, disgusting, revolting, repulsive, nasty, foul, vile
OPPOSITE pleasant

offer VERB
❶ *He **offered** to do the washing-up.*
• to volunteer, to propose
❷ *She **offered** a reward for anyone who found her cat.*
• to propose, to put forward, to make available

offer NOUN
*I accepted their **offer** of help.*
• a proposal, a suggestion

official *ADJECTIVE*
*The teacher told us she is leaving, but there hasn't been an **official** announcement yet.*
• formal, authorised, proper
OPPOSITE unofficial

often *ADVERB*
❶ *It **often** rains in April.*
• frequently, regularly, routinely
❷ *To my annoyance, he was **often** late.*
• frequently, regularly, time after time, again and again, repeatedly, constantly

old *ADJECTIVE*

 OVERUSED WORD

Try to use a more interesting word when you want to say **old**. Here are some ideas and examples:

FOR AN OLD PERSON:

• aged, elderly, senior
— Use **venerable** for someone old and respected.
OPPOSITE young
'What are you doing here?' said someone, sharply. An aged face was poking at him out of the shadows.
—GOALKEEPER, Sally Prue

FOR AN OLD OBJECT:

• ancient, old-fashioned, out-of-date
— Use **antique** or **vintage** for something old and valuable.
— Use **historical** for something from the past.
OPPOSITES new, modern

an antique phonogram

[The] rock was not rock. It was a door. An ancient wooden door which had aged to the same colour as the rock around them.—DARK SUMMER, Ali Sparkes

an old-fashioned typewriter

FOR SOMETHING OLD AND WORN-OUT:

• worn, shabby, scruffy, tatty, tattered, battered, threadbare
They pulled on their battered old boots and their shabby hats, picked up their walking sticks and set out into the world.—THE NIGHTMARE GAME, Gillian Cross

old-fashioned *ADJECTIVE*
*That hairstyle is quite **old-fashioned** now.*
• out-of-date, out-of-fashion
OPPOSITES modern, up-to-date

omit *VERB*
*His name was **omitted** from the list.*
• to exclude, to leave out, to miss out, to overlook, to skip

ooze *VERB*
*The filling started to **ooze** from my sandwich.*
• to leak, to seep, to escape, to dribble, to drip

opaque *ADJECTIVE*
*The condensation had turned the window **opaque**.*
• cloudy, obscure, unclear, hazy, murky
OPPOSITE transparent

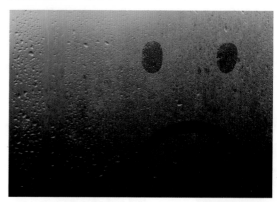

open *ADJECTIVE*
❶ *Someone had left the door **open** and the dog got out.*
• unlocked, unfastened, ajar
OPPOSITE closed
❷ *The library is **open** on Saturdays.*
• accessible, operating, usable
OPPOSITES closed, shut

open *VERB*
❶ *Someone knocked on the door and I went to **open** it.*
• to unfasten, to unlock, to unbolt
❷ *I can't wait to **open** my birthday presents!*
• to undo, to unwrap, to untie
— To open a map is to **unfold** or **unroll** it.
— To open an umbrella is to **unfurl** it.
❸ *The summer fair **opens** at 10 a.m.*
• to begin, to start, to commence
OPPOSITES to close, to shut

opening NOUN
❶ *The sheep got out through an **opening** in the fence.*
• a gap, a hole, a break, a split
– Use a **chink**, a **crack**, a **slit** or a **slot** for a narrow opening.
– A **vent** is an opening to let out gas or let in air.
❷ *The film has a very dramatic **opening**.*
• a beginning, a start

operate VERB
❶ *Do you know how to **operate** this machine?*
• to use, to work, to handle
– Use to **drive** for operating a vehicle.
❷ *The surgeon **operated** to remove her appendix.*
• to carry out an operation, to perform surgery

operation NOUN
❶ *Trying to defuse a bomb is a dangerous **operation**.*
• a task, an activity, an exercise, a mission, a process, a procedure
❷ *He had an **operation** to remove his tonsils.*
• surgery

opinion NOUN
*What's your **opinion** about what we should do?*
• a view, a judgement, an impression, a belief, an attitude, a point of view, a thought, a conclusion

opponent NOUN
*The knight fought bravely against his **opponent**.*
• an enemy, a foe, a rival, a challenger
– Your opponents in a game are the **opposition**.
OPPOSITE ally

opportunity NOUN
*You will have the **opportunity** to ask questions.*
• a chance, an occasion, a moment, time, scope

oppose VERB
*Many people **opposed** the plan to expand the school.*
• to object to, to disapprove of, to disagree with, to be against, to fight against, to resist
OPPOSITES to support, to back

opposite ADJECTIVE
❶ *My friend lives on the **opposite** side of the road.*
• facing, other
❷ *We came to **opposite** conclusions about what happened.*
• contrasting, different, opposing, conflicting, contrary
OPPOSITE similar

opposite NOUN
*She says one thing and does the **opposite**.*
• the contrary, the reverse

opposition NOUN
❶ *There was fierce **opposition** to his plan.*
• resistance, disapproval, disagreement, hostility
OPPOSITE support
❷ *The **opposition** were stronger than our team expected.*
• the opponents, the rivals

optional ADJECTIVE
*Staying after school for homework club is **optional**.*
• voluntary, non-compulsory
OPPOSITE compulsory

oral ADJECTIVE
*She had to take an **oral** exam in French.*
• spoken, verbal
OPPOSITE written

order NOUN
❶ *The captain gave the **order** to abandon ship.*
• a command, an instruction, a direction, a decree
❷ *I've put in an **order** for the new phone.*
• a request, a demand, a reservation, a booking
❸ *The words are in alphabetical **order**.*
• a sequence, an arrangement, a series

order VERB
❶ *She **ordered** them to be quiet.*
• to command, to instruct, to direct, to tell
❷ *He **ordered** the book before it came out.*
• to request, to reserve, to apply for, to book

orderly ADJECTIVE
❶ *The library has an **orderly** system for sorting books.*
• organised, ordered, tidy, neat, methodical
OPPOSITE untidy
❷ *Please form an **orderly** queue.*
• well-behaved, controlled, disciplined
OPPOSITE disorderly

ordinary ADJECTIVE
❶ *It began as a very **ordinary** day.*
• normal, typical, usual, customary, routine
❷ *This is not just an **ordinary** car.*
• standard, average, common, conventional, regular
❸ *It was a very **ordinary** game.*
• mediocre, unexceptional
OPPOSITES special, unusual

a
b
c
d
e
f
g
h
n
o
u
v
w
x
y
z

organisation NOUN
❶ *She works for a charity **organisation**.*
• an institution, a group, an enterprise, a company
❷ *Mum did all the **organisation** for the party.*
• planning, arrangement, organising

organise VERB
❶ *We are **organising** a concert.*
• to plan, to make arrangements for, to arrange, to set up, to hold
❷ *The librarian has to **organise** the books in the library.*
• to arrange, to put in order, to sort, to classify

original ADJECTIVE
❶ *The settlers drove out the **original** inhabitants.*
• earliest, first, initial, native, aboriginal
❷ *The story was very **original**.*
• inventive, new, novel, creative, fresh, imaginative, unusual
❸ *Is that an **original** work of art or a copy?*
• genuine, real, authentic, actual

ornament NOUN
*A few **ornaments** will make the room more attractive.*
• a decoration
— A **bauble** is an ornament you hang on a Christmas tree.

outbreak NOUN
❶ *There was an **outbreak** of flu.*
• an epidemic
❷ *After the **outbreak** of war they left the city.*
• the beginning, the start

outdoor ADJECTIVE
*The hotel had an **outdoor** swimming pool.*
• open-air, out of doors, outside
OPPOSITE indoor

outer ADJECTIVE
*The fishermen wore waterproof **outer** garments.*
• external, exterior, outside
OPPOSITE inner

outfit NOUN
*Katie bought a new **outfit** for the wedding.*
• clothes, a costume, a suit
— A **uniform** is a special outfit someone has to wear for work or school.

outing NOUN
*We went on a family **outing** to the beach.*
• a trip, an excursion, an expedition

outlaw NOUN
*A band of **outlaws** held up the train.*
• a bandit, a brigand, a robber, a criminal, a fugitive

outline NOUN
*We could see the **outline** of some trees in the distance.*
• the profile, the shape, the silhouette, the form

outline VERB
*He **outlined** his plan.*
• to summarise, to sketch out, to give a summary of
➤ **to be outlined against something**
*The mountains were **outlined against** the sky.*
• to be silhouetted, to be cut out, to stand out

outside ADJECTIVE
*Lookouts were stationed on the **outside** wall of the castle.*
• exterior, external, outer

outside NOUN
*Insects have their skeletons on the **outside** of their bodies.*
• the exterior, the shell, the surface
OPPOSITE the inside

outsider NOUN
*She's lived in the village for years, but still feels like an **outsider**.*
• a newcomer, a stranger, a foreigner, an immigrant

outskirts NOUN
*We live on the **outskirts** of town.*
• the edge, the fringe, the outer part
— The **suburbs** are the outskirts of a city.
OPPOSITE the centre

oven NOUN
*The meat was roasting in the **oven**.*
• a cooker, a stove
— A **kiln** is a special oven for baking pottery or bricks.

overwhelm VERB
❶ *The enemy **overwhelmed** us.*
• to defeat, to overcome, to overpower, to crush, to conquer
❷ *A huge wave **overwhelmed** the village.*
• to engulf, to flood, to swamp, to submerge, to swallow up, to bury

own VERB
*It was the first bike she had **owned**.*
• to be the owner of, to have, to possess

owner NOUN
*The **owner** of the shop asked us what we wanted.*
• the manager, the proprietor, the boss

Pp

⚙ A tree and a cactus are two types of plant. Can you think of 3 more?

⚙ Do you know a word for a young plant?
S _ _ D _ _ _ G

⚙ Check the thesaurus to find answers!

pack NOUN
There were four candles in each **pack**.
• a packet, a package, a bundle, a set

pack VERB
❶ It was hard to **pack** everything into the car.
• to load, to cram, to squeeze, to stuff, to jam
❷ They **packed** all the books in boxes.
• to put away, to stow, to load, to store

package NOUN
The postman delivered a big **package**.
• a parcel, a packet

page NOUN
❶ Several **pages** have been torn out of this book.
• a sheet, a leaf
❷ He wrote two **pages** of notes.
• a side
❸ Visit our **page** for more information and games.
• a web page, a website, a site, a screen

paid (past tense of **pay**)

pain NOUN
❶ I have a **pain** in my stomach.
• soreness
— Discomfort is slight pain.
— An **ache** is a dull steady pain.
— A **twinge** or a **pang** is a sudden short pain.
— A **cramp** is a pain caused by a muscle tightening suddenly.
— Agony, torment or torture is very great pain.
❷ Their cruel remarks caused her a lot of **pain**.
• anguish, suffering

😊 **WRITING TIPS**

Here are some helpful words for writing about **pain**:

WORDS TO DESCRIBE PAIN:
• sharp, burning, searing, stabbing, shooting, stinging, throbbing, excruciating, agonising, intense, acute

THINGS SOMEONE IN PAIN MIGHT DO:
• to wince, to gasp, to grimace, to writhe, to twist, to moan, to groan, to yelp, to shriek, to howl, to bellow
A searing pain shot through her leg and she closed her eyes and clamped her teeth together. She would not cry out.—THE HIDDEN KINGDOM, Ian Beck

painful ADJECTIVE
❶ Is your knee still **painful**?
• sore, aching, tender, hurting, stinging, throbbing
OPPOSITE painless
❷ Going there again brought back **painful** memories.
• upsetting, distressing, sad, unpleasant

paint VERB
❶ We **painted** the walls green.
• to colour, to decorate
❷ I **painted** a jug of flowers.
• to depict, to portray, to represent

painting NOUN
» Look at **picture**.

pair NOUN
We worked in **pairs**.
• twos, partners
We worked with **partners**.
— A **couple** is two people who are married or going out together.
— A **duet** or **duo** is two people who sing or play music together.

palace NOUN
» For types of building look at **building**.

pale ADJECTIVE
❶ Are you all right? You look **pale**.
• white, pallid, pasty, ashen, sickly
— To **blanch** is to go pale.
OPPOSITES ruddy, flushed
❷ I used a **pale** blue for the sky.
• light, pastel, faded, faint
OPPOSITES bright, deep

panic NOUN
People fled the streets in **panic**.
• alarm, fright, terror, hysteria

panic VERB

If a fire starts, don't panic!
• to be alarmed, to take fright, to become hysterical, to lose your head

pant VERB

I was panting when I got to the top.
• to gasp, to be out of breath, to wheeze, to puff, to huff and puff

paper NOUN

❶ *The story was on the front page of the paper.*
• a newspaper, a journal
❷ *The doctor had some important papers to sign.*
• a document, a certificate, a deed

 WORD WEB

SOME TYPES OF PAPER:

• card, cardboard, newspaper, notepaper, tissue paper, toilet paper, tracing paper, wrapping paper, writing paper
—A **sheet** or a **leaf** of paper is a piece of it.
—**Papyrus** is paper made from the stems of reeds, used in ancient Egypt.
—**Parchment** is a kind of heavy paper originally made from animal skins.

parade NOUN

A parade passed along the street.
• a procession, a march
— A **pageant** is a parade of people in costumes.

parade VERB

The brass band paraded through the town.
• to march, to troop, to file past

paralysed ADJECTIVE

I was paralysed with fear.
• frozen, immobilised, rooted to the spot

parcel NOUN

The postman delivered a bulky parcel.
• a package, a packet

park NOUN

At lunchtime, we went for a walk in the park.
• gardens, recreation ground
— An **estate** is a park with fields and trees around a big house.

park VERB

He parked his van outside the building.
• to leave, to stop, to position

part NOUN

❶ *The machine has tiny parts.*
• a bit, a component, an element, a portion,

a fraction, a segment, a unit
❷ *She works in another part of the company.*
• a department, a division, a branch
❸ *Granny lives in a nice part of town.*
• an area, a district, a neighbourhood
❹ *The TV series is in four parts.*
• a section, an episode, an instalment
❺ *She got a part in the school play.*
• a character, a role
➤ **to take part**
The whole school is taking part in the show.
• to participate, to engage, to join, to be involved

part VERB

❶ *It was the first time she'd been parted from her parents.*
• to separate, to divide, to remove
OPPOSITE to join
❷ *We parted at the bus stop and each went home.*
• to leave, to depart, to say goodbye, to go your separate ways
OPPOSITE to meet

participate VERB

She participates in a lot of after-school activities.
• to take part, to be involved, to engage, to join

particular ADJECTIVE

❶ *The tickets must be used on a particular day.*
• specific, certain, definite, exact, precise
❷ *The cat's very particular about his food.*
• fussy, awkward, hard to please

partly ADVERB

It was partly my fault that we were late.
• in part, to some extent, up to a point
OPPOSITE entirely

partner NOUN

Choose a partner to work with on the project.
• a friend, a companion, a colleague, a helper
— A **spouse** is a marriage partner.

party NOUN

❶ *We had a class party at the end of term.*
• a celebration, festivities, a gathering, a reception
❷ *A party of tourists was going round the museum.*
• a group, a band, a crowd, a gang

a disco ball

 WORD WEB

SOME KINDS OF PARTY:

• a ball, a banquet, a barbecue, a birthday party, a dance, a disco, a fancy dress party, a wedding reception

pass *VERB*
❶ *She tried to* **pass** *the bike in front.*
• to move past, to go by, to overtake
❷ *Will you* **pass** *me a cup?*
• to hand, to give, to offer
❸ *Do you think you will* **pass** *your music exam?*
• to be successful in, to succeed in, to get through
OPPOSITE to fail

passage *NOUN*
❶ *A secret* **passage** *led from the chamber to the outside.*
• a passageway, a corridor, a tunnel, a path, a route
❷ *Our homework is to choose a favourite* **passage** *from a book.*
• an extract, an episode, a section, a piece, a quotation

passenger *NOUN*
The bus has seats for 55 **passengers**.
• a traveller
— A **commuter** is a passenger who travels regularly to work.

passion *NOUN*
❶ *'Romeo and Juliet' is a story of youthful* **passion**.
• love, emotion
❷ *She has a great* **passion** *for sport.*
• enthusiasm, keenness, love, obsession, zeal

passionate *ADJECTIVE*
❶ *She made a* **passionate** *speech about her beliefs.*
• emotional, intense, powerful, moving
OPPOSITE unemotional
❷ *He is a* **passionate** *football fan.*
• eager, keen, committed, avid, enthusiastic, fervent
OPPOSITE apathetic

past *NOUN*
In the **past**, *things were different.*
• past times, the old days, the olden days, days gone by
OPPOSITE the future

past *ADJECTIVE*
Things were very different in **past** *centuries.*
• earlier, former, previous, old
OPPOSITE future

pat *VERB*
She **patted** *the dog gently.*
• to tap, to touch, to stroke

patch *NOUN*
There's a burnt **patch** *on the grass.*
• an area, a spot, a mark, a blotch

patchy *ADJECTIVE*
There was **patchy** *snow on the ground.*
• uneven, irregular, spotty

path *NOUN*
❶ *We walked along the* **path** *through the gardens.*
• a pathway, a track, a trail, a footpath, a lane, a walk, a walkway
— A **bridleway** is a path for horse-riding.
— A **promenade** is a path for walking by the sea.
— The **pavement** is a path with a hard surface along the side of a street.
» *Look at* **road**.
❷ *The diagram shows the* **path** *of the meteor.*
• a route, a line
— A **circuit** is the path of an electric current.
— An **orbit** is the curved path of something moving around an object in space.

pathetic *ADJECTIVE*
❶ *The abandoned kittens were a* **pathetic** *sight.*
• moving, touching, pitiful, distressing, heartbreaking, sad
❷ *That was a* **pathetic** *effort.*
• hopeless, useless, feeble, terrible

patience *NOUN*
A teacher needs to have a lot of **patience**.
• calmness, tolerance, restraint, self-control, persistence
OPPOSITE impatience

patient *ADJECTIVE*
❶ *The nurse was very* **patient** *with the children.*
• calm, composed, even-tempered, easy-going, tolerant
❷ *It took a lot of* **patient** *work to repair the engine.*
• persevering, persistent, untiring, steady, determined
OPPOSITE impatient

patrol *VERB*
Guards **patrolled** *the area at night.*
• to guard, to keep watch over, to inspect, to tour

patter *NOUN, VERB*
» *For various sounds look at* **sound**.

pattern *NOUN*
Do you like the **pattern** *on this wallpaper?*
• a design, a decoration

 WORD WEB

SOME KINDS OF PATTERN:

• checked, chequered, dotted or dotty, floral or flowery, plaid, a swirl, a spiral, spotted or spotty, striped or stripy, tartan, zigzag

a
b
c
d
e
f
g
h
i
j
k
l
m
n
o
p
q
r
s
t
u
v
w
x
y
z

pause NOUN
*There was a **pause** while she got her breath back.*
• a break, a gap, a halt, a rest, a lull, an interlude, a delay
— An **interval** or an **intermission** is a pause in the middle of a performance.

pause VERB
*I **paused** for a moment before knocking on the door.*
• to hesitate, to wait, to delay, to hang back, to stop

pay VERB **pays, paying, paid**
❶ *How much did you **pay** for your new bike?*
• to spend, to give, to hand over
❷ *Who's going to **pay** the bill?*
• to pay off, to repay, to settle

pay NOUN
*He gave all his **pay** to his mother.*
• wages, salary, income, earnings

payment NOUN
*You can borrow a bike for a **payment** of £5.*
• a charge
— A **fare** is a payment for using public transport.
— A **fee** is a payment for doing a piece of work.
— A **bonus** is an extra payment that someone gets for their work.
— A **tip** is an extra payment given to someone who helps you, such as a waiter or taxi driver.
— A **deposit** is a payment that is part of a larger payment, or that you can get back after you return something.
— A **fine** is a payment someone must make as a punishment.

peace NOUN
❶ *After the war there was a period of **peace**.*
• agreement, harmony, friendliness
— A **truce** is an agreement to stop fighting for a while.
❷ *She enjoys the **peace** of the countryside.*
• calm, peacefulness, quiet, tranquillity, calmness, stillness, silence

peaceful ADJECTIVE
*They enjoyed a **peaceful** day fishing.*
• calm, quiet, relaxing, tranquil, restful, serene, undisturbed, untroubled, soothing
OPPOSITES noisy, troubled

peak NOUN
❶ *The **peak** of the mountain was covered in snow.*
• the summit, the cap, the crest, the crown, the top, the tip
❷ *She is at the **peak** of her career as an athlete.*
• the top, the height, the high point, the climax

peculiar ADJECTIVE
*What's that **peculiar** sound?*
• strange, odd, unusual, curious, extraordinary, funny, weird, bizarre
— Use **eerie** or **uncanny** for something peculiar and slightly frightening.
OPPOSITE ordinary

peel NOUN
*Orange **peel** is used in marmalade.*
• rind, skin

penetrate VERB
*Sunlight could not **penetrate** the thick jungle.*
• to pierce, to get through, to push through, to enter, to infiltrate

people NOUN
❶ *How many **people** are you inviting?*
• persons *(formal)*, individuals, folk
— People as opposed to animals are **humans** or **human beings**.
❷ *The government is elected by the **people**.*
• the population, the citizens, the public

perceive VERB
❶ *They **perceived** something moving in the bushes.*
• to make out, to notice, to observe, to become aware of, to catch sight of, to spot
❷ *I **perceived** that what he said was not true.*
• to realise, to see, to understand, to comprehend, to grasp

perfect *(say per-fikt)* ADJECTIVE
*This is a **perfect** place for a picnic.*
• ideal, excellent, faultless, flawless

perfect *(say per-fekt)* VERB
*Gymnasts spend years **perfecting** their technique.*
• to improve, to refine, to polish, to make something perfect

perform VERB
❶ *Is this your first time **performing** on stage?*
• to appear, to act, to play, to dance, to sing
❷ *The class **performed** a play about pirates.*
• to present, to stage, to produce, to put on
❸ *We **performed** an experiment.*
• to do, to carry out, to conduct

perfume NOUN
*The **perfume** of roses filled the room.*
• a smell, a scent, a fragrance

perhaps ADVERB
Perhaps the weather will improve soon.
• maybe, possibly
OPPOSITE definitely

peril NOUN
*The crew faced many **perils** on their voyage.*
• a danger, a hazard, a risk, a menace, a threat
OPPOSITE safety

perimeter NOUN
*There is a fence around the **perimeter** of the field.*
• the edge, the border, the boundary
— The **circumference** is the line or distance around the edge of a circle.

period NOUN
❶ *After a long **period** of hard work they had a rest.*
• a time, a stretch
❷ *The book is about the Victorian **period**.*
• an age, an era

permanent ADJECTIVE
❶ *Sugar can do **permanent** damage to your teeth.*
• lasting, long-lasting, long-term, everlasting
❷ *Traffic noise is a **permanent** problem in the city centre.*
• never-ending, perpetual, persistent, constant
OPPOSITE temporary

permission NOUN
*They had the teacher's **permission** to leave.*
• consent, agreement, approval

permit *(say* per-mit*)* VERB
*We don't **permit** fishing in the lake.*
• to allow, to consent to, to give permission for, to authorise, to tolerate

permit *(say* per-mit*)* NOUN
*You need a **permit** to park here.*
• a licence, a pass, authorisation

persecute VERB
*People were **persecuted** for their religious beliefs.*
• to oppress, to discriminate against, to harass, to intimidate, to bully, to terrorise

persevere VERB
*The rescuers **persevered** despite the bad weather.*
• to continue, to persist, to carry on, to keep going
OPPOSITE to give up

persist VERB
*The rain **persisted** all day.*
• to continue, to carry on, to go on, to keep on, to last
OPPOSITE to stop
➤ **to persist in**
*She **persisted in** asking questions.*
• to persevere in, to keep on, to continue, to insist on

persistent ADJECTIVE
❶ *She was very **persistent** and wouldn't leave until he had answered her questions.*
• determined, resolute, relentless, persevering, stubborn, obstinate
❷ *There was a **persistent** drip from the tap.*
• constant, continual, incessant, never-ending, non-stop

person NOUN
*She's a very nice **person**.*
• an individual, a character
— A person as opposed to an animal is a **human** or a **human being**.

personal ADJECTIVE
❶ *The book is based on the writer's **personal** experience.*
• own, individual, particular
❷ *The contents of the letter are **personal**.*
• confidential, private, secret, intimate

personality NOUN
❶ *He has a lovely **personality**.*
• a character, a nature, a disposition, a temperament
❷ *A TV **personality** came to speak at our school.*
• a celebrity, a star, a VIP

persuade VERB
*I **persuaded** my friend to join the choir.*
• to convince, to encourage, to coax, to induce, to talk someone into
*I **talked** my friend **into** joining the choir.*
OPPOSITE to dissuade

persuasive ADJECTIVE
*She used some very **persuasive** arguments.*
• convincing, effective, sound, strong, valid
OPPOSITE unconvincing

pest NOUN
❶ *Slugs are garden **pests**.*
— **Vermin** are animals or insects that damage crops or food, or carry disease.
— A **parasite** is an animal that lives on or inside another creature.
❷ *Don't be a **pest**!*
• a nuisance, a bother, an annoyance, a pain *(informal)*

pester VERB
*Please don't **pester** me when I'm busy!*
• to annoy, to bother, to trouble, to harass, to badger, to plague

a
b
c
d
e
f
g
h
i
j
k
l
m
n
o
p
q
r
s
t
u
v
w
x
y
z

pet NOUN

🕸 **WORD WEB**

SOME ANIMALS KEPT AS PETS:

• a budgerigar, a cat, a dog, a ferret, a fish, a gerbil, a goldfish, a guinea pig, a hamster, a mouse, a parrot, a rabbit, a snake, a tortoise
» *For other animals look at* **animal**.

phase NOUN
Going to school is the start of a new phase in your life.
• a period, a time, a stage, a step

phone NOUN
Can I use your phone?
• a telephone, a mobile, a mobile phone, a mobile device
— A **smartphone** is a mobile phone that can access the Internet.

phone VERB
He phoned to say that he'd be late.
• to call, to ring, to ring up, to telephone, to give someone a ring

photograph NOUN
We're having our class photograph taken today.
• a photo, a shot, a picture
— A **selfie** is a photograph that you take of yourself.
— A **print** is a photograph printed on paper.

photograph VERB
Dad photographed some birds in the garden.
• to take a picture of, to shoot, to snap

phrase NOUN
Do you know what this phrase means?
• an expression, a saying, an idiom

physical ADJECTIVE
❶ *Physical illness can be linked to mental illness.*
• bodily
OPPOSITE mental
❷ *Are you talking about a physical object?*
• material, solid, concrete

pick VERB
❶ *You can pick any flavour you like.*
• to choose, to select, to decide on, to settle on, to opt for, to take
❷ *We picked some blackberries for tea.*
• to gather, to collect, to pluck
➤ **to pick up**
The box was too heavy for me to pick up.
• to lift, to raise
Dad will pick us up from school today.
• to collect, to get, to fetch

picture NOUN

🕸 **WORD WEB**

❶ *There's a picture of a pyramid in this book.*
• an illustration, an image, a depiction
— A **painting** is a painted picture.
— A **drawing** is a picture made with pencils, crayons or chalk.
— A **sketch** is a quick or rough drawing.
— A **portrait** is a picture of a person.
— A **self-portrait** is a picture you paint or draw of yourself.
— A **cartoon** is a picture that is funny or tells a joke.
— A **landscape** is a picture showing a view of an area of land.
— A **mural** is a picture painted on a wall.
— **Graphics** are pictures on a computer.
❷ *Mum took some pictures of us building a sandcastle.*
• a photo, a photograph
— A **selfie** is a picture you take of yourself.

picture VERB
❶ *The girl is pictured riding a horse.*
• to depict, to illustrate, to represent, to show, to portray
❷ *Can you picture what the world will be like in 100 years?*
• to imagine, to visualise

pie NOUN
We had a chicken pie for dinner.
• a pastry, a pasty, a tart

piece NOUN
❶ *Would you like another piece of cake?*
• a bit, a slice
» *For more ways to say 'piece' look at* **bit**.
❷ *I always have a piece of fruit in my lunch box.*
• an item
— An **article** of clothing is a piece.
❸ *I've lost one of the pieces of the puzzle.*
• a part, an element, a component

pier NOUN
The passengers waited at the pier to board the ship.
• a quay, a wharf, a jetty

pierce VERB
The arrow had pierced the knight's armour.
• to enter, to go through, to make a hole in, to penetrate
— To **spear** something is to stick a long sharp object into it: *He speared a sausage with his fork.*

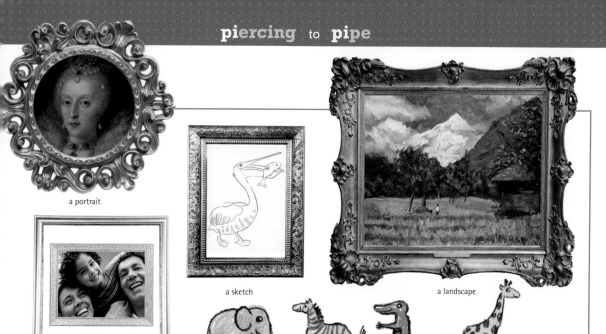

a portrait

a sketch

a landscape

drawings

a photograph

piercing *ADJECTIVE*
*We heard a **piercing** shriek.*
• high-pitched, shrill, deafening, ear-splitting

pig *NOUN*

 WORD WEB

— A female pig is a **sow**.
— A male pig is a **boar** or **hog**.
— A young pig is a **piglet**.
— A family of piglets is a **litter**.
— A wild pig is a **wild boar**.
— An old word for pigs is **swine**.
— When pigs make a sound, they **grunt**, **oink** or **squeal**.

pile *NOUN*
*Where did this **pile** of rubbish come from?*
• a heap, a mound, a mountain, a stack, a mass
— A **drift** is a pile of snow or sand.

pile *VERB*
Pile the clean clothes on that chair.
• to heap, to stack, to collect, to gather
➤ **to pile up**
*Dead leaves **piled up** in the playground.*
• to build up, to accumulate

pill *NOUN*
*Take one **pill** every four hours.*
• a tablet, a capsule
— A **lozenge** is a sweet containing medicine for a sore throat.

pillar *NOUN*
*The roof was supported by tall **pillars**.*
• a column, a post, a prop, a beam

pinch *VERB*
❶ *My sister **pinched** my arm.*
• to nip, to squeeze, to press, to grip
❷ *(informal) Who's **pinched** my calculator?*
• to steal, to take, to snatch, to swipe *(informal)*, to nick *(informal)*

pink *NOUN, ADJECTIVE*

 WORD WEB

SOME SHADES OF PINK:

• coral, fuchsia, peach, rose pink, salmon pink

pip *NOUN*
*Make sure there are no **pips** in the lemon juice.*
• a seed

pipe *NOUN*
*The water flows away along this **pipe**.*
• a tube, a hose
— A **pipeline** is a pipe carrying oil, gas or water over a long distance.

pipe *VERB*
*Water is **piped** from the reservoir to the town.*
• to carry, to convey, to channel

pirate NOUN

The ship was attacked by pirates.

• a buccaneer, a brigand, a raider

— A **Viking** was a pirate or trader from Scandinavia.

 WRITING TIPS

Here are some helpful words for writing about pirates:

SOME WORDS TO DESCRIBE A PIRATE:

• bearded, bloodthirsty, cruel, fearless, fierce, heartless, merciless, murderous, one-eyed, peg-legged, pitiless, ruthless, savage, swashbuckling, vicious, villainous

SOME THINGS A PIRATE MIGHT USE OR CARRY:

• a bottle of rum, breeches, a cutlass, a dagger, an eye patch, a hook, a musket, a parrot, a pigtail, a pistol, a treasure map, a treasure chest, a wooden leg

— A pirate flag is called the **Jolly Roger** or a skull-and-crossbones.

 » Look at **boat**.

 » Look at **treasure**.

[He] was the blood-thirstiest pirate on all the seven seas and hated her friend Peter Pan more than Death itself . . . —PETER PAN IN SCARLET, Geraldine McCaughrean

pit NOUN

The evil wizard fell into a deep pit.

• a hole, a shaft, a crater, a cavity, a pothole

— A **chasm** or an **abyss** is a very deep hole in the ground that seems to have no bottom.

pitch NOUN

❶ *The pitch was frozen, so we couldn't play.*

• a ground, a field, a playing field

❷ *She can sing at a very high pitch.*

• a tone, a frequency

pitch VERB

❶ *Scott pitched the ball back over the fence.*

• to throw, to toss, to fling, to hurl, to sling, to cast

❷ *It was hard trying to pitch the tent in the wind.*

• to erect, to put up, to set up

pitiful ADJECTIVE

❶ *We could hear pitiful cries for help.*

• pathetic, distressing, mournful, heartbreaking, touching, moving, sad

❷ *The goalie made a pitiful attempt to stop the ball.*

• hopeless, useless, feeble, pathetic

pity NOUN

The pirates showed no pity towards the captives.

• mercy, compassion, sympathy, humanity, kindness, concern, feeling

➤ **a pity**

It's a pity that you have to leave so early.

• a shame, unfortunate, bad luck

pity VERB

We pitied anyone who was caught up in the storm.

• to feel sorry for, to feel for, to sympathise with, to take pity on

place NOUN

❶ *This is a safe place to wait.*

• a location, a position, a site, a spot, a point

❷ *They live in a lovely place.*

• an area, a district, a neighbourhood, a region, a vicinity

❸ *Save me a place on the bus.*

• a seat, a space

place VERB

❶ *She placed a jug of flowers on the table.*

• to put down, to set down, to lay

❷ *They placed markers at the corners of the field.*

• to position, to locate, to put

plague NOUN

❶ *Doctors worked hard to prevent the plague from spreading.*

• an epidemic, an outbreak

❷ *There was a plague of wasps this summer.*

• an invasion, a swarm

plague VERB

Stop plaguing me with questions!

• to bother, to pester, to trouble, to annoy, to badger, to harass

plain ADJECTIVE

❶ *The furniture in the room was very plain.*

• simple, modest, basic, undecorated

OPPOSITES elaborate, ornate

❷ *He made his feelings plain.*

• clear, evident, obvious, apparent, unmistakable

OPPOSITE unclear

plan NOUN

❶ *The captain explained her plan to the rest of the team.*

• an idea, a proposal, a scheme, a strategy, a policy, a project, a suggestion

— A **plot** is a plan to do something bad.

❷ *They looked at a plan of the town centre.*

• a map, a drawing, a diagram, a chart

plan VERB

❶ *The outlaws planned their attack.*

• to prepare, to organise, to work out, to design, to devise

— To **plot** is to plan something bad.

❷ *What do you plan to do next?*

• to intend, to aim, to propose, to mean

plane NOUN
» *Look at* **aircraft**.

planet NOUN
The new space probe will travel to distant planets.
• a world

an asteroid

WORD WEB

THE PLANETS OF THE SOLAR SYSTEM (IN ORDER FROM THE SUN) ARE:

• Mercury, Venus, Earth, Mars, Jupiter, Saturn, Uranus, Neptune
— Pluto is classified as a **dwarf planet**.
— Minor planets orbiting the sun are **asteroids**.

— Something which orbits a planet is a **satellite**.
— The earth's large satellite is the **moon**.
— The path followed by a planet is its **orbit**.
» *Look at* **space**.

WRITING TIPS

Here are some helpful words for writing about a **planet**:

WORDS FOR DESCRIBING A PLANET:

• alien, strange, distant, far-off, remote, arid, barren, bleak, desolate, frozen, icy, inhospitable, lifeless, rocky, earthlike, fertile, green, lush

A CREATURE THAT LIVES ON A PLANET:

• an alien, a being, a creature, an extraterrestrial, an inhabitant, a life form
On Uriel there had been the magnificent creatures. On Camazotz the inhabitants had at least resembled people. But what were these three strange things approaching?—A WRINKLE IN TIME, Madeleine L'Engle

a rocky inhospitable planet

a lush green planet

plant NOUN

🕸 **WORD WEB**

SOME TYPES OF PLANT:

• algae, a bush, a cactus, a cereal, a creeper,
a fern, a flower, a fungus, a grass, a herb,
a house plant, ivy, lichen, moss, a shrub, a tree,
a vegetable, a vine, a weed, a wild flower
— A **seedling** is a young plant.
— **Vegetation** is plants in general.
» *Look at* **flower**, **fruit**, **herb**,
tree *and* **vegetable**.

flowers

fruit

cereal

a cactus

wild
flowers

fungi

a vine

plant VERB
*They **planted** sunflowers.*
• to sow, to grow, to put in the ground
— To **transplant** a plant is to dig it up and plant it in
a different place.

plate NOUN
❶ *She put the fruit on a **plate**.*
• a dish, a platter
— A **bowl** is a deep plate.
❷ *The robot's body was formed of
metal **plates**.*
• a panel, a sheet

play VERB
❶ *The children were **playing** outside.*
• to enjoy yourself, to amuse yourself, to have fun,
to romp about, to frolic
❷ *My sister loves **playing** football.*
• to take part in, to participate in, to compete in
❸ *Liverpool **play** Arsenal next week.*
• to compete against, to take on, to challenge,
to oppose
❹ *I'm learning to **play** the guitar.*
• to perform on
❺ *I **played** the king in our performance.*
• to act as, to take the part of, to portray,
to represent

play NOUN
We are putting on a play for our parents.
• a show, a drama, a performance, a production

player NOUN
❶ *You need four players for this game.*
• a contestant, a participant, a competitor
— Someone who plays a sport is a **sportsperson,** **sportsman** or **sportswoman.**
❷ *How many players are in the orchestra?*
• a performer, a musician
» *For people who play various instruments look at* **music.**

playful ADJECTIVE
She was in a playful mood.
• lively, spirited, frisky, mischievous, frivolous, jokey, light-hearted
OPPOSITE serious

plead VERB
➤ to plead with
I pleaded with my parents to let me go.
• to beg, to entreat, to implore, to appeal to

pleasant ADJECTIVE
❶ *The owner of the shop is always pleasant to us.*
• kind, friendly, likeable, charming, gracious, agreeable, good-natured, hospitable
❷ *We had a pleasant day in the park.*
• pleasing, enjoyable, agreeable, delightful, lovely
— Use **wonderful** or **fantastic** for something very pleasant.
❸ *The weather is quite pleasant today.*
• fine, fair, mild, sunny, warm
OPPOSITE unpleasant

pleased ADJECTIVE
Why are you looking so pleased?
• glad, happy, contented, satisfied
— Use **thrilled, delighted, joyful** or **elated** to mean very pleased.
— Use **grateful** or **thankful** when you are pleased because someone has been kind to you.
OPPOSITE annoyed

pleasure NOUN
I get a lot of pleasure from riding my bike.
• happiness, satisfaction, enjoyment, contentment, gladness
— Use **delight, joy, bliss** or **ecstasy** to mean very great pleasure.

pledge NOUN
The knights swore a pledge of loyalty to the king.
• an oath, a vow, a promise

plentiful ADJECTIVE
There is a plentiful supply of food in the fridge.
• generous, large, lavish, liberal
OPPOSITE scarce

plenty NOUN
➤ plenty of
We've still got plenty of time.
• a lot of, lots of, more than enough, loads of *(informal),* masses of *(informal)*

plod VERB
The hikers plodded on through the mud.
• to tramp, to trudge, to lumber
» *For other ways of walking look at* **walk.**

plot NOUN
❶ *They had a secret plot to steal the jewels.*
• a plan, a scheme, a conspiracy
❷ *It was hard to follow the plot of the film.*
• the story, the storyline, the narrative
» *Look at* **story.**

plot VERB
He was plotting to get the crown for himself.
• to scheme, to plan

plug NOUN
They removed the plug in the side of the barrel.
• a stopper, a cork, a seal

plug VERB
I managed to plug the leak in the pipe.
• to block, to stop up, to close, to fill, to seal

plump ADJECTIVE
We saw a small plump man.
• chubby, fat, tubby, podgy, round, stout
— **Stocky** means short and solidly built.
OPPOSITE skinny

plunge VERB
❶ *One by one, the girls plunged into the pool.*
• to dive, to jump, to leap
❷ *I plunged my hand in the cold water.*
• to immerse, to submerge, to dip, to lower

poem NOUN

We each wrote a **poem** about the seaside.

• a rhyme

— **Verse** or **poetry** is poems in general.

— A **stanza** is a group of lines forming a section of a poem.

WORD WEB

SOME KINDS OF POEM:

• an acrostic, a ballad, a haiku, a limerick, a nursery rhyme, a rap, a sonnet

point NOUN

❶ Be careful—that knife has a very sharp **point**.

• a tip, an end, a spike, a prong

❷ What is the **point** of this exercise?

• a purpose, a reason, an aim, an object, a use, a meaning

❸ I agree with your last **point**.

• an idea, an argument, a thought, an opinion

❹ He marked on the map the **point** where the treasure lay.

• a location, a place, a position, a spot, a site

❺ At that **point** the rain started to come down.

• a moment, an instant, a time

point VERB

❶ She **pointed** the way.

• to indicate, to point out, to show, to signal

❷ She **pointed** her telescope at the moon.

• to aim, to direct

pointless ADJECTIVE

It's **pointless** arguing with him—he's so stubborn.

• useless, futile, senseless

— You can also say there is **no point** doing something.

OPPOSITE worthwhile

poison NOUN

The potion contained deadly **poison**.

— **Venom** is poison from a snake.

— An **antidote** is a substance which can save you from the effects of a poison.

poisonous ADJECTIVE

Some of those mushrooms may be **poisonous**.

• toxic, harmful

— If something is **deadly** or **lethal**, it is poisonous enough to kill you.

— A poisonous snake is **venomous**.

poke VERB

Someone **poked** me in the back with an umbrella.

• to prod, to dig, to jab, to nudge, to stab, to thrust

➤ to poke out

The kitten's head was **poking out** of the basket.

• to stick out, to protrude

polar ADJECTIVE

The **polar** expedition will study birds and sea life.

— **Arctic** means to do with the North Pole.

— **Antarctic** means to do with the South Pole.

❯❯ For writing about ice look at **ice**.

pole NOUN

Four **poles** marked the corners of the field.

• a post, a bar, a rod, a stick

— A **mast** or a **spar** is a pole to support sails on a ship.

— A **stake** is a thick pole with a point to stick in the ground.

police officer NOUN

A **police officer** stood in front of the door.

• a policeman or policewoman, an officer, a constable

— A **detective** is a police officer who investigates crimes.

— A **cadet** is someone being trained for the police force.

— A **sergeant** is a police officer above an ordinary constable in rank.

— An **inspector** is a police officer above a sergeant in rank.

❯❯ Look at **detective**.

policy NOUN

The leaflet explains the school's **policy** on bullying.

• an approach, a strategy

polish VERB

He **polished** his boots.

• to rub down, to shine, to buff

polite *ADJECTIVE*
*He is very **polite** and always says thank you.*
• courteous, well-mannered, respectful, civil, gracious
— Use **diplomatic** or **tactful** when someone is careful not to offend anyone.
— **Refined** means very polite and cultured.
— A **gallant** man is polite or brave, especially towards women.
OPPOSITES rude, impolite

pollute *VERB*
*The river has been **polluted** by chemicals.*
• to contaminate, to infect, to poison

pond *NOUN*
» *Look at **pool**.*

pool *NOUN*
❶ *The surface of the **pool** was covered with frogspawn.*
• a pond
— A **puddle** is a small shallow pool of water.
— A **rock pool** is a pool among rocks on a seashore.
— A **lake** is a large area of water surrounded by land.
— A **loch** is a lake in Scotland.
— A **lagoon** is a saltwater lake.
❷ *At the weekend dad took me to the **pool**.*
• a swimming pool, a swimming baths

poor *ADJECTIVE*
❶ *He came from a **poor** family.*
• badly off, needy, penniless, hard-up *(informal)*, broke *(informal)*
— **Poverty** is the state of being poor.
OPPOSITE rich

❷ *His spelling is very **poor**.*
• bad, weak, unsatisfactory, inferior
OPPOSITES good, superior
❸ *They pitied the **poor** animals standing in the rain.*
• unfortunate, unlucky, pitiful, wretched
OPPOSITE fortunate

poorly *ADJECTIVE*
*He stayed at home because he felt **poorly**.*
• ill, sick, unwell
OPPOSITE well

popular *ADJECTIVE*
❶ *She is a **popular** children's writer.*
• well-liked, well-known, celebrated, favourite, famous
OPPOSITE unpopular
❷ *Those trainers are very **popular** at the moment.*
• fashionable, current, in demand
OPPOSITE unfashionable

population *NOUN*
*About ten per cent of the **population** of the world is left-handed.*
• inhabitants, residents, occupants, citizens, people

port *NOUN*
*A large cruise ship sailed into the **port**.*
• a harbour, a dock

portion *NOUN*
❶ *Can I have a **portion** of chips?*
• a helping, a serving, a ration, a quantity
❷ *I only got a small **portion** of pie.*
• a piece, a slice, a bit, a share, a fraction

portrait *NOUN*
*There's a **portrait** of the Queen on every stamp.*
• a picture, an image, a likeness, a representation

pose *VERB*
*The film star **posed** for the cameras.*
• to model, to sit
➤ **to pose as someone**
*The spy **posed** as a newspaper reporter.*
• to impersonate, to pretend to be, to pass yourself off as

posh *ADJECTIVE*
*(informal) We went to a **posh** restaurant for a treat.*
• smart, stylish, high-class, elegant, fashionable, luxurious, luxury

a
b
c
d
e
f
g
h
i
j
k
l
m
n
o
p
q
r
s
t
u
v
w
x
y
z

position NOUN
❶ Mark the **position** on the map.
• a location, a place, a point, a spot, a site
❷ He shifted his **position** to avoid getting cramp.
• a pose, a posture
❸ You have put me in a difficult **position**.
• a situation, a state, a condition, circumstances

positive ADJECTIVE
❶ I am **positive** I saw him.
• certain, sure, convinced, confident
OPPOSITE uncertain
❷ The changes have had some **positive** effects.
• good, helpful, useful, worthwhile, beneficial, constructive, desirable
OPPOSITE negative

positive NOUN
We listed all the negatives and **positives** of the plan.
• an advantage, a benefit, a plus, a good point, an asset
OPPOSITE a negative

possess VERB
They don't **possess** a computer.
• to have, to own

possessions NOUN
The refugees had lost all of their **possessions**.
• belongings, goods, property

possibility NOUN
❶ There's a **possibility** that it may rain later.
• a chance, a likelihood, a prospect
— A danger or a risk is a possibility of something bad.
❷ There are all sorts of **possibilities** if you want to do a summer sports course.
• an option, an opportunity, a choice

possible ADJECTIVE
❶ Is it **possible** that life exists on other planets?
• likely, probable
❷ It wasn't **possible** to shift the piano.
• feasible, practical
OPPOSITE impossible
❸ She is a **possible** national champion.
• potential, promising, likely, future

possibly ADVERB
'Will you see him today?'–'**Possibly**.'
• maybe, perhaps

post NOUN
❶ The farmer put up some **posts** for a new fence.
• a pole, a pillar, a shaft, a stake, a support, a prop
❷ The **post** arrived late.
• mail, letters, delivery

post VERB
❶ Did you **post** those letters?
• to mail, to send, to dispatch
❷ The names of the winners will be **posted** on the website.
• to display, to put up, to announce, to advertise

poster NOUN
We made a **poster** about our summer fair.
• a notice, a sign, an advertisement, an announcement

post

postpone VERB
They **postponed** the match because of bad weather.
• to put off, to defer, to delay

pot NOUN
On the table were little **pots** of jam and honey.
• a jar, a dish, a bowl, a tub
— A pan, a saucepan or a casserole is a pot used for cooking.

potential ADJECTIVE
He's a **potential** champion.
• possible, future, likely, probable, promising

potential NOUN
Her coach sees a lot of **potential** in her.
• promise, possibility, hope, talent

poultry NOUN
They keep all sorts of **poultry**.
• fowl

a turkey

🌐 WORD WEB
KINDS OF POULTRY:
• a chicken, a duck, a goose, a hen, a turkey

pounce VERB
➤ to pounce on
The cat **pounced on** the mouse.
• to jump on, to leap on, to spring on, to swoop down on, to lunge at, to attack

pour VERB
❶ *Water **poured** through the hole.*
• to flow, to run, to gush, to stream, to spill, to spout
❷ *I **poured** some milk into my cup.*
• to tip, to serve

poverty NOUN
*Many of the people were living in **poverty**.*
• hardship, need
OPPOSITE wealth

powder NOUN
*The fairy sprinkled some magic **powder** in the air.*
• dust, particles

power NOUN
❶ *The empress had **power** over all the people.*
• authority, command, control, domination
❷ *The wizard had magic **powers**.*
• an ability, a skill, a talent
❸ *They were amazed by the **power** of the wave.*
• strength, force, might
❹ *We use renewable **power** as much as we can.*
• energy, fuel, electricity

powerful ADJECTIVE
❶ *The queen was a very **powerful** person.*
• influential, important, dominant, senior
❷ *This is a **powerful** magic potion.*
• strong, formidable, potent, mighty

powerless ADJECTIVE
*The good witch was **powerless** to undo the spell.*
• helpless, unable
— Use **defenceless**, **vulnerable** or **weak** if someone is unable to protect themselves.

practical ADJECTIVE
❶ *She's a very **practical** person.*
• sensible, capable, competent
OPPOSITE impractical
❷ *The plan was not very **practical**.*
• realistic, sensible, achievable
OPPOSITE impractical

practically ADVERB
*Keep going—we're **practically** there!*
• almost, just about, nearly, virtually

practice NOUN
*We have extra football **practice** this week.*
• training, exercises, drill
— A **rehearsal** is a practice for a performance.

practise VERB
❶ *I need to **practise** my speech.*
• to rehearse, to go through, to run through, to work on
— To **rehearse** is to practise a performance.
❷ *The team meets once a week to **practise**.*
• to train, to do exercises

praise VERB
*The teacher **praised** my story.*
• to compliment, to commend, to applaud, to admire
— To **rave about** something is to praise it very enthusiastically.
OPPOSITE to criticise

praise NOUN
*She received a lot of **praise** for her actions.*
• approval, admiration, compliments, congratulations, applause

precious ADJECTIVE
❶ *Her most **precious** possession was an old photograph.*
• treasured, cherished, valued, prized, dear, beloved
❷ *The crown glittered with **precious** gems.*
• valuable, costly, expensive, priceless
» *For precious stones look at **jewel**.*
OPPOSITE worthless

precise ADJECTIVE
❶ *Can you tell me the **precise** time, please?*
• exact, accurate, correct, true, right
OPPOSITE rough
❷ *She gave us very **precise** instructions.*
• careful, detailed, specific, particular, definite
OPPOSITE vague

predict VERB
*You can't **predict** what may happen in the future.*
• to forecast, to foresee, to foretell, to prophesy, to anticipate

prefer VERB
*Would you **prefer** juice or lemonade?*
• to like, to choose, to opt for, rather have
*Would you **rather have** juice or lemonade?*

preference NOUN
❶ *Sandy has a **preference** for sweet things.*
• a liking, a fancy, an inclination
❷ *There is a choice of meals so please write your **preference** here.*
• a choice, a selection, an option, a wish

a b c d e f g h i j k l m n o **p** q r s t u v w x y z

prejudice NOUN
The school does not allow any kind of prejudice.
• bias, discrimination, intolerance, unfairness
OPPOSITES fairness, tolerance

prepare VERB
We are all busy preparing for the party.
• to get ready, to make arrangements for, to organise, to plan, to set up
➤ **to be prepared to**
I am prepared to help you.
• to be willing to, to be ready to, to be happy to

presence NOUN
Your presence is required.
• attendance
OPPOSITE absence

present (say prez-ent) ADJECTIVE
❶ *Is everyone present?*
• here, in attendance
OPPOSITE absent
❷ *Who is the present world chess champion?*
• current, existing
OPPOSITES past, future

present (say prez-ent) NOUN
What would you like for your birthday present?
• a gift, a prezzie (informal)

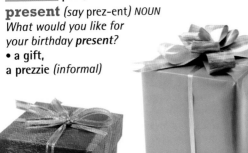

present
(say pri-zent) VERB
❶ *The head presents the prizes on sports day.*
• to award, to hand over, to give out
We presented our work in assembly.
• to show, to display
— To put on or perform a play is to **present** it.
❸ *Who will present the show tonight?*
• to introduce, to host

preserve VERB
❶ *A fridge is best for preserving food.*
• to keep, to save, to store
❷ *It's important to preserve these animals' habitat.*
• to protect, to look after, to conserve, to defend, to safeguard, to maintain

press VERB
❶ *Press the fruit through a sieve to get rid of the seeds.*
• to push, to force, to squeeze, to squash, to crush
❷ *Don't press any of the buttons.*
• to push, to touch, to activate

press NOUN
The press were outside waiting to ask questions.
• the media, the papers, journalists, reporters

pressure NOUN
❶ *Pressure built up inside the container.*
• force, compression, weight
❷ *The team was under a lot of pressure to win.*
• stress, strain, obligation

pretend VERB
❶ *She's not really crying—she's only pretending.*
• to put on an act, to act, to fake, to bluff, to kid (informal)
❷ *Let's pretend that we're pirates.*
• to imagine, to make believe, to play

pretty ADJECTIVE
We saw a pretty little cottage.
• attractive, beautiful, lovely, nice, pleasing, charming, dainty, picturesque, quaint, cute (informal)
— A common simile is **as pretty as a picture**.
OPPOSITE ugly

prevent VERB
❶ *The driver could not prevent the accident.*
• to stop, to avert, to avoid
❷ *The police managed to prevent a bank robbery.*
• to foil, to hinder, to block, to stop

previous ADJECTIVE
❶ *I had been there on a previous occasion.*
• earlier, former, preceding
❷ *The previous owners of the house have gone abroad.*
• former
OPPOSITE subsequent

price NOUN
The bill shows the total price.
• the cost, the charge, the rate, the fee, the amount, the payment, the sum
— The **price** for using public transport is the **fare**.

prick VERB
Jamie burst the balloon by pricking it with a pin.
• to pierce, to puncture, to stab, to jab

prickle NOUN
A hedgehog uses its prickles for defence.
• a spike, a spine, a needle
— A porcupine's prickles are its **quills**.
— A **thorn** is a prickle on a rose, blackberry or other bush.

pride NOUN
❶ *He blushed with pride.*
• satisfaction, pleasure, glee, triumph
OPPOSITE shame
❷ *I had to forget my pride and ask for help.*
• self-esteem, self-respect, dignity
— Use **arrogance**, **vanity** or **conceit** when someone has too much pride.
OPPOSITE humility

priest NOUN
The priest conducted the ceremony.
• a clergyman or clergywoman, a minister, a vicar
— A Hindu or Sikh religious leader is a **guru**.
— A Muslim religious leader is an **imam**.
— A Jewish religious leader is a **rabbi**.

primary ADJECTIVE
Their primary aim was to win the match.
• main, chief, central, key, principal, foremost, major, basic, essential, fundamental

principal ADJECTIVE
Our principal goal is to raise money.
• main, chief, primary, foremost, most important, major, fundamental, essential, basic

principle NOUN
It is against her principles to wear fur.
• a rule, a standard, a code

print NOUN
❶ *She found the tiny print difficult to read.*
• lettering, letters, printing, type, font
❷ *Her thumb left a print on the glass.*
• a mark, a trace, a track
— A **fingerprint** is a mark left by a finger.
— A **footprint** is a mark left by a foot or shoe.

prison NOUN
He was sentenced to six months in prison.
• jail, imprisonment
— A **dungeon** is an underground prison.
— A **cell** is a prisoner's room in a prison.

prisoner NOUN
The prisoner tried to escape from jail.
• a convict, a captive, an inmate
— A **hostage** is someone who is held prisoner until a demand is met.

private ADJECTIVE
❶ *She has her own private room.*
• personal, individual
❷ *Everything I write in my diary is private.*
• secret, confidential, personal, intimate
❸ *Let's go somewhere private to talk.*
• quiet, secluded, hidden, concealed
OPPOSITE public

privilege NOUN
Club members have special privileges.
• an advantage, a benefit, a right

prize NOUN
Our team won a prize.
• an award, a reward, a trophy, a medal

prize VERB
She prized her grandmother's ring above all else.
• to treasure, to value, to cherish, to hold dear

probable ADJECTIVE
A burst pipe was the probable cause of the flood.
• likely, expected, possible, predicted
OPPOSITE improbable

problem NOUN
❶ *I'm having a problem with my computer.*
• a difficulty, trouble, an issue, a worry
— A **hitch** or a **snag** is a small unexpected problem.
— A **bug** is a problem in a computer program.

an echidna's spines

a b c d e f g h i j k l m n o p q r s t u v w x y z

❷ *Our maths teacher set us a difficult **problem**.*
• a puzzle, a question
❸ *We solved the **problem** of the missing piece.*
• a mystery, a riddle, a puzzle

proceed *VERB*
❶ *We **proceeded** slowly along the path.*
• to advance, to move forward, to progress
❷ *They decided not to **proceed** with their plan.*
• to continue, to go ahead, to carry on

process *NOUN*
*I made the first card, then repeated the **process** for all the others.*
• method, procedure, operation, system, technique

process *VERB*
*The oil is **processed** at a refinery.*
• to treat, to refine, to prepare, to convert

procession *NOUN*
*The **procession** made its way slowly down the hill.*
• a parade, a march, a column, a line

prod *VERB*
*Someone **prodded** me in the back with an umbrella.*
• to poke, to dig, to jab, to nudge, to push

produce *VERB*
❶ *Some lorries **produce** a lot of fumes.*
• to create, to generate, to cause, to give out, to emit
— To **belch** smoke or fumes is to produce them.
— To **radiate** heat is to produce it.
❷ *The tree **produced** a good crop of apples this year.*
• to yield, to grow
❸ *The factory **produces** cars and vans.*
• to make, to manufacture, to assemble, to build, to construct
❹ *She **produced** a camera and took a photo.*
• to bring out, to take out, to reveal

product *NOUN*
*They sell household **products**.*
• an item, an article, goods

production *NOUN*
❶ *They are involved in food **production**.*
• creation, producing, output
— **Manufacturing** is the production of goods using machines.
❷ *We went to see a **production** of 'The Sound of Music'.*
• a performance, a show

profession *NOUN*
*Nursing is an important **profession**.*
• a career, a job, an occupation, a trade, work, employment

professional *ADJECTIVE*
❶ *The plans were drawn by a **professional** architect.*
• qualified, skilled, trained, experienced
❷ *Her ambition is to be a **professional** footballer.*
• paid, full-time
OPPOSITE amateur
❸ *The show was very **professional**.*
• skilful, skilled, high-quality, competent
OPPOSITE incompetent

programme *NOUN*
❶ *There was a really good **programme** on TV last night.*
• a show, a broadcast, a production
❷ *We worked out a **programme** for sports day.*
• a plan, a schedule, a timetable
— An **agenda** is a list of items to be discussed at a meeting.

progress *(say proh-gress) NOUN*
❶ *I traced their **progress** on the map.*
• a journey, a route, movements, travels
❷ *You have made great **progress** this term.*
• advances, development, growth, improvement
— A **breakthrough** is an important piece of progress.

progress *(say pro-gress) VERB*
❶ *They **progressed** slowly along the track.*
• to proceed, to advance, to travel, to move forward, to continue
OPPOSITE to retreat
❷ *Your writing has really **progressed**.*
• to improve, to make progress, to develop, to come on

project *(say pro-ject) NOUN*
❶ *I did a **project** on the Romans.*
• a task, an assignment, an activity, research
❷ *There is a **project** to create a bird sanctuary in the area.*
• a plan, a proposal, a scheme

project *(say pro-ject) VERB*
❶ *A rock **projects** from the cliff.*
• to extend, to protrude, to stick out, to jut out
❷ *The lighthouse **projects** a beam of light.*
• to cast, to shine, to throw out light

promise NOUN
❶ *She made me a **promise** that she wouldn't tell.*
• an assurance, a guarantee, a commitment, a vow
— An **oath** or a **pledge** is a serious promise, especially at a special ceremony.
❷ *That young player shows **promise**.*
• potential, possibility, talent

promise VERB
*Dad **promised** that we'd go camping this summer.*
• to swear, to guarantee, to give your word, to vow, to pledge, to assure
*Dad **assured** me that we'd go camping this summer.*
— To **undertake** to do something is to promise to do it.

promote VERB
❶ *She was **promoted** to captain.*
• to move up, to advance
❷ *The singer is on tour to **promote** her new album.*
• to advertise, to market, to sell
❸ *The school is trying to **promote** healthy eating.*
• to encourage, to support

prompt ADJECTIVE
*I received a **prompt** reply to my email.*
• punctual, quick, rapid, swift, immediate, instant
OPPOSITE delayed

proof NOUN
*There is no **proof** that he is a secret agent.*
• evidence, confirmation

prop VERB
*Kenny **propped** his bike against the kerb.*
• to lean, to rest, to stand

prop NOUN
*The bridge is supported by steel **props**.*
• a support, a strut, a post

proper ADJECTIVE
❶ *This is the **proper** way to hold a bat.*
• correct, right, suitable, appropriate, accurate
OPPOSITES wrong, incorrect
❷ *He can fly a **proper** plane.*
• real, genuine, actual

property NOUN
❶ *This office deals with lost **property**.*
• belongings, possessions, goods
❷ *He was very rich and owned a lot of **property**.*
• buildings, houses, land, premises
❸ *Many herbs have healing **properties**.*
• a quality, a characteristic, a feature

proportion NOUN
❶ *Water covers a large **proportion** of the earth's surface.*
• a part, a section, a share, a fraction
❷ *What is the **proportion** of girls to boys in your class?*
• the ratio, the balance

propose VERB
*He **proposed** a change in the rules.*
• to suggest, to recommend, to put forward

protect VERB
❶ *Guards **protect** the palace.*
• to defend, to guard, to safeguard, to keep safe
— To **fortify** a place is to protect it with strong walls.
❷ *Always **protect** your skin from the sun.*
• to shield, to shade, to screen

protection NOUN
*The tent gave us **protection** from the rain.*
• shelter, defence, cover, a shield

protest (say proh-test) NOUN
*There were **protests** at the plan to make playtime shorter.*
• complaints, objections, an outcry, an uproar

protest (say pro-test) VERB
*We **protested** when the swimming pool was closed down.*
• to complain, to object, to make a protest, to express disapproval

protrude VERB
*His stomach **protrudes** above his belt.*
• to stick out, to poke out, to bulge, to swell, to project, to jut out

proud ADJECTIVE
❶ *My parents were **proud** when I sang at the concert.*
• delighted, pleased
OPPOSITE ashamed
— A common simile is **as proud as a peacock**.
❷ *He is too **proud** to admit he needs help.*
• arrogant, haughty, conceited, big-headed, vain, self-important
OPPOSITE humble

prove VERB
*The evidence will **prove** that he is innocent.*
• to confirm, to demonstrate, to establish
OPPOSITE to disprove

a
b
c
d
e
f
g
h
i
j
k
l
m
n
o
p
q
r
s
t
u
v
w
x
y
z

provide VERB
❶ The school **provides** paper and pencils.
• to supply, to offer, to lay on, to give out
❷ We can **provide** you with boots and waterproofs.
• to supply, to equip

provisions NOUN
We had enough **provisions** for two weeks.
• food, rations, stores, supplies

provoke VERB
❶ Stop trying to **provoke** your sister!
• to annoy, to irritate, to anger, to infuriate,
to exasperate, to tease, to taunt
OPPOSITE to pacify
❷ His words **provoked** laughter.
• to arouse, to produce, to cause, to generate,
to induce, to stimulate, to inspire

prowl VERB
The leopard **prowled** through the long grass.
• to slink, to creep, to roam, to sneak, to steal

public ADJECTIVE
❶ This is a **public** park.
• common, communal, general, open, shared
OPPOSITE private
❷ These facts are **public** knowledge.
• well-known, acknowledged, published,
open, general
OPPOSITE secret

public NOUN
➤ the public
This part of the castle is not open to **the public**.
• people in general, everyone, the community
➤ in public
I'm too shy to sing **in public**.
• publicly, openly, in front of an audience
OPPOSITE in private

publicity NOUN
Did you see the **publicity** for the book fair?
• advertising, advertisements, marketing

publish VERB
❶ The magazine is **published** every week.
• to issue, to print, to produce, to bring out,
to release, to circulate
❷ When will they **publish** the results?
• to announce, to declare, to disclose, to make
known, to make public, to report, to reveal
— To **broadcast** information is to publish it on
TV or radio.

puff VERB
❶ The dragon **puffed** green smoke from its nostrils.
• to blow out, to send out, to emit, to belch
❷ By the end of the race I was **puffing**.
• to breathe heavily, to pant, to gasp, to wheeze
❸ The sails **puffed** out as the wind rose.
• to billow, to swell, to inflate

puff NOUN
❶ A **puff** of wind caught his hat.
• a gust, a breath, a flurry
❷ A **puff** of smoke rose from the chimney.
• a cloud, a wisp
— A **column** or **plume** of smoke is a line of it.

pull VERB
❶ She **pulled** her chair nearer to the desk.
• to drag, to draw, to haul, to lug
❷ I grabbed the handle and **pulled** hard.
• to tug, to yank, to heave
❸ She **pulled** her hand away.
• to tear, to wrench, to snatch, to drag, to rip
❹ The car was **pulling** a caravan.
• to tow, to trail, to draw
OPPOSITE to push
➤ to pull out
The dentist **pulled out** one of my teeth.
• to extract, to take out, to remove

pump VERB
The fire brigade **pumped** water out of the cellar.
• to drain, to draw off, to empty

punch VERB
❶ The boxer **punched** his opponent.
• to thump, to strike, to hit
》 For other ways of hitting look at **hit**.
❷ This tool **punches** holes in paper.
• to bore, to pierce

punctual ADJECTIVE
The bus was **punctual** today.
• on time, prompt
OPPOSITE late

punish VERB
*Those responsible for the damage will be **punished**.*
• to penalise, to discipline, to chastise

punishment NOUN
*There were harsh **punishments** for stealing.*
• a penalty
— **Detention** is the punishment of being made to stay behind after school.
— A **fine** is money that someone must pay as a punishment.
— A **sentence** is a punishment given in court, usually a period of time in prison.
— **Execution** is being killed as a punishment.
— **Exile** or **banishment** is being sent away as a punishment.

pupil NOUN
*There are 33 **pupils** in our class.*
• a student, a schoolchild, a learner

pure ADJECTIVE
❶ *The bracelet is made of **pure** gold.*
• real, solid, unmixed, authentic, genuine
❷ *All our dishes are made from **pure** ingredients.*
• natural, wholesome, fresh
❸ *They swam in the **pure** clear water of the lake.*
• clean, fresh, unpolluted
OPPOSITE impure

purple NOUN, ADJECTIVE

WORD WEB

SOME SHADES OF PURPLE:
• lavender, lilac, magenta, mauve, plum, violet

purpose NOUN
❶ *What is the **purpose** of the exercise?*
• the intention, the aim, the goal, the target, the objective
❷ *Does this invention have any particular **purpose**?*
• a point, a use, usefulness, value

purse NOUN
*I always keep some loose change in my **purse**.*
• a wallet, a pouch, a bag

push VERB
❶ *We **pushed** the table into a corner.*
• to shove, to move, to heave
OPPOSITE to pull
❷ *They **pushed** their way through the crowd.*
• to shove, to thrust, to force, to barge, to elbow, to jostle

❸ *She **pushed** me in the back.*
• to shove, to poke, to nudge, to jog, to jostle
❹ *He **pushed** a stick into the ground.*
• to thrust, to force, to plunge, to stab
❺ *Pete **pushed** his things into a bag.*
• to pack, to stuff, to press, to cram, to crush, to compress, to ram, to jam, to squash, to squeeze

put VERB puts, putting, put
❶ *You can **put** your bags in the corner.*
• to place, to set down, to leave, to drop
— To **dump** or **plonk** (informal) something is to put it somewhere carelessly.
❷ *Where are they planning to **put** the car park?*
• to locate, to situate, to position
❸ *The dog **put** its head on my lap.*
• to lay, to lean, to rest
❹ *I'll **put** some pictures on the wall.*
• to attach, to fasten, to fix, to hang
➤ **to put something in**
Put in the disk and press 'Start'.
• to insert, to install
➤ **to put someone off**
*Not many people came because the bad weather **put** them **off**.*
• to deter, to discourage, to dissuade
➤ **to put something off**
*He **put off** the party because he was ill.*
• to delay, to postpone, to defer
➤ **to put something up**
*It doesn't take long to **put up** the tent.*
• to set up, to construct, to erect, to assemble
*I'm going to buy a new bike before they **put up** the price.*
• to increase, to raise
➤ **to put up with something**
*I don't know how you **put up with** that noise.*
• to bear, to stand, to tolerate, to endure, to withstand

puzzle NOUN
❶ *The website has lots of games and **puzzles**.*
• a riddle, a question, a problem, a brainteaser
❷ *The disappearance of the keys was a **puzzle**.*
• a mystery, a riddle, an enigma
puzzle VERB
*The message **puzzled** him.*
• to confuse, to baffle, to bewilder, to mystify, to perplex

pyramid NOUN
» *For some things to do with ancient Egypt look at* **museum**.

a b c d e f g h i j k l m n o **p** q r s t u v w x y z

Qq

⚙ Can you think of a word to describe
a) a quiet voice
b) a quiet person
c) a quiet place?

⚙ Do you know a word meaning 'so quiet you can't hear it'?
I N _ _ D _ _ _ E

⚙ Check the thesaurus to find answers!

quake *VERB*
*The ground **quaked** with the thud of the giant's footsteps.*
• to shake, to shudder, to tremble, to quiver, to shiver, to vibrate, to rock, to sway, to wobble

qualification *NOUN*
*What **qualifications** do you need to be a vet?*
• a diploma, a certificate, a degree, knowledge, training, skill

quality *NOUN*
❶ *We only use ingredients of the highest **quality**.*
• a standard, a class, a grade
❷ *Stretchiness is a **quality** of rubber.*
• a characteristic, a feature, a property

quantity *NOUN*
*A huge **quantity** of food is wasted every day.*
• an amount, a mass, a volume, a load
— A **number** is a quantity that can be counted: *We had a huge **number** of sandwiches left over.*

quarrel *NOUN*
*She had a **quarrel** with her best friend.*
• an argument, a disagreement, a dispute, a row, a squabble, a clash, a fight
— A **feud** is a bitter quarrel that lasts a long time.

quarrel *VERB*
*They **quarrelled** over who should sit in the front.*
• to disagree, to argue, to row, to squabble, to clash, to fight, to fall out

quay *NOUN*
*The ship unloaded its cargo on to the **quay**.*
• a dock, a harbour, a pier, a wharf, a jetty

quest *NOUN*
*The knights set out on a **quest** to find the enchanted tower.*
• an expedition, a mission, a search, a hunt

question *NOUN*
*Does anyone have any **questions**?*
• an enquiry, a query

question *VERB*
❶ *The detective **questioned** everyone who was in the house.*
• to ask, to interview, to quiz, to interrogate, to examine, to probe
— To **grill** someone is to ask them a lot of questions in a severe way.
❷ *He **questioned** the judge's decision.*
• to challenge, to dispute, to argue over, to quarrel with, to object to, to query, to doubt

queue *NOUN*
*There was a **queue** of people outside the cinema.*
• a line, a file, a column, a string
— A **jam** or a **tailback** is a queue of traffic.

queue *VERB*
*Please **queue** at the door.*
• to line up, to form a queue

quick *ADJECTIVE*
❶ *You'd better be **quick** the bus leaves in 10 minutes.*
• fast, swift, rapid, speedy, hasty
— A common simile is as **quick** as a flash.
OPPOSITE slow
❷ *We had a **quick** chat.*
• short, brief
OPPOSITES long, lengthy

quicken *VERB*
*The runners **quickened** their pace.*
• to accelerate, to speed up, to hurry up, to hasten

quiet *ADJECTIVE*
❶ *The deserted house was still and **quiet**.*
• silent, noiseless, soundless
— A common simile is **as quiet as a mouse**.
`OPPOSITE` noisy
❷ *The children spoke in **quiet** whispers.*
• hushed, muffled, low, soft
— Use **inaudible** for something so quiet that you can't hear it.
`OPPOSITE` loud
❸ *Amy has always been a **quiet** child.*
• shy, reserved, withdrawn
`OPPOSITE` talkative
❹ *We found a **quiet** place for a picnic.*
• peaceful, secluded, isolated, restful, tranquil, calm, serene
`OPPOSITE` busy

quiet *NOUN*
*Can we have some **quiet**, please?*
• peace, silence
— A **lull** is a quiet period during a storm or a lot of noise.
`OPPOSITE` noise

quieten *VERB*
*The teacher tried to **quieten** the class.*
• to calm, to hush, to pacify, to soothe

quit *VERB* **quits, quitting, quitted, quit**
*She **quit** her job to travel round the world.*
• to give up, to leave, to resign from

quite *ADVERB*
❶ *They played **quite** well but not brilliantly.*
• fairly, reasonably, moderately
❷ *Are you **quite** sure?*
• completely, totally, utterly, entirely, absolutely

quiz *NOUN*
*Our class took part in a general knowledge **quiz**.*
• a test, a questionnaire, a contest

quotation *NOUN*
*I copied a short **quotation** from the book.*
• an extract, a passage, a piece

quote *VERB*
*He **quoted** some lines from a poem.*
• to recite, to repeat

⚙ Can you think of 3 different ways to say 'run'?

⚙ Can you think of a verb meaning 'to run with short steps'?

⚙ Check the thesaurus to find answers!

race *NOUN*
*We had a **race** to see who was the fastest.*
• a competition, a contest, a chase

🕸 **WORD WEB**

SOME TYPES OF RACE:

• a marathon, a sprint, a relay race, hurdles, a cross-country race, a horse race
— A **heat** is a race to decide who will race in the final.
— A **lap** is one time around a racetrack.

race *VERB*
❶ *We **raced** each other to the end of the road.*
• to have a race with, to run against, to compete with
❷ *The train **raced** towards him.*
• to rush, to dash, to fly, to tear, to hurry, to sprint, to whizz, to zoom

rack *NOUN*
*Cooking pots hung from a **rack** on the wall.*
• a frame, a framework, a shelf, a support

rage *NOUN*
*Derek slammed the door in **rage**.*
• anger, fury
— A **tantrum** or a **fit of temper** is an outburst of rage, especially by a child.

ragged *ADJECTIVE*
*They met a traveller wearing **ragged** clothes.*
• tattered, tatty, threadbare, torn, frayed, ripped, shabby, worn-out

a
b
c
d
e
f
g
h
i
j
k
l
m
n
o
p
q
r
s
t
u
v
w
x
y
z

raid NOUN
The enemy **raid** caught them by surprise.
• an attack, an assault, a strike, an invasion

raid VERB
❶ Long ago, Vikings **raided** the towns on the coast.
• to attack, to invade, to ransack, to plunder, to loot
❷ Police **raided** the house at dawn.
• to descend on, to storm, to swoop on

rail NOUN
The fence was made of iron **rails**.
• a bar, a rod, a post, a pole, a spar

railway NOUN
» Look at **train**

rain NOUN
There was some **rain** this morning.
• a shower
— **Drizzle** is very light rain.
— A **deluge** or a **downpour** is a very heavy fall of rain.
— **Rainfall** is the amount of rain that falls somewhere in a period of time.
— A **drought** is a long time when there is no rain.

rain VERB
It's still **raining**.
— To **drizzle** or to **spit** is to rain lightly.
— To **pour** is to rain heavily.

😀 **WRITING TIPS**

Here are some useful words for writing about **rain**:

THINGS RAIN DOES:

• to drip, to fall, to patter, to pour, to drum, to beat, to hammer, to lash, to pelt, to stream down, to drench someone, to soak someone

The sky rumbled loudly above them and the rain continued to pour down, bouncing on the lane and running into little streams.—GOODNIGHT MISTER TOM, Michelle Magorian

WAYS TO DESCRIBE RAIN:

• heavy, incessant, driving, pouring, pelting, torrential, light, gentle, soft, drizzling

---

rainy ADJECTIVE
We play indoors on **rainy** days.
• wet, showery
— Use **drizzly** or **damp** if it is slightly rainy.

raise VERB
❶ **Raise** your hand if you need help.
• to hold up, to put up, to lift

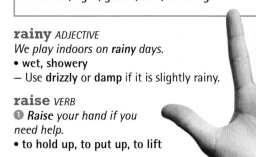

❷ The sunken treasure was **raised** from the ocean bed.
• to lift, to pick up, to hoist, to haul up
❸ The bus company is **raising** their fares.
• to increase, to put up
❹ We **raised** £1000 for charity.
• to collect, to gather, to take in, to make
❺ **Raising** children is hard work.
• to bring up, to rear, to look after, to care for
— To **adopt** a child is to take it into your family and make it legally your own child.
— To **foster** a child is to take it into your home and look after it, but without adopting it.

rampage VERB
An angry mob **rampaged** through the streets.
• to run wild, to go wild, to go berserk, to race about, to rush about

ran (past tense of **run**)

random ADJECTIVE
They picked a **random** group of pupils.
• chance, unplanned, casual
OPPOSITE deliberate

rang (past tense of **ring**)

range NOUN
❶ Supermarkets sell a wide **range** of goods.
• a variety, an assortment, a selection, a choice
❷ The books are aimed at the 8–11 age **range**.
• a group, a band, a span, a scope
❸ There is a **range** of mountains to the south.
• a chain, a line, a row, a series, a string

range VERB
Prices **range** from five to twenty pounds.
• to vary, to differ, to extend, to span

rank NOUN
A black belt is the highest **rank** in judo.
• a grade, a level, a position, a status

rare ADJECTIVE
These animals are now very **rare**.
• uncommon, unusual, infrequent, scarce, sparse
OPPOSITE common

rate NOUN
The cyclists were pedalling at a furious **rate**.
• a pace, a speed, a frequency

rather ADVERB
It's **rather** chilly today.
• quite, fairly, moderately, slightly, somewhat, a bit, a little

➤ **would rather**
I would rather stay at home.
• would prefer to, would sooner, would preferably

ratio NOUN
The ratio of boys to girls is about 50–50.
• the proportion, the balance

ration NOUN
The pirates each had a daily ration of rum.
• a portion, a quota, a share, an allowance,
a helping, a measure
➤ **rations**
The astronauts took enough rations to last a month.
• food, provisions, stores, supplies

ration VERB
We had to ration the food.
• to limit, to restrict

rattle NOUN, VERB
» *For various sounds look
at sound.*

raw ADJECTIVE
❶ *The salad is made with raw carrots.*
• uncooked
OPPOSITE cooked
❷ *These are the raw materials for making steel.*
• crude, natural, unprocessed, untreated
OPPOSITES manufactured, processed

ray NOUN
A ray of light shone through the crack in the door.
• a beam, a shaft, a stream

reach VERB
❶ *They hoped to reach Oxford by lunchtime.*
• to arrive at, to get to, to get as far as, to make it to
❷ *I'm not tall enough to reach the top shelf.*
• to touch, to get hold of, to grasp, to access
➤ **to reach out**
Reach out your hands.
• to extend, to hold out, to put out, to stick out,
to stretch out

reach NOUN
❶ *The shelf was just within his reach.*
• grasp
❷ *The shops are within easy reach.*
• distance, range

react VERB
How did he react when he read the letter?
• to respond, to behave, to answer, to reply

reaction NOUN
What was her reaction when you said you were sorry?
• a response, an answer, a reply

read VERB reads, reading, read
❶ *Have you read this book?*
— To **skim** is to read something quickly in order to
get the general idea.
— To **scan** is to quickly read through something
looking for particular information.
— To **browse** is to read through magazines, books or
the Internet looking at several different parts.
— To **pore over** something is to read it carefully for a
long time.
❷ *They couldn't read the doctor's handwriting.*
• to make out, to understand, to decipher
— Something that you cannot read is **illegible**.

ready ADJECTIVE
❶ *When will tea be ready?*
• prepared, done, finished
OPPOSITE not ready
❷ *I'm ready to go.*
• set, poised, waiting
OPPOSITE not ready
❸ *He's always ready to help.*
• willing, prepared, glad, pleased,
happy
OPPOSITE unwilling

real ADJECTIVE
❶ *History is about real events.*
• actual, true, factual
OPPOSITES fictitious, imaginary
❷ *The necklace was made from real rubies.*
• authentic, genuine, natural
OPPOSITES artificial, fake
❸ *She rarely shows her real feelings.*
• true, sincere, genuine, honest
OPPOSITE insincere

realise VERB
We began to realise that something was wrong.
• to understand, to appreciate, to grasp,
to comprehend, to recognise, to see

realistic ADJECTIVE
❶ *The portrait is very realistic.*
• lifelike, true to life, faithful, convincing,
recognisable
❷ *It's not realistic to expect a baby to be quiet all
the time.*
• practical, sensible, possible, feasible
OPPOSITE unrealistic

reality NOUN
It's time to face reality.
• the facts, the real world, the truth

really *ADVERB*
❶ *I saw a really good film last night.*
• very, extremely, exceptionally
❷ *Are you really leaving?*
• actually, definitely, truly, in fact, genuinely, honestly

reason *NOUN*
❶ *What was the reason for the delay?*
• the cause, the explanation
❷ *Did you have a reason for not telling the truth?*
• a motive, a justification, an excuse, grounds
❸ *They tried to make him see reason.*
• sense, common sense, logic

reason *VERB*
➤ **to reason with someone**
We tried to reason with him, but he wouldn't change his mind.
• to argue with, to persuade, to talk round

reasonable *ADJECTIVE*
❶ *That seems like a reasonable plan.*
• sensible, intelligent, rational, logical, sane
OPPOSITE irrational
❷ *£10 for that T-shirt is reasonable.*
• fair, acceptable, right, appropriate
OPPOSITE unreasonable

reassure *VERB*
The teacher reassured us that the test was not hard.
• to calm, to comfort, to encourage, to console
OPPOSITE to threaten

rebel *VERB*
The king feared that the people would rebel.
• to revolt, to rise up
— To **mutiny** is to rebel against the captain of a ship.
OPPOSITE to obey

rebellion *NOUN*
The protest soon became a widespread rebellion.
• a revolt, a revolution, an uprising
— A **mutiny** is a rebellion on a ship.

receive *VERB*
❶ *I received lots of presents.*
• to get, to be given, to be sent
OPPOSITE to give
❷ *Some passengers received minor injuries.*
• to experience, to suffer, to undergo, to sustain
OPPOSITE to inflict

recent *ADJECTIVE*
Have you seen her recent film?
• current, latest, new

recently *ADVERB*
Have you read any good books recently?
• lately, in recent weeks

recipe *NOUN*
This is my mum's recipe for pancakes.
• directions, instructions
— The **ingredients** are the food items in a recipe.

reckless *ADJECTIVE*
It was reckless to run across the road like that.
• careless, irresponsible, thoughtless, foolish, rash, impulsive
OPPOSITE careful

reckon *VERB*
❶ *How many do you reckon we need?*
• to calculate, to work out, to estimate, to assess, to figure, to suppose
❷ *I reckon it's about to rain.*
• to think, to believe, to guess, to imagine, to feel

recognise *VERB*
❶ *I recognised his face.*
• to identify, to know, to be familiar with, to recall, to recollect, to remember
❷ *He refused to recognise that he was to blame.*
• to acknowledge, to admit, to accept, to grant, to concede, to confess, to realise

recommend *VERB*
❶ *I had the strawberry ice cream because my friend recommended it.*
• to praise, to commend, to compliment, to advise
❷ *I recommend you see a doctor.*
• to advise, to counsel, to suggest
• to encourage: *I encourage you to see a doctor.*

record *NOUN*
The zookeepers keep a record of the animals' diet.
• an account, a report, a register
— A **diary** or a **journal** is a daily record.
— A **log** is a record of what happens on a journey.

record *VERB*
❶ *The concert is being recorded by the BBC.*
• to tape, to video, to film
❷ *She recorded our names in a notebook.*
• to write down, to note, to set down, to put down, to enter

recover *VERB*
❶ *He soon recovered after his illness.*
• to get better, to feel better, to recuperate, to rally, to revive, to heal, to improve
❷ *The police have recovered the stolen car.*
• to get back, to retrieve, to reclaim, to find, to trace

recycle VERB
We try to recycle as much plastic as we can.
• to reuse, to reprocess, to salvage, to use again

red ADJECTIVE, NOUN
❶ *His face was red with embarrassment.*
• flushed, glowing, rosy, ruddy, blushing
— Common similes are **as red as a beetroot** or **as red as a lobster**.
❷ *Her eyes were red from lack of sleep.*
• bloodshot, inflamed, red-rimmed
❸ *The fairy queen had flaming red hair.*
• ginger, auburn, coppery

 WORD WEB

SOME SHADES OF RED:

• blood red, brick red, cherry, crimson, maroon, ruby, scarlet, wine
Autumn leaves, blood red, floated on the dark waters of the loch and clogged together round the edges of the shore.–SKY HAWK, Gill Lewis
» Look at **pink**.

reduce VERB
❶ *She's reduced the amount of sugar in her diet.*
• to decrease, to lessen, to lower, to cut
OPPOSITE to increase
❷ *This medicine will reduce the pain.*
• to ease, to relieve, to lessen, to soothe

reflection NOUN
Gus could see his reflection in the pond.
• an image, a likeness

refresh VERB
They refreshed themselves with a glass of lemonade.
• to revive, to restore, to invigorate, to cool, to freshen

refreshing ADJECTIVE
We went for a refreshing dip in the pool.
• reviving, invigorating, cooling, stimulating

refuge NOUN
❶ *They stayed safe in their mountain refuge.*
• a haven, a sanctuary, a hideout
❷ *There was no refuge from the storm.*
• shelter, protection, cover

refuse (say ri-fewz) VERB
❶ *He refused my offer of help.*
• to decline, to reject, to turn down, to say no to
OPPOSITE to accept
❷ *They refused us permission to enter.*
• to deny
OPPOSITES to give, to grant

refuse (say ref-yooss) NOUN
Dispose of your refuse carefully.
• rubbish, waste, trash, litter

regard VERB
❶ *I regard her as a friend.*
• to think of, to consider, to judge
❷ *She regarded him suspiciously.*
• to look at, to eye, to view, to watch, to observe

regarding PREPOSITION
We received a letter regarding the trip.
• about, concerning, on the subject of, with reference to, with regard to

region NOUN
❶ *The Arctic and Antarctic are polar regions.*
• an area, a place, a land, a territory, a zone, a part of the world
❷ *We live in the north-west region.*
• an area, a district, a county

regret VERB
She regretted the mean things she had said.
• to be sorry for, to repent, to feel sad about, to feel remorse for

regular ADJECTIVE
❶ *They have regular meetings.*
• frequent, evenly spaced
— Use **daily**, **weekly**, etc. for something that happens every day, week, etc.
— Use **annual** or **yearly** for something that happens every year.
OPPOSITES irregular, occasional
❷ *The drummer kept up a regular rhythm.*
• constant, consistent, steady, uniform
— A common simile is **as regular as clockwork**.
OPPOSITE erratic
❸ *She has very regular teeth.*
• even, symmetrical, straight
OPPOSITES irregular, uneven
❹ *Is this your regular route to school?*
• normal, usual, customary, habitual, ordinary, routine
OPPOSITE unusual

a b c d e f g h i j k l m n o p q r s t u v w x y z

regulate VERB
This button **regulates** the temperature.
• to control, to set, to adjust, to alter, to change, to moderate

regulation NOUN
There are new **regulations** on school uniform.
• a rule, a requirement
— A **law** is a regulation that everyone in a country must obey.

rehearsal NOUN
The actors had to learn their words before the **rehearsal**.
• practice, preparation, run-through
— A **dress rehearsal** is a final practice in which actors wear their costumes.

rehearse VERB
We had to **rehearse** the scene all over again.
• to go over, to practise, to run through

reign VERB
Which British monarch **reigned** the longest?
• to rule, to govern, to be on the throne, to be king or queen

reject VERB
At first, she **rejected** their offer of help.
• to decline, to refuse, to turn down, to say no to
OPPOSITE to accept

relate VERB
❶ Does anything **relate** these two crimes?
• to connect, to link, to associate
❷ She **related** what had happened to her on her journey.
• to tell, to narrate, to report, to describe
➤ **relate to**
The letter **relates to** your great-grandfather.
• to be about, to refer to, to have to do with, to concern

relation NOUN
❶ Are you a **relation** of hers?
• a relative, a member of the family
— Your **kin** are your relations: She was happy to be reunited with her **kin**.
❷ There is no **relation** between the two events.
• a connection, a link, an association

relationship NOUN
❶ There is a **relationship** between your diet and health.
• a connection, a link, an association
— A **ratio** is the relationship between two numbers.

❷ The twins have a close **relationship**.
• a bond, an attachment, a friendship, an understanding

relax VERB
❶ I like to **relax** by listening to music.
• to unwind, to rest
❷ Once we had caught the train I started to **relax**.
• to calm down, to become calm, to stop worrying
❸ **Relax** your shoulder muscles.
• to loosen, to ease, to let go
OPPOSITES to tighten, to contract

relaxed ADJECTIVE
❶ I felt very **relaxed** lying in the sun
• calm, peaceful, carefree
OPPOSITE tense
❷ Our classroom usually has quite a **relaxed** atmosphere.
• easy-going, informal, calm, casual, laid-back (informal)
OPPOSITE stressful

release VERB
❶ They **released** all the prisoners.
• to free, to let go, to set free, to liberate
OPPOSITE to imprison
❷ He **released** the catch on the safety belt.
• to unfasten, to undo
OPPOSITE to fasten

relevant ADJECTIVE
His remarks were not **relevant** to the discussion.
• related, connected, linked, appropriate, applicable
OPPOSITE irrelevant

reliable ADJECTIVE
❶ She is my most **reliable** friend.
• dependable, trustworthy, faithful, loyal, staunch, true
❷ I'm surprised at George being so silly—he's usually very **reliable**.
• dependable, trustworthy, steady, sensible, serious
OPPOSITE unreliable

relief NOUN
❶ It was such a **relief** when we reached dry land.
• a comfort, a blessing, a pleasure
❷ The medicine gave some **relief** from the pain.
• comfort, ease, help

relieve VERB
Rubbing your knee might **relieve** the pain.
• to ease, to help, to lessen, to diminish, to soothe
OPPOSITE to intensify

religion NOUN
People from all religions went to the meeting.
• a faith, a belief
— A **cult** is a small religion, especially one that is considered strange.

 WORD WEB

SOME MAJOR WORLD RELIGIONS AND BELIEVERS:

— A **Buddhist** follows **Buddhism.**
— A **Christian** follows **Christianity.**
— A **Hindu** follows **Hinduism.**
— A **Jew** follows **Judaism.**
— A **Muslim** follows **Islam.**
— A **Sikh** follows **Sikhism.**
» *For religious leaders look at* **priest.**

religious ADJECTIVE
❶ *There was a religious ceremony.*
• sacred, holy, divine
OPPOSITE secular
❷ *My grandparents are very religious.*
• devout, pious, spiritual

reluctant ADJECTIVE
She was reluctant to answer my question.
• unwilling, hesitant, slow
OPPOSITE eager

rely VERB
Are you sure that we can rely on their help?
• to depend on, to count on, to have confidence in, to trust

remain VERB
❶ *It will remain warm and sunny all weekend.*
• to continue, to stay
❷ *The boys were told to remain behind after school.*
• to stay, to wait, to linger
❸ *Little remained of the house after the fire.*
• to be left, to survive

remains NOUN
They cleared away the remains of the picnic.
• remnants, leftovers, fragments, traces, scraps
— **Debris** is scattered remains left after something has been destroyed.
— **Ruins** are remains still standing after a building has been destroyed.
— A **relic** is something that has survived from an ancient time.

remark VERB
He remarked that it was a nice day.
• to say, to state, to comment, to note, to declare, to mention, to observe, to point out
» *For more ways to say things look at* **say.**

remark NOUN
They exchanged a few remarks about the weather.
• a comment, an observation, a word, a statement, a thought

remarkable ADJECTIVE
The Northern Lights are a remarkable sight.
• astonishing, astounding, incredible, extraordinary, staggering, unforgettable, breathtaking, sensational, tremendous, wonderful, marvellous, impressive

remember VERB
❶ *Can you remember his name?*
• to recall, to recollect
❷ *He was trying to remember his lines for the play.*
• to learn, to memorise, to keep in mind
OPPOSITE to forget

remind VERB
Mum reminded me to take my bag.
• to prompt, to jog someone's memory
➤ **to remind someone of something**
What does this tune remind you of?
• to make you think of, to take you back to

reminder NOUN
❶ *I sometimes need a reminder to take my lunch.*
• a prompt, a cue, a hint, a nudge
❷ *The photographs are a reminder of our holiday.*
• a souvenir

remote ADJECTIVE
❶ *They live on a remote farm.*
• distant, faraway, isolated, inaccessible
OPPOSITE accessible
❷ *The chances of us winning are remote.*
• poor, slender, slight, small
OPPOSITE high

remove VERB
❶ *Please remove your rubbish.*
• to clear away, to take away
❷ *The dentist removed my bad tooth.*
• to extract, to pull out, to take out, to withdraw
❸ *We removed our muddy shoes.*
• to take off, to kick off, to slip off
❹ *The rowdy passengers were removed from the bus.*
• to throw out, to eject, to expel
— To **evict** someone is to remove them from a place where they are living.
❺ *I decided to remove the last paragraph.*
• to cut, to delete, to erase, to get rid of, to cross out

rent VERB
You can rent a bike for the day.
• to hire, to lease

repair VERB
Dad said he could repair my bike.
• to mend, to fix, to put right

repay VERB repays, repaying, repaid
❶ *I can repay you the money next week.*
• to pay back
— To **refund** someone's money is to give it back because they are not happy with what they bought.
❷ *How can we ever repay your kindness?*
• to return, to pay back

repeat VERB
❶ *Could you repeat that, please?*
• to say again, to echo
❷ *He repeated a few lines of the poem.*
• to recite, to quote, to read back
❸ *The actors had to repeat the opening scene.*
• to redo, to do again

repeatedly ADVERB
We warned them repeatedly about the danger.
• again and again, over and over, regularly, time after time, frequently, often

repel VERB
❶ *They managed to repel the invaders.*
• to drive back, to beat back, to push back, to fend off, to ward off, to keep away
❷ *The smell repelled us.*
• to disgust, to revolt, to sicken, to offend

replace VERB
❶ *The spy carefully replaced the missing document.*
• to put back, to return, to restore
❷ *Who will replace the head teacher when she retires?*
• to follow, to succeed, to take over from, to take the place of

reply NOUN
I haven't had a reply to my email.
• a response, an answer, a reaction, an acknowledgement
— A **retort** is an angry reply.

reply VERB
She took a long time to reply.
• to answer, to respond, to react, to give a response, to give a reply

report VERB
The newspapers reported what happened.
• to give an account of, to record, to state, to describe, to tell, to narrate

report NOUN
❶ *We had to write a report of the experiment.*
• an account, a description
❷ *There was a report about our school in the local newspaper.*
• an article, a story, a piece

reporter NOUN
The film star was being interviewed by a TV reporter.
• a journalist, a correspondent

represent VERB
❶ *The graph represents the favourite foods of everyone in the class.*
• to portray, to show, to depict, to illustrate
❷ *A dove is often said to represent peace.*
• to stand for, to symbolise
❸ *I represent our class on the school council.*
• to speak for, to act for

reproduce VERB
❶ *The computer can reproduce a human voice.*
• to copy, to duplicate, to imitate, to mimic
❷ *Mice reproduce very quickly.*
• to breed, to produce offspring, to multiply

reproduction NOUN
Is that an original painting or a reproduction?
• a copy, a replica, an imitation, a likeness, a duplicate
— A **fake** or a **forgery** is a reproduction which is intended to deceive people.

reptile NOUN

✺ **WORD WEB**

SOME REPTILES:

• an alligator, a chameleon, a crocodile, a dinosaur, a gecko, a lizard, a snake, a terrapin, a tortoise, a turtle
» *For writing about snakes look at* **snake**.
» *For other animals look at* **animal**.

a terrapin

a lizard

an alligator

reputation NOUN
❶ *The school has a good reputation.*
• a name, an image
❷ *Her reputation as a singer spread quickly.*
• fame, celebrity

request VERB
I requested more time to finish my story.
• to ask for, to appeal for, to apply for, to plead for

request NOUN
They have ignored our request for help.
• an appeal, a plea, a call
— An **application** is a request for a job or to join something.
— A **petition** is a request signed by a lot of people.

require VERB
We will give you any help that you require.
• to need, to want
➤ **to be required to**
Visitors are required to sign the register.
• must, have to, to be obliged to, to be instructed to, to be requested to, to be directed to

rescue VERB
❶ *The brave firefighters rescued them from the tower.*
• to save, to free, to liberate, to release, to set free
❷ *The divers rescued some items from the sunken ship.*
• to retrieve, to recover, to save, to salvage

resemblance NOUN
It's easy to see the resemblance between the two sisters.
• a likeness, a similarity
OPPOSITE a difference

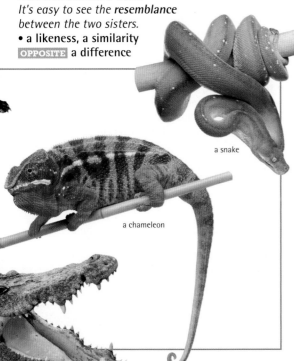

a snake

a chameleon

resemble VERB
The device resembles a fork.
• to look like, to be similar to

resent VERB
I resented him winning because I thought I deserved it.
• to be annoyed about, to be resentful about, to begrudge, to grudge

reservation NOUN
❶ *Mum made a reservation at a restaurant.*
• a booking
❷ *She had reservations about whether the plan would work.*
• a doubt, a hesitation
— If you have reservations about something, you are **sceptical** about it.

reserve VERB
❶ *Reserve some sugar to sprinkle on top.*
• to keep, to put aside, to set aside, to save, to preserve
❷ *Have you reserved your seats on the train?*
• to book, to order

reserve NOUN
❶ *The climbers kept a reserve of food in their base camp.*
• a stock, a store, a supply, a hoard
❷ *The wildlife reserve has many different species of birds.*
• a reservation, a park, a sanctuary

resign VERB
The manager of the football team resigned.
• to leave, to quit, to stand down

resist VERB
❶ *They resisted the Roman invasion.*
• to oppose, to defy, to stand up to
OPPOSITES to yield to, to surrender to
❷ *The material can resist high temperatures.*
• to withstand, to tolerate, to endure, to survive
❸ *I can't resist chocolate cake.*
• to hold back from, to refuse

resolve VERB
❶ *There was a meeting to try to resolve the dispute.*
• to settle, to sort out, to end, to overcome
❷ *I resolved to try harder next time.*
• to decide, to determine, to make up your mind

respect NOUN
❶ *Her team is full of respect for her.*
• admiration, regard, honour, reverence
OPPOSITE contempt

❷ *Have some **respect** for other people's feelings.*
• consideration, regard, sympathy, thought, concern
OPPOSITE disrespect
❸ *It's a strange story in some **respects**.*
• way, point, aspect, feature, characteristic, detail, particular

respect VERB
❶ *Everyone **respects** her for her courage.*
• to admire, to revere, to honour, to look up to
OPPOSITES to scorn, to despise
❷ *We should **respect** their wishes.*
• to obey, to follow, to observe, to consider
OPPOSITE to ignore

respectable ADJECTIVE
*He came from a very **respectable** family.*
• decent, honest, honourable, upright, worthy

respond VERB
*I asked a question, but he didn't **respond**.*
• to reply, to answer, to react

response NOUN
*Did you get a **response** to your letter?*
• a reply, an answer, a reaction, an acknowledgement
– A **retort** is an angry response.

responsible ADJECTIVE
*He's a very **responsible** boy.*
• reliable, sensible, dependable, trustworthy, conscientious, dutiful
OPPOSITE irresponsible
➤ **to be responsible for**
❶ *The teacher is **responsible for** the children on the trip.*
• to be in charge of, to supervise, to look after, to manage
❷ *Who **was responsible for** this mistake?*
• to be to blame for, to be at fault for, to be guilty of

rest NOUN
*I was tired so I had a **rest**.*
• a break, a pause, a lie-down, a nap
➤ **the rest**
❶ *If you've finished, the dog will eat **the rest**.*
• the remainder, the remains, the leftovers
❷ *A few people have arrived and **the rest** are coming later.*
• the others, the remainder

rest VERB
❶ *I think we should stop and **rest** for a while.*
• to have a rest, to have a break, to lie down, to relax, to have a nap

❷ *I **rested** my bike against the wall.*
• to lean, to prop, to stand, to place, to support

restaurant NOUN

 WORD WEB

SOME TYPES OF RESTAURANT:
• a buffet, a cafe, a cafeteria, a canteen, a takeaway

restrict VERB
*The new law **restricts** the sale of fireworks.*
• to control, to limit, to regulate, to restrain

result NOUN
❶ *The water shortage is a **result** of a long drought.*
• the consequence, the effect, the outcome
– The result of a trial is the **verdict**.
❷ *If you subtract one number from the other, what is the **result**?*
• the answer, the total
– The **sum** is the result of adding numbers together.
– The **product** is the result of multiplying numbers together.
– The **score** is the result at the end of a game or test.

result VERB
*He had a bruise which **resulted** from a fall.*
• to be caused by, to be the result of, to follow
➤ **to result in**
*Severe flooding **resulted in** chaos on the roads.*
• to cause, to bring about, to lead to, to precede

retreat VERB
*We **retreated** to a safe position.*
• to move back, to draw back, to withdraw, to retire
– To **recoil** is to move back suddenly, because you are shocked or disgusted.
– If flood water moves back, it **recedes**.

return VERB
❶ *They **returned** to the spot the next day to search again.*
• to go back to, to revisit
❷ *What time will she **return** from school?*
• to come back, to get back, to come home, to get home
❸ *Please **return** the books you borrowed.*
• to give back, to put back, to restore
– To **repay** money is to give it back.
❹ *The game didn't work so I **returned** it.*
• to send back, to take back

reveal VERB
❶ *The spy refused to reveal his real identity.*
• to declare, to disclose, to make known, to confess, to admit, to announce, to publish, to tell
❷ *She drew back the curtain to reveal a secret door.*
• to uncover, to unveil, to expose
OPPOSITE to hide

revenge NOUN
He wanted revenge for what they had done.
• vengeance, retribution
➤ **to take revenge on**
He threatened to take revenge on them all.
• to take vengeance on, to get even with, to repay

reverse NOUN
The picture had some writing on the reverse.
• the other side, the back
➤ **in reverse**
The image appears in reverse.
• backwards, back to front, reversed

reverse VERB
❶ *The mirror reverses the image.*
• to turn round, to invert
❷ *He tried to reverse into the space.*
• to back, to go backwards

review NOUN
We had to write a review of the book.
• a criticism, an evaluation, an assessment
• a report: *We had to write a report on the book.*

revolting ADJECTIVE
What is that revolting smell?
• disgusting, repulsive, sickening, appalling, offensive, foul, horrible, nasty, nauseating, loathsome, vile, gross (informal)
OPPOSITE pleasant

revolve VERB
The earth revolves once every 24 hours.
• to rotate, to turn
— To **spin** or to **whirl** is to revolve quickly.
— To **circle** or to **orbit** something is to revolve around it.

reward NOUN
There is a reward for finding the missing cat.
• a prize, a bonus, a payment, an award
OPPOSITE a punishment

reward VERB
Her kindness was rewarded.
• to repay, to compensate, to pay someone back, to give someone a reward

rewarding ADJECTIVE
Being a vet must be a rewarding job.
• satisfying, pleasing, worthwhile
OPPOSITE thankless

rhythm NOUN
We tapped our feet to the rhythm of the music.
• the beat, the pulse

rich ADJECTIVE
❶ *He came from a rich family.*
• wealthy, affluent, prosperous, well-off
OPPOSITE poor
❷ *The palace was full of rich furnishings.*
• luxurious, lavish, costly, expensive, splendid, ornate

riches NOUN
They acquired riches beyond their wildest dreams.
• wealth, money, affluence, prosperity, fortune, treasure

rid VERB rids, ridding, rid
He rid the town of rats.
• to clear, to free, to empty
➤ **to get rid of**
We decided to get rid of some of our old toys.
• to dispose of, to discard, to throw away, to throw out, to dispense with, to dump (informal)

ridden (past participle of **ride**)

riddle NOUN
They had to solve the riddle to find the treasure.
• a puzzle, a mystery, a question, a problem

ride VERB rides, riding, rode, ridden
My little brother is learning to ride a bike.
• to control, to handle, to manage, to steer

ride NOUN
They took us for a ride in their new car.
• a journey, a trip, a drive

ridiculous ADJECTIVE
❶ *You look ridiculous in that hat.*
• absurd, silly, ludicrous, foolish, daft, funny, comical
❷ *What a ridiculous thing to say!*
• absurd, ludicrous, senseless, nonsensical, outrageous, unreasonable, illogical, crazy, idiotic, stupid
OPPOSITE sensible

a
b
c
d
e
f
g
h
i
j
k
l
m
n
o
p
q
r
s
t
u
v
w
x
y
z

right ADJECTIVE
❶ *Is this the **right** spelling?*
• correct, accurate, true, exact
OPPOSITE wrong
❷ *She was waiting for the **right** moment to tell him.*
• proper, appropriate, suitable, ideal
OPPOSITE wrong
❸ *It's not **right** to steal.*
• fair, good, honest, decent, just, honourable, moral, righteous
OPPOSITE wrong

right ADVERB
*She stood **right** in the middle.*
• exactly, precisely, just, completely

right NOUN
*Women wanted the **right** to vote.*
• freedom, liberty, the power, the authority

rigid ADJECTIVE
*The frame of the tent is very **rigid**.*
• solid, stiff, firm, hard

rim NOUN
*Some water spilled over the **rim** of the bucket.*
• the brim, the edge, the lip

ring NOUN
❶ *He wore a gold **ring** on his finger.*
• a band, a hoop
❷ *The dancers stood in a **ring**.*
• a circle, a round, a loop

ring VERB rings, ringing, rang, rung
❶ *Somewhere a bell **rang**.*
• to chime, to peal, to jangle, to jingle, to tinkle, to sound
» *Look at **bell**.*
❷ ***Ring** me tomorrow evening.*
• to phone, to call, to telephone, to ring up

riot NOUN
*The police moved in to stop the **riot**.*
• a commotion, a disorder, a disturbance, a turmoil, an uproar
— A **rebellion** is a disturbance involving people who refuse to obey the authorities or government.

riot VERB
*The crowds were **rioting** in the streets.*
• to run riot, to run wild, to rampage
— To **revolt** or to **rebel** is to refuse to obey the authorities or government.

rip VERB
*She snatched the letter and **ripped** it to pieces.*
• to tear, to shred

ripe ADJECTIVE
*Some of the plums on the tree are **ripe** now.*
• mature, ready to eat
— To become ripe is to **ripen**.

rise VERB rises, rising, rose, risen
❶ *The kite **rose** high into the air.*
• to climb, to mount, to fly up, to ascend, to lift, to soar
OPPOSITE to fall
❷ *A high wall **rose** before us.*
• to tower, to loom, to reach up, to stick up
❸ *The sun **rises** in the east.*
• to come up, to appear
OPPOSITE to set
❹ *The audience **rose** and applauded.*
• to get up, to stand up
OPPOSITES to sit down, to lie down
❺ *Bus fares have **risen** again.*
• to go up, to increase
— To **soar** is to suddenly rise a lot.
— To **double** is to become twice as much.
OPPOSITE to fall

rise NOUN
*There was a **rise** in temperature.*
• an increase, a jump
OPPOSITE a fall

risen (past participle of **rise**)

risk VERB
*The firefighter **risked** his life to save them.*
• to endanger, to put at risk, to gamble with

risk NOUN
❶ *We knew the mission would involve **risk**.*
• danger, hazard, peril, uncertainty
❷ *Telling him the truth was a **risk**.*
• a gamble
❸ *There's a **risk** the river could flood.*
• a chance, a possibility, a danger
➤ **at risk**
*While the animals are out in the open they are at **risk**.*
• vulnerable, in danger, exposed

rival NOUN
*She is his main **rival** for the prize.*
• a competitor, a challenger, an opponent

river NOUN

 WORD WEB

— A **stream** or **brook** is a small river.
— A **tributary** is a small river that flows into a larger river.
— A river's **source** is the place where it begins.
— A river **basin** is the area of land where it comes from.
— A river's **mouth** is the place where it flows into the sea.
— An **estuary** or *(Scottish)* **firth** is a wide river mouth.
— A **delta** is a triangular area at the mouth of a river where it splits into branches.

— A **fork** in the river is a place where it divides.
— A **ford** is a shallow place where you can cross a river.
— **Rapids** are a place where a river flows very fast.
— A **canyon** is a deep valley with a river running through it.
— **Downstream** is the direction that a river flows.
— **Upstream** is the opposite direction.

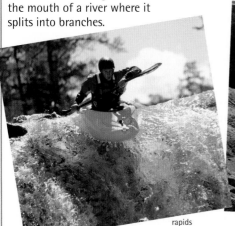

rapids

a canyon

WRITING TIPS

Here are some helpful words for writing about a **river**:

HOW A RIVER FLOWS:

• to cascade, to flood, to gush, to run, to rush, to sweep, to plunge, to swirl, to glide, to meander, to snake, to twist, to weave, to wind, to fork

HOW A RIVER SOUNDS:

• to babble, to burble, to gurgle, to murmur, to ripple, to roar, to splash, to thunder

WORDS TO DESCRIBE A RIVER:

• narrow, broad, wide, mighty, fast-flowing, rushing, slow, placid, shining, meandering, winding, dried-up

Below was the dense tangle of the jungle and beyond that vast grassy plains with a wide river snaking through towards their hill.—DINOSAUR COVE 2: CHARGE OF THE THREE-HORNED MONSTER, Rex Stone

road NOUN

*We live on the same **road**.*

• a street
— An **avenue** is a wide road, usually with trees on each side.
— A **lane** is a narrow road, especially in the country.
— An **alley** is a narrow street or passage.
— A **close** is a street that is closed at one end.
— A **drive** is a private road going up to a house.
— A **motorway** is a very large road for fast traffic travelling between cities.
— An **underpass** is a place where one road passes under another.
— A **viaduct** is a bridge carrying a road (or railway) across a valley.
» *Look at* **path**.

roar NOUN, VERB

*The dragon lifted its mighty head and **roared**.*

• to bellow, to yell, to bawl, to howl, to cry out

rob VERB

The thieves planned to rob a bank.

• to steal from, to break into, to burgle, to hold up, to raid

— To **loot** or **plunder** a place is to violently steal things from it, especially during war.

— To **ransack** a place is to go through it finding things to steal, causing mess and damage.

robber NOUN

» Look at **thief**.

robot NOUN

The robot spoke in a flat metallic voice.

• an automaton, an android

— A **cyberman** is a creature in stories that is part-robot and part-human.

WRITING TIPS

Here are some helpful words for writing about a **robot**:

THINGS A ROBOT MIGHT DO:

• to beep, to bleep, to clank, to flash, to jerk, to judder, to lurch, to lumber, to trundle

SOME WAYS TO DESCRIBE A ROBOT:

• gleaming, metallic, silver, automated, emotionless, mechanical, machine-like, intelligent, lifelike, superhuman

Lydia watched in horror as he began to turn to tin: his hands became metallic gauntlets; his whole body covered in dull grey tones. Soon there was nothing left of the man but an emotionless robot in armoured clothes.—LYDIA'S TIN LID DRUM, Neale Osborne

rock NOUN

We clambered over the rocks on the seashore.

• a boulder, a stone

— A **pebble** is a small rock.

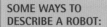

WORD WEB

SOME KINDS OF ROCK:

• chalk, flint, granite, limestone, marble, pumice, quartz, sandstone, slate

— **Permeable** rock lets water soak through it. **Impermeable** rock does not.

— **Ore** is rock with metal in it.

rock VERB

❶ *The cradle rocked gently.*

• to sway, to swing

❷ *The ship rocked violently in the storm.*

• to roll, to toss, to lurch, to pitch

rod NOUN

The framework is held together by steel rods.

• a bar, a rail, a pole, a strut, a shaft, a stick

rode (past tense of **ride**)

rogue NOUN

Don't trust him—he's a rogue.

• a rascal, a villain, a cheat

role NOUN

❶ *Plants have an important role in keeping the air clean.*

• a job, a task, a function

❷ *I got the main role in the play.*

• a character, a part

roll VERB

❶ *The wheels of the carriage began to roll.*

• to move round, to turn, to revolve, to rotate, to spin

❷ *She rolled the dough into a ball.*

• to curl, to wind, to wrap, to shape

— To **furl** a sail, flag or umbrella is to roll and fasten it.

romantic ADJECTIVE

❶ *My mum likes romantic films.*

• sentimental, emotional, soppy (informal)

❷ *The life of an explorer sounds very romantic.*

• glamorous, exciting, exotic

room NOUN

❶ *Is there room in the car for another suitcase?*

• space, capacity

❷ *How many rooms are there in your house?*

— An old word for room is **chamber**.

WORD WEB

ROOMS IN A HOUSE:

• an attic, a basement, a bathroom, a bedroom, a cellar, a conservatory, a dining room, an entrance hall, a hall, a kitchen, a living room, a lounge, a pantry, a parlour, a sitting room, a study, a toilet or **lavatory** or (informal) **loo**

— A **studio** is a room where an artist works.

ROOMS IN PUBLIC BUILDINGS:

• a classroom, a cloakroom, a corridor, a gym, a hall, a laboratory, a library, an office,

rope NOUN
*The sailors threw a **rope** to the men in the water.*
• a cable, a cord, a line
— A **lasso** is a rope with a loop at the end, for catching cattle.
— A **noose** is a rope with a loop in it that tightens when it is pulled.

rose *(past tense of **rise**)*

rot VERB
*The wooden fence had begun to **rot**.*
• to decay, to decompose, to become rotten, to disintegrate, to crumble
— If metal rots, it **corrodes**.
— If rubber rots, it **perishes**.
— If food rots, it **goes bad**.

rotate VERB
*The globe **rotates** on its axis.*
• to revolve, to turn
— To **spin**, to **whirl** or to **twirl** is to rotate quickly.
— To **pivot** or to **swivel** is to rotate from a fixed point.
— To **twist** is to turn your body around.
— To **wheel** is to move in a curve or circle.

rotten ADJECTIVE
❶ *The fridge smelled of **rotten** food.*
• bad, mouldy, decayed
OPPOSITE fresh
❷ *(informal) We had **rotten** weather.*
• awful, unpleasant, abysmal, dreadful, terrible
OPPOSITE good

rough ADJECTIVE
❶ *We walked across **rough** ground.*
• bumpy, uneven, irregular, rocky, stony, rugged, craggy, jagged
OPPOSITES even, smooth

a staffroom, a storeroom, toilets or lavatories or *(informal)* loos
— A **dormitory** is a room in a boarding school where pupils sleep.
— A **ward** is a room in a hospital where patients sleep.
— A **cell** is a small room for a prisoner.
— A **crypt** is a room underneath a church, often for burials.
— A **vault** is a secure room for keeping money or valuables.

❷ *The sea was **rough** and the boat lurched from side to side.*
• stormy, turbulent
— Use **choppy** when the sea is rough with small waves.
OPPOSITE calm
❸ *The prisoners had suffered **rough** treatment.*
• harsh, severe, cruel, hard, tough, violent
OPPOSITE gentle
❹ *Just make a **rough** guess.*
• approximate, vague, inexact, imprecise, general
OPPOSITES exact, precise

roughly ADVERB
*The cinema can seat **roughly** a hundred people.*
• approximately, about, around, close to, nearly

round ADJECTIVE
*Holly bushes have small **round** berries.*
• rounded, spherical
— Use **circular** for something flat and round.

round NOUN
*The winners go through to the next **round**.*
• a stage, a part, a heat, a contest, a game

route NOUN
*We drove home by the quickest **route**.*
• a path, a road, a way, a course, a direction, a journey

routine NOUN
*Brushing my teeth is part of my morning **routine**.*
• a procedure, a habit, a custom, a way, a practice

row (rhymes with **go**) NOUN
*The gardener planted the vegetables in **rows**.*
• a column, a line, a string, a series, a sequence
row (rhymes with **cow**) NOUN
❶ *I had a **row** with my sister.*
• an argument, a quarrel, a squabble, a fight,
a disagreement, a dispute
❷ *The class next door was making a terrible **row**.*
• a noise, a racket, a din, a commotion,
a disturbance, an uproar

royal ADJECTIVE
*She sat proudly on her **royal** throne.*
• regal, majestic, queenly, kingly
» *For kings and queens look at **ruler**.*

rub VERB
❶ *I **rubbed** my sore elbow.*
• to stroke, to massage
❷ *He **rubbed** the mirror until it gleamed.*
• to polish, to wipe, to shine
➤ **to rub something out**
*Can you **rub out** those pencil marks?*
• to erase, to delete, to remove, to wipe out

rubbish NOUN
❶ *Will you take the **rubbish** out to the bin?*
• refuse, waste, trash, garbage, junk, litter, scrap
❷ *Don't talk **rubbish**!*
• nonsense, drivel, gibberish, gobbledegook

rude ADJECTIVE
❶ *It's **rude** to talk with your mouth full.*
• impolite, bad-mannered, ill-mannered,
discourteous, disrespectful, insulting, offensive
— Use **cheeky** to mean rude or disrespectful without
being nasty.
— Use **impertinent**, **impudent** or **insolent** when
someone does not show enough respect for someone
important or in authority.
OPPOSITE polite
❷ *Some of the jokes in the film are rather **rude**.*
• coarse, crude, vulgar, offensive
OPPOSITE decent

ruffle VERB
*A breeze **ruffled** the surface of the lake.*
• to stir, to ripple, to shake

ruin VERB
*The storm had **ruined** the farmer's crops.*
• to damage, to destroy, to spoil, to wreck,
to devastate
— To destroy a building is to **demolish** it.
— To **annihilate** something is to completely destroy
it so it no longer exists.

ruin NOUN
➤ **ruins**
*Archaeologists found some Roman **ruins**.*
• remains, relics, remnants, fragments
➤ **in ruins**
*Our dream of winning the cup was **in ruins**.*
• destroyed, shattered, wrecked, crushed,
devastated

rule NOUN
*Players must stick to the **rules** of the game.*
• a regulation, a principle, a requirement
— A **law** is a rule that everyone in a country must obey.
rule VERB
❶ *The Romans **ruled** a vast empire.*
• to command, to govern, to control, to direct,
to lead, to manage, to run
❷ *Queen Victoria **ruled** for many years.*
• to reign, to be ruler, to be on the throne

ruler NOUN
*The people feared their **ruler**.*
• a leader, a head, a chief

✳ **WORD WEB**
SOME KINDS OF RULER:
• an emperor, an empress,
a king, a lord, a monarch,
a pharaoh, a president,
prince, a princess, a queen,
a sultan, a sovereign

Tutankhamen, a pharaoh

— A **dictator** or a
tyrant is a single
ruler who has
complete power and
does not allow any
disagreement.

Queen Victoria

rumour NOUN
*There was a **rumour** that she was going to leave.*
• a story, a report, gossip, talk

run VERB **runs, running, ran, run**
❶ *He **ran** towards the door.*
• to race, to sprint, to dash, to dart, to bolt, to pelt,
to speed, to streak, to rush, to hurry, to hurtle,
to fly, to whizz, to zoom
— To **jog** is to run at a gentle pace.
— To **bound** is to run with leaping steps.

— To **scamper**, to **scurry** or to **scuttle** is to run with short steps.

— Use to **gallop**, to **canter** or to **trot** for a horse.

[The wolf] hurtled across the enclosure towards the opposite fence . . . . [and] bounded off into the forest, in the direction of the mountains.—OLAF THE VIKING, Martin Conway

❷ *Tears ran down the mermaid's cheeks.*
• to flow, to pour, to stream, to gush, to flood, to cascade, to spill, to trickle, to dribble

❸ *She runs the drama club.*
• to be in charge of, to manage, to direct, to organise, to control, to supervise

❹ *The High Street runs through the city centre.*
• to pass, to go, to extend, to stretch

➤ **to run away** or **off**
The thieves ran off when they heard footsteps.
• to bolt, to flee, to fly, to escape

➤ **to run out**
The ink in the printer has run out.
• to finish, to be used up

— Use to **expire** when a ticket or document runs out so it is no longer valid.

run *NOUN*
She goes for a run in the park every morning.
• a jog

— A **sprint** or a **dash** is a fast run over a short distance.

runaway *NOUN*
A runaway had hidden on board the ship.
— A **fugitive** or an **outlaw** is someone running away from the law.

rung *(past participle of **ring**)*

runner *NOUN*
The runners were ready to start the race.
• an athlete, a competitor

— A **sprinter** is an athlete who runs fast over short distances.
— A **jogger** is someone who runs to keep fit.

runny *ADJECTIVE*
This sauce is too runny.
• watery, thin, liquid
OPPOSITE thick

rural *ADJECTIVE*
They live in a peaceful rural area.
• country, rustic, agricultural
OPPOSITE urban

rush *VERB*
I rushed home with the good news.
• to hurry, to hasten, to make haste *(formal)*, to race, to run, to sprint, to fly

— To **scamper**, to **scurry** or to **scuttle** is to rush somewhere with short steps.

— To **stampede** is to rush somewhere together in a large group.

rush *NOUN*
We've got plenty of time, so what's the rush?
• hurry, haste, urgency

rut *NOUN*
The tractor left ruts along the track.
• a furrow, a groove, a channel

ruthless *ADJECTIVE*
He was ruthless in destroying his enemies.
• pitiless, merciless, heartless, relentless, cruel, callous, brutal, fierce, vicious, savage, ferocious, violent
OPPOSITE merciful

Ss

⚙ Can you think of 3 different words you could use instead of 'storm'?

⚙ Can you think of 3 adjectives for describing a bad storm?

⚙ Check the thesaurus to find answers!

sack NOUN
*He was carrying a **sack** of potatoes.*
• a bag, a pack

sack VERB
*The team **sacked** their manager.*
• to dismiss, to give someone the sack, to get rid of, to fire *(informal)*

sacred ADJECTIVE
*The Koran is a **sacred** book.*
• holy, religious, divine, spiritual

sacrifice VERB
*I **sacrificed** my lunch break to practise guitar.*
• to give up, to surrender, to go without

sad ADJECTIVE

sadden VERB
*The news of her best friend's illness **saddened** her.*
• to distress, to upset, to depress, to grieve, to disappoint
OPPOSITE to cheer up

safe ADJECTIVE
❶ *We will be **safe** here until the storm blows over.*
• protected, sheltered, secure, out of danger
OPPOSITES vulnerable, in danger
❷ *The building was destroyed, but all the people were **safe**.*
• unharmed, unhurt, uninjured
OPPOSITES hurt, injured
❸ *The secret code is in **safe** hands.*
• reliable, trustworthy, dependable
❹ *Is the tap water **safe**?*
• harmless, healthy, wholesome
— If something is **drinkable** it is safe to drink.
— If something is **edible** it is safe to eat.
OPPOSITE dangerous

safety NOUN
❶ *You must wear a seat belt for your own safety.*
• protection, security, well-being
OPPOSITE danger
❷ *I wanted to get to the **safety** of my bed.*
• a refuge, a sanctuary, a haven

sag VERB
*The mattress **sags** in the middle.*
• to sink, to dip, to droop, to drop, to flop

said *(past tense of **say**)*

😮 **OVERUSED WORD**

Try to use a more interesting word when you want to say **sad**. Here are some ideas and examples:

FOR A SAD MOOD OR SAD PERSON:

• unhappy, miserable, dejected, depressed, desolate, downcast, forlorn, gloomy, glum, melancholy, tearful, upset, wretched
— Use **devastated** or **heartbroken** to mean extremely sad: *They were **devastated** because their homes had been destroyed.*
— Use **grieving** to mean sad because someone has died: *People helped the **grieving** widow to a chair.*
— Use **homesick** to mean sad because you miss your home.

— Use **wistful** to mean thinking sadly about something you would like to have: *She felt **wistful** when she thought about last summer.*
OPPOSITE happy
The Big Friendly Giant looked suddenly so forlorn that Sophie got quite upset. 'I'm sorry,' she said. 'I didn't mean to be rude.'—THE BFG, Roald Dahl
— To **regret** something is to feel sad or sorry that it has happened: *He **regretted** all the trouble he had caused.*
— To **grieve** or to **mourn** is to feel very sad because someone has died.
— To **pine** is to feel very sad because you miss something or someone: *I was **pining** for home.*

sail VERB
❶ They **sailed** to far-off lands.
• to go by ship, to set sail, to voyage
❷ We watched the yachts **sailing** on the lake.
• to float, to glide, to drift, to bob
❸ None of them knew how to **sail** the ship.
• to pilot, to steer, to navigate

sailor NOUN
He was a **sailor** who had travelled all over the world.
• a seaman, a seafarer

salary NOUN
He had to live on a very small **salary**.
• income, pay, earnings, wages

same ADJECTIVE
➤ **the same**
❶ All the houses look **the same**.
• matching, alike
— Identical means exactly the same.
— Similar means the same in some ways.
— Equivalent means the same in value, importance or meaning: They cost ten euros or the **equivalent** amount in pounds.
❷ Her feelings have remained **the same**.
• unchanged, unchanging, constant
OPPOSITE different

sample NOUN
The detective asked for a **sample** of her handwriting.
• a specimen, an example, an instance, an illustration

This is a sample of my handwriting written today by me.

FOR A SAD STORY OR SAD SOUND:

• depressing, dismal, melancholy, mournful, moving, plaintive, touching
[The kites made] a desolate, ghostly howling which seemed to echo off the dome of the sky, a dismal, mournful, supernatural noise.—THE KITE RIDER, Geraldine McCaughrean
OPPOSITES cheerful, cheering

FOR A SAD SITUATION OR SAD NEWS:

• unfortunate, unpleasant, upsetting, distressing, grave, serious, tragic, painful, grim, grievous
The letter contained some **painful** news.
OPPOSITES cheerful, pleasant

sample VERB
Would you like to **sample** some home-made jam?
• to taste, to test, to try

sane ADJECTIVE
No **sane** person would stand out in the pouring rain!
• sensible, rational, reasonable
OPPOSITE insane

sang (past tense of **sing**)

sank (past tense of **sink**)

sarcastic ADJECTIVE
He made a **sarcastic** remark about my hat.
• mocking, ironic, sneering, taunting

sat (past tense of **sit**)

satisfaction NOUN
She gets a lot of **satisfaction** from her job.
• happiness, pleasure, enjoyment, contentment, fulfilment, pride
OPPOSITE dissatisfaction

satisfactory ADJECTIVE
Your work is **satisfactory**, but I think you can do better.
• acceptable, good enough, all right, adequate, fair, passable, tolerable
— Sufficient means satisfactory in amount.
OPPOSITE unsatisfactory

satisfied VERB
I was not **satisfied** with the meal.
• pleased, content, happy
OPPOSITE dissatisfied

save VERB
❶ They managed to **save** most of the books from the flood.
• to rescue, to retrieve, to recover, to salvage
❷ Firefighters **saved** them from the burning building.
• to rescue, to free, to liberate, to release, to set free
❸ I **saved** you a piece of my birthday cake.
• to keep, to reserve, to set aside, to hold on to
❹ Turn the lights out to **save** energy.
• to conserve, to preserve
OPPOSITE to waste

saw (past tense of **see**)

saw NOUN
» For various tools look at **tool**.

a
b
c
d
e
f
g
h
i
j
k
l
m
n
o
p
q
r
s
t
u
v
w
x
y
z

say VERB says, saying, said
❶ He found it hard to **say** what he meant.
• to express, to communicate, to put into words, to convey, to get across
❷ I would like to **say** a few words before we start.
• to utter, to speak

OVERUSED WORD

Try to use a more interesting word instead of **say**, especially with direct speech. Here are some ideas and examples:

TO SAY LOUDLY:

• to call, to cry, to exclaim, to bellow, to bawl, to shout, to yell, to roar

TO SAY QUIETLY:

• to whisper, to mumble, to mutter
'That woman,' I **whispered**, 'is a secret agent.'

TO SAY FIRMLY:

• to state, to announce, to declare, to pronounce, to propose, to insist, to demand, to maintain
'You must be loopy, Shanks,' **declared** the President. 'You're dotty as a doughnut!'—CHARLIE AND THE GREAT GLASS ELEVATOR, Roald Dahl

TO SAY CASUALLY:

• to remark, to comment, to observe
'It's rather late,' he **remarked**.

TO SAY ANGRILY:

• to snap, to snarl, to growl, to thunder, to bark, to rant, to rave

TO SAY QUICKLY OR UNCLEARLY:

• to babble, to blurt out, to burble, to gabble, to stammer, to stutter
'I'm sorry,' he **gabbled**. 'Sorry, sorry, sorry.' —THE NIGHTMARE GAME, Gillian Cross

TO SAY IN SURPRISE OR ALARM:

• to gasp, to cry, to squeal, to scream
'I feel most peculiar!' **gasped** Violet.—CHARLIE AND THE CHOCOLATE FACTORY, Roald Dahl

TO SAY SOMETHING AS A JOKE:

• to joke, to laugh, to tease
— To **sneer**, to **scoff**, to **mock**, to **taunt** or to **jeer** is to make fun of someone in an unkind way.
'You think a kid like you is tough enough to work with soldiers like us?' one of the men **jeered**.—BEYOND THE BARRICADE, Deborah Ellis

TO MAKE A REQUEST OR AN EXCUSE:

• to beg, to entreat, to implore, to plead, to urge
'I didn't mean it!' **pleaded** poor Alice. 'But you're so easily offended, you know!'—ALICE'S ADVENTURES IN WONDERLAND, Lewis Carroll

saying NOUN
'Too many cooks spoil the broth' is a common **saying**.
• an expression, a phrase, a motto, a proverb
— A **slogan** is a saying used in advertising or politics.
— A **cliché** is a saying that is used too much.

scandal NOUN
❶ The way he was treated was a **scandal**.
• a disgrace, an embarrassment, a shame, an outrage
❷ That newspaper is just full of **scandal**.
• gossip, rumours

scar NOUN
The warrior had a **scar** across his forehead.
• a mark, a blemish, a wound

scarce ADJECTIVE
Water is very **scarce** in the desert.
• rare, uncommon, unusual, scanty, lacking
— Use **sparse** when there is not much of something

and it is thinly spread out: There was only **sparse** vegetation.
OPPOSITE plentiful

scarcely ADVERB
She was so tired that she could **scarcely** walk.
• barely, hardly, only just

scare NOUN
The explosion gave them a nasty **scare**.
• a fright, a shock, an alarm

scare VERB
My brother tried to **scare** us by making ghost noises.
• to frighten, to alarm
— To **terrify** or to **petrify** someone is to frighten them very much.
— To **startle** or to **shock** someone is to frighten them by being unexpected.
— To **panic** someone is to frighten them so that they do not know what to do.
OPPOSITE to reassure

scared *ADJECTIVE*
Lily was too scared to move.
• afraid, frightened, alarmed, fearful
— Use **terrified** or **petrified** to mean very scared.
— Use **startled** or **shocked** to mean scared by something unexpected.
— Use **panicky** when someone is scared and does not know what to do.
» *For some ideas for writing about being scared look at* **frightened**.

scary *ADJECTIVE (informal)*
I had to close my eyes at the scary bits in the film.
• alarming, frightening, chilling
— Use **terrifying, horrifying** or **petrifying** if something is very scary.
— Use **creepy, spooky, eerie** or **uncanny** for something that is strange and slightly scary.
— Use **sinister** or **menacing** if something is scary because it seems evil or harmful.
— Use **startling** for something that makes you jump.

scatter *VERB*
❶ *She scattered the seeds on the ground.*
• to spread, to sprinkle
OPPOSITE to collect
❷ *The animals scattered when the children ran towards them.*
• to separate, to disperse, to break up
OPPOSITE to gather

scene *NOUN*
❶ *The police arrived quickly at the scene of the crime.*
• a location, a position, a site, a place, a situation, a spot
❷ *They were rehearsing a scene from the play.*
• an episode, a part, a section

scenery *NOUN*
We admired the scenery from the top of the hill.
• the landscape, the scene, the view

scent *NOUN*
The roses have a beautiful scent.
• a smell, a fragrance, a perfume, an aroma
» *Look at* **smell**.

schedule *NOUN*
The athletes had a rigorous training schedule.
• a programme, a timetable, a plan, a calendar, a diary
— An **agenda** is a schedule of things to be discussed at a meeting.

scheme *NOUN*
They worked out a scheme to raise some money.
• a plan, a proposal, a project

scheme *VERB*
The smugglers were scheming against each other.
• to plot, to conspire

school *NOUN*

 WORD WEB

SOME KINDS OF SCHOOL:

• an academy, a boarding school, a comprehensive school, a high school, an infant school, a junior school, a kindergarten, a nursery school, a playgroup, a primary school, a secondary school

science *NOUN*

 WORD WEB

SOME TYPES OF SCIENCE AND SCIENTISTS:

— An **astronomer** studies **astronomy**.
— A **biologist** studies **biology**.
— A **botanist** studies **botany**.
— A **chemist** studies **chemistry**.
— A **computer scientist** studies **computer science**.
— An **engineer** studies **engineering**.
— A **geologist** studies **geology**.
— A **doctor** studies **medicine**.
— A **meteorologist** studies **meteorology**.
— A **physicist** studies **physics**.
— A **psychologist** studies **psychology**.
— A **vet** studies **veterinary medicine**.
— A **zoologist** studies **zoology**.

scold *VERB*
He scolded us for being late.
• to tell off, to reproach, to shout at

score *NOUN*
What was your final score?
• mark, points, total, result

score *VERB*
❶ *We scored two goals.*
• to get, to win, to gain, to make
❷ *Some lines were scored into the bark of the tree.*
• to cut, to gouge, to mark, to scrape, to scratch

scorn *NOUN*
She dismissed my suggestion with scorn.
• contempt, derision, disrespect, ridicule
OPPOSITES admiration, respect

scramble VERB
*We **scrambled** over the rocks to safety.*
• to clamber, to climb, to crawl

scrap NOUN
❶ *They fed **scraps** of food to the birds.*
• a bit, a piece, a morsel, a crumb
— A **fragment** is a small broken piece.
— A **splinter** is a small sharp piece.
— A **flake** is a small light scrap of something.
— A **shred** is a scrap of cloth.
— A **speck** or a **particle** is a very small piece.
❷ *He took a pile of **scrap** to the tip.*
• rubbish, waste, junk, refuse, litter

scrap VERB
*I decided to **scrap** the last paragraph.*
• to discard, to get rid of, to abandon, to cancel, to drop, to dump *(informal)*

scrape VERB
❶ *She **scraped** her knee when she fell over.*
• to graze, to scratch
❷ *I tried to **scrape** the mud off my trainers.*
• to rub, to scour, to scrub, to clean

scratch VERB
*Someone **scratched** the side of the car.*
• to mark, to scrape
— To **score** or to **gouge** something is to make a deep scratch in it.
— To **graze** something is to scratch it lightly.

scratch NOUN
*Who made this **scratch** on the side of the car?*
• a scrape, a mark, a line
— A **groove** is a long narrow cut.
— A **gash** is a long deep cut.

scream NOUN
*We heard a **scream**.*
• a shriek, a screech, a shout, a yell, a cry
— A **squeal** is a high sound of fear or excitement.
— A **yelp** is a short high sound of pain.
— A **howl** or a **wail** is a long loud sad cry.

scream VERB
*Everyone **screamed** when they saw the spider.*
• to shriek, to squeal, to screech, to cry out
» *For ways to say something look at* **say**.

screen NOUN
*The room was divided into two by a **screen**.*
• a curtain, a partition, a panel

screen VERB
*Thick bushes **screened** their den.*
• to cover, to hide, to mask, to shelter, to shield, to protect, to shade

scribble VERB
*He **scribbled** his phone number on a scrap of paper.*
• to scrawl, to jot down, to write
— To **doodle** is to scribble drawings or words when you are bored or thinking about something else.

scrub VERB
*Cinderella had to **scrub** the floors.*
• to scour, to rub, to brush, to clean, to wash

scruffy ADJECTIVE
*He always wears those **scruffy** jeans.*
• untidy, messy, ragged, tatty, tattered, worn-out, shabby
OPPOSITE smart

sculpture NOUN
*The temple was full of marble **sculptures**.*
• a carving, a figure, a statue

sea NOUN
*They sailed across the **sea**.*
• the ocean, the water, the waves, the deep

🕸 **WORD WEB**

LAND AND SEA FEATURES:

• a bay, a beach, a cape, a cave, a cliff, a coastline, a fjord, a gulf, a headland, an inlet, a lagoon, a strait, a reef
» *Look at* **river**.

THINGS YOU MIGHT SEE ON THE SEA:

• a boat, a ship, a yacht, a lifeboat, a lighthouse, a raft, a shipwreck, a lifebelt, a buoy, driftwood, an iceberg, a wave, a tsunami, a breaker, a roller, surf

a lifebelt

SEA CREATURES AND PLANTS:

• coral, a crab, a dolphin, an eel, a fish, a killer whale, a manatee, an octopus, plankton, a porpoise, a seahorse, a seal, a sea lion, seaweed, a shark, shellfish, a sponge, a starfish, a stingray, a turtle, a walrus, a whale
— A **kraken** is a sea monster in Norse myth.
— A **mermaid** is a creature in stories with a woman's upper body and a fish's tail.
— Creatures that live in the sea are **marine** creatures.
» *For sea birds look at* **bird**.
» *For fish look at* **fish**.
» *For shellfish look at* **shellfish**.
» *Look at* **seaside**.

WRITING TIPS

Here are some useful words for writing about **the sea**:

TO DESCRIBE A CALM SEA:

• calm, tranquil, glassy, crystal clear, sparkling, unruffled

TO DESCRIBE A ROUGH SEA:

• choppy, raging, rough, stormy, tempestuous, turbulent, wild

He's heading for the narrow gap between the harbour walls. It seems impossible to aim for in the raging sea.
—WHITE DOLPHIN, Gill Lewis

search VERB
❶ *They searched everywhere for the dog.*
• to hunt, to look, to seek
❷ *The police searched the house but didn't find anything.*
• to check, to inspect, to examine, to scour, to comb
— To **ransack** something is to search everywhere in it, causing mess and damage.
— To **rummage** is to feel inside something trying to find something: *I rummaged in my bag for a pen.*

search NOUN
After a long search, she found her keys.
• a hunt, a look
— A **quest** is a long journey in search of something.

seashore NOUN
We explored the seashore, looking for shells and fossils.
• the seaside, the beach, the shore, the coast
» *For sea birds look at* **bird**.
» *For shellfish look at* **shellfish**.
» *For other sea creatures look at* **sea**.
» *Look at* **seaside**.

seaside NOUN
If it's sunny tomorrow, we might go to the seaside.
• the beach, the sands, the seashore

WORD WEB

THINGS YOU MIGHT SEE AT THE SEASIDE:

• a beach ball, beach huts, a bucket and spade, a fishing net, a funfair, a harbour, an ice cream, a jetty, pebbles, a pier, a promenade, rock pools, a sandcastle, sand dunes, seaweed, shells, shingle, a snorkel, a swimming costume, a towel, a wetsuit

seat NOUN
We found two empty seats at the back.
• a chair, a place, a space

WORD WEB

SOME TYPES OF SEAT:

• an armchair, a bench, a couch, a high chair, a rocking chair, a settee, a sofa, a stool
— A **pew** is a long wooden seat in a church.
— A **throne** is a seat for a king or queen.
— A **saddle** is a seat on a bicycle or horse.

seat VERB
The hall seats two hundred people.
• to have seats for, to accommodate, to hold, to take

second NOUN
I'll be there in a second.
• an instant, a moment, a flash

second-hand ADJECTIVE
The shop sells second-hand phones.
• used, pre-owned
OPPOSITE new

secret ADJECTIVE
❶ *She wrote everything down in her secret diary.*
• private, confidential, personal, intimate
❷ *There was a secret passageway into the castle.*
• hidden, concealed, disguised
» *For secret agents look at* **spy**.

secretive ADJECTIVE
They were very secretive about what they were doing.
• furtive, mysterious, stealthy, sneaky, sly
OPPOSITE open

section NOUN
The website has a special section aimed at children.
• a part, a division, a portion, a segment, a bit
— A **chapter** is one of the sections a book is divided into.
— An **extract** or a **passage** is a small section from a book or text.
— A **stage** is a section of a journey or competition.

THINGS YOU MIGHT DO AT THE SEASIDE:

• to build sandcastles, to collect shells, to fish, to paddle, to paddleboard, to sail, to scuba dive, to snorkel, to splash, to sunbathe, to surf, to swim, to waterski, to windsurf

a b c d e f g h i j k l m n o p q r **s** t u v w x y z

secure ADJECTIVE
❶ *The ladder was not very secure.*
• steady, firm, solid, fixed, safe
OPPOSITES insecure, unsafe
❷ *They felt secure inside the castle.*
• safe, guarded, protected, defended

secure VERB
❶ *The door wasn't properly secured.*
• to fasten, to lock, to seal, to bolt
❷ *He managed to secure two tickets for the match.*
• to get hold of, to acquire, to obtain

security NOUN
We check everyone's bags for your security.
• protection, safety

see VERB sees, seeing, saw, seen
❶ *If you watch carefully, you might see a dragonfly.*
• to catch sight of, to spot, to notice, to observe, to make out, to distinguish, to perceive, to recognise, to spy
— To **glimpse** or to **catch a glimpse of** something is to see it very briefly.
— To **witness** something is to see an unusual event.
❷ *We saw a good film.*
• to watch, to view, to look at
❸ *I saw my friend in town.*
• to meet, to run into, to bump into, to encounter
❹ *I'm going to see my grandma tomorrow.*
• to visit, to call on, to pay a visit to
❺ *I see what you mean.*
• to understand, to appreciate, to comprehend, to follow, to grasp, to realise
❻ *Please see that the windows are shut.*
• to make sure, to make certain, to ensure, to check

seed NOUN
I planted some seeds in the garden.
— A **pip** is the seed of an apple, pear, orange or lemon.
— A **stone** is the seed of a peach or plum.
— A **grain** is the seed of a cereal plant.

seek VERB seeks, seeking, sought
He sought his long-lost brother everywhere.
• to search for, to hunt for, to look for

seem VERB
She seemed annoyed.
• to appear, to look, to give the impression of being

seen (past participle of **see**)

seize VERB
I seized the end of the rope.
• to grab, to grasp, to catch, to snatch, to take hold of, to grip, to clutch

seldom ADVERB
It seldom rains in the desert.
• rarely, infrequently, hardly ever
OPPOSITE often

select VERB
❶ *You can select your character for the game from this menu.*
• to choose, to pick, to decide on, to opt for
❷ *They had to select a team captain.*
• to choose, to appoint, to nominate, to name, to elect, to vote for

select ADJECTIVE
Only a select few were invited to the party.
• special, chosen, privileged

selection NOUN
They sell a wide selection of games.
• a choice, a range, a variety, an assortment

selfish ADJECTIVE
It's very selfish not to share your sweets with your friends.
• greedy, mean, thoughtless
OPPOSITES unselfish, generous

sell VERB sells, selling, sold
The corner shop sells newspapers and sweets.
• to stock, to deal in, to trade in
》 For people who sell things look at **shop**.
OPPOSITE to buy

send VERB sends, sending, sent
I sent my friends a postcard.
• to post, to mail, to dispatch
➤ **to send for**
They sent for a doctor.
• to call, to summon
➤ **to send something out**
The device was sending out green smoke.
• to emit, to issue, to give off, to discharge, to generate, to produce
— To **belch** smoke is to send out a lot of it.
— To send out heat, light or energy is to **radiate** it.

sense NOUN
❶ *A baby learns about the world through its senses.*
— Your five senses are **hearing**, **sight**, **smell**, **taste** and **touch**.
❷ *If you had any sense you'd stay at home.*
• wisdom, intelligence, reason, judgement, wit, brains
➤ **to make sense of something**
They couldn't make sense of the garbled message.
• to understand, to make out, to interpret, to decipher, to decode

sense *VERB*
He sensed that someone was watching him.
• to perceive, to be aware, to realise, to feel, to guess, to notice, to suspect, to detect

sensible *ADJECTIVE*
It would be sensible to wait until the weather improves.
• wise, intelligent, shrewd, rational, reasonable, careful, prudent, logical
OPPOSITE stupid

sensitive *ADJECTIVE*
❶ *He's very sensitive about his hair.*
• easily offended, easily upset, easily hurt
❷ *I tried to ask the questions in a sensitive way.*
• tactful, considerate, diplomatic, thoughtful, sympathetic, understanding
OPPOSITE insensitive
❸ *She has sensitive skin which gets sunburnt.*
• delicate, tender, fine, soft

sentimental *ADJECTIVE*
I hate sentimental films.
• romantic, emotional, soppy *(informal)*

separate *(say sep-er-at) ADJECTIVE*
❶ *I keep my things separate from my sister's.*
• apart, separated, distinct, independent
OPPOSITE together
❷ *The sports hall is in a separate building.*
• different, detached, unattached, individual
OPPOSITES attached, shared

separate *(say sep-er-ayt) VERB*
❶ *A strip of grass separates the path from the road.*
• to cut off, to divide, to keep apart, to disconnect
OPPOSITES to join, to connect
❷ *We separated the egg yolks and the egg whites.*
• to split, to divide, to set apart, to remove
OPPOSITES to combine, to mix
❸ *They walked along together until their paths separated.*
• to split, to branch, to fork
OPPOSITES to merge, to converge

sequence *NOUN*
The detective tried to understand the sequence of events.
• an order, a progression, a series, a succession, a string, a chain, a train

series *NOUN*
❶ *The detective asked her a series of questions.*
• a succession, a sequence, a string, a set
❷ *Are you watching the new series of Dr Who?*
• a serial, a season

serious *ADJECTIVE*
❶ *She looked serious.*
• solemn, sombre, grave, grim, stern
OPPOSITE cheerful
❷ *Are you serious about wanting to learn to ski?*
• sincere, genuine, in earnest
OPPOSITE joking
❸ *He was taken to hospital with serious injuries.*
• severe, bad, major, grave, terrible, appalling, dreadful
OPPOSITE minor
❹ *This is a serious matter.*
• important, critical, crucial, vital, significant
OPPOSITE trivial

servant *NOUN*
This part of the house was where the servants lived.
• staff, domestic staff
— A **maid** is a female servant.
— A **butler** is a male servant in charge of other servants in a large house.
— The servant of a medieval knight was a **page** or **squire**.

serve *VERB*
❶ *When everyone had sat down they served the first course.*
• to give out, to dish up, to pass round, to distribute
❷ *The shopkeeper was busy serving customers.*
• to help, to assist, to aid

service *NOUN*
They were grateful for his services.
• help, assistance, aid
➤ **of service**
I'm glad I could be of service.
• useful, helpful, beneficial, obliging

session *NOUN*
We have a training session on Saturday mornings.
• a period, a time

set *VERB* sets, setting, set
❶ *She set the jug carefully on the floor.*
• to place, to put, to stand, to position
❷ *I helped Dad to set the table.*
• to lay, to arrange, to set out
❸ *Have they set a date for the wedding?*
• to decide, to fix, to choose, to establish, to specify, to settle
❹ *Wait for the concrete to set.*
• to solidify, to harden, to become firm

a b c d e f g h i j k l m n o p q r s t u v w x y z

⑤ *The sun was just beginning to set.*
• to go down, to sink

➤ **to set off**
The knights set off on their quest.
• to depart, to leave, to set out, to start out

➤ **to set something up**
They're trying to set up an after-school club.
• to establish, to create, to found, to start, to begin, to organise

set NOUN
There is a set of measuring spoons in the drawer.
• a collection, a batch, a kit

setting NOUN
The setting for the story is a medieval village.
• location, place, background, surroundings

settle VERB
① *To settle the argument, we looked the word up in the dictionary.*
• to resolve, to sort out, to deal with, to end
② *The cat had just settled on the sofa.*
• to sit down, to relax, to get settled
③ *A robin settled on a nearby branch.*
• to land, to alight
④ *The family settled in Canada.*
• to emigrate to, to move to, to set up home, to go to live

several DETERMINER
We have been there several times.
• a number of, some, a few, various

severe ADJECTIVE
① *The teachers were very severe with them.*
• harsh, strict, stern, disapproving, unkind, unsympathetic
OPPOSITES **kind, gentle**
② *Ruby has a severe case of chickenpox.*
• bad, serious, acute, grave
OPPOSITE **mild**

sew VERB sews, sewing, sewed, sewn or sewed
Mum sewed a name tag on to my coat.
• to stitch
— To **embroider** something is to sew a picture or design.

shade NOUN
① *They sat in the shade of a chestnut tree.*
• shadow
② *This is a nice shade of blue.*
• a hue, a tint, a tone, a colour
③ *The porch had a shade to keep out the sun.*
• a screen, a blind, a canopy
— A **parasol** is a type of umbrella used as a sunshade.

shade VERB
She shaded her eyes from the sun.
• to shield, to screen, to protect, to hide

shadow NOUN
Her face was deep in shadow.
• shade, darkness, gloom

shadow VERB
The detective was shadowing the suspect.
• to follow, to pursue, to tail, to stalk, to track, to trail

shady ADJECTIVE
They found a shady spot under a tree.
• shaded, shadowy, cool, dark
OPPOSITE **sunny**

shake VERB shakes, shaking, shook, shaken
① *The storm made the whole house shake.*
• to quake, to quiver, to shudder, to rock, to vibrate, to sway, to wobble, to rattle
② *He was so nervous he was shaking.*
• to tremble, to quiver, to quaver
— To **shiver** is to shake with cold.
— To **shudder** is to shake with fear or disgust.
③ *I picked up the money box and shook it.*
• to rattle, to waggle, to joggle
④ *The giant shook his fist angrily.*
• to wave, to brandish, to flourish, to wag, to waggle

shaken (past participle of **shake**)

shaky ADJECTIVE
① *She was balancing on a shaky stool.*
• unsteady, wobbly, insecure, rickety, flimsy, weak
② *He spoke in a shaky voice.*
• quavering, trembling, quivering, faltering, nervous
OPPOSITE **steady**

shallow ADJECTIVE
The stream is quite shallow here.
OPPOSITE **deep**

shame NOUN
① *I hung my head in shame.*
• embarrassment, guilt, remorse, humiliation
OPPOSITE **pride**
② *He brought shame on his family.*
• dishonour, disgrace, embarrassment, humiliation
OPPOSITE **honour**

➤ **a shame**
It's a shame that you can't come.
• a pity, unfortunate

shape NOUN
*We saw a dark **shape** moving outside.*
• a form, a figure

— An **outline** is a line showing the shape of something.
— A **silhouette** is a dark shape or outline seen against a dark background.

WORD WEB

FLAT SHAPES:

• a circle, a crescent, a diamond or a rhombus, an ellipse or an oval, a heptagon, a hexagon, an oblong or a rectangle, an octagon, a parallelogram, a pentagon, a semicircle, a square, a star, a trapezium, a triangle
— A **polygon** is any flat shape with many sides.
— A **quadrilateral** is any flat shape with four straight sides.

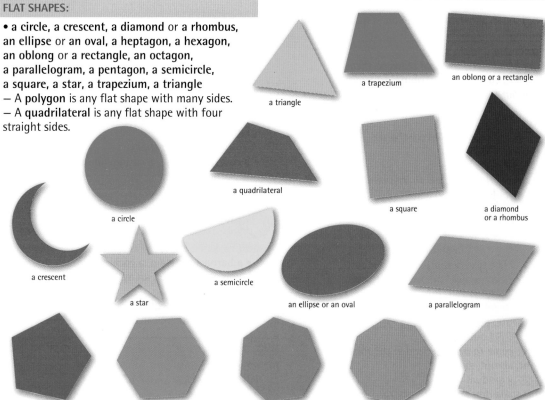

a triangle

a trapezium

an oblong or a rectangle

a quadrilateral

a square

a diamond or a rhombus

a circle

a crescent

a star

a semicircle

an ellipse or an oval

a parallelogram

a pentagon

a hexagon

a heptagon

an octagon

a polygon

THREE-DIMENSIONAL SHAPES:

• a cone, a cube, a cylinder, a hemisphere, a pyramid, a sphere
— A **solid** is any three-dimensional shape.

— A **tetrahedron** is a solid shape with four triangular sides.
— A **prism** is a solid shape with parallel ends that are equal triangles or polygons.

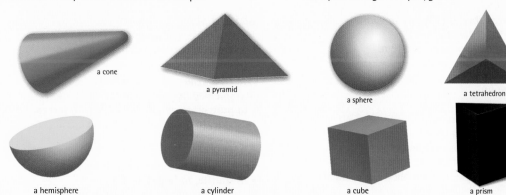

a cone

a pyramid

a sphere

a tetrahedron

a hemisphere

a cylinder

a cube

a prism

shape VERB
The potter **shaped** the clay into a vase.
• to form, to mould, to fashion

share NOUN
We each got a **share** of sweets.
• a ration, an allowance, a portion, a quota, a helping

share VERB
The robbers **shared** the gold between them.
• to divide, to split, to distribute, to allocate, to deal out

sharp ADJECTIVE
❶ These scissors are very **sharp**.
• keen, sharpened
OPPOSITE blunt
❷ Barbed wire has **sharp** points all along it.
• pointed, spiky, jagged
OPPOSITE smooth
❸ Eagles have **sharp** eyes.
• keen, powerful, observant, perceptive
OPPOSITE unobservant
❹ She is very **sharp** and learns fast.
• clever, quick, shrewd, perceptive
OPPOSITES dull, slow
❺ He felt a **sharp** pain in his side.
• acute, piercing, stabbing
OPPOSITE dull
❻ We came to a **sharp** bend in the road.
• tight, abrupt, sudden
OPPOSITE gradual
❼ This salad dressing is a bit **sharp**.
• sour, tart, bitter
OPPOSITES mild, sweet

shed NOUN
I keep my bike in the **shed**.
• a hut, a shack, a shelter

shed VERB sheds, shedding, shed
❶ Some trees **shed** their leaves in winter.
• to drop, to let fall, to lose
❷ Snakes **shed** their skin each year.
• to cast off, to slough off

sheep NOUN
— A female sheep is a **ewe**.
— A male sheep is a **ram**.
— A young sheep is a **lamb**.
— Meat from sheep is **mutton** or **lamb**.
— The woolly coat of a sheep is its **fleece**.
— When sheep make a sound, they **baa** or **bleat**.

sheet NOUN
❶ She started her diary on a fresh **sheet** of paper.
• a page, a leaf, a piece
❷ The pond was covered with a thin **sheet** of ice.
• a layer, a film, a covering, a surface
❸ The sculpture is made from a thin **sheet** of metal.
• a panel, a plate
— A **pane** is a sheet of glass.

shelf NOUN
She put the books back on the **shelf**.
• a ledge, a rack
— A **mantelpiece** is a shelf above a fireplace.

shell NOUN
Tortoises have hard **shells**.
• a covering, a case, a casing, an outside, an exterior

shellfish NOUN

⬡ **WORD WEB**

SOME TYPES OF SHELLFISH:

• a barnacle, a clam, a cockle, a crab, a limpet, a lobster, a mussel, an oyster, a prawn, a shrimp, a whelk
— Shellfish with legs such as crabs, lobsters and prawns are **crustaceans**.

shelter NOUN
We found **shelter** under a rock.
• cover, protection, safety, refuge, sanctuary

shelter VERB
❶ We **sheltered** under the trees.
• to take refuge, to take shelter, to hide
❷ The hedge **shelters** the garden from the wind.
• to protect, to screen, to shield, to guard, to defend

shield NOUN
He used a piece of wood as a **shield**.
• a screen, a barrier, a defence, a guard, a protection

shield VERB
She **shielded** her eyes from the sun.
• to protect, to defend, to shelter, to screen, to shade, to guard

shift VERB
❶ He **shifted** uncomfortably in his seat.
• to shuffle, to fidget, to stir
❷ The big wardrobe was difficult to **shift**.
• to move, to remove, to reposition

shine VERB shines, shining, shined or shone
❶ *A light **shone** from an upstairs window.*
• to beam, to glow, to gleam
— To **blaze** or to **glare** is to shine very brightly.
» *For other ways to describe light shining look at **light**.*
❷ *The sun **shone** all day.*
• to blaze down, to beat down, to be out
❸ *He **shone** his torch into the cave.*
• to point, to direct

shiny ADJECTIVE
*She polished the mirror until it was **shiny**.*
• shining, bright, gleaming, glistening, polished
— Use **glossy** for something that is shiny and looks wet.
— Use **sleek** for shiny fur or hair.
OPPOSITE dull

ship NOUN
» *Look at **boat**.*
ship VERB
*The firm **ships** goods all over the world.*
• to transport, to send, to deliver

shiver VERB
*Ali waited outside, **shivering** with cold.*
• to tremble, to shake, to quiver, to shudder
— To **quake** is to shiver with fear.

shock NOUN
❶ *Hearing about the accident was a big **shock**.*
• a blow, a surprise, a fright, an upset
❷ *We felt **shock** and disgust when we heard what he had done.*
• outrage, offence, horror
shock VERB
*The terrible news **shocked** us all.*
• to horrify, to appal, to startle, to alarm, to stun, to stagger, to astonish, to astound, to dismay, to upset

shocked ADJECTIVE
❶ *She was really **shocked** at their bad behaviour.*
• appalled, horrified, disgusted, indignant, offended, outraged, aghast
❷ *I felt quite **shocked** when I realised I had won.*
• surprised, astounded, astonished, staggered, stunned

shocking ADJECTIVE
❶ *I think it's **shocking** that nobody helped her.*
• appalling, disgusting, outrageous, horrifying, awful, terrible, shameful
❷ *The **shocking** news was on the front page of every paper.*
• sensational, startling, scandalous, staggering, stunning

shoe NOUN

 WORD WEB

SOME TYPES OF SHOE OR BOOT:

• ballet shoes, boots, clogs, flip-flops, football boots, high heels, ice skates, moccasins, plimsolls, pumps, roller skates, sandals, slippers, trainers, wellingtons or *(informal)* wellies

shone *(past tense of **shine**)*

shook *(past tense of **shake**)*

shoot VERB shoots, shooting, shot
*Robin Hood **shot** an arrow into the air.*
• to fire, to discharge, to launch, to aim
shoot NOUN
*Young **shoots** grow in the spring.*
• a bud, a sprout

shop NOUN

 WORD WEB

SHOPS AND SHOPKEEPERS:

• a baker, a barber, a beautician, a butcher, a chemist, a fishmonger, a florist, a greengrocer, a grocer, a hairdresser, a jeweller, a newsagent
Then old Mrs. Rabbit took a basket and her umbrella, and went through the wood to the baker's. She bought a loaf of brown bread and five currant buns.
—PETER RABBIT, Beatrix Potter

SOME OTHER SHOPS:

• an antique shop, a bookshop, a boutique, a clothes shop, a corner shop, a delicatessen, a department store, a garden centre, a gift shop, a music shop, a pet shop, a pharmacy, a post office, a shoe shop, a supermarket, a sweet shop, a toy shop
— A **shopping centre** or **shopping mall** is a place with a lot of different shops.

shopping NOUN
*Just put the **shopping** in the boot of the car.*
• goods, purchases

short *ADJECTIVE*
❶ *My grandma is quite **short**.*
• small, little, tiny
— **Squat** means short and fat.
`OPPOSITE` tall
❷ *My brother has **short** black hair.*
• cropped
`OPPOSITE` long
❸ *It's only a **short** walk to the shops.*
• little
`OPPOSITE` long
❹ *It was a very **short** visit.*
• brief, quick, fleeting, hasty
`OPPOSITE` long
➤ **to be short of**
*We are **short** of chairs.*
• to be lacking, to lack, not to have enough

shortage *NOUN*
*In some areas there is a **shortage** of housing.*
• a scarcity, a lack
— A **drought** is a shortage of water.
— A **famine** is a shortage of food.

shorten *VERB*
*She had to **shorten** the speech because it was too long.*
• to cut down, to reduce, to cut
— To **abbreviate** a word or phrase is to shorten it by writing it with fewer letters.
— To **trim** something is to shorten it by cutting off part of it.
`OPPOSITE` to lengthen

shot *(past tense of* **shoot***)*

shot *NOUN*
❶ *I heard a noise like the **shot** of a pistol.*
• a bang, a blast, a crack
❷ *Did you get any **shots** of the school trip?*
• a photograph, a photo, a picture
❸ *That was a great **shot** by the striker!*
• a strike, a hit, a kick

shout *VERB*
*There's no need to **shout**.*
• to yell, to roar, to bawl, to bellow
— To **scream** or to **shriek** is to shout in a high loud way because you are very angry or very frightened.
— To **rant** or to **rave** is to keep shouting angrily about something.
— To **cheer** is to shout praise or encouragement.
» *For ways to say something look at* **say**.
`OPPOSITE` to whisper

shout *NOUN*
*We heard a **shout** from far away.*
• a call, a cry, a yell, a bellow, a roar

shove *VERB*
*He **shoved** me rudely out of the way.*
• to push, to thrust, to barge, to force, to elbow

show *VERB* **shows, showing, showed, shown**
❶ *She **showed** her picture to me.*
• to present, to display, to exhibit, to reveal
❷ *The dance teacher **showed** them what to do.*
• to explain to, to demonstrate to, to teach, to tell,
• to instruct: *The dance teacher **instructed** them in what to do.*
❸ *I'll **show** you to your seats.*
• to guide, to lead, to escort, to usher, to direct
❹ ***Show** me where the accident happened.*
• to point out, to point to, to indicate
❺ *The photo **shows** my grandparents on holiday.*
• to portray, to depict, to illustrate, to represent
❻ *The evidence **shows** that he was right.*
• to prove, to demonstrate, to indicate, to reveal
❼ *His vest **showed** through his shirt.*
• to be seen, to be visible, to appear
➤ **to show off**
*He is always **showing off** about how much money he's got.*
• to boast, to brag, to gloat, to swagger

show *NOUN*
❶ *There is a **show** of artwork in the hall.*
• a display, an exhibition, a presentation
❷ *We went to see a comedy **show** at the theatre.*
• a performance, a production, a spectacle, an entertainment
— A **programme** or a **broadcast** is a TV or radio show.

shred *NOUN*
*The police couldn't find a **shred** of evidence.*
• a bit, a piece, a scrap, a trace
➤ **shreds**
*The gale ripped the tent to **shreds**.*
• tatters, ribbons, rags

shrill *ADJECTIVE*
*They heard the **shrill** sound of a whistle.*
• high, high-pitched, piercing, sharp
`OPPOSITES` low, soft

shrink *VERB*
❶ *The pile of cookies was **shrinking**.*
• to dwindle, to diminish, to disappear, to get smaller
`OPPOSITE` to grow
❷ *My jeans have **shrunk** in the wash.*
• to become smaller, to contract
`OPPOSITE` to expand

shrivel VERB
The plants shrivelled in the heat.
• to wilt, to wither, to droop, to dry up, to wrinkle, to shrink

shut VERB **shuts, shutting, shut**
❶ *Please shut the door behind you.*
• to close, to fasten, to seal, to secure
— To **slam** something is to shut it noisily.
OPPOSITE **to open**
❷ *They shut the dog in the back room.*
• to confine, to lock up, to detain, to imprison, to keep, to enclose
❸ *The shop shuts at 5.*
• to close, to close its doors
OPPOSITE **to open**

shy ADJECTIVE
The little girl was too shy to say anything.
• bashful, timid, reserved, hesitant, self-conscious
OPPOSITE **bold**

sick ADJECTIVE
❶ *Katie is off school because she's sick.*
• ill, unwell, poorly
OPPOSITE **well**
❷ *The rough sea made me feel sick.*
• nauseous, queasy
➤ **to be sick of**
I'm sick of this rain!
• to be fed up with, to be tired of, to have had enough of

sickly ADJECTIVE
He was a sickly child.
• unhealthy, weak, delicate, frail
OPPOSITES **healthy, strong**

sickness NOUN
» Look at **illness**.

side NOUN
❶ *A cube has six sides.*
• a face, a surface
❷ *The path runs along the side of the field.*
• the edge, the border, the boundary, the fringe, the perimeter, the margin
— A **verge** is the side of a road or path.
❸ *I could see both sides of the argument.*
• a point of view, a view, an angle, an aspect
❹ *We're on the same side.*
• a team

side VERB
➤ **to side with someone**
My mum sided with my brother in our argument.
• to support, to favour, to take someone's side, to agree with, to back

sift VERB
Sift the flour to get rid of any lumps.
• to sieve, to strain, to filter

sigh NOUN, VERB
'I'll never be good at tennis,' sighed Libby.
• to moan, to lament, to grumble, to complain

sight NOUN
❶ *Owls have very good sight.*
• eyesight, vision
❷ *The woods in autumn are a lovely sight.*
• a spectacle, a display, a show, a scene
❸ *We went to London to see the sights.*
• an attraction, a landmark
➤ **to be in sight**
At last, land was in sight.
• to be visible, to appear, to come into view
➤ **to be out of sight**
He waved until they were out of sight.
• to be invisible, to disappear, to disappear from view

sign NOUN
❶ *Write a minus sign before the number.*
• a symbol, a mark
— A **numeral** is a sign that represents a number.
— A **logo** is a sign used by a company on its products.
❷ *The sign said 'No Entry'.*
• a notice, a placard, a poster, a signpost
❸ *She made a sign to be quiet.*
• a signal, a gesture, a movement, an action
❹ *Green shoots are a sign that spring is coming.*
• an indication, a clue, a hint, a signal
— A **warning** is a sign that something bad is going to happen.
— An **omen** is an event that people believe is a sign that something will happen.

sign VERB
Please sign here.
• to write your name, to write your signature

signal NOUN
The soldiers waited for the signal to attack.
• a sign, an indication, a prompt, a cue

signal VERB
The diver signalled that he was going up.
• to give a sign or signal, to gesture, to indicate, to motion

a
b
c
d
e
f
g
h
i
j
k
l
m
n
o
p
q
r
s
t
u
v
w
x
y
z

significance NOUN
What's the significance of that mark?
• importance, meaning, message, point, relevance

significant ADJECTIVE
❶ *Climate change is having a significant effect on wildlife.*
• noticeable, considerable, perceptible, striking, substantial, meaningful
❷ *The article lists some significant events in the history of science.*
• important, major, notable, influential
OPPOSITE insignificant

silence NOUN
There was silence while we read our books.
• quiet, hush, stillness, calm, peace
OPPOSITE noise

silent ADJECTIVE
❶ *The house was silent.*
• quiet, noiseless, soundless, still
OPPOSITE noisy
❷ *The others talked, but I stayed silent.*
• quiet, speechless, mute
OPPOSITE talkative

silly ADJECTIVE
❶ *It was silly of you to come out without your coat.*
• foolish, stupid, idiotic, thoughtless, unwise
— Immature, juvenile, childish or babyish means silly in a way that is like a young child.
❷ *That was a really silly idea.*
• stupid, absurd, ridiculous, ludicrous, daft, mad, crazy, dotty (informal)
OPPOSITE sensible

similar ADJECTIVE
The two cars are similar.
• alike, the same
— Identical means exactly the same.
OPPOSITE different
➤ **similar to**
Her new book is similar to the previous one.
• like, close to, comparable to
OPPOSITES unlike, different from

similarity NOUN
There are some similarities between the two stories.
• a resemblance, a likeness
OPPOSITE a difference

simple ADJECTIVE
❶ *Can you answer this simple question?*
• easy, elementary, straightforward
OPPOSITE difficult

❷ *The help file is written in simple language.*
• clear, uncomplicated, understandable, intelligible
OPPOSITE complicated
❸ *The girl wore a simple cotton dress.*
• plain, undecorated
OPPOSITE elaborate
❹ *They live in a simple cottage.*
• ordinary, humble, modest, basic
OPPOSITE fancy

simply ADVERB
❶ *Try to explain it simply.*
• clearly, straightforwardly, in simple terms, in plain terms
❷ *I was simply trying to help.*
• just, merely, only

sin NOUN
They believed God would punish them for their sins.
• evil, wickedness, wrongdoing

sincere ADJECTIVE
Please accept my sincere apologies.
• genuine, honest, true, truthful, real, earnest
OPPOSITE insincere

sing VERB sings, singing, sang, sung
❶ *He was singing quietly to himself.*
• to hum
— To croon is to sing softly or lovingly.
— To chant is to sing or say repeated words in a rhythmic way.
❷ *The birds were singing in the trees.*
• to chirp, to cheep, to tweet, to twitter, to warble

single ADJECTIVE
We only found one single example of this type of leaf.
• individual, lone, solitary, isolated, unique

single VERB
➤ **to single someone out**
They singled her out as the best player.
• to pick out, to select, to choose, to identify

sink VERB sinks, sinking, sank, sunk
❶ *The ship hit the rocks and sank.*
• to go down, to become submerged
— To capsize is to turn upside down in the water.
— To scuttle a ship is to sink it deliberately by making holes in it.
❷ *The sun had sunk behind the hills.*
• to drop, to descend, to subside, to dip, to set, to fall

sit *VERB* **sits, sitting, sat**
*I was **sitting** on the sofa reading.*
• to settle, to be seated, to rest
— To **perch** is to sit on the edge of something or on something small.
— To **loll**, to **lounge** or to **slouch** is to sit in a very relaxed lazy position.
— To **squat** is to sit on your heels.
— To **crouch** is to be in a low position with legs and arms bent.
— To **straddle** something is to sit with one leg on either side of it.
— To **bask** is to sit or lie comfortably in the sun.
➤ **to sit down**
*Please **sit down** and open your books.*
• to take a seat, to be seated
— To **flop** is to sit down heavily.

site *NOUN*
*This is the **site** of an ancient burial ground.*
• a location, a place, a position, a setting

situation *NOUN*
*I found myself in an awkward **situation**.*
• position, circumstances, condition, state of affairs
— A **plight** or a **predicament** is a bad situation.

size *NOUN*
*What **size** is the garden?*
• dimensions, proportions, area, extent, scale
— The **length** of something is how long it is.
— The **height** of something is how tall or high it is.
— The **width** or **breadth** of something is how wide it is.
— The **depth** of something is how deep it is.
— The **capacity** or the **volume** of something is the amount of space inside it.

sketch *NOUN*
*She drew a quick **sketch** of her cat.*
• a drawing, a picture, an outline
— A **doodle** is a sketch you do while you are bored or thinking about something else.

sketch *VERB*
*He **sketched** a rough design for the poster.*
• to draw, to draft, to outline

skilful *ADJECTIVE*
*She is a very **skilful** player.*
• skilled, able, capable, talented, expert
— Use **deft** or **agile** if someone is physically skilful and quick.
OPPOSITE incompetent

skill *NOUN*
❶ *It takes a lot of **skill** to fly the plane.*
• ability, aptitude, talent, capability, competence, craft
❷ *There's a special **skill** to tossing the pancakes.*
• a knack, a trick

skin *NOUN*
*The cave people wore animal **skins**.*
• a fur, a hide, a pelt
— The skin of a fruit or vegetable is its **peel** or **rind**.
— Your **complexion** is the appearance of the skin on your face.

skip *VERB*
❶ *The children **skipped** along the pavement.*
• to hop, to jump, to leap, to bound, to prance
❷ *You can **skip** the last paragraph.*
• to pass over, to miss out, to ignore, to omit, to leave out

sky *NOUN*
*The kite soared up into the **sky**.*
• the air, the heavens

WRITING TIPS

Here are some helpful words for writing about the sky:

TO DESCRIBE THE SKY BY DAY:

• blue, clear, cloudless, sunny, sunless, cloudy, grey, overcast, stormy, thundery
The sky was overcast and still. Thin wisps of mist clung to the tops of the pine trees, and the oak and wild cherry were bare-leaved, waiting for spring.
—SKY HAWK, Gill Lewis

TO DESCRIBE THE SKY AT NIGHT:

• moonless, moonlit, pitch-black, starless, starlit, starry, star-studded

slack *ADJECTIVE*
*The rope went **slack**.*
• loose, limp
OPPOSITE tight

slam *VERB*
*Don't **slam** the door!*
• to bang, to shut loudly

slant *VERB*
*Her handwriting **slants** backwards.*
• to slope, to lean, to tilt, to incline, to be at an angle

a b c d e f g h i j k l m n o p q r s t u v w x y z

slant NOUN
The floor of the caravan was at a *slant*.
• a slope, an angle, a tilt, an incline, a gradient
— A **diagonal** is a slanting line joining opposite corners of something.
— A **ramp** is a slope joining two different levels.

slap VERB
He *slapped* his hand down on the table.
• to smack, to strike, to hit, to whack
— To **spank** someone is to slap them as a punishment, usually on the bottom.

sledge NOUN
We dragged our *sledges* up the snowy slope.
• a toboggan
— A **sleigh** is a large sledge pulled by horses.

sleep VERB sleeps, sleeping, slept
The baby was *sleeping* upstairs.
• to be asleep, to have a nap, to doze, to snooze, to snore, to rest, to slumber *(old use)*
— To **hibernate** is to have a long sleep through the winter.

sleep NOUN
Mr Khan had a short *sleep* after lunch.
• a nap, a rest, a doze, a snooze
— **Hibernation** is the long sleep some animals have through the winter.
➤ **to go to sleep**
Dad *went to sleep* in front of the TV.
• to fall asleep, to doze off, to drop off, to nod off

sleepy ADJECTIVE
The giant was usually *sleepy* after dinner.
• drowsy, tired, weary
OPPOSITE wide awake

slice NOUN
Would you like a *slice* of pie?
• a piece, a slab, a bit, a portion

slice VERB
I'll *slice* the cake.
• to cut
— To slice a large piece of meat is to **carve** it.
» For other ways of cutting things look at **cut**.

slide VERB
Everyone was *sliding* around on the ice.
• to slip, to skid, to slither, to glide

slight ADJECTIVE
❶ There are some *slight* differences.
• minor, unimportant, small, insignificant, trifling, trivial
OPPOSITES important, major

❷ She is very small and *slight*.
• slim, slender, thin, light, delicate
OPPOSITES stout, tall

slightly ADVERB
I got the answer *slightly* wrong.
• a little, a bit, somewhat
OPPOSITE seriously

slim ADJECTIVE
❶ A tall *slim* figure appeared out of the fog.
• slender, lean, thin
OPPOSITE fat
❷ Their chances of winning are *slim*.
• small, poor, slight, slender, remote
OPPOSITE good
❸ They won by a *slim* margin.
• narrow, small, slender
OPPOSITE wide

slime NOUN
The snails had left a trail of *slime*.
• ooze, sludge, mud, gunk *(informal)*, goo *(informal)*

slimy ADJECTIVE
The floor of the tunnel was covered with *slimy* mud.
• slippery, slithery, sticky, oozy, gooey *(informal)*

slip VERB
❶ I *slipped* and fell over.
• to trip, to stumble
— To **skid**, to **slide** or to **slither** is to slip on something slippery such as ice.
❷ The lifeboat *slipped* into the water.
• to glide, to slide
❸ He *slipped* out before anyone was awake.
• to sneak, to steal, to creep, to slink, to tiptoe

slip NOUN
❶ One *slip* and you could fall into the river.
• a trip, a stumble
❷ The pianist made a few tiny *slips*.
• a mistake, an error, a fault
— A **blunder** is a serious mistake.
❸ She wrote her phone number on a *slip* of paper.
• a piece, a scrap

slippery ADJECTIVE
Take care—the floor is *slippery*.
• slithery, slippy, smooth, glassy, icy, greasy, oily
— A common simile is as **slippery as an eel**.

slit NOUN
The archers shot arrows through the *slits* in the castle wall.
• an opening, a chink, a gap, a slot

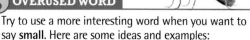

— A **split** is a slit where something has burst or separated.

— A **tear** or a **rip** is a slit where something has torn.

— A **vent** is a slit for letting out gas or smoke.

slit VERB

» For ways to cut things look at **cut**.

slope VERB

The beach **slopes** gently to the sea.

• to incline, to slant

— To **fall**, to **drop** or to **dip** is to slope downwards.

— To **rise** is to slope upwards.

slope NOUN

It was hard work pushing my bike up the **slope**.

• a hill, a rise, a bank, a ramp, an incline, a gradient

— An **ascent** is an upward slope.

— A **descent** is a downward slope.

sloppy ADJECTIVE

❶ The cake mixture was too **sloppy**.

• runny, watery, liquid, wet

❷ This is a very **sloppy** piece of work.

• careless, messy, untidy, shoddy

slouch VERB

Don't **slouch**—sit up straight!

• to hunch, to stoop, to slump, to droop, to flop, to loll, to lounge, to sprawl

slow ADJECTIVE

❶ Tortoises move at a **slow** pace.

• steady, unhurried, leisurely, gradual, plodding, dawdling

OPPOSITE fast

❷ She was **slow** to answer.

• hesitant, reluctant

OPPOSITE quick

slow VERB

➤ **to slow down**

Slow down—I can't keep up with you!

• to go slower, to slow your pace

— To **brake** is to make a car or bicycle slow down.

OPPOSITES to speed up, to accelerate

sly ADJECTIVE

The old man was very **sly**.

• crafty, cunning, clever, wily, tricky, sneaky, devious

— A common simile is **as sly as a fox**.

OPPOSITE straightforward

smack VERB

She **smacked** me on the hand.

• to slap, to strike, to hit, to whack, to cuff

» For other ways of hitting look at **hit**.

---

small ADJECTIVE

😮 **OVERUSED WORD**

Try to use a more interesting word when you want to say **small**. Here are some ideas and examples:

FOR A SMALL OBJECT OR A SMALL PERSON OR CREATURE:

• little, dainty, tiny, minute, compact, slight, miniature, microscopic, wee (Scottish), titchy (informal)

OPPOSITES big, large

Coral grew everywhere, shaped like miniature cauliflowers and coloured white, tan and pinkish grey.—THE FLIP-FLOP CLUB: WHALE SONG, EllenRichardson

FOR A SMALL HELPING OR PORTION:

• meagre, insufficient, scanty, stingy, skimpy

OPPOSITES large, generous

Interesting smells rose from the camp-kitchens, and Snibril thought sadly of the meagre rations he carried in his pack.—DRAGONS AT CRUMBLING CASTLE, Terry Pratchett

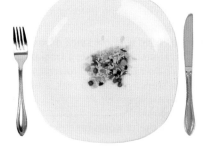

FOR A SMALL PROBLEM OR CHANGE:

• minor, slight, unimportant, insignificant, trivial, trifling, petty

OPPOSITES major, substantial

I shivered guiltily, and reminded myself that my injuries were trifling. I had been fortunate.—THE LADY IN THE TOWER, Marie-Louise Jensen

smart ADJECTIVE

❶ Everyone looked **smart** at the wedding.

• elegant, well-dressed, stylish, neat

OPPOSITE scruffy

❷ He was **smart** and realised immediately what they were up to.

• clever, intelligent, shrewd, quick, sharp

OPPOSITE stupid

smart VERB

The smoke from the barbecue made our eyes **smart**.

• to sting, to hurt, to prick, to prickle, to tingle

A
B
C
D
E
F
G
H
I
J
K
L
M
N
O
P
Q
R
S
T
U
V
W
X
Y
Z

smash *VERB*
❶ *The vase rolled off the table and smashed on the floor.*
• to break, to shatter, to crack
— To **demolish**, to **destroy** or to **wreck** something is to smash it completely.
— When wood smashes it **splinters**.
❷ *A wave smashed against the side of the boat.*
• to crash, to smack, to hit, to whack

smear *VERB*
The baby had smeared jam all over the walls.
• to spread, to wipe, to rub, to dab, to smudge, to daub

smear *NOUN*
There were smears of paint all over the carpet.
• a streak, a smudge, a blotch, a splodge, a mark

smell *VERB* smells, smelling, smelt
or smelled
❶ *Smell these lovely flowers.*
• to sniff
❷ *Your feet smell!*
• to stink, to reek, to pong *(informal)*

smell *NOUN*
❶ *The air was filled with the smell of roses.*
• a scent, an aroma, a perfume, a fragrance
❷ *There was a horrible smell of rotten eggs.*
• an odour, a stench, a stink, a reek, a whiff

 WRITING TIPS

Here are some useful words for describing a **smell**:

TO DESCRIBE A GOOD SMELL:

• aromatic, fragrant, perfumed, scented, sweet, sweet-smelling
In the garden below were lilac-trees purple with flowers, and their dizzily sweet fragrance drifted up to the window on the morning wind.—ANNE OF GREEN GABLES, L. M. Montgomery

TO DESCRIBE A BAD SMELL:

• acrid, fetid, foul, musty, odorous, rancid, rank, reeking, rotten, smelly, stinking, stinky *(informal)*
There was the same musty smell about the place that I had noticed in the Ballroom. It was the stench of witches.—THE WITCHES, Roald Dahl

TO DESCRIBE A STRONG SMELL:

• pungent, overpowering, lingering
The smell was a pungent mixture of almonds and rotten oranges.—TOM SCATTERHORN 2: THE HIDDEN WORLD, Henry Chancellor

smile *VERB*
The stranger smiled and introduced himself.
— To **grin** or to **beam** is to give a big happy smile.
— To **leer** is to smile unpleasantly.
— To **smirk** is to smile in an annoying self-satisfied way.

smile *NOUN*
She waved at me with a smile.
— A **grin** or a **beam** is a big happy smile.
— A **leer** is an unpleasant smile.
— A **smirk** is an annoying self-satisfied smile.

 WRITING TIPS

Here are some useful words for describing a **smile**:
• broad, wide, big, beaming, bright, radiant, cheerful,
• warm, pleasant, friendly, charming
• faint, slight, small, weak
• shy, nervous, tight
• wry, sly, knowing, smug, satisfied
• crooked, lopsided

smoke *NOUN*
Puffs of green smoke came from the dragon's nostrils.
• fumes, gas
— **Steam** or **vapour** is a mass of tiny drops of liquid in the air.
— **Exhaust** is the smoke given out by a car.
— **Smog** is a mixture of smoke and fog.

smooth *ADJECTIVE*
❶ *This part of the road is smooth and good for cycling.*
• flat, even, level
OPPOSITE uneven
❷ *There was no wind and the lake was smooth.*
• calm, still, unruffled, undisturbed, glassy
OPPOSITE rough
❸ *Otters have smooth and shiny coats.*
• silky, sleek, velvety
OPPOSITE coarse
❹ *Stir the cake mixture until it is smooth.*
• creamy, flowing, runny
OPPOSITE lumpy
❺ *The journey was very smooth.*
• comfortable, steady
OPPOSITE bumpy

smooth *VERB*
He smoothed his hair.
• to flatten, to pat, to stroke, to rub
— To **iron** clothes is to smooth them with an iron.

smother VERB
❶ *She smothered the toast with butter.*
• to cover, to coat, to plaster
❷ *Her hug almost smothered me.*
• to suffocate, to stifle

snake NOUN
The snake coiled itself around a branch.
• a serpent

 WORD WEB

SOME KINDS OF SNAKE:

• an adder, a boa constrictor, a cobra, a grass snake, a mamba, a python, a rattlesnake, a viper — A **basilisk** is a kind of snake found in stories and myths, that can kill people by looking at them.

PARTS OF A SNAKE:

• fangs, a forked tongue, scales, skin, venom

 WRITING TIPS

Here are some helpful words for writing about a **snake**:

THINGS A SNAKE DOES:

• to coil, to dart, to glide, to slide, to slither, to twine, to twist, to wind, to wriggle, to writhe, to shed its skin, to slough off its skin, to hiss, to bite, to strike

WORDS FOR DESCRIBING A SNAKE:

• deadly, fanged, venomous, slimy, smooth, coiled, twisting, writhing

[The snake] slithered out of a crevice, tasting a peculiar scent on the air with its quivering forked tongue . . . At once, its dull mantle of scales split from end to end, and a new snake emerged, shining and brightly coloured. Then it was gone, leaving behind the transparent husk of its sloughed skin.—GILGAMESH THE HERO, Geraldine McCaughrean

snatch VERB
The thief snatched the bag and ran off.
• to grab, to seize, to grasp, to pluck, to take

sneak VERB sneaks, sneaking, sneaked
I managed to sneak in without anyone seeing.
• to slip, to steal, to creep, to slink, to tiptoe

sneer VERB
➤ to sneer at
He sneered at my attempt to write a poem.
• to make fun of, to mock, to ridicule, to scoff at, to jeer at

snip VERB
Snip off the loose threads.
• to cut, to chop, to clip, to trim

snoop VERB
They caught a man snooping round the building.
• to sneak, to pry, to poke, to rummage, to spy

snort NOUN, VERB
» *For various sounds look at* **sound**.

snow NOUN

 WRITING TIPS

Here are some useful words for writing about **snow**:

SOME WORDS FOR DESCRIBING SNOW:

• crisp, powdery, soft, deep, patchy, slushy, floating, drifting, whirling, swirling, driving, blinding

SOME THINGS SNOW DOES:

• to fall, to drift, to float, to fly, to settle, to lie, to cover things, to blanket things
Through the swirling snow, the hound's form was blurred and it was difficult to see it properly.
—THE HOUNDS OF THE MORRIGAN, Pat O'Shea
— A **flurry** is a sudden gusty fall of snow.
— A **bank** or a **drift** is a pile of snow blown together by the wind.
— A **blanket** or a **mantle** of snow is a layer of it.

soak VERB
Days of rain had soaked the cricket pitch.
• to drench, to saturate, to wet thoroughly

soaking ADJECTIVE
My socks are absolutely soaking!
• wet through, drenched, dripping, wringing wet, saturated, sodden, sopping wet, soggy
— Ground that has been soaked by rain is **waterlogged**.

society NOUN
❶ *Ancient Egypt was a society ruled by pharaohs.*
• a community, a civilisation
❷ *He's joined the drama society.*
• a club, a group, an association, an organisation

soft ADJECTIVE
❶ *The baby can only eat soft food.*
• pulpy, spongy, squashy
OPPOSITE hard

❷ *I lay down on the **soft** bed.*
• supple, springy, flexible, comfortable
OPPOSITES firm, rigid
❸ *The rabbit's fur felt very **soft**.*
• smooth, silky, sleek, velvety
OPPOSITES coarse, rough
❹ *A **soft** breeze stirred the leaves.*
• gentle, light, mild, delicate
OPPOSITES rough, strong
❺ *She spoke in a **soft** voice.*
• quiet, low, faint
OPPOSITE loud

sold *(past tense of **sell**)*

soldier NOUN
*He was a **soldier** in the emperor's army.*
• a fighter, a warrior
— A **mercenary** is a soldier who can be paid to fight on any side.
— **Infantry** are soldiers trained to fight on foot.

solid ADJECTIVE
❶ *A cricket ball is **solid**.*
OPPOSITE hollow
❷ *The water turned into **solid** ice.*
• hard, firm, dense, compact, rigid, stiff
— A common simile is **as solid as a rock**.
OPPOSITES soft, liquid
❸ *The crown was made of **solid** gold.*
• pure, unmixed, real
❹ *The bars of the climbing frame are quite **solid**.*
• firm, robust, sound, strong, stable, sturdy, substantial
OPPOSITES weak, unstable

solitary ADJECTIVE
❶ *He was a **solitary** man and rarely spoke to others.*
• unsociable, isolated, lonely
OPPOSITE sociable
❷ *There was a **solitary** tree in the middle of the field.*
• single, sole, one, only

solitude NOUN
*On the island, there was total peace and **solitude**.*
• privacy, seclusion
— Use **isolation** or **loneliness** for solitude that makes someone unhappy.

solve VERB
*No one has been able to **solve** this ancient riddle.*
• to interpret, to explain, to answer, to work out, to find the solution to, to unravel, to decipher, to decode

song NOUN

 WORD WEB

SOME KINDS OF SONG:

• an anthem, a ballad, a carol, a chant, a folk song, a hymn, a jingle, a lullaby, a nursery rhyme, a pop song, a psalm, a rap, a shanty
— The **lyrics** of a song are its words.
— The **melody** of a song is its tune.
— A **verse** of a song is one part of it, that has a repeated **chorus** sung in between.

soon ADVERB
*Dinner will be ready **soon**.*
• shortly, before long, in a minute, presently, quickly

sophisticated ADJECTIVE
❶ *Frida looked very **sophisticated** with her hair up.*
• grown-up, mature, cultured, refined
OPPOSITE naive
❷ *They use very **sophisticated** equipment.*
• advanced, complex, complicated, intricate, elaborate
OPPOSITES primitive, simple

sore ADJECTIVE
*My feet are still **sore** from the walk.*
• painful, aching, hurting, smarting, tender, sensitive
» For ways to say that something is sore look at **hurt**.

sorrow NOUN
❶ *Those were years of **sorrow** for the family.*
• sadness, unhappiness, misery, woe, anguish, distress, despair, melancholy, gloom, wretchedness
— **Depression** is a very sad mood that lasts for a long time.
— **Grief** or **mourning** is deep sorrow because someone has died.
— **Homesickness** is sorrow because you miss your home.
OPPOSITE happiness
❷ *He expressed his **sorrow** for what he had done.*
• regret, remorse, repentance, apologies

sorry ADJECTIVE
*He was very **sorry** for what he had done.*
• apologetic, regretful, remorseful, repentant
• ashamed: *He was very **ashamed** of what he had done.*
OPPOSITE unapologetic
➤ **to feel sorry for someone**
*Everyone **felt sorry for** the losers.*
• to pity, to sympathise with, to feel pity for, to feel sympathy for, to feel compassion for, to feel for

sort NOUN
*What **sort** of fruit is it?*
• a kind, a type, a variety, a style, a category
– A **breed** of dog is a sort of dog.
– A **species** of animal is a sort of animal.

sort VERB
*We **sorted** the books according to size.*
• to arrange, to organise, to class, to classify, to group, to categorise
OPPOSITE to mix
➤ **to sort something out**
*Did you manage to **sort out** the problem?*
• to settle, to resolve, to clear up, to cope with, to deal with

sought *(past tense of seek)*

sound NOUN
*We heard the **sound** of footsteps approaching.*
• a noise
– A **din** or a **racket** is a loud unpleasant sound.
– A **cacophony** is a loud unpleasant mixture of sounds.

✹ WORD WEB

SOME LOUD SOUNDS:

• bang, bawl, bellow, blare, boom, clang, clank, clap, clatter, crash, crunch, drum, grate, howl, jangle, pop, rattle, ring, scrape, scream, shout, shriek, slam, snap, splash, thud, thunder, wail, wham, whoop

SOME GENTLE SOUNDS:

• chime, chink, click, clink, crackle, creak, croak, drone, fizz, gurgle, hiss, hum, moan, murmur, patter, plop, purr, rumble, rustle, scrunch, sigh, sizzle, squeak, squelch, swish, tick, tinkle, wheeze, whirr, whoosh

rattle

☺ WRITING TIPS

Here are some useful words for describing a **sound**:

TO DESCRIBE A PLEASANT SOUND:

• sweet, harmonious, melodious, smooth
*It sounded like the **sweet** singing of a mermaid.*

TO DESCRIBE AN UNPLEASANT SOUND:

• grating, harsh, jarring, piercing, rasping, shrill, tinny, cacophonous
A startled raven burst upward uttering its harsh, grating alarm cry . . .–THE EAGLE OF THE NINTH, Rosemary Sutcliff

sour ADJECTIVE
❶ *These apples are a bit **sour**.*
• tart, bitter, sharp, acid, tangy
OPPOSITE sweet
❷ *The guard opened the door with a **sour** look on his face.*
• cross, bad-tempered, grumpy, disagreeable

source NOUN
*What was the **source** of this information?*
• the origin, the starting point

bellow
scream
shriek
wail
blare

SOME ELECTRONIC SOUNDS:

• beep, bleep, buzz, hum, ping, zap
Great whooshes of sound filled the air as the beam engine started to move, then generators started to hum, and power surged through the sizing machine.
—HERE BE MONSTERS!, Alan Snow
» *For sounds made when speaking look at **say**.*
» *For sounds made by animals look at **cat**, **bird**, **dog**, **sheep**, etc.*

TO DESCRIBE A LOUD SOUND:

• blaring, deafening, noisy, thunderous

TO DESCRIBE A QUIET SOUND:

• low, muffled, muted, soft
In the distance they could hear the muted sound of traffic going round Hyde Park Corner.—THE BFG, Roald Dahl

sweet singing

a b c d e f g h i j k l m n o p q r s t u v w x y

space NOUN

❶ *There wasn't much **space** to move about.*
• room, area

❷ *Leave a **space** on the shelf for my picture.*
• a gap, a place
— A **vacuum** is a space with nothing in it, including air.
— An **interval** is a space of time.

❸ *The astronauts will spend ten days in **space**.*
• outer space
— The **universe** or the **cosmos** is everything that exists in space.
— **Cosmic** means relating to space or the universe.

WRITING TIPS

Here are some helpful words you could use when writing about **space**:

THINGS THAT TRAVEL THROUGH SPACE:

• a capsule, a module, a pod, a lunar lander, a rocket, a spacecraft, a spaceship, a space shuttle, a space station, a satellite, a starship, a flying saucer, an alien craft, a UFO

WORDS FOR TRAVELLING THROUGH SPACE:

• to launch, to orbit, to blast off, to touch down, to splash down, to beam up

THINGS FOUND IN SPACE:

• an asteroid, a black hole, a comet, a constellation, a galaxy, a meteor, a meteorite, a moon, a nebula, a planet, a shooting star, a star

Wilbur unfurled his map. Then he began to poke at screens and pull levers and push buttons until—lurch! swerve!—the spaceship was suddenly whizzing through space, heading towards Earth.—WINNIE SHAPES UP, Laura Owen & Korky Paul

» *Look at* **planet**.

spacious ADJECTIVE

*The living room is **spacious** and bright.*
• big, large, roomy
OPPOSITES small, cramped

spare ADJECTIVE

❶ *The **spare** tyre is in the boot.*
• additional, extra, reserve, emergency

❷ *Is there any **spare** food?*
• leftover, remaining, unused, unwanted

spare VERB

*Can you **spare** any money for a good cause?*
• to afford, to give, to provide, to do without

a satellite   a moon

an astronaut

a spaceship

spark NOUN
*There was a **spark** of light as he struck the match.*
• a flash, a gleam, a glint, a flicker, a sparkle

sparkle VERB
*The diamond ring **sparkled** in the sunlight.*
• to glitter, to glisten, to glint, to twinkle, to shine, to wink

speak VERB speaks, speaking, spoke, spoken
*I opened my mouth to **speak**.*
• to communicate, to express yourself, to talk, to say something, to utter something
» *For ways to say something look at* **say**.

spear NOUN
— A **lance** is a long spear used by medieval knights.
— A **javelin** is a light spear thrown in sport.
— A **harpoon** is a spear attached to a rope, used to catch whales.

special ADJECTIVE
❶ *Today is a very **special** day.*
• important, significant, extraordinary, exceptional, unusual, out of the ordinary, memorable, notable
OPPOSITES ordinary, average
❷ *My granny has her own **special** way of making porridge.*
• unique, individual, personal, characteristic, distinctive, different, peculiar, particular, specific

speciality NOUN
*Pancakes are my **speciality**.*
• a strength, a strong point, a special skill

specific ADJECTIVE
*Can you be more **specific** about what you want?*
• detailed, precise, exact, definite, particular
OPPOSITES general, vague

speck NOUN
*She brushed a **speck** of dust from her shoes.*
• a bit, a dot, a spot, a fleck, a grain, a particle, a trace, a mark
» *Look at* **bit**.

speckled ADJECTIVE
*A brown **speckled** egg lay on the nest.*
• spotted, spotty, mottled, freckled, dappled

spectacular ADJECTIVE
*The acrobats gave a **spectacular** performance.*
• dramatic, exciting, impressive, thrilling, magnificent, sensational, breathtaking

spectator NOUN
*The **spectators** enjoyed the fireworks.*
• the audience, the crowd
— A **viewer** is a person watching TV.
— A **witness** is someone who sees an accident or a crime.
— An **onlooker** is someone who sees an event but is not involved in it.

speech NOUN
❶ *His **speech** was slow and he looked tired.*
• speaking, talking, pronunciation
❷ *The head teacher give a **speech** at prize day.*
• a talk, an address
— A **lecture** is a formal speech about a subject.
— A **sermon** is a speech given by a preacher.
— A **monologue** is a speech in a play or film delivered by one actor.

speed NOUN
❶ *They were going at a **speed** of 20 miles per hour.*
• a pace, a rate
— The **tempo** is the speed of a piece of music.
— **Velocity** is a formal word for speed in a particular direction.
❷ *They ate with amazing **speed**.*
• quickness, rapidity, swiftness
OPPOSITE slowness

speed VERB speeds, speeding, sped
*The skiers **sped** down the mountain.*
• to race, to rush, to dash, to fly, to dart, to hurry, to hurtle, to streak, to tear, to whizz, to shoot, to zoom
➤ **to speed up**
*He **sped** up to overtake his rival.*
• to accelerate, to increase your pace, to hurry, to hasten
OPPOSITES to slow down, to decelerate

spell NOUN
*The witch used a **spell** to turn him into a toad.*
• a charm, magic
» *For other words to do with magic look at* **magic**.

spend VERB spends, spending, spent
❶ *Have you **spent** all your pocket money already?*
• to pay out, to use up, to get through
— To **squander** money is to spend it wastefully.
❷ *We **spent** the day in the park.*
• to pass, to occupy, to fill
— To **waste** time is to spend it doing something useless.

sphere NOUN
*The earth is a **sphere**.*
• a ball, a globe

a
b
c
d
e
f
g
h
i
j
k
l
m
n
o
p
q
r
s
t
u
v
w
x
y
z

spice NOUN

🕸 **WORD WEB**

SOME SPICES USED IN COOKING:

• chilli, cinnamon, curry powder, ginger, nutmeg, paprika, pepper

paprika   nutmeg   cinnamon

spicy ADJECTIVE
The meat was cooked in a **spicy** chilli sauce.
• hot, peppery, fiery

spike NOUN
His shirt got caught on a metal **spike**.
• a point, a prong, a spear, a stake, a barb

spill VERB spills, spilling, spilt or spilled
❶ Don't **spill** juice on your picture.
• to tip, to splash, to pour, to slop, to slosh
❷ The treasure chest fell open, **spilling** gold coins everywhere.
• to shed, to tip, to scatter, to drop

spin VERB spins, spinning, spun
The rear wheels of the truck **spun** round.
• to turn, to rotate, to revolve, to whirl, to twirl

spine NOUN
❶ Vertebrates are animals that have a **spine**.
• a backbone, a spinal column
❷ A porcupine has sharp **spines**.
• a needle, a quill, a point, a spike, a prickle, a bristle

spiral NOUN
The staircase wound upwards in a long **spiral**.
• a coil, a twist, a corkscrew
— A **vortex** is a whirling spiral of air or water.

spirit NOUN
❶ They believe the **spirit** lives on after death.
• soul
❷ He carried a charm to keep evil **spirits** away.
• a ghost, a ghoul, a phantom, a spectre, a demon
≫ Look at **ghost**.
❸ They played with great **spirit**.
• energy, liveliness, enthusiasm, vigour, zest, zeal

spite NOUN
I think she broke the bracelet on purpose out of **spite**.
• malice, bitterness, resentment, spitefulness, maliciousness

spiteful ADJECTIVE
He made some really **spiteful** comments.
• malicious, mean, nasty, vicious, unkind, horrible
OPPOSITE kind

splash VERB
The bus **splashed** water over us.
• to shower, to spray, to spatter, to sprinkle, to squirt, to slop, to slosh, to spill

splendid ADJECTIVE
❶ The queen organised a **splendid** banquet.
• magnificent, grand, great, lavish, luxurious, impressive, imposing, dazzling, glorious, elegant, majestic
❷ That's a **splendid** idea!
• excellent, superb, tremendous, marvellous, wonderful, fantastic, terrific

splendour NOUN
They admired the **splendour** of the palace.
• magnificence, glory, majesty, richness, brilliance

split VERB splits, splitting, split
❶ The bag has **split**.
• to rip, to tear, to burst
❷ He **split** the log with an axe.
• to chop, to cut up, to crack open, to splinter
❸ The robbers **split** the gold between them.
• to divide, to share out, to distribute
❹ The path **splits** here.
• to divide, to branch, to fork, to separate

split NOUN
He had a **split** in the seat of his trousers.
• a rip, a tear, a slash, a slit

spoil VERB spoils, spoiling, spoilt or spoiled
❶ Bad weather **spoiled** the holiday.
• to ruin, to wreck, to upset, to mess up
❷ The water had **spoilt** some of the books.
• to damage, to harm, to destroy
❸ My grandparents always **spoil** me.
• to indulge, to pamper, to make a fuss of

spoke (past tense of **speak**)

spoken (past tense of **speak**)

spoken ADJECTIVE
Her **spoken** French is excellent.
• oral, verbal
OPPOSITE written

spooky ADJECTIVE
It's very **spooky** in the graveyard at night.
• sinister, creepy, frightening, scary, uncanny, eerie, ghostly

sport *NOUN*

*I enjoy doing **sport** at school.*

• exercise, games

✦ WORD WEB

SOME TEAM SPORTS:

• American football, baseball, basketball, cricket, football

— **Soccer** is another word for football, used especially in America.

• hockey, netball, rounders, rugby, volleyball

SOME INDIVIDUAL SPORTS:

• archery, athletics, badminton, boxing, bowling, cycling, fishing, golf, gymnastics, horse racing, jogging, judo, karate, kick-boxing, mountaineering, orienteering, running, skateboarding, snooker, squash, table tennis, taekwondo, tennis, trampolining, weightlifting

SOME WINTER SPORTS:

• ice hockey, ice skating, skiing, snowboarding, tobogganing

SOME WATER SPORTS:

• canoeing, diving, kayaking, rowing, sailing, scuba diving, surfing, swimming, waterskiing, windsurfing

» *For individual athletic events look at **athletics**.*

football

karate

skateboarding

ice hockey

---

spot *NOUN*

❶ *There were several **spots** of paint on the carpet.*

• a mark, a stain, a blot, a smudge, a dot, a fleck, a speck

— A **freckle** is a small brown spot on your skin.

— A **mole** is a small dark spot or lump on your skin.

— A **birthmark** is a mark someone is born with on their skin.

— A **rash** is a lot of red spots on your skin.

❷ *Here's a nice **spot** for a picnic.*

• a place, a position, a location, a site

spot *VERB*

*Nina **spotted** her friend in the crowd.*

• to see, to sight, to spy, to catch sight of, to notice, to observe, to make out, to recognise, to detect

spray *VERB*

*I **sprayed** the plants with water.*

• to shower, to spatter, to splash, to sprinkle, to scatter

A B C D E F G H I J K L M N O P Q R **S** T U V W X Y Z

spread *VERB* spreads, spreading, spread
❶ *I spread the map on the table.*
• to lay out, to open out, to unfold, to unfurl, to unroll
❷ *The spilled oil spread over a wide area.*
• to expand, to extend, to stretch
— Use to **billow** when a cloth, flag or sail spreads in the wind.
❸ *She spread the bread with butter.*
• to smear, to coat, to cover, to plaster
❹ *He spread the seeds evenly over the ground.*
• to scatter, to disperse
❺ *The school website is a good way of spreading news.*
• to communicate, to share, to circulate, to distribute, to transmit, to make known, to pass on
❻ *The news spread fast.*
• to travel, to be transmitted, to be passed on

spring *VERB* springs, springing, sprang, sprung
Suddenly a rabbit sprang over the fence.
• to jump, to leap, to bound, to hop, to vault
— To **pounce** on something is to spring on top of it to catch it.

springy *ADJECTIVE*
The bed felt soft and springy.
• bouncy, elastic, stretchy, flexible
OPPOSITE rigid

sprinkle *VERB*
He sprinkled flakes of chocolate over the cake.
• to scatter, to shower, to spray, to dust

spun (*past tense of* **spin**)

spy *NOUN*
The spy was on a top-secret mission.
• an agent, a secret agent
— **Intelligence** is secret information that a spy tries to find out.

spy *VERB*
❶ *Have you been spying on me?*
• to snoop, to pry, to watch
— To **stalk** someone is to follow them secretly.
— To **eavesdrop** is to listen secretly to someone's conversation.
❷ *We spied a ship on the horizon.*
• to spot, to see, to catch sight of, to notice, to observe, to make out, to detect

squabble *VERB*
The children were squabbling in the car.
• to quarrel, to argue, to fight

squash *VERB*
❶ *My sandwich got squashed at the bottom of my school bag.*
• to crush, to flatten, to press, to compress, to mangle, to mash
❷ *We squashed our sleeping bags into our rucksacks.*
• to squeeze, to stuff, to force, to cram, to pack, to ram

squeak *NOUN, VERB*
》 *For various sounds look at* **sound**.

squeeze *VERB*
❶ *She squeezed the water out of the sponge.*
• to press, to wring, to compress, to crush
— To squeeze something between your thumb and finger is to **pinch** it.
❷ *We all squeezed into the lift.*
• to squash, to cram, to crowd, to stuff, to push, to ram, to shove

squirt *VERB*
Orange juice squirted in my eye.
• to spurt, to spray, to gush, to spout, to shoot, to jet

stab *VERB*
❶ *He stabbed the sausage with his fork.*
• to spear, to jab, to pierce
❷ *She stabbed a stick into the soft earth.*
• to stick, to thrust, to push, to jab, to plunge
stab *NOUN*
Jake felt a sudden stab of pain.
• a pang, a sting, a twinge

stable *ADJECTIVE*
The ladder doesn't look very stable.
• steady, secure, firm, fixed, solid, balanced
OPPOSITES wobbly, unstable

stack *NOUN*
There were stacks of books all over the floor.
• a pile, a heap, a mound, a tower

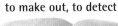

stacks of books

stack VERB
Stack the papers on the desk.
• to pile up, to heap up, to gather, to collect, to assemble

staff NOUN
There was a party at the hospital for all the staff.
• workers, employees, team
— The staff on a ship or aircraft are its **crew**.

stage NOUN
❶ *They went up on the stage to collect their prizes.*
• a platform
❷ *The final stage of the journey was made by coach.*
• a phase, a part, a portion, a stretch
❸ *What stage have you reached with your project?*
• a point, a step, a level

stagger VERB
❶ *The wounded knight staggered and fell.*
• to reel, to stumble, to lurch, to trip, to sway, to totter, to flounder, to lumber, to wobble
❷ *The size of the pyramid staggered us.*
• to amaze, to astonish, to astound, to surprise, to stun, to startle, to shock

stain NOUN
There was a stain on the tablecloth.
• a mark, a spot, a blot, a blemish, a smear, a smudge

stain VERB
The ink has stained the carpet.
• to mark, to soil, to dirty
— To stain metal is to **tarnish** it.

stale ADJECTIVE
The bread had gone stale.
• dry, hard, old, mouldy, musty
OPPOSITE fresh

stalk NOUN
We used a stalk of celery.
• a stem, a shoot, a twig, a stick
— A **trunk** is the main stem of a tree.

stalk VERB
❶ *The tiger stalked its prey.*
• to hunt, to pursue, to track, to trail, to follow, to shadow, to tail
❷ *She stalked angrily out of the room.*
• to stride, to march, to strut
» *For other ways to walk look at* **walk**.

stammer VERB
Angela went red and started stammering.
• to stutter, to splutter

stamp VERB
You stamped on my toe.
• to step, to tread, to trample

stand VERB stands, standing, stood
❶ *The newborn calf was too weak to stand.*
• to get up, to rise
— To **arise** is an old word meaning 'to stand'.
❷ *They stood the ladder against the wall.*
• to put, to place, to set, to position, to erect
❸ *I can't stand the smell any longer.*
• to bear, to abide, to endure, to put up with, to tolerate, to suffer
➤ **to stand for something**
What do these initials stand for?
• to mean, to indicate, to signify, to represent, to be short for

stand NOUN
The tablet computer comes with a stand.
• a support, a holder
— A **tripod** is a three-legged stand for a camera or telescope.
— A **pedestal** or **plinth** is a stand for a statue or column.

standard NOUN
❶ *Their writing is of a very high standard.*
• a grade, a level, a quality
❷ *We expect you to follow certain behaviour standards.*
• a guideline, a rule, an ideal, a model

standard ADJECTIVE
These are standard units used for measuring.
• normal, usual, conventional, accepted, established, typical, customary, common
OPPOSITE non-standard

star NOUN
The show featured a lot of big stars.
• a celebrity, an idol
» *For objects found in space look at* **space**.

stare VERB
He stared into the distance.
• to gaze, to look
— To **gape** is to stare with your mouth wide open.
— To **peer** is to stare at something closely or with difficulty.
— To **glare** or to **glower** is to stare angrily.

stare NOUN
I gave him a hard stare.
• a look, a gaze
— A **glare** is an angry stare.

start VERB
❶ *The concert starts at 7.30.*
• to begin, to commence
OPPOSITES to finish, to end
❷ *We are planning to start a book club.*
• to create, to set up, to establish, to found
❸ *I've started learning the violin.*
• to begin, to embark on, to undertake
❹ *The explosion started an avalanche.*
• to trigger, to cause, to bring about, to produce
❺ *She started the computer.*
• to switch on, to turn on
OPPOSITE to shut down

start NOUN
❶ *Try not to miss the start of the film.*
• the beginning, the opening
OPPOSITES the end, the close
❷ *This line is the start of the race.*
• the beginning, the starting point,
the starting line
OPPOSITES the end, the finish line
❸ *This was the start of an exciting new adventure.*
• the beginning, the dawn
OPPOSITE the end

starving ADJECTIVE
What's for dinner? I'm starving!
• hungry, famished, ravenous

state NOUN
❶ *The room was in a really bad state.*
• condition, shape
❷ *Slovakia became an independent state.*
• a country, a nation, a land

state VERB
Her passport states that she is an Australian citizen.
• to declare, to announce, to report, to say,
to proclaim, to pronounce

statement NOUN
The witness made a statement to the police.
• a declaration, a report, an announcement,
a comment

statue NOUN
We saw a statue of Millicent Fawcett.
• a figure, a sculpture, a carving

status NOUN
His gold cloak was a symbol of his high status.
• a rank, a level, a position, a grade, importance

stay VERB
❶ *Can you stay there for a minute?*
• to wait, to remain, to linger
OPPOSITE to leave

❷ *I tried to stay calm.*
• to keep, to remain
❸ *On holiday we stayed on a campsite.*
• to sleep, to lodge, to dwell

steady ADJECTIVE
❶ *Make sure the ladder is steady.*
• stable, secure, firm, fixed, balanced, solid
— A common simile is **as steady as a rock**.
OPPOSITES unsteady, shaky
❷ *The plants need a steady supply of water.*
• continuous, uninterrupted, non-stop, consistent
OPPOSITE intermittent
❸ *The runners kept up a steady pace.*
• regular, constant, unchanging, even
OPPOSITE irregular

steady VERB
He managed to steady his breathing.
• to regulate, to stabilise, to calm, to balance

steal VERB steals, stealing, stole, stolen
❶ *The burglars stole his laptop.*
• to take, to snatch, to make off with,
to pinch (*informal*), to swipe (*informal*),
to nick (*informal*)
— To **rob** a place is to steal from it.
— To **loot** or **plunder** a place is to violently steal
things from it, especially during war.
❷ *He stole away in the night.*
• to creep, to slip, to sneak, to tiptoe, to slink

steam NOUN
Clouds of steam were coming from the cauldron.
• vapour, mist, haze
— **Condensation** is steam on a cold window.

steep ADJECTIVE
The bus inched its way slowly up the steep slope.
• abrupt, sharp, sudden
— Use **sheer** or **vertical** if something is so steep that
it is almost straight up and down.
OPPOSITES gradual, gentle

steer VERB
She steered the car into the parking space.
• to direct, to guide, to manoeuvre
— You **drive** a vehicle.
— You **navigate** or **pilot** a boat or aircraft.

stem NOUN
The flower has a tall stem.
• a stalk, a shoot, a twig, a stick
— A **trunk** is the main stem of a tree.

step NOUN
❶ *She took a few steps towards me.*
• a footstep, a pace, a stride

❷ *Be careful not to trip on the **step**.*
• a doorstep
− **Stairs** are usually indoors while steps are usually outdoors.
− A **flight of stairs** or a **staircase** is a set of steps inside a house.
− **Rungs** are the steps of a ladder.
❸ *The first **step** in making a cake is to weigh the ingredients.*
• a stage, a phase, an action

step VERB
*Don't **step** in the puddle!*
• to tread, to put your foot, to walk
− To **stamp** is to step hard on something.
− To **trample** something is to crush it by stepping on it.

stick NOUN
❶ *They collected **sticks** to make a fire.*
• a twig, a branch, a stalk
❷ *The old lady walked with a **stick**.*
• a cane, a rod, a staff, a pole
− A **baton** is a stick used by a conductor.
− A **truncheon** is a stick carried by a police officer.
− A **wand** is a magic stick used by a magician, wizard, witch or fairy.

a wand

stick VERB sticks, sticking, stuck
❶ *He **stuck** his fork into the potato.*
• to poke, to prod, to stab, to thrust, to dig, to jab, to plunge
❷ *I **stuck** a stamp on the envelope.*
• to glue, to paste, to attach, to seal
❸ *The wheels of the caravan **stuck** in the mud.*
• to jam, to wedge, to become trapped
➤ **to stick out**
*A rock **stuck out** from the side of the cliff.*
• to jut out, to poke out, to protrude, to project

sticky ADJECTIVE
*There was a **sticky** mess on the table.*
• gummy, gluey, sludgy, slimy, gooey (informal)

stiff ADJECTIVE
❶ *He mounted the picture on **stiff** card.*
• rigid, inflexible, thick
− A common simile is **as stiff as a poker**.
OPPOSITE bendy
❷ *Make a **stiff** paste with flour and water.*
• firm, thick, solid
OPPOSITE soft
❸ *Her legs were **stiff** after the long walk.*
• aching, achy, painful, taut, tight
OPPOSITE supple

still ADJECTIVE
❶ *They stood **still** and listened.*
• motionless, unmoving, stationary, immobile
− If someone suddenly stands still, you can say that they **freeze** or **halt**.
❷ *We looked out at the **still** lake.*
• calm, quiet, peaceful, tranquil, serene
− **Stagnant** water is not flowing or fresh.
❸ *Can I have some **still** water please?*
• flat, plain
OPPOSITES fizzy, sparkling

stink NOUN
*The mouldy cheese gave off a dreadful **stink**.*
• a stench, an odour, a reek, a bad smell

stink VERB stinks, stinking, stank, stunk
*The ogre's breath **stank**.*
• to reek, to smell
» *Look at **smell**.*

stir VERB
❶ ***Stir** the mixture until it is smooth.*
• to mix, to beat, to blend, to whisk
❷ *The giant **stirred** in his sleep.*
• to shift, to move slightly
➤ **to stir something up**
*She was always **stirring up** trouble.*
• to cause, to arouse, to provoke, to set off, to trigger, to whip up

stock NOUN
❶ ***Stocks** of food were running low.*
• a supply, a store, a reserve, a hoard
❷ *The shopkeeper arranged his new **stock**.*
• goods, merchandise, wares

stock VERB
❶ *They **stock** all kinds of books.*
• to sell, to have, to trade in, to deal in, to have in stock
❷ *They **stocked** the fridge with cold drinks.*
• to load, to pack, to fill, to supply

stole (past tense of **steal**)

stolen (past participle of **steal**)

stomach NOUN
❶ *I had a pain in my **stomach**.*
• belly, gut, tummy (informal)
❷ *He rolled over and lay on his **stomach**.*
• abdomen, front, belly

stone NOUN
❶ *The columns of the temple were carved from **stone**.*
• rock
» *For types of stone look at **rock**.*

a b c d e f g h i j k l m n o p q r s t u v w x y z

❷ *Someone threw a* **stone**.
- a rock, a pebble
- A **boulder** is a large rounded stone.
- **Shingle** is pebbles on the beach.
- **Gravel** is a mixture of sand and small stones.
» *For precious stones look at* **jewel**.
» *Look at* **seed**.

stood *(past tense of* **stand***)*

stop *VERB*
❶ *I'll go out when the rain* **stops**.
- to cease, to end, to finish
`OPPOSITE` to start
❷ *Can you* **stop** *talking?*
- to cease, to refrain from, to quit, to give up
`OPPOSITES` to continue, to go on
❸ *We had to* **stop** *the game.*
- to pause, to interrupt, to break, to halt, to hold up, to suspend
`OPPOSITES` to continue, to resume
❹ *We need to* **stop** *this unfairness.*
- to eliminate, to abolish, to put an end to, to end
❺ *Suddenly the bus* **stopped**.
- to come to a stop, to come to a halt, to come to a standstill, to halt, to pull up, to draw up, to stall
❻ *Guards,* **stop** *that man!*
- to hold, to detain, to seize, to catch, to capture, to restrain
❼ *They tried to* **stop** *him from going.*
- to prevent, to obstruct, to bar, to hinder, to hamper, to foil
❽ *She* **stopped** *the leak with a piece of rubber.*
- to close, to plug, to seal, to block up

stop *NOUN*
Everything suddenly came to a **stop**.
- an end, a finish, a halt, a standstill

store *VERB*
Squirrels need to **store** *food for the winter.*
- to save, to set aside, to stow away, to hoard, to reserve, to stash

store *NOUN*
❶ *She works in a grocery* **store**.
- a shop
» *For types of shop look at* **shop**.
❷ *He had a large* **store** *of food in the cellar.*
- a hoard, a supply, a stock, a quantity, a reserve
❸ *The building is used as a grain* **store**.
- a storeroom
- A **warehouse** is a large building for storing goods.
- A **vault** is a secure place for storing valuables.
- A **larder** or a **pantry** is a small room for storing food.

storm *NOUN*
Crops were damaged in the heavy **storms**.
- a squall, a tempest, a hurricane, a gale, a tornado, a typhoon, a thunderstorm
- A **blizzard** or a **snowstorm** is a storm with a lot of snow.

😊 **WRITING TIPS**

Here are some helpful words for writing about a storm:

THINGS A STORM DOES:

- to brew, to grow, to break, to break out, to blow up, to rage, to hit, to strike, to batter, to whip, to tear, to engulf somewhere, to sweep somewhere, to ease, to abate, to calm, to die down, to pass

WORDS FOR DESCRIBING A STORM:

- dreadful, fearful, ferocious, fierce, pitiless, raging, severe, terrible, terrific, violent, tropical, Arctic

By noon the storm had broken, and the white, lashing swathes of rain were sweeping across the downs before the gale. —THE EAGLE OF THE NINTH, Rosemary Sutcliff

storm *VERB*
❶ *He* **stormed** *out of the room.*
- to stalk, to stride
❷ *The soldiers* **stormed** *the castle.*
- to charge at, to rush at, to attack, to raid

story *NOUN*
❶ *'Peter Pan' is a* **story** *about a boy who never grew up.*
- a tale, an account, a narrative, a yarn *(informal)*
- **Fiction** is invented stories in general.
- A **novel** is a book that tells a long fictional story.
❷ *It was the front-page* **story** *in all the papers.*
- an article, an item, a feature, a report, a piece

story

WORD WEB

SOME TYPES OF STORY:

• an adventure story, a detective story, a fable, a fairy tale, a fantasy, a folk tale, a ghost story, a horror story, a legend, a love story, a mystery, a myth, a parable, a saga, a science fiction story, a spy story
» *For other types of writing look at* **writing**.

WRITING TIPS

Here are some useful words for describing a **story**:

SOME ELEMENTS OF A STORY:

• a character, the plot, the narrator, the hero, the heroine, the villain, the setting, the opening or start, the ending

SOME POSITIVE WAYS TO DESCRIBE A STORY:

• action-packed, dramatic, engrossing, eventful, gripping, intriguing, riveting, spellbinding, thrilling
• believable, convincing, lifelike, realistic
• amusing, comic, entertaining, hilarious, humorous
• creative, imaginative, interesting, original, thought-provoking
• moving, powerful, romantic, touching
This is a **riveting action-packed** *story that should appeal to anyone who likes adventure.*

SOME NEGATIVE WAYS TO DESCRIBE A STORY:

• boring, dreary, dry, dull, monotonous, slow, uneventful
• absurd, far-fetched, improbable, ludicrous, unbelievable, unconvincing
• unoriginal, obvious
• sentimental, soppy *(informal)*
I liked the opening of the story, but some of the events were **far-fetched** *and the ending was* **sentimental**.

straight ADJECTIVE
❶ *They walked in a* **straight** *line.*
• direct, unswerving
— A common simile is **as straight as an arrow**.
OPPOSITES crooked, curved
❷ *She has* **straight** *black hair.*
• flat, smooth
OPPOSITES curly, wavy
❸ *Is this picture* **straight**?
• level
OPPOSITES tilted, sloping

a store of acorns

straight ADVERB
I was tired so I went **straight** *to bed.*
• directly, immediately, at once

strain VERB
❶ *The dog was* **straining** *at its lead.*
• to pull, to tug, to stretch
❷ *I* **strained** *my eyes trying to see the screen.*
• to tire, to exhaust, to weaken, to hurt, to damage
❸ *People were* **straining** *to hear what he said.*
• to struggle, to strive, to make an effort, to try, to attempt

strain NOUN
The rope broke under the **strain**.
• stress, pressure, tension, weight

strange ADJECTIVE
❶ *It's* **strange** *that nobody noticed him.*
• odd, peculiar, curious, funny, extraordinary, remarkable, unusual, surprising, weird, bizarre, inexplicable, puzzling, baffling, mysterious, mystifying, perplexing, bewildering
OPPOSITES normal, unsurprising
❷ *I heard a* **strange** *noise.*
• odd, funny, peculiar, mysterious, weird, bizarre
— Use **uncanny** or **eerie** for something strange and slightly frightening.
OPPOSITE ordinary
❸ *I find it hard to get to sleep in a* **strange** *bed.*
• unfamiliar, unknown, new, alien
OPPOSITE familiar

stranger NOUN
He was a **stranger** *in the town.*
• an unknown, a newcomer, an outsider, a visitor, a foreigner

strangle VERB
She hugged me so hard she almost **strangled** *me!*
• to throttle, to choke, to suffocate, to stifle

strap NOUN
The trunk was fastened with a leather **strap**.
• a belt, a band, a strip

stray VERB
Some sheep had **strayed** *on to the road.*
• to wander, to drift, to roam, to rove, to straggle, to meander, to ramble

a
b
c
d
e
f
g
h
i
j
k
l
m
n
o
p
q
r
s
t
u
v
w
x
y
z

streak NOUN
There was a muddy **streak** on the cloth.
• a band, a mark, a line, a stripe, a strip, a smear, a stain

stream NOUN
❶ They dipped their feet in the cool **stream**.
• a brook
❷ There was a constant **stream** of traffic.
• a flow, a flood, a current, a tide

stream VERB
Warm sunlight **streamed** through the window.
• to pour, to flow, to flood, to issue, to gush, to spill

street NOUN
» Look at **road**.

strength NOUN
❶ It took huge **strength** to move the rock.
• power, might, muscle, force
OPPOSITE weakness
❷ Her main **strength** as a player is her speed.
• a strong point, an asset, an advantage
OPPOSITE a weakness

strengthen VERB
❶ Regular exercise **strengthens** your muscles.
• to make stronger, to build up, to toughen, to harden
❷ Concrete was used to **strengthen** the tunnel.
• to fortify, to reinforce, to bolster, to prop up
OPPOSITE to weaken

stress NOUN
❶ In the word 'rabbit' the **stress** is on the first syllable.
• emphasis, weight, importance
❷ The hospital staff were working under a lot of **stress**.
• strain, pressure, tension, worry, anxiety

stress VERB
She **stressed** the importance of checking your work.
• to emphasise, to draw attention to, to highlight, to underline

stretch VERB
❶ He **stretched** the rubber band until it snapped.
• to expand, to extend, to draw out, to pull, to lengthen
❷ She **stretched** her arms wide.
• to extend, to spread, to open
❸ The road **stretched** into the distance.
• to extend, to continue

stretch NOUN
This **stretch** of the river is very wide.
• a section, a length, a piece, a part, an area

strict ADJECTIVE
❶ The club has **strict** rules about who can join.
• rigid, inflexible
OPPOSITE flexible
❷ She was known as a **strict** teacher.
• severe, stern, harsh, firm
OPPOSITE lenient
❸ We were given **strict** instructions on what to do.
• exact, precise
OPPOSITE loose

strike VERB strikes, striking, struck
❶ The car skidded and **struck** a tree.
• to hit, to crash into, to knock into, to collide with, to bang into, to bump into
❷ She **struck** the thief on the head with her handbag.
• to hit, to swipe, to knock, to bang, to cuff

string NOUN
❶ She tied some **string** round the parcel.
• rope, cord, twine
» For musical instruments with strings look at **music**.
❷ I had to remember a **string** of numbers.
• a series, a succession, a sequence, a chain

string VERB strings, stringing, strung
We **strung** lights on the Christmas tree.
• to hang, to arrange, to thread

strip NOUN
Cut a **strip** of paper.
• a band, a length, a ribbon
— A **verge** is a strip of grass by the road.

strip VERB
❶ I **stripped** the sheets from the bed.
• to remove, to pull, to peel
❷ He **stripped** and got into the bath.
• to get undressed, to undress
OPPOSITE to dress

stripe NOUN
The tablecloth was white with blue **stripes**.
• a line, a strip, a band, a bar

stroke VERB
Jess was curled up on the sofa, **stroking** the cat.
• to pat, to caress, to rub, to touch

stroke NOUN
He split the log with a single **stroke**.
• a blow, a hit, a movement, a motion

strong ADJECTIVE

 OVERUSED WORD

Try to use a more interesting word when you want to say **strong**. Here are some ideas and examples:

FOR A STRONG PERSON OR STRONG BODY:

• powerful, muscular, mighty, fit, healthy, hearty, athletic, vigorous
— **Burly** means big and strong.
— **Wiry** means thin and strong.
— **Stocky** means short, solid and strong.
— **Hardy** means able to endure cold or difficult conditions.
— A common simile is **as strong as an ox.**
*He was grabbed by a **burly** security guard.*
OPPOSITE weak, puny

FOR STRONG MATERIAL OR A STRONG OBJECT:

• tough, sturdy, solid, stout, substantial
— A **fortified** place has been made strong against attack.
She stamped on the ground with her sturdy boots.—THE MAGIC FACTORY: COLD SPELL, Theresa Breslin
OPPOSITES flimsy, fragile

FOR A STRONG IMPACT OR A STRONG BLOW:

• heavy, hard, powerful, forceful, intense, mighty
Barn lumbered over, picked up a table and computer with one mighty heave and staggered towards the door.—BUNKER 10, J. A. Henderson
OPPOSITES light, gentle

FOR A STRONG LIGHT OR STRONG COLOUR:

• bright, brilliant, dazzling, glaring
Blessed Street was half in grey shadow, and half in glaring sunshine.—GOLDKEEPER, Sally Prue
OPPOSITES faint, pale

FOR A STRONG FEELING:

• deep, profound, intense, powerful, passionate, overwhelming
*I had an **intense** feeling of relief.*
OPPOSITES slight, faint

FOR A STRONG WILL OR STRONG PERSONALITY:

• resolute, determined, firm, decisive, single-minded, persistent, resilient
OPPOSITE weak

FOR A STRONG FLAVOUR OR STRONG SMELL:

• overpowering, pungent, powerful
— A **concentrated** flavour or drink is strong and not watered down.
Holding an arm over his face he drew closer, shielding himself from the pungent acid smell that was now almost overpowering.—TOM SCATTERHORN 2: THE HIDDEN WORLD, Henry Chancellor
OPPOSITES faint, slight

FOR A STRONG INTEREST OR STRONG SUPPORTER:

• enthusiastic, ardent, avid, fervent, firm, fierce, keen, passionate, staunch, loyal
*She is a **passionate** supporter of animal charities.*
OPPOSITE unenthusiastic

---

struck *(past tense of* **strike***)*

structure NOUN
❶ *Look at the **structure** of the leaf.*
• a design, a plan, a shape, an arrangement
❷ *The tower is a tall **structure**.*
• a building, a construction

struggle VERB
❶ *The captives **struggled** to get free.*
• to strain, to strive, to wrestle, to writhe, to wriggle, to fight
❷ *The expedition had to **struggle** through a snowstorm.*
• to stagger, to battle, to stumble, to flounder

struggle NOUN
*It was a **struggle** to keep going in the blazing heat.*
• an effort, a battle, a fight

stubborn ADJECTIVE
*She's too **stubborn** to admit that she was wrong.*
• obstinate, strong-willed, uncooperative, inflexible, wilful, awkward, difficult
— A common simile is **as stubborn as a mule.**

stuck *(past tense of* **stick***)*

student NOUN
*There are 250 **students** at the school.*
• a pupil
— A **scholar** is an old word for a student.

study VERB
❶ *We have been **studying** the Romans at school.*
• to learn about, to find out about, to research
❷ *The spy **studied** the document carefully.*
• to examine, to inspect, to analyse, to investigate, to look closely at, to scrutinise, to pore over, to survey

stuff NOUN
❶ *What's that sticky* **stuff** *on the carpet?*
• substance, material, matter
❷ *You can put your* **stuff** *in one of the lockers.*
• belongings, possessions, things, kit

stuff VERB
❶ *We managed to* **stuff** *everything into the boot of the car.*
• to pack, to push, to shove, to squeeze, to ram, to force, to cram, to jam
❷ *The cushions are* **stuffed** *with foam rubber.*
• to fill, to pad

stuffy ADJECTIVE
Open a window—it's **stuffy** *in here.*
• musty, stifling, humid
OPPOSITE airy

stumble VERB
❶ *He* **stumbled** *on the path and twisted his ankle.*
• to trip, to stagger, to totter, to fall
❷ *I* **stumbled** *over my words.*
• to stammer, to stutter, to falter, to hesitate

stupid ADJECTIVE
That was a **stupid** *thing to do.*
• silly, foolish, dumb, idiotic, imbecilic, senseless, daft, crazy, unintelligent
OPPOSITE clever

style NOUN
❶ *The book is written in an informal* **style.**
• a manner, a tone
❷ *I had my hair cut in a new* **style.**
• a design, a pattern, a fashion
❸ *I like this* **style** *of cooking.*
• a type, a kind, a way, a variety
❹ *She always dresses with* **style.**
• elegance, stylishness, taste, sophistication

subject NOUN
We have to write an essay on any **subject** *we choose.*
• a matter, an issue, a question, a topic, a point, a theme

submerge VERB
❶ *The submarine* **submerged** *slowly.*
• to dive, to go down, to go under
OPPOSITE to surface
❷ *The flood* **submerged** *the fields.*
• to engulf, to cover, to flood, to drown, to immerse

substance NOUN
What's this sticky **substance** *on my shoe?*
• material, matter, stuff

substitute VERB
You can **substitute** *oil for butter in the recipe.*
• to exchange, to swap, to switch
— You can say that oil can **take the place of** butter.
— You can also say that you can **replace** the butter with oil.

substitute NOUN
The manager brought on a **substitute.**
• a replacement, a reserve, a standby

subtle ADJECTIVE
❶ *The flowers had a* **subtle** *smell.*
• faint, slight, mild, delicate
OPPOSITE powerful
❷ *I tried to give her a* **subtle** *hint.*
• gentle, tactful, indirect, discreet
OPPOSITE obvious

subtract VERB
If you **subtract** *5 from 20, you have 15.*
• to take away, to deduct, to remove
OPPOSITE to add

succeed VERB
❶ *You have to work hard if you want to* **succeed.**
• to be successful, to do well, to prosper, to flourish, to thrive
OPPOSITE to fail
❷ *Everyone hoped that the plan would* **succeed.**
• to be effective, to be a success, to work
OPPOSITE to fail
➤ **to succeed in something**
She **succeeded in** *her ambition to read all the Harry Potter books.*
• to accomplish, to achieve, to fulfil, to manage

success NOUN
❶ *She had a lot of* **success** *as an actress.*
• achievement, attainment, fame
❷ *We congratulated the team on their* **success.**
• triumph, victory, win
OPPOSITE failure
❸ *His last film was a great* **success.**
• a hit
OPPOSITES a failure, a disaster

successful ADJECTIVE
❶ *Our team was* **successful** *in the competition.*
• victorious, triumphant

submerge

❷ *She runs a* **successful** *business.*
• thriving, flourishing, prosperous, profitable, popular
OPPOSITE failing

sudden ADJECTIVE
❶ *He made a* **sudden** *dash for the door.*
• unexpected, rushed, impulsive, hasty, hurried
OPPOSITE expected
❷ *The bus came to a* **sudden** *halt.*
• abrupt, sharp, swift
OPPOSITE gradual

suffer VERB
❶ *I hate to see animals* **suffer.**
• to feel pain, to be hurt
❷ *They* **suffered** *some terrible experiences.*
• to endure, to go through, to undergo, to experience, to be subjected to

suffering NOUN
There was great **suffering** *during the war.*
• hardship, misery, anguish, pain, distress, an ordeal

suffocate VERB
The firefighters were nearly **suffocated** *by the fumes.*
• to choke, to stifle, to smother
— To **strangle** or to **throttle** someone is to suffocate them by squeezing their throat.

suggest VERB
I **suggest** *you use a light colour for the background.*
• to propose, to advise, to recommend

suggestion NOUN
They didn't like his **suggestion.**
• a proposal, a plan, an idea, a proposition, a recommendation

suit VERB
❶ *Does it* **suit** *you to meet here?*
• to be convenient for, to be suitable for
❷ *That colour really* **suits** *you.*
• to look good on, to look nice on, to flatter

suitable ADJECTIVE
❶ *Please wear shoes* **suitable** *for walking.*
• appropriate, fitting, proper, right
• suited: *Please wear shoes* **suited** *to walking.*
OPPOSITE unsuitable
❷ *Is this a* **suitable** *time to have a chat?*
• convenient, acceptable, satisfactory
OPPOSITE inconvenient

sulk VERB
I was **sulking** *because I got told off.*
• to be sulky, to be sullen, to mope, to brood, to pout

sulky ADJECTIVE
What are you so **sulky** *about?*
• sullen, moody, grumpy, bad-tempered, sour
OPPOSITES cheerful, good-tempered

summit NOUN
The **summit** *of the mountain was shrouded in mist.*
• the peak, the top, the cap, the tip
OPPOSITE the base

sun NOUN
They sat out in the **sun.**
• the sunshine, the sunlight
» *For things found in space look at* **space.**

sung (past participle of sing)

sunk (past participle of sink)

sunlight NOUN
Most plants can only grow in **sunlight.**
• daylight, sun, sunshine
— A **sunbeam** is a ray of light from the sun.

sunny ADJECTIVE
❶ *It was a beautiful* **sunny** *day.*
• fine, clear, cloudless
OPPOSITE cloudy
❷ *The flat has a large* **sunny** *living room.*
• bright, sunlit, cheerful
OPPOSITE gloomy

sunrise NOUN
The magic spell wears off at **sunrise.**
• dawn, daybreak
OPPOSITE sunset

sunset NOUN
They arranged to meet at **sunset.**
• sundown, dusk, twilight, evening, nightfall
OPPOSITE sunrise

superhero NOUN

 WORD WEB

THINGS A SUPERHERO MIGHT HAVE:

• a cape, a costume, a force field, a mask, invisibility, an outfit, a secret identity, superhuman strength, a superpower, X-ray vision

Zack had a force field and we had to know how powerful it was. Clearly the easiest way to find out was to throw things at him. –MY BROTHER IS A SUPERHERO, David Solomons

superior ADJECTIVE
❶ *They only sell chocolate of superior quality.*
• excellent, first-class, highest, top, best
OPPOSITES inferior, worse
❷ *A colonel is superior in rank to a captain.*
• senior, higher, greater
OPPOSITES inferior, lower

supply VERB
We will supply you with paper and pens.
• to provide, to equip, to furnish

supply NOUN
They had a good supply of fuel for the winter.
• a stock, a store, a reserve, a hoard, a quantity
➤ **supplies**
We bought supplies for the camping trip.
• provisions, stores, rations, food, necessities

support VERB
❶ *The beams support the roof.*
• to prop up, to hold up, to bear, to carry, to reinforce
❷ *His friends supported him when he was in trouble.*
• to back, to help, to aid, to assist, to encourage, to stand by, to stick up for
❸ *Which football team do you support?*
• to be a supporter of, to follow

support NOUN
❶ *She thanked them for their support.*
• assistance, backing, aid, encouragement, help
❷ *The supports prevented the wall from collapsing.*
• a prop, a brace, a strut
— A **crutch** is a support for someone who has difficulty walking.

suppose VERB
I suppose he's tired.
• to expect, to presume, to assume, to guess, to believe, to think, to reckon
➤ **to be supposed to do something**
The bus is supposed to leave at nine o'clock.
• to be meant to, to be due to, to be expected to
— You can also say something **ought to** or **should** happen.

suppress VERB
He managed to suppress a smile.
• to hold back, to control, to repress, to restrain, to stifle, to conceal

sure ADJECTIVE
❶ *Are you sure that's right?*
• certain, convinced, confident, definite, positive
OPPOSITES unsure, uncertain
❷ *He's sure to complain.*
• bound, certain

— If something is sure to happen you can say it is inevitable.
OPPOSITE unlikely
❸ *A high temperature is a sure sign of illness.*
• clear, definite, true, undoubted, undeniable
OPPOSITES unclear, doubtful

surface NOUN
❶ *The surface of the ball is smooth.*
• the exterior, the outside
— The inner surface is the **inside** or the **interior**.
— A **crust** or a **shell** is a hard outer surface.
— The **enamel** is the hard surface of your teeth.
OPPOSITE the centre
❷ *A dice has dots on each surface.*
• a face, a side
❸ *Oil floated on the surface of the water.*
• the top
OPPOSITE the bottom

surface VERB
The submarine surfaced.
• to rise to the surface, to come up, to emerge, to appear
OPPOSITE to submerge

surprise NOUN
❶ *It was a big surprise to see him there.*
• a shock, a revelation
— A **marvel** is something wonderful and surprising.
❷ *She looked at me in surprise.*
• amazement, astonishment, wonder, shock

surprise VERB
It surprised me that she could sing so well.
• to amaze, to astonish, to astound, to stagger, to startle, to stun, to take someone aback, to take someone by surprise

surprised ADJECTIVE
I was so surprised I didn't know what to say.
• amazed, astonished, astounded, staggered, flabbergasted, shocked, taken aback

☺ **WRITING TIPS**

Here are some things someone might do if they feel **surprised**:
• to stare wide-eyed, to be open-mouthed, to open your mouth, to have your mouth hanging open, to gape, to gaze, to gawp, to gasp, to blink, to be speechless, to marvel, to wonder
As the last of the paper fell away Olga blinked in astonishment. 'Wheeeeee!' she squeaked, her eyes growing larger and larger. 'A new water bowl!'
—THE TALES OF OLGA DA POLGA, Michael Bond
» *For things you might say when surprised look at* **exclamation**.

surrender VERB
The outlaws refused to surrender.
• to admit defeat, to give in, to give way, to yield, to submit

surround VERB
The garden was surrounded by a stone wall.
• to enclose, to border, to encircle

surroundings NOUN
The hotel is set in very pleasant surroundings.
• a setting, a location, an environment

survey NOUN
We did a survey to find out what people thought of the new building.
• a poll, a questionnaire, a study, an investigation

survive VERB
❶ *He managed to survive alone on the island for six months.*
• to stay alive, to last, to live, to keep going, to carry on, to continue
OPPOSITE to die
❷ *Will the plants survive this cold weather?*
• to endure, to withstand, to live through

suspect VERB
❶ *His strange behaviour made us suspect him.*
• to mistrust, to doubt, to be suspicious of, to have suspicions about
OPPOSITE to trust
❷ *I suspect that you're right.*
• to expect, to imagine, to guess, to sense, to feel

suspicion NOUN
I have a suspicion that he is lying.
• a feeling, a hunch, an inkling, an intuition, an impression

suspicious ADJECTIVE
❶ *There is something about her which makes me suspicious.*
• doubtful, distrustful, mistrustful, unsure, uneasy, wary
OPPOSITE trusting
❷ *Do you think his behaviour is suspicious?*
• questionable, dubious, untrustworthy
OPPOSITE trustworthy

swallow VERB
He swallowed loudly.
• to gulp
» *For ways to eat and drink look at eat and drink.*

surface

swam (past tense of **swim**)

swap (also **swop**) VERB
We swapped seats so I could sit with my friend.
• to change, to exchange, to switch

sway VERB
The tall grass swayed in the breeze.
• to wave, to swing, to rock, to bend, to lean

swear VERB swears, swearing, swore, sworn
❶ *The knight swore that he would protect the unicorn.*
• to pledge, to promise, to vow, to give your word, to take an oath
❷ *He swore when he hit his thumb with the hammer.*
• to curse, to use bad language

sweat VERB
We were sweating after our run.
• to perspire

sweep VERB
❶ *She swept the floor with an old broom.*
• to brush, to clean, to dust
❷ *The bus swept past.*
• to shoot, to speed, to rush, to fly, to whizz, to zoom
➤ **to sweep something away**
The flood swept away several houses.
• to destroy, to wash away, to flatten

sweet ADJECTIVE
❶ *The pudding is too sweet for me.*
• sickly, sugary, sweetened
OPPOSITES acid, bitter, savoury
❷ *The sweet smell of roses filled the room.*
• pleasant, fragrant
OPPOSITE foul
❸ *What a sweet little cottage!*
• attractive, charming, dear, lovely, pretty, quaint, cute
OPPOSITE unattractive

sweet NOUN
❶ *The bag contained a mixture of sweets.*
— **Candy** is sweets. This word is mostly used in American English.
❷ *We had apple pie as our sweet.*
• a dessert, a pudding

sweet

bubblegum

WORD WEB

SOME SWEETS:

• bubblegum, caramels, chewing gum, chocolates, fudge, jelly beans, liquorice, a lollipop, a lozenge, marshmallow, marzipan, mints, peppermints, toffees

a lollipop

jelly beans

swell VERB swells, swelling, swelled, swollen or swelled
The balloon *swelled* as it filled with hot air.
• to expand, to inflate, to bulge, to grow, to enlarge, to puff up, to billow
OPPOSITE to shrink

swelling NOUN
He had a painful *swelling* on his foot.
• a lump, an inflammation, a bump, a growth

swerve VERB
The bike *swerved* to avoid a hedgehog.
• to veer, to turn, to dodge

swim VERB swims, swimming, swam, swum
We *swam* in the sea on our holiday.
• to go swimming, to go for a swim, to bathe
— To go for a dip is to have a short swim.

WORD WEB

SOME SWIMMING STROKES:

• backstroke, breaststroke, butterfly, crawl

EQUIPMENT FOR SWIMMING:

• a bikini, flippers, goggles, a mask, a snorkel, a swimming costume, a swimsuit, swimming trunks

swing VERB swings, swinging, swung
A rope *swung* from the branch.
• to hang, to dangle, to sway, to flap

swirl VERB
Clouds of dust *swirled* up in the desert wind.
• to spin, to twirl, to whirl, to churn

switch VERB
❶ Please remember to *switch* off the light.
• to turn
❷ The teams will *switch* ends at half-time.
• to change, to swap, to exchange, to shift

swollen ADJECTIVE
My feet were *swollen* from walking all day.
• inflamed, bloated, puffed up, puffy

swoop VERB
The owl *swooped* and caught the mouse.
• to dive, to drop, to plunge, to descend, to pounce

swop VERB
» Look at **swap**.

sword NOUN
» For types of weapon look at **weapon**.

swore (past tense of **swear**)

sworn (past participle of **swear**)

swum (past participle of **swim**)

symbol NOUN
The dove is a *symbol* of peace.
• a sign, an emblem, an image, a token
— A **numeral** is a symbol that represents a number.
— A **logo** is a symbol used by a company on its products.
— An **icon** is a small symbol on a computer screen.
— A **pictogram** is a symbol that stands for a word or phrase.

sympathetic ADJECTIVE
They were *sympathetic* when my mother was ill.
• understanding, compassionate, concerned, caring, comforting, kind, supportive
OPPOSITE unsympathetic

sympathise VERB
➤ to sympathise with
We *sympathised with* the losers.
• to be sympathetic towards, to feel sorry for, to feel for, to feel compassion for

sympathy NOUN
Did you feel any *sympathy* for the characters in the story?
• understanding, compassion, pity, tenderness

system NOUN
❶ The city has an efficient transport *system*.
• an organisation, a structure, a network, a framework
❷ We have a *system* for organising the reading books.
• a procedure, a process, a scheme, an arrangement, a method, a routine

Tt

⚙ Can you think of any other ways to say 'very thin'?

⚙ Do you know a word that means 'thin and long or tall'? S P _ _ _ _ Y

⚙ Check the thesaurus to find answers!

tackle *VERB*
❶ *They left him to* **tackle** *the washing-up.*
• to deal with, to cope with, to attend to, to handle, to manage, to grapple with
❷ *Another player* **tackled** *her and got the ball.*
• to challenge, to intercept, to take on

tackle *NOUN*
❶ *He kept his fishing* **tackle** *in a special case.*
• gear, equipment, kit
❷ *The referee said it was a fair* **tackle**.
• a challenge, an interception

tactful *ADJECTIVE*
She gave him a **tactful** *reminder about her birthday.*
• subtle, discreet, diplomatic, sensitive, thoughtful
OPPOSITE tactless

tactics *NOUN*
They discussed their **tactics** *for the next game.*
• plan, methods, moves, manoeuvres
— A **strategy** is an overall plan to achieve or win something.

tag *NOUN*
The price is marked on the **tag**.
• a label, a sticker, a ticket

tag *VERB*
➤ **to tag along with someone**
She **tagged along with** *her brothers.*
• to accompany, to follow, to go with, to join

£6.99

tail *NOUN*
He joined the **tail** *of the queue.*
• the end, the back, the rear

tail *VERB*
The detective **tailed** *the suspect to this address.*
• to follow, to pursue, to track, to trail, to shadow, to stalk

take *VERB* **takes, taking, took, taken**
❶ *Naomi* **took** *her sister's hand.*
• to take hold of
— To **clutch**, to **clasp**, to **grasp** or to **grip** something is to take and hold it firmly.
— To **snatch**, to **seize** or to **grab** something is to take it quickly.
❷ *Someone has* **taken** *my pen.*
• to steal, to remove, to go off with, to pinch *(informal)*, to nick *(informal)*, to swipe *(informal)*
❸ *I will* **take** *you to the head's office.*
• to lead, to accompany, to conduct, to escort, to show
❹ *The bus* **took** *us right to the station.*
• to bring, to carry, to convey, to transport
❺ *If you* **take** *2 from 8 you get 6.*
• to subtract, to take away, to deduct
➤ **to take something apart**
I **took** *the clock* **apart** *to see how it worked.*
• to dismantle, to take something to pieces, to break something up
➤ **to take off**
Our flight **took off** *on time.*
• to depart, to lift off, to leave
➤ **to take part in something**
We all **took part in** *the discussion.*
• to participate in, to be involved in, to join in, to engage in
➤ **to take place**
When did the accident **take place**?
• to happen, to occur, to come about

taken *(past participle of* **take**)

tale *NOUN*
Pinocchio is a **tale** *about a boy made of wood.*
• a story, a narrative, an account, a yarn *(informal)*
» *For types of story look at* **story**.

talent *NOUN*
She has a great **talent** *for music.*
• a gift, an ability, an aptitude, a skill, a flair
— **Genius** is unusually great talent.

talk *VERB*
❶ *Doug was trying to teach his parrot to* **talk**.
• to speak, to communicate, to express yourself
» *For ways to talk look at* **say**.
❷ *We* **talked** *about what we did in our holidays.*
• to discuss, to converse, to chat
— To **chatter** is to talk quickly and a lot.

a b c d e f g h i j k l m n o p q r s t u v w x y z

talk NOUN
❶ *I need to have a **talk** with you.*
• a conversation, a discussion, a chat
— **Dialogue** is talk between characters in a story.
❷ *She gave a **talk** about ancient Egypt.*
• a lecture, a presentation, a speech, an address
— A **sermon** is a talk given by a preacher.

tall ADJECTIVE
❶ *Jasmine is **tall** for her age.*
• big
OPPOSITE short
❷ *Singapore has many **tall** buildings.*
• high, lofty, towering, soaring
— **Spindly** means tall and thin:
*The flowers grew on **spindly** stems.*
OPPOSITE low

tame ADJECTIVE
*The guinea pigs are **tame** and used to people.*
• gentle, docile, domesticated, obedient
OPPOSITE wild

tamper VERB
➤ to tamper with something
*Someone had **tampered with** the lock.*
• to meddle with, to mess about with, to fiddle with, to interfere with, to touch

tangle VERB
❶ *The wires have **tangled** together.*
• to entangle, to twist, to knot, to jumble, to muddle
❷ *Dolphins can get **tangled** in fishing nets.*
• to catch, to trap, to ensnare, to entangle

tangle NOUN
*The computer cables have got into a **tangle**.*
• a muddle, a jumble, a knot, a twist

tangled ADJECTIVE
*The fisherman's nets were all **tangled**.*
• knotted, twisted, entangled
— **Matted** hair is very tangled and stuck together.

tap VERB
*Someone **tapped** three times on the door.*
• to knock, to rap, to strike

target NOUN
*Her **target** was to swim thirty lengths.*
• a goal, an aim, an objective, an intention, a purpose, a hope, an ambition

task NOUN
*The teacher gave us a **task** to do.*
• a job, an assignment, an exercise
— A **chore** is a boring task you have to do at home.
— An **errand** is a task that involves a short journey to take a message or to fetch something.

taste VERB
❶ ***Taste** the soup to see if you like it.*
• to try, to sample, to test, to sip
❷ *This curry **tastes** delicious.*
» For ways to say food tastes good or bad look at **food**.
» For ways to describe flavours look at **flavour**.

taste NOUN
❶ *I love the **taste** of ginger.*
• a flavour
❷ *We have similar **taste** in books.*
• preferences, choices, likes and dislikes, judgement

tasty ADJECTIVE
*The pie was very **tasty**.*
• delicious, appetising, mouth-watering, flavoursome
— Use **savoury** for something that is tasty and not sweet.
» Look at **food**.

taught (past tense of **teach**)

taunt VERB
*The boxer **taunted** his opponent.*
• to insult, to jeer at, to laugh at, to make fun of, to mock, to ridicule, to sneer at

teach VERB teaches, teaching, taught
❶ *Miss Darcy **taught** me last year.*
• to educate, to be someone's teacher
— To **train** or to **coach** someone is to teach them a sport.
— To **tutor** someone is to teach them in a small group or on their own.
❷ *My dad **taught** me how to make pancakes.*
• to inform, to instruct, to show, to tell

teacher NOUN
*We have a new art **teacher**.*
• a tutor, a trainer
— An **instructor** is usually someone who teaches you a skill, such as driving a car or skiing.
— A **coach** is someone who teaches you in a sport.
— A **lecturer** or a **professor** is a teacher at a university.
— A **governess** was a woman who taught children in their home in the past.

team NOUN
*She's in the school swimming **team**.*
• a side, a club

tear VERB tears, tearing, tore, torn
*I've **torn** my jeans.*
• to rip, to split, to slit
— To **snag** is to catch and tear slightly on something sharp.
— To **shred** something is to tear it into many small pieces.

spindly

tear NOUN
There was a tear in one of the sails.
• a rip, a cut, a split, a hole, a slit

tease VERB
They teased him about his new haircut.
• to make fun of, to mock, to laugh at
— To **ridicule** someone is to tease them in an unkind way.
— To **taunt** someone is to tease them in an insulting way.

technical ADJECTIVE
The computer manual uses technical language.
• specialised, scientific

technique NOUN
There is a special technique for flipping the pancake.
• a method, a skill, a procedure

tedious ADJECTIVE
It was a tedious bus journey.
• boring, dreary, dull, tiresome, monotonous, unexciting, uninteresting
OPPOSITE exciting

teenager NOUN
The film will appeal to teenagers.
• an adolescent, a teen, a youth

telephone NOUN, VERB
(see **phone**)

tell VERB tells, telling, told
❶ *Tell me what you saw.*
• to describe: *Describe what you saw.*
to explain, to report, to reveal, to state, to say
❷ *Tell us when you have finished.*
• to let someone know, to inform, to notify, to announce
❸ *We told each other scary ghost stories.*
• to narrate, to relate
❹ *He told them to stop making so much noise.*
• to order, to command, to direct, to instruct
❺ *She couldn't tell where she was in the dark.*
• to make out, to recognise, to identify, to perceive, to see, to distinguish
➤ **to tell someone off**
She told them off for being late.
• to scold, to reproach, to tick off (informal)

temper NOUN
❶ *Why are you in such a bad temper?*
• a mood, a humour, a state of mind
❷ *She flew into a temper.*
• a rage, a fury, a fit of anger, a tantrum
➤ **to lose your temper**
Finally she lost her temper and started shouting.
• to get angry, to lose patience, to fly into a rage, to go mad (informal)
» *For things people do when they lose their temper look at* **angry**.

temple NOUN
» *For places of worship look at* **building**.

temporary ADJECTIVE
❶ *They made a temporary shelter for the night.*
• makeshift, provisional
OPPOSITE permanent
❷ *It was just a temporary problem.*
• fleeting, brief, momentary
OPPOSITE lasting

tempt VERB
The witch tempted them into her house with sweets.
• to lure, to attract, to invite, to coax, to persuade

tend VERB
❶ *This room tends to get cold.*
• to be inclined, to have a tendency, to be liable, to be likely
— You can also say that someone or something **often** or **frequently** does something:
This room frequently gets cold.
❷ *She tended the young plants.*
• to take care of, to care for, to attend to, to look after

tennis NOUN

⊕ **WORD WEB**

SOME TERMS USED IN TENNIS:

• a ballboy or ballgirl, a court, a racket or racquet, the net, singles, doubles, a rally, a serve, an ace, the umpire

tense ADJECTIVE
❶ *The muscles in her shoulders were tense.*
• taut, tight, strained, stretched
❷ *I felt tense as I waited for the result.*
• anxious, nervous, apprehensive, fidgety, jumpy
❸ *It was a tense moment for all of us.*
• stressful, worrying
OPPOSITE relaxed

A B C D E F G H I J K L M N O P Q R S **T** U V W X Y Z

tension NOUN
The **tension** of waiting was almost unbearable.
• stress, strain, anxiety, nervousness, suspense, pressure, worry, uncertainty, drama

tent NOUN

 WORD WEB

SOME KINDS OF TENT:
• a marquee, a circus tent, a pavilion, a tepee, a yurt
— To put up a tent is to **pitch** it.

terrible ADJECTIVE
We heard there had been a **terrible** accident.
• awful, dreadful, horrible, appalling, shocking, ghastly, horrific, frightful
» For other ways to describe something bad look at **bad**.

terrify VERB
The thunder **terrified** the dog.
• to frighten, to scare, to startle, to alarm, to panic, to horrify, to petrify
» For things someone might do when they are terrified look at **frightened**.

territory NOUN
They had entered enemy **territory**.
• land, area, ground, country, a district, a region
• a zone: They had entered an enemy **zone**.

terror NOUN
The noise filled me with **terror**.
• fear, fright, horror, panic, alarm, dread

test NOUN
❶ Every week we have a spelling **test**.
• an exam, a quiz
— An **audition** is a test to see if an actor or musician is suitable for a part.
❷ This is a **test** to see if the printer works.
• an experiment, a trial, a check

test VERB
❶ The optician will **test** your eyes.
• to examine, to check, to assess
❷ He is **testing** a new formula for invisible ink.
• to experiment with, to try out, to trial

texture NOUN
Silk has a smooth **texture**.
• feel, feeling, touch, quality

thanks NOUN
She sent them a card to show her **thanks**.
• gratitude, appreciation

thaw VERB
The snow began to **thaw**.
• to melt, to dissolve
OPPOSITE to freeze

theatre NOUN

 WORD WEB

PARTS OF A THEATRE:
• the balcony, the circle, the gallery, the stalls, the set, the stage, backstage, the box office, the foyer

PERFORMERS:
• an actor, an actress, a ballerina, a comedian, a dancer, a magician, a musician, a singer, an understudy

OTHER PEOPLE WHO WORK IN THE THEATRE:
• a director, a playwright, an usher

theft NOUN
He was found guilty of **theft**.
• robbery, stealing

theme NOUN
What is the **theme** of the poem?
• a subject, a topic, an idea

theory NOUN
The detective has a **theory** about the case.
• an explanation, an idea, a view, a belief, a notion, a suggestion
➤ in theory
In **theory** you should return the book within 7 days.
• theoretically, in principle, officially

therapy NOUN
This **therapy** is used to help people who stammer.
• a treatment, a remedy

thick ADJECTIVE
❶ The wall was almost a metre **thick**.
• wide, broad
❷ The cabin was made from **thick** logs.
• stout, chunky, heavy, solid, substantial
OPPOSITES thin, slender
❸ The area is covered with **thick** vegetation.
• dense, closely packed, compact, lush
OPPOSITES thin, sparse
❹ Whip the cream until it is **thick**.
• stiff, dense, heavy
OPPOSITES thin, watery

thief *NOUN*

*The police managed to catch the **thief**.*
• a robber
— A **burglar** is a thief who steals from people's homes.
— A **highwayman** was a thief who used to steal from travellers in the past.

thin *ADJECTIVE*

❶ *The old man was tall and **thin**.*
• slender, bony, lean
— **Slim** means thin in an attractive way.
— **Skinny** means very thin.
— **Gaunt** means very thin and tired-looking.
— **Slight** means thin and light.
— **Wiry** means thin but strong.
— **Spindly** means long or tall and thin: *The baby giraffe stood on its **spindly** legs.*
— A common simile is **as thin as a rake**.
OPPOSITE fat
❷ *The fairy wore a cloak of **thin** silk.*
• fine, light, delicate
— **Flimsy** means thin and not very strong.
OPPOSITE thick
❸ *He had **thin** hair.*
• sparse, fine
OPPOSITES thick, dense
❹ *The icing was too **thin** and dribbled everywhere.*
• runny, watery
OPPOSITE thick

thing *NOUN*

❶ *What's that round blue **thing**?*
• an object, an item, an article
❷ *We had a lot of **things** to talk about.*
• a matter, an affair, an issue, a topic, a subject, a point
❸ *Some strange **things** have been happening.*
• an event, a happening, an occurrence, an incident
❹ *I have only one **thing** left to do.*
• a job, a task, an act, an action
❺ *You can leave your **things** here.*
• belongings, possessions, stuff, equipment, gear

think *VERB* **thinks, thinking, thought**

❶ ***Think** before you do anything rash.*
• to consider, to contemplate, to reflect, to ponder
— To **meditate** is to think deeply and seriously, usually in silence.
— To **concentrate** is to think hard about what you are doing.
— To **brood** is to keep thinking and worrying about something.
— To **muse** is to think or wonder in a casual way about something.

This is a scarab. To find out more look in the Oxford Primary Illustrated Dictionary!

❷ *Do you **think** this is a good idea?*
• to believe, to feel, to consider, to judge, to conclude
❸ *What do you **think** this ring is worth?*
• to reckon, to suppose, to imagine, to estimate, to guess, to expect
➤ **to be thinking of something**
*We're **thinking of** moving house next year.*
• to consider, to plan to, to intend to
➤ **to think something up**
*They **thought up** a good plan.*
• to invent, to make up, to conceive of, to devise, to come up with

thirsty *ADJECTIVE*

*They were **thirsty** after their long walk.*
• dry, parched
— Use **dehydrated** if someone is so thirsty they are ill.

thorn *NOUN*

*The creature had a **thorn** in its paw.*
• a prickle, a spike, a needle

thorough *ADJECTIVE*

*The doctor gave him a **thorough** examination.*
• full, careful, methodical, detailed, intensive, comprehensive, conscientious
OPPOSITE superficial

thought *(past tense of **think**)*

thought *NOUN*

❶ *Please tell me your **thoughts**.*
• an opinion, an idea, a notion, a conclusion, a belief
❷ *I can see you've put a lot of **thought** into this.*
• consideration, contemplation, reflection, study, thinking

thoughtful *ADJECTIVE*

❶ *He had a **thoughtful** look on his face.*
• reflective, absorbed, preoccupied
OPPOSITES blank, vacant
❷ *It was very **thoughtful** of you to visit me in hospital.*
• caring, considerate, kind, sensitive, sympathetic, unselfish
OPPOSITE thoughtless

thoughtless *ADJECTIVE*

*His **thoughtless** remark hurt her feelings.*
• inconsiderate, insensitive, uncaring, unthinking, unsympathetic, unkind
OPPOSITE thoughtful

a
b
c
d
e
f
g
h
i
j
k
l
m
n
o
p
q
r
s
t
u
v
w
x
y
z

thread NOUN
❶ *There was a loose **thread** hanging from her dress.*
• a strand, a fibre
❷ *He picked up a needle and **thread**.*
• cotton, yarn, silk
— A **reel** or a **spool** is a cylindrical object on which thread is wound.

threat NOUN
❶ *I didn't take his **threats** seriously.*
• a warning, a curse
❷ *There is a constant **threat** of earthquakes here.*
• a danger, a menace, a hazard, a risk

threaten VERB
❶ *An ogre was **threatening** the villagers.*
• to make threats against, to menace, to intimidate, to terrorise, to bully
❷ *Pollution **threatens** our oceans.*
• to endanger, to put at risk, to be a threat to, to be a danger to

threw (past tense of **throw**)

thrive VERB thrives, thriving, thrived or throve, thrived or thriven
*She is **thriving** at her new school.*
• to do well, to flourish, to succeed, to prosper

throb VERB
*She could feel the blood **throbbing** through her veins.*
• to beat, to pound, to pulse

throw VERB throws, throwing, threw, thrown
*I **threw** some bread into the pond for the ducks.*
• to fling, to cast, to toss, to sling
— To **hurl** or to **pitch** something is to throw it with a lot of force.
— To **pelt** or to **bombard** someone with something is to throw a lot of things at them.
— To **bowl** is to throw the ball in cricket or rounders.
➤ **to throw away**
*We **threw away** a pile of old junk.*
• to get rid of, to dispose of, to discard, to dump, to scrap

thrown (past participle of **throw**)

thrust VERB thrusts, thrusting, thrust
*He **thrust** his hands into his pockets.*
• to push, to force, to shove

thunder NOUN, VERB

 WRITING TIPS

Here are some words for describing the sound of thunder:
• to boom, to crash, to resound, to echo, to roar, to rumble
— A burst of thunder is a **clap**, a **crack**, a **peal**, a **roll** or a **rumble** of thunder.
The clouds had turned purple and grey, like a dark bruise spreading across the sky. To the south, thunder rumbled over the mountains.—SKY HAWK, Gill Lewis

tick VERB
» *For various sounds look at **sound**.*

ticket NOUN
*You need a **ticket** to get in.*
• a pass, a permit, a token, a voucher, a coupon

tidy ADJECTIVE
*He always keeps his bedroom **tidy**.*
• neat, orderly, clean, trim, smart
OPPOSITE untidy

tie VERB
*Zoe **tied** a pink ribbon round the parcel.*
• to bind, to fasten, to hitch, to knot, to loop, to secure
— To **bundle** things is to tie them together.
— To **lash** something to something else is to tie it tightly.
— To tie a shoe or boot is to **lace** it.
— To tie up a boat is to **moor** it.
— To tie up an animal is to **tether** it.
OPPOSITE to untie

tight ADJECTIVE
❶ *These jeans are a bit **tight**.*
• small, tight-fitting, close-fitting
OPPOSITES loose, baggy
❷ *Make sure the lid is **tight**.*
• firm, secure
OPPOSITE loose
❸ *Is the rope **tight**?*
• taut, tense, stretched
OPPOSITE slack

tighten VERB
❶ *He tried to **tighten** the screw.*
• to make something tighter, to screw in or on
OPPOSITE to loosen

❷ *You need to **tighten** the guy ropes.*
• to make something taut, to pull something tight, to stretch
OPPOSITE to slacken

tilt VERB
*She **tilted** her head to one side.*
• to lean, to incline, to tip, to slant, to slope, to angle

timber NOUN
❶ *He bought some **timber** to build a shed.*
• wood, lumber, logs, planks
❷ *The old **timbers** of the house creaked.*
• a plank, a beam, a panel, a post, a pole

time NOUN
❶ *We've been waiting for a long **time**.*
• a period, a while, a term
❷ *Is this a good **time** to talk?*
• a moment, an occasion, an opportunity
❸ *This was a sad **time** in her life.*
• a phase, a period
— A **season** is a time of year.
❹ *Shakespeare lived in the **time** of Elizabeth I.*
• the era, the age, the days, the period
➤ **on time**
*Please try to be **on time**.*
• punctual, prompt

🕸 **WORD WEB** | a stopwatch

UNITS FOR MEASURING TIME:
• a second, a minute, an hour, a day, a week, a fortnight, a month, a year, a decade, a century, a millennium

CLOCKS AND OTHER INSTRUMENTS FOR MEASURING TIME:
• an alarm clock, a cuckoo clock, a grandfather clock, a stopwatch, a sundial, a timer, a watch

timid ADJECTIVE
*At first, I was too **timid** to say anything.*
• shy, bashful, modest, nervous, sheepish
— A common simile is **as timid as a mouse**.
OPPOSITES brave, confident

tingle VERB
*My ears were **tingling** with the cold.*
• to prickle, to sting, to tickle

a grandfather clock

tiny ADJECTIVE
*Inside the shell was a **tiny** creature.*
• little, minute, miniature, microscopic, titchy (informal)
OPPOSITES big, large

tip NOUN
❶ *The **tip** of his nose felt cold.*
• the end, the point
❷ *The **tip** of the mountain was covered in snow.*
• the summit, the cap, the peak, the top
❸ *He gave them some useful **tips** on making a website.*
• a hint, a piece of advice, a suggestion, a clue, an idea
❹ *They took a load of rubbish to the **tip**.*
• the dump, the rubbish heap

tip VERB
❶ *She **tipped** the bucket to one side.*
• to tilt, to lean, to incline, to slant
❷ *Sophie **tipped** the box of crayons on to the table.*
• to empty, to turn out, to dump
➤ **to tip over**
*The boat **tipped over** in the storm.*
• to capsize, to overturn
➤ **to tip something over**
*He **tipped** a chair **over** by accident.*
• to knock over, to overturn, to topple

tire VERB
➤ **to tire someone out**
*Running in the playground had **tired** us all **out**.*
• to exhaust, to wear out
OPPOSITES to refresh, to invigorate

tired ADJECTIVE
*Have a lie-down if you're **tired**.*
• exhausted, weary, worn out, sleepy
— **Listless** means tired and not interested in anything.
➤ **to be tired of something**
*I'm **tired of** this game.*
• to be bored with, to be fed up with, to be sick of, to have had enough of

tiring ADJECTIVE
*Digging is **tiring** work.*
• exhausting, demanding, difficult, hard, laborious, tough
OPPOSITE refreshing

title NOUN
*She couldn't think of a **title** for the story.*
• a name, a heading
— A **headline** is the title above a newspaper story.
— A **caption** is a title or brief description next to a picture.

a
b
c
d
e
f
g
h
i
j
k
l
m
n
o
p
q
r
s
t
u
v
w
x
y
z

toilet NOUN
Can you tell me where the toilet is?
• the lavatory, the bathroom, the loo (informal)

BOYS GIRLS

told (past tense of tell)

tolerant ADJECTIVE
We try to be **tolerant** of people who have different ideas to us.
• understanding, easy-going, open-minded, sympathetic, forgiving, liberal
OPPOSITE intolerant

tolerate VERB
We will not **tolerate** fighting in school.
• to accept, to permit, to allow, to put up with

tomb NOUN
Inside the **tomb** were several ancient skeletons.
• a burial chamber, a crypt, a grave, a vault

tone NOUN
❶ She spoke with an impatient **tone** in her voice.
• a note, a sound, a quality, a manner
❷ The room is painted in neutral **tones**.
• a colour, a hue, a shade, a tint

took (past tense of take)

tool NOUN
This is a **tool** for unscrewing the bike wheel.
• an implement, an instrument, a utensil, a device, a gadget, an appliance, an apparatus

WORD WEB

SOME TOOLS FOR CUTTING, HOLDING AND MAKING THINGS:

• an axe, a chisel, a drill, a file, a hammer, a knife, a pickaxe, a pair of pincers, a plane, a pair of pliers, a saw, a pair of scissors, a screwdriver, a spanner, a pair of tongs, a vice, a wrench

SOME GARDEN AND FARM TOOLS:

• a fork, a hoe, a plough, a rake, a scythe, a pair of shears, a shovel, a spade, a trowel

tooth NOUN

WORD WEB

a molar

TYPES OF TEETH:

• **canines** or **canine teeth**, **incisors, molars, wisdom teeth**
— A **fang** is a long sharp tooth, usually a canine tooth.
— A **tusk** is one of the long pointed teeth of an elephant, walrus or boar.

tusks

WRITING TIPS

Here are some helpful words for writing about **teeth**:

WORDS FOR DESCRIBING TEETH:

• **sharp, pointed, razor-sharp, needle-sharp, jagged, gleaming, pearly**
I knew of the Hydra . . . A monstrous dragon creature of the marshes, with nine great heads, each one full of razor-sharp teeth.—MEASLE AND THE DOOMPIT, Ian Ogilvy

THINGS TEETH DO:

• **to bite, to chew, to chomp, to clench, to gnash, to grind, to munch, to puncture, to rip, to snap, to tear, to flash, to gleam, to chatter with cold**
— To **grit your teeth** is to clench them in pain or determination.
— To **bare your teeth** is to show them in a fierce way.

top NOUN
❶ They climbed to the **top** of the hill.
• the peak, the summit, the tip, the crest
OPPOSITES the bottom, the base
❷ Please put the **top** back on the jar.
• a lid, a cap, a cover, a covering

top ADJECTIVE
❶ Their office is on the **top** floor.
• highest, topmost, upper, uppermost
OPPOSITES bottom, lowest
❷ The car can go at a **top** speed of 120 miles per hour.
• greatest, maximum, highest
❸ He is one of the city's **top** chefs.
• best, leading, finest, principal, superior
OPPOSITE junior

top VERB
We **topped** the cake with fudge icing.
• to cover, to decorate, to garnish

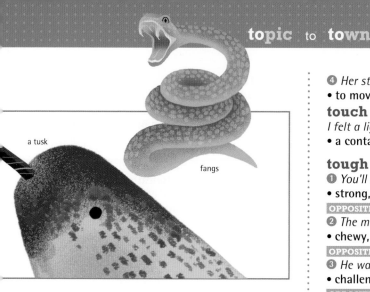

a tusk

fangs

topic NOUN
What **topic** are you going to write about?
• a subject, a theme, an issue, a matter, a question

tore (past tense of **tear**)

torment VERB
❶ Nightmares **tormented** him.
• to torture, to plague, to distress
❷ Stop **tormenting** your brother.
• to annoy, to bother, to harass, to pester, to plague, to tease
— To **bully** or to **persecute** someone weaker is to torment them in a cruel way.

torn (past participle of **tear**)

total NOUN
What is the **total** when you add it all together?
• the sum, the result, the amount

total ADJECTIVE
❶ The bill shows the **total** amount due.
• full, complete, whole, entire
❷ There was **total** silence.
• complete, utter, absolute
— Use **downright** or **sheer** to emphasise something bad: That is **sheer** rubbish!

total VERB
The donations **total** almost £300.
• to add up to, to amount to, to come to, to make

touch VERB
❶ Some animals don't like to be **touched**.
• to feel, to handle, to pat, to stroke, to caress
❷ Please don't **touch** the exhibits.
• to fiddle with, to meddle with, to play with, to handle, to pick up
❸ The car just **touched** the gatepost.
• to brush, to graze, to come into contact with

❹ Her story **touched** us.
• to move, to affect

touch NOUN
I felt a light **touch** on my arm.
• a contact, a pat, a stroke, a tap, a caress

tough ADJECTIVE
❶ You'll need **tough** shoes for hiking.
• strong, sturdy, solid, stout, substantial
OPPOSITE flimsy
❷ The meat was **tough**.
• chewy, leathery, rubbery
OPPOSITE tender
❸ He was given a **tough** assignment.
• challenging, difficult, hard, strenuous
OPPOSITE easy
❹ She is very **tough** and not easily frightened.
• brave, strong, hardy, rough
OPPOSITES weak, sensitive

tour NOUN
They went on a sightseeing **tour**.
• a journey, a trip, an excursion, an expedition, an outing

tourist NOUN
The town was full of **tourists**.
• a sightseer, a holidaymaker, a traveller, a visitor

tournament NOUN
She reached the semi-final of the chess **tournament**.
• a championship, a competition, a contest, a series

tow VERB
Horses used to **tow** barges up and down the river.
• to pull, to tug, to drag, to haul, to draw

tower NOUN
— A **turret** is a small tower on a castle or house.
— A castle's **keep** is a strong tower.
— A **steeple** is a church tower.
— A **spire** is the pointed top of a steeple.
— A **minaret** is a tall tower on a mosque.
— A **pagoda** is a Buddhist tower.

a pagoda

tower VERB
➤ **to tower above something**
The castle **towers above** the village.
• to rise above, to stand above, to dominate, to loom over

town NOUN
They could see a **town** in the distance.
• a city, a settlement
— A **borough** is a town with its own local government.
— A word meaning to do with a town or city is **urban**.

a b l m n o p q r s t u v w x y z

toxic ADJECTIVE

The flask contained a **toxic** gas.

• poisonous, harmful

— **Deadly** or **lethal** means toxic enough to kill you.

— A poisonous snake is **venomous**.

OPPOSITE harmless

toy NOUN

 WORD WEB

SOME TOYS:

• a ball, a balloon, building blocks, a computer game, a doll, a doll's house, a jigsaw, a kaleidoscope, a kite, a puppet, a puzzle, a rattle, a remote-control car, roller skates, a see-saw, a skateboard, a teddy bear, a top, a train set, a trampoline, a video game, a yo-yo

» Look at **game**.

trace VERB

Police are trying to **trace** the witness.

• to track down, to discover, to find

trace NOUN

❶ The burglar left no **trace** of his presence.

• evidence, a sign, a mark, an indication, a hint, a clue, a track, a trail

❷ They found **traces** of blood on the carpet.

• a spot, a speck, a drop, a particle

track NOUN

❶ They followed the deer's **tracks** for miles.

• a footprint, a trail, a trace, a mark

❷ A rough **track** leads past the farm.

• a path, a pathway, a footpath, a trail

❸ The train sped along the **track**.

• the line, the rails

❹ The athletes were warming up on the **track**.

• a racetrack, a circuit, a course

track VERB

They **tracked** the bear through the forest.

• to follow, to trace, to pursue, to chase, to tail, to trail

trade NOUN

❶ The cake stall was doing a lot of **trade**.

• business, dealing, buying and selling

❷ He is learning a **trade** as a plumber.

• a craft, a skill, an occupation, a profession

trade VERB

➤ **to trade in something**

The company **trades** in second-hand computers.

• to deal in, to do business in, to buy and sell

» For people who sell things look at **shop**.

tradition NOUN

It's a **tradition** to sing 'Auld Lang Syne' on New Year's Eve.

• a custom, a convention, a habit, a routine

traditional ADJECTIVE

❶ The dancers wore **traditional** costumes.

• national, regional, historical

❷ It is **traditional** to send cards at Christmas.

• customary, usual, normal, accepted, typical

❸ I went to a very **traditional** school.

• old-fashioned, conventional

tragedy NOUN

❶ The accident was a terrible **tragedy**.

• a disaster, a catastrophe, a calamity, a misfortune

❷ 'Romeo and Juliet' is a **tragedy**.

OPPOSITE a comedy

tragic ADJECTIVE

He died in a **tragic** accident.

• catastrophic, disastrous, devastating, dreadful, terrible, appalling

trail NOUN

❶ We walked along a **trail** through the woods.

• a path, a track, a route

❷ They followed his **trail** across the fields.

• tracks, traces, marks

— A ship's **wake** is the trail it leaves in the water.

trail VERB

❶ The children **trailed** after us.

• to follow, to pursue, to tail, to track, to straggle, to dawdle

❷ She **trailed** her suitcase behind her.

• to pull, to tow, to drag, to draw, to haul

train NOUN

 **WORD WEB**

SOME TYPES OF TRAIN:

• an express (train), a goods train or freight train, a shuttle, a steam train, a tram, an underground train

SOME PARTS OF A TRAIN:

• a berth, the buffet car, the cab, a carriage, a coach, the engine or the locomotive, a goods truck

SOME PARTS OF A RAILWAY:

• an embankment, a platform, a railway bridge, a railway junction, a railway line, the rails or the track, a station, a stop, the ticket office

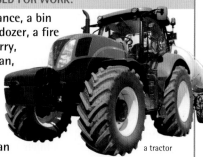
a scooter

train VERB
❶ She **trains** dogs to work as guide dogs.
• to teach, to instruct, to coach
❷ She is **training** hard for the race.
• to practise, to exercise, to prepare yourself, to work out

trainer NOUN
❶ I need some new **trainers**.
• running shoes, sports shoes
» For other types of shoe or boot look at **shoe**.
❷ Their **trainer** makes them work hard.
• a coach, an instructor, a teacher

trample VERB
Don't **trample** the flowers!
• to crush, to flatten, to squash, to tread on, to walk over, to stamp on

transfer VERB
We **transferred** the books into the new library.
• to move, to remove, to shift, to transport

transform VERB
The caterpillar **transforms** into a butterfly.
• to change, to turn, to convert, to develop, to alter

translate VERB
I had to **translate** the letter for my grandma.
• to interpret, to decode

transmit VERB
❶ The alien craft was **transmitting** a signal.
• to send out, to relay, to emit, to broadcast, to communicate
OPPOSITE to receive
❷ Can the disease be **transmitted** to humans?
• to pass on, to spread, to carry, to transfer

transparent ADJECTIVE
The box had a **transparent** lid.
• clear, see-through
— Something that allows light through is **translucent**.

transport (say trans-port) VERB
The goods are **transported** by sea.
• to take, to carry, to ship, to transfer, to move

transmit

transport (say trans-port) NOUN

⬡ **WORD WEB**

VEHICLES WHICH CARRY PEOPLE:
• a buggy, a bus, a cab, a car, a caravan, a coach, a hovercraft, a minibus, a motorcycle or motorbike, a sledge, a taxi, a toboggan, a train, a tram
» Look at **aircraft**, **bicycle**, **boat**, **car** and **train**.
» For space vehicles look at **space**.

VEHICLES USED FOR WORK:
• an ambulance, a bin lorry, a bulldozer, a fire engine, a lorry, a removal van, a pick-up truck, a police car, a tank, a tractor, a truck, a van

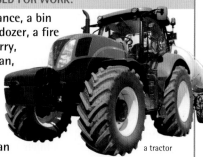
a tractor

HORSE-DRAWN VEHICLES:
• a carriage, a cart, a chariot, a coach, a sleigh, a wagon

a caravan

a car

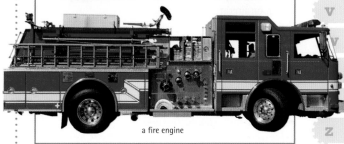
a fire engine

trap NOUN
❶ *The animal was caught in a* **trap**.
• a snare, a net
❷ *He thought the invitation might be a* **trap**.
• a trick, an ambush

trap VERB
❶ *We tried to* **trap** *the mouse.*
• to capture, to catch, to snare, to corner
❷ *They* **trapped** *him into a confession.*
• to trick, to corner, to ambush

travel VERB
We **travel** *to school by bus.*
• to go, to journey
— To **tour** an area is to travel around it.
— To **commute** is to travel from home to work and back again.

⬡ **WORD WEB**

SOME WAYS TO TRAVEL:

• to cruise, to cycle, to drive, to fly or go by air, to go by rail or by train, to hitch-hike, to ride, to row, to sail, to trek, to voyage or go by sea, to walk
— When birds travel from one country to another they **migrate**.
— When people travel to another country to live there they **emigrate**.
» *For ways of walking look at* **walk**.
» *For methods of transport look at* **aircraft**, **boat**, **train** *and* **vehicle**.

traveller NOUN
The **travellers** *saw many amazing things on their journey.*
• an explorer, a voyager
— A **tourist** is someone who travels for a holiday.
— A **commuter** is someone who travels from home to work and back again.
— A **nomad** is someone who travels as a way of life, instead of living in one place.
— A **pilgrim** is someone who travels to a religious place.
— A **stowaway** is someone who travels secretly on a ship or aircraft.

tread VERB treads, treading, trod, trodden
Try not to **tread** *on the flowers.*
• to step, to walk, to stand, to trample, to stamp

treasure NOUN
The pirates buried their **treasure** *on the island.*
• a hoard, loot, riches, fortune
» *For some things you might find as treasure look at* **jewel**.

treasure VERB
She **treasures** *the photograph of her grandmother.*
• to cherish, to value

treat NOUN
❶ *We were allowed to stay up late as a* **treat**.
• a reward, a favour
❷ *The cake shop sells lots of tasty* **treats**.
• a delicacy, a snack

treatment NOUN
❶ *Their* **treatment** *of their animals was cruel.*
• handling, care, management
• behaviour: *Their* **behaviour** *towards their animals was cruel.*
❷ *She needed medical* **treatment** *in hospital.*
• care, therapy, a remedy
— **First aid** is emergency treatment at the scene of an accident.
» *For some types of medical treatment look at* **medicine**.

treaty NOUN
The two sides signed a peace **treaty**.
• an agreement, a pact, a contract

tree NOUN

⬡ **WORD WEB**

— **Deciduous** trees lose their leaves in winter.
— **Evergreen** trees have leaves all year round.
— **Conifers** are trees which grow cones.
— A **sapling** is a young tree.
— A **shrub** is a small low tree or bush.

SOME VARIETIES OF TREE:

• an ash, a banyan, a baobab, a beech, a birch, a cedar, a chestnut, a cypress, an elder, an elm, a eucalyptus, a fir, a hawthorn, a hazel, a holly, a laburnum, a larch, a lime, a magnolia, a maple, an oak, an olive, a palm, a pine, a poplar, a spruce, a sycamore, a willow, a yew
[They] clambered into the trees . . . The climb was exhausting. Thin boughs snapped under their feet. Fir needles pricked at them. Bark came loose under their fingers and the smell of resin made them dizzy.—PETER PAN IN SCARLET, Geraldine McCraughrean

a cone

magnolia blossom

a
b
c
d
e
f
g
h
i
j
k
l
m
n
o
p
q
r
s
t
u
v
w
x
y
z

😊 WRITING TIPS

Here are some words you could use for describing trees:
• gnarled, twisted, ancient, tall, lofty, giant, towering, whispering, rustling, shady, cool, dark, dead, hollow, fallen

She pelted through the skinny young trees until she came to an oak, gnarled and ancient.—ICE MAIDEN, Sally Prue

tremble *VERB*
*The little fairy was **trembling** with cold.*
• to shake, to shiver, to quake, to quiver, to shudder

trend *NOUN*
*There is a **trend** towards healthier eating.*
• a tendency, a movement, a shift

trial *NOUN*
❶ *Witnesses gave evidence at the **trial**.*
• a case, a hearing
❷ *Scientists are conducting **trials** on a new medicine.*
• a test, an experiment

trick *NOUN*
❶ *Lucy played a **trick** on her brother.*
• a joke, a prank, a hoax
❷ *It was all a **trick** to get his money.*
• a deception, a fraud, a trap, a pretence, a cheat

trick *VERB*
*He **tricked** them into believing he was a police officer.*
• to fool, to deceive, to mislead, to cheat, to hoax, to con *(informal)*

trickle *VERB*
*Water **trickled** from the tap.*
• to dribble, to drip, to leak, to seep
— Use to **ooze** for a thick liquid.
OPPOSITE to gush

tricky *ADJECTIVE*
❶ *This is a **tricky** question to answer.*
• difficult, challenging, awkward, complex, hard
OPPOSITES straightforward, easy
❷ *The gnome was **tricky** and mean.*
• crafty, cunning, sly, wily

trim *VERB*
❶ *He asked the barber to **trim** his beard.*
• to cut, to clip, to shorten, to crop, to tidy

PARTS OF A TREE:

• the bark, the base, blossom, a bough or a branch, a cone, the foliage or the leaves, the needles, sap or resin, the trunk, a twig

PLACES WHERE TREES GROW:

• a forest, a grove, a jungle, a plantation, a wood, woodland
— An **orchard** is an area planted with fruit trees.

olive fruits

a maple branch

a palm

baobabs

❷ *The cloak was **trimmed** with fur.*
• to decorate, to border, to hem

trim ADJECTIVE
*Mr Stanley always keeps his garden **trim**.*
• neat, orderly, tidy, smart
OPPOSITE untidy

trip NOUN
*They went on a **trip** to the seaside.*
• a journey, a visit, an outing, an excursion, an expedition

trip VERB
*I **tripped** on the step.*
• to stumble, to fall, to slip, to stagger

trivial ADJECTIVE
*Don't bother me with **trivial** details.*
• unimportant, minor, insignificant, trifling, petty, slight, small
OPPOSITE important

trod (past tense of **tread**)

trodden (past participle of **tread**)

troop NOUN
❶ ***Troops** marched on the town.*
• soldiers, an army
❷ *A **troop** of riders crossed the river.*
• a group, a band, a party

troop VERB
*The children **trooped** along the road.*
• to march, to parade, to walk, to proceed
— To file somewhere is to walk one behind the other.

trouble NOUN
❶ *My friends would always help me if I was in trouble.*
• difficulty, hardship, suffering, unhappiness, distress, misfortune, pain, sadness, sorrow, a plight, a predicament, an ordeal
❷ *I'm very sorry to have caused you so much **trouble**.*
• worry, bother, inconvenience
• a problem: *I'm very sorry to have caused so many problems.*
❸ *There was some **trouble** at the football match.*
• disorder, unrest, disturbance, commotion, fighting, violence
❹ *The **trouble** with this computer is that it's very slow.*
• a problem, a difficulty, a disadvantage, a drawback

trouble VERB
❶ *Something seemed to be **troubling** him.*
• to distress, to upset, to bother, to worry, to concern
❷ *I'm sorry to **trouble** you, but I need the key.*
• to disturb, to interrupt, to bother, to pester

troublesome ADJECTIVE
❶ *The case was solved except for one **troublesome** detail.*
• awkward, tricky, difficult, inconvenient, annoying, irritating, worrying, concerning
❷ *The children can be very **troublesome**.*
• badly behaved, disorderly, rowdy, unruly, disobedient, naughty

true ADJECTIVE
❶ *Do you think what he said is **true**?*
• accurate, correct, right, factual, honest
OPPOSITES untrue, false
❷ *This is a **true** story.*
• real, actual, genuine, authentic
OPPOSITES fictional, invented
❸ *Esther has always been a **true** friend.*
• loyal, faithful, devoted, firm, staunch, reliable, dependable, trustworthy, trusty
OPPOSITE unreliable

trust VERB
*I **trusted** her to keep my secret.*
• to rely on, to depend on, to count on, to believe in, to be sure of, to have confidence in, to have faith in

trust NOUN
*I have **trust** in your ability.*
• belief, confidence, faith

trustworthy ADJECTIVE
*She was my most **trustworthy** friend.*
• reliable, dependable, loyal, trusty, true, honourable, responsible
OPPOSITE untrustworthy

truth NOUN
❶ *I just want to know the **truth**.*
• the facts, the reality
OPPOSITE lies
❷ *The police doubted the **truth** of his story.*
• accuracy, authenticity, correctness, genuineness, reliability, truthfulness, validity
OPPOSITES inaccuracy, falseness

truthful ADJECTIVE
❶ *She is normally a **truthful** person.*
• honest, frank, sincere, straightforward, reliable, trustworthy
❷ *He gave a **truthful** answer.*
• accurate, correct, proper, right, true, valid
OPPOSITE dishonest

A B C D E F G H I J K L M N O P Q R S T U V W X Y Z

try *VERB*
❶ *We **tried** to be quiet.*
• to attempt, to aim, to endeavour, to make an effort
— To **strive**, to **struggle** or to **battle** to do something is to try hard to do something difficult.
❷ *Would you like to **try** a new flavour?*
• to test, to try out, to experiment with

try *NOUN*
*We may not succeed, but it's worth a **try**!*
• an attempt, an effort, a go

tube *NOUN*
*Roll the paper into a **tube**.*
• a cylinder, a roll
— A **pipe** is a tube for carrying water, gas or oil.
— A **hose** is a long flexible tube.
— A **duct** is a tube through which air or gas passes.

tuft *NOUN*
*The goat stood munching on a **tuft** of grass.*
• a clump, a bunch
— A **crest** or a **plume** is a tuft of feathers.

tune *NOUN*
*I can remember the **tune** but not the words.*
• a melody, a song, music

tunnel *NOUN*
*There is a secret **tunnel** under the castle.*
• a passage, a passageway
— A **subway** or an **underpass** is a tunnel beneath a road.
— A **burrow** is a tunnel dug by an animal such as a rabbit.
— A **warren** is an area where there are many burrows.

tunnel *VERB*
*They **tunnelled** under the wall.*
• to dig, to excavate, to burrow

turn *VERB*
❶ *The wheels started to **turn**.*
• to go round, to revolve, to rotate, to spin, to roll
❷ *She **turned** to look at him.*
• to twist round, to spin round, to twirl round, to swivel round, to wheel round, to pivot
— To **whirl** round is to turn quickly.
❸ *The car **turned** at the traffic lights.*
• to change direction, to turn left or right
— To **swerve** or **veer** is to suddenly change direction.
❹ *The weather has **turned** cold.*
• to become, to go, to grow
❺ *They **turned** the attic into a playroom.*
• to convert, to adapt, to change, to alter, to modify, to transform
❻ *Can we **turn** the TV on?*
• to switch, to put

➤ **to turn into something**
*The frog **turned into** a handsome prince.*
• to become, to transform into, to change into, to develop into
➤ **to turn out**
*Everything **turned out** well in the end.*
• to end up, to come out, to happen
➤ **to turn up**
*A friend **turned up** unexpectedly.*
• to arrive, to appear, to drop in

turn *NOUN*
*Now it's my **turn**.*
• a go, an opportunity, a chance, a try

twin *NOUN*
*The two of them looked like **twins**.*
• a double, a duplicate, a clone

twinkle *VERB*
*The stars **twinkled** in the sky.*
• to sparkle, to shine, to glitter, to glisten, to glimmer, to glint

twirl *VERB*
❶ *The dancers **twirled** faster and faster.*
• to spin, to turn, to whirl, to rotate, to revolve
❷ *He **twirled** his cane.*
• to twiddle, to spin, to rotate

twist *VERB*
❶ *The heat has **twisted** the metal.*
• to bend, to buckle, to warp, to crumple, to distort
❷ *She **twisted** a bandage round her wrist.*
• to wind, to loop, to coil, to curl, to entwine
❸ ***Twist** the lid to remove it.*
• to turn, to rotate, to twiddle, to unscrew
❹ *The road **twists** through the hills.*
• to wind, to weave, to curve, to zigzag, to meander

twisted *ADJECTIVE*
*The trunk of the olive tree was **twisted** with age.*
• warped, gnarled, bent, curved

type *NOUN*
*What **type** of films do you like to watch?*
• a kind, a sort, a variety, a style, a category
— A **breed** of dog is a type of dog.
— A **species** of animal is a type of animal.

typical *ADJECTIVE*
❶ *The weather is **typical** for this time of year.*
• normal, usual, standard, ordinary, average, unsurprising
OPPOSITE unusual
❷ *It is **typical** of her to be late!*
• characteristic, habitual, usual, common
OPPOSITE uncharacteristic

a
b
c
d
e
f
g
h
i
j
k
l
m
n
o
p
q
r
s
t
u
v
w
x
y
z

🔧 Can you think of 3 different words for describing someone as unfriendly?

🔧 Some synonyms for **unfriendly** are to do with **coldness**. Can you think of any?

🔧 Check the thesaurus to find answers!

ugly ADJECTIVE
We screamed when we saw the **ugly** monster.
• horrible, hideous, frightful, grotesque, repulsive, revolting, monstrous, unattractive
OPPOSITE beautiful

unaware ADJECTIVE
➤ **unaware of**
They were **unaware of** the dangers that lay ahead.
• ignorant of, oblivious to, unconscious of

unbearable ADJECTIVE
The stench in the cave was **unbearable**.
• unendurable, intolerable, impossible to bear

unbelievable ADJECTIVE
❶ I found his story about seeing a ghost **unbelievable**.
• unconvincing, unlikely, far-fetched, improbable, incredible
❷ The flavour of this ice cream is **unbelievable**.
• amazing, astonishing, extraordinary, wonderful, fantastic, sensational

uncertain ADJECTIVE
❶ I was **uncertain** what to do next.
• unsure, doubtful, unclear, unconfident
OPPOSITES certain, clear
❷ She was **uncertain** about some parts of his story.
• doubtful, dubious, sceptical, unconvinced
OPPOSITES certain, convinced
❸ They are facing an **uncertain** future.
• indefinite, unknown, undecided
OPPOSITES certain, definite

uncomfortable ADJECTIVE
❶ She complained that her shoes were **uncomfortable**.
• tight, cramped, stiff
❷ The sofa was very **uncomfortable**.
• hard, stiff, lumpy
❸ He spent an **uncomfortable** night sleeping on the floor.
• restless, troubled, disagreeable, uneasy
OPPOSITE comfortable

uncover VERB
❶ Archaeologists have **uncovered** two more skeletons.
• to dig up, to unearth, to expose, to reveal, to disclose
❷ He **uncovered** the truth about his family's past.
• to discover, to find out, to unearth, to detect, to come across
OPPOSITES to cover up, to hide

understand VERB understands, understanding, understood
❶ I couldn't **understand** the instructions.
• to comprehend, to grasp, to follow, to take in, to work out, to fathom
❷ I can't **understand** all of the words.
• to read, to interpret, to make out, to make sense of, to decipher
— To decode something is to understand something written in code.
❸ I **understand** why you are annoyed.
• to see, to realise, to appreciate, to recognise

understanding NOUN
❶ The book will increase your **understanding** of science.
• comprehension, grasp, knowledge, appreciation, awareness
❷ Thank you for your **understanding**.
• sympathy, tolerance, compassion, consideration, thoughtfulness

understanding ADJECTIVE
Martha is an **understanding** person.
• sympathetic, caring, kind, tolerant, considerate, thoughtful

undo VERB undoes, undoing, undid, undone
❶ I **undid** the ribbon on the package.
• to unfasten, to untie, to loosen, to release, to open
❷ The good witch tried to **undo** the spell.
• to reverse, to cancel out, to wipe out

undress VERB
*He **undressed** quickly and got into bed.*
• to get undressed, to take off your clothes, to strip
OPPOSITE to dress

uneasy ADJECTIVE
*I felt **uneasy**, as if I was being watched.*
• anxious, nervous, worried, apprehensive, tense, uncomfortable, troubled, concerned, preoccupied, fearful
OPPOSITE confident

uneven ADJECTIVE
❶ *The surface was very **uneven**.*
• rough, bumpy, irregular
OPPOSITE smooth
❷ *It was a very **uneven** contest.*
• one-sided, unbalanced, unequal, unfair
OPPOSITE balanced

unexpected ADJECTIVE
*He gave an **unexpected** laugh.*
• sudden, abrupt, surprising, startling, unforeseen
OPPOSITE expected

unfair ADJECTIVE
❶ *Do you think that the referee was **unfair**?*
• unjust, unreasonable, wrong, prejudiced, biased, unbalanced
OPPOSITES fair, just
❷ *I felt that her criticism of my work was **unfair**.*
• undeserved, unjustified
OPPOSITES fair, deserved

unfamiliar ADJECTIVE
*The astronauts looked on an **unfamiliar** landscape.*
• strange, unusual, curious, alien
➤ to be unfamiliar with
*They were **unfamiliar with** the local customs.*
• unaccustomed to, unused to, unaware of

unfortunate ADJECTIVE
❶ *The **unfortunate** couple had lost all their possessions.*
• unlucky, poor, unhappy, wretched, pitiful
❷ *It is **unfortunate** that you had to leave early.*
• regrettable, a shame, a pity
OPPOSITE fortunate

unfriendly ADJECTIVE
*The housekeeper seemed rather **unfriendly**.*
• unwelcoming, cold, chilly, icy, frosty, distant, gruff, forbidding, stern, abrupt, unpleasant, hostile, aggressive
OPPOSITE friendly

unhappy ADJECTIVE
❶ *You look **unhappy**—what's the matter?*
• sad, miserable, dejected, depressed, downhearted, despondent, gloomy, glum, downcast, forlorn
» *For more ways to say unhappy look at **sad**.*
OPPOSITES happy, cheerful
❷ *I was **unhappy** with my score.*
• dissatisfied, disappointed, displeased, discontented
OPPOSITES satisfied, pleased

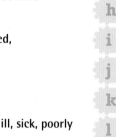

unhealthy ADJECTIVE
❶ *He was an **unhealthy** child.*
• unwell, sickly, weak, delicate, frail, ill, sick, poorly
OPPOSITES healthy, strong
❷ *She eats an **unhealthy** diet.*
• unwholesome, harmful, bad for you
OPPOSITES healthy, wholesome

unimportant ADJECTIVE
*Don't worry about **unimportant** details.*
• insignificant, minor, trivial, trifling, irrelevant, slight, small, petty
OPPOSITE important

unique ADJECTIVE
*Each person's fingerprints are **unique**.*
• distinctive, different, individual, special, particular

unite VERB
❶ *The king managed to **unite** the two kingdoms.*
• to join, to merge, to combine, to link, to unify, to bring together
OPPOSITE to separate
❷ *They all **united** to help in the rescue.*
• to join together, to come together, to cooperate
OPPOSITE to compete

universal ADJECTIVE
*Pollution is a **universal** problem.*
• general, widespread, global, worldwide, international

a b c d e f g h i j k l m n o p q r s t u v w x

unkind *ADJECTIVE*
*It was an **unkind** thing to say.*
• cruel, mean, nasty, callous, uncaring, heartless, harsh, unpleasant, spiteful, malicious
— Use **thoughtless** or **inconsiderate** if someone is unkind without meaning to be.
OPPOSITE kind

unknown *ADJECTIVE*
❶ *It was painted by an **unknown** artist.*
• unidentified, unrecognised, nameless
— Use **anonymous** if someone does not want their name to be known.
OPPOSITE known
❷ *The explorers entered **unknown** territory.*
• unfamiliar, alien, new, foreign, undiscovered, unexplored
OPPOSITE familiar

unlike *ADJECTIVE*
*The food was **unlike** anything I had tasted before.*
• different from, distinct from
OPPOSITE similar to

unlikely *ADJECTIVE*
❶ *It is **unlikely** that he'll win.*
• not likely, improbable
— If something is unlikely, you can say there is **a slim chance** or **not much chance** it will happen.
OPPOSITE likely
❷ *Her excuse sounded very **unlikely**.*
• unbelievable, unconvincing, improbable, incredible, far-fetched
OPPOSITES convincing, believable

unlucky *ADJECTIVE*
❶ *The **unlucky** travellers had been robbed by bandits.*
• unfortunate, poor, unhappy, wretched, pitiful
❷ *By an **unlucky** chance, their plan was discovered.*
• unfortunate, regrettable, unwelcome
OPPOSITE lucky

unnatural *ADJECTIVE*
❶ *It's **unnatural** for cats to eat vegetables.*
• unusual, not normal, odd, strange, weird, bizarre
❷ *The strawberries were an **unnatural** colour.*
• artificial, fake, man-made, manufactured
OPPOSITE natural

unnecessary *ADJECTIVE*
*I'm deleting any **unnecessary** apps from my phone.*
• unneeded, unwanted, inessential, excessive, extra
OPPOSITE necessary

unpleasant *ADJECTIVE*
*He was very **unpleasant** and told us to go away.*
• disagreeable, horrible, nasty, unkind, mean, malicious, spiteful, rude
» *To describe unpleasant smells look at* **smell**.
» *To describe food that tastes unpleasant look at* **food**.
» *To describe unpleasant sounds look at* **sound**.
» *To describe other unpleasant things look at* **bad**.

unpopular *ADJECTIVE*
*The new coach was **unpopular** at first.*
• disliked, hated, despised
OPPOSITE popular

unsafe *ADJECTIVE*
» *Look at* **dangerous**.

unsteady *ADJECTIVE*
*The table was a bit **unsteady**.*
• unstable, shaky, wobbly, insecure, rickety
OPPOSITES stable, steady

unnatural

unsure *ADJECTIVE*
» *Look at* **uncertain**.

untidy *ADJECTIVE*
❶ *Your desk is very **untidy**.*
• messy, disorderly, muddled, cluttered, disorganised, chaotic
❷ *His work was **untidy** and full of mistakes.*
• careless, thoughtless, messy, disorganised, sloppy
❸ *She arrived looking **untidy** and flustered.*
• dishevelled, bedraggled, rumpled, unkempt, scruffy
OPPOSITES tidy, neat

untrue *ADJECTIVE*
» *Look at* **false**.

unusual *ADJECTIVE*
❶ *The weather was **unusual** for the time of year.*
• extraordinary, out of the ordinary, exceptional, remarkable, odd, peculiar, strange, curious, surprising, weird, bizarre, unexpected, unconventional, irregular
OPPOSITE ordinary
❷ *Woodpeckers are **unusual** in this part of the country.*
• uncommon, rare, unfamiliar, scarce
OPPOSITE common

unwilling *ADJECTIVE*
» *Look at* **reluctant**.

upper *ADJECTIVE*
*My bedroom is on the **upper** floor.*
• higher, upstairs
OPPOSITE lower

upright ADJECTIVE
The car seat should be in an upright position.
• vertical, erect, perpendicular
OPPOSITE horizontal

upset ADJECTIVE
She seemed very upset about something.
• unhappy, sad, distressed, troubled, dismayed
— Use **hurt** or **offended** if you are upset by something unkind that someone has done.

upset VERB
❶ *Something in the letter had upset her.*
• to distress, to trouble, to bother, to disturb, to displease, to offend, to dismay
❷ *I upset a whole bottle of milk.*
• to knock over, to spill, to tip over, to topple

upside down ADJECTIVE
I can't read the writing if it's upside down.
• the wrong way up, inverted, topsy-turvy (informal)
OPPOSITE the right way up

upward ADJECTIVE
He started on the steep upward climb.
• uphill, ascending, rising
OPPOSITE downward

urban ADJECTIVE
Most of the population live in urban areas.
• built-up, busy, densely populated
OPPOSITE rural

urge VERB
He urged her to think carefully about her decision.
• to advise, to counsel, to encourage, to appeal to, to beg, to implore, to plead with

urge NOUN
I had a sudden urge to burst into song.
• an impulse, a desire, a wish, a longing, a yearning

urgent ADJECTIVE
It is urgent that we do something about the leak.
• essential, important, critical, crucial, vital
OPPOSITE unimportant

use (say yooz) VERB
❶ *She used a calculator to add up the figures.*
• to make use of, to utilise, to employ
— To **exploit** something or someone is to use them selfishly.
— To **harness** something is to control and use it: *They were able to harness the power of the wind.*
❷ *Can you show me how to use the photocopier?*
• to operate, to work, to handle, to manage

❸ *You've used all the hot water.*
• to use up, to go through, to consume, to finish

use (say yooss) NOUN
❶ *Can you find a use for this box?*
• a purpose, a function
❷ *Shouting is no use—they can't hear you.*
• help, benefit, advantage
— You can also say **there is no point** doing something.

useful ADJECTIVE
❶ *A flask is useful for keeping food warm.*
• convenient, handy, effective, efficient, practical
❷ *The website offers some useful advice.*
• good, helpful, valuable, worthwhile, constructive, invaluable
OPPOSITE useless

useless ADJECTIVE
❶ *This old vacuum cleaner is useless.*
• ineffective, inefficient, impractical, unusable
OPPOSITES useful, effective
❷ *My efforts to persuade him were useless.*
• worthless, pointless, futile, fruitless, unhelpful, unsuccessful
OPPOSITE useful
❸ *(informal) I'm useless at drawing.*
• bad, poor, incompetent, rubbish (informal), hopeless (informal)
OPPOSITE good

usual ADJECTIVE
❶ *I'll meet you at the usual time.*
• normal, customary, familiar, habitual, regular, standard
❷ *It's usual to knock before entering.*
• common, accepted, conventional, traditional
OPPOSITE unusual

usually ADVERB
We usually go swimming on Saturdays.
• normally, typically, generally, ordinarily, as a rule

utter VERB
The robot could only utter a few phrases.
• to say, to speak, to express, to pronounce

utter ADJECTIVE
They stared at the unicorn in utter amazement.
• complete, total, absolute, sheer
— Use **downright** to emphasise something bad: *That's a downright lie!*

⚙ Can you think of
   a) 3 green vegetables
   b) 3 root vegetables
   c) 3 other vegetables?

⚙ Do you know
   a word for an
   animal that eats
   only vegetables
   (plants)?

⚙ Check the thesaurus to find answers!

vacancy NOUN
*They have a **vacancy** for a shop assistant.*
• a job, a post, a position, work

vacant ADJECTIVE
❶ *The house over the road is still **vacant**.*
• unoccupied, uninhabited, deserted, empty
OPPOSITE occupied
❷ *He stared out of the window with a **vacant** look.*
• blank, expressionless, mindless, absent-minded
OPPOSITE alert

vague ADJECTIVE
❶ *The description she gave was a bit **vague**.*
• imprecise, broad, general, indefinite, unclear, confused
OPPOSITES exact, detailed
❷ *A **vague** shape could be seen through the mist.*
• blurred, blurry, indistinct, unclear, hazy, fuzzy, shadowy, obscure
OPPOSITES definite, clear

vain ADJECTIVE
❶ *The evil queen was **vain** about her appearance.*
• arrogant, proud, conceited, haughty
OPPOSITE modest
❷ *He made a **vain** attempt to tidy the room.*
• unsuccessful, ineffective, useless, worthless, fruitless, futile, pointless
OPPOSITE successful

valid ADJECTIVE
*Your ticket is not **valid**.*
• current, legal, acceptable, usable, permitted, approved, authorised
OPPOSITE invalid

valley NOUN
*A stream ran through the **valley**.*
• a dale, a glen (Scottish)
— A **gorge**, a **ravine** or a **canyon** is a deep valley with steep sides.

valuable ADJECTIVE
❶ *Apparently the painting is very **valuable**.*
• expensive, costly, dear, precious, priceless
❷ *He gave her some **valuable** advice.*
• useful, helpful, constructive, good, worthwhile, invaluable
OPPOSITE worthless
Note that *invaluable* is not the opposite of *valuable*, as it means very valuable.

value NOUN
❶ *The house has recently increased in **value**.*
• price, cost, worth
❷ *He stressed the **value** of regular exercise.*
• advantage, benefit, merit, use, usefulness, importance

value VERB
*I **value** your opinion.*
• to appreciate, to respect, to have a high opinion of
— To **prize** or to **treasure** a possession is to value it.

vanish VERB
*The magician **vanished** in a puff of smoke.*
• to disappear, to go away, to dissolve
OPPOSITE to appear

variation NOUN
*There have been slight **variations** in temperature.*
• a difference, a change, an alteration, a shift

variety NOUN
❶ *The school offers a **variety** of clubs.*
• an assortment, a mixture, an array
❷ *The supermarket has several **varieties** of pasta.*
• a kind, a sort, a type, a make, a brand
— A **breed** is a variety of animal.
❸ *Try to have more **variety** in the words you choose.*
• variation, diversity, change, difference

various ADJECTIVE
*The T-shirt is available in **various** colours.*
• different, assorted, several, varying, differing, a variety of, diverse

vary VERB
❶ *The weather **varies** a lot here.*
• to change, to alter, to differ
❷ *The school cafeteria tries to **vary** the menu.*
• to change, to modify, to adjust, to alter

vast ADJECTIVE

❶ *The miser accumulated a **vast** fortune.*
• large, huge, enormous, great, immense, massive, colossal
❷ *They looked out on a **vast** stretch of desert.*
• broad, wide, extensive
OPPOSITES small, tiny

vegetable NOUN

WORD WEB

SOME GREEN VEGETABLES:

• broccoli, Brussels sprouts, a cabbage, a cauliflower, a lettuce, spinach

SOME BEANS AND PEAS:

• broad beans, chickpeas, lentils, peas, runner beans, soya beans

SOME ROOT VEGETABLES:

• beetroot, a carrot, a parsnip, a radish, a swede, a sweet potato, a turnip

vegetarian NOUN

*My sister is a **vegetarian** so she doesn't eat chicken.*
— A **vegan** is a person who eats only plants, not animal products such as eggs or milk.
— A **herbivore** is an animal that eats only plants.
— A **carnivore** is an animal that eats meat.
— An **omnivore** is an animal that eats plants and meat.

SOME OTHER VEGETABLES:

• an aubergine, an avocado, celery, a courgette, a cucumber, garlic, a leek, a marrow, a mushroom, an onion, a pepper, a potato, a pumpkin, spring onions, a squash, sweetcorn, a tomato, a yam

a pepper

broad beans

radishes

garlic

celery

lentils

sweetcorn

a courgette

broccoli

chickpeas

spring onion

spinach

peas

an onion

a cucumber

Brussels sprouts

an aubergine

lettuce

a mushroom

a parsnip

a yam

soya beans

a squash

a potato

a turnip

a cabbage

a runner bean

a swede

a carrot

a cauliflower

a leek

a pumpkin

beetroot

vegetation *NOUN*
The rainforest is filled with lush **vegetation**.
• foliage, greenery, growth, plants

vein *NOUN*
— A **vein** carries blood towards the heart.
— An **artery** carries blood away from the heart.
— A **blood vessel** is a vein or an artery.

venture *VERB*
They **ventured** out into the snow.
• to journey, to set out, to dare to go

venture *NOUN*
She decided to try a new business **venture**.
• an enterprise, an undertaking, a project, a scheme

verdict *NOUN*
What was the jury's **verdict**?
• a conclusion, a decision, a judgement, an opinion

version *NOUN*
❶ Everyone gave different **versions** of what happened.
• an account, a description, a story, a report
❷ A new **version** of the computer game will be released in May.
• a design, a model, a form, a variation

vertical *ADJECTIVE*
The fence posts must be **vertical**.
• erect, perpendicular, upright
— Use **sheer** for a vertical drop or cliff.
OPPOSITE horizontal

very *ADVERB*
Charlotte is a **very** talented player.
• extremely, highly, enormously, exceedingly, truly, especially, particularly, remarkably, unusually, outstandingly, really
OPPOSITES slightly, fairly

vessel *NOUN*
❶ They saw a fishing **vessel**.
• a boat, a ship, a craft
» For types of boat or ship look at **boat**.
❷ Archaeologists found clay **vessels** at the site.
• a pot, a dish, a bowl, a jar, a bottle, a container

vibrate *VERB*
When you pluck the string it **vibrates**.
• to shake, to shudder, to tremble, to throb, to quake, to quiver, to rattle

vicious *ADJECTIVE*
❶ It was a **vicious** attack.
• brutal, barbaric, cruel, savage, inhuman, bloodthirsty, violent, merciless, pitiless, ruthless, callous

❷ They faced a **vicious** beast.
• fierce, ferocious, savage, wild

victim *NOUN*
❶ Ambulances took the **victims** to hospital.
• a casualty
— You can also say that victims of an accident are the injured.
❷ The hawk carried its **victim** in its talons.
• prey
❸ He was the **victim** of cruel jokes.
• the target, the subject, the object

victorious *ADJECTIVE*
The **victorious** team celebrated.
• winning, triumphant, successful
OPPOSITE defeated

victory *NOUN*
The team had a great **victory** over their rivals.
• a win, a success, a triumph
OPPOSITE a defeat

view *NOUN*
❶ There's a lovely **view** from the top of the hill.
• a scene, scenery, landscape
— A **glimpse** is a brief view.
— A **bird's-eye view** is a view from above.
— A **cross-section** is a view of something that has been cut through.
❷ We'd like to hear your **views** on the new show.
• an opinion, a perspective, a point of view, a reaction, an attitude, a thought, an idea, a belief

view *VERB*
Thousands of people came to **view** the exhibits.
• to see, to look at, to examine, to eye
— To **watch** a programme or film is to view it.
— To **gaze at** something is to look at it for a long time.
— To **contemplate** something is to look at and think about it.

viewer *NOUN*
Millions of **viewers** watched the show.
— A show's **audience** is its viewers.
— A **spectator** is someone who views a performance.
— A **witness** is someone who sees an accident or a crime.
— An **onlooker** is someone who sees an event but is not involved in it.

villain *NOUN*
She felt sure that the man was a **villain**.
• a rogue, a wrongdoer, a criminal, an offender, a crook (informal)
— The villain in a story is the **baddy** (informal).
OPPOSITE hero
» For types of criminal look at **criminal**.

violence NOUN
❶ *They don't believe in using **violence**.*
• force, brutality, fighting, aggression, war, bloodshed
OPPOSITE non-violence
❷ *We weren't prepared for the **violence** of the storm.*
• force, power, strength, severity, intensity, ferocity, fierceness, fury
OPPOSITES gentleness, mildness

violent ADJECTIVE
❶ *It was a **violent** attack.*
• aggressive, forceful, rough, fierce, frenzied, vicious, brutal, bloodthirsty, warlike
OPPOSITE gentle
❷ *The bridge was washed away in a **violent** storm.*
• severe, powerful, forceful, raging, turbulent
OPPOSITES weak, mild

virtually ADVERB
*The two images are **virtually** identical.*
• almost, nearly, practically, as good as, in effect

virtue NOUN
❶ *He preached to them about **virtue**.*
• goodness, decency, righteousness, honesty
OPPOSITE vice
❷ *One **virtue** of this phone is that it's cheap.*
• an advantage, a benefit, an asset, a good point, a merit, a strength

visible ADJECTIVE
*There was no **visible** damage to the car.*
• noticeable, obvious, evident, apparent, conspicuous, clear, distinct, recognisable, detectable
OPPOSITE invisible

vision NOUN
❶ *He began to have problems with his **vision**.*
• eyesight, sight
❷ *He saw his grandfather in a **vision**.*
• a dream, a hallucination
— A **mirage** is something you see that is not there, especially water in a desert.

visit VERB
*Our cousins are **visiting** us this weekend.*
• to call on, to come to see, to go to see, to stay with

visit NOUN
❶ *My grandmother is coming for a **visit**.*
• a call, a stay
❷ *We went on a **visit** to the museum.*
• a trip, an excursion, an outing

visitor NOUN
❶ *They've got some **visitors** staying with them.*
• a guest, a caller, company
❷ *Rome has millions of **visitors** every year.*
• a tourist, a holidaymaker, a sightseer, a traveller

vital ADJECTIVE
*It is **vital** that you remember the secret password.*
• essential, crucial, important, necessary, critical
OPPOSITE unimportant

voice NOUN
*I recognised my dad's **voice**.*
• tone, way of speaking, speech

 WRITING TIPS

Here are some words you could use to describe a voice:
• deep, low, gruff, croaky, husky, hoarse, harsh, soft, quiet, gentle, high-pitched, squeaky, shrill, piercing, clear, loud, booming, thunderous, droning, monotonous
The small, shrill voice in the distance was growing louder every second, frantic, piercing, non-stop.
—DANNY THE CHAMPION OF THE WORLD, Roald Dahl

voice VERB
*They **voiced** some concerns about the plan.*
• to express, to communicate, to state, to declare

volcano NOUN
— A **crater** is the mouth of a volcano.
— **Lava** is molten rock that pours from a volcano.
— **Igneous** rock is formed from lava.
— A **dormant** volcano is not erupting or not likely to erupt soon.
— An **active** volcano is erupting or likely to erupt.
— An **extinct** volcano will no longer erupt.

a b c d e f g h i j k l m n o p q r s t u v w x y z

voluntary *ADJECTIVE*
❶ *There is no charge for the museum, but you can make a **voluntary** contribution.*
• optional
OPPOSITE compulsory
❷ *She does **voluntary** work for a charity.*
• unpaid
OPPOSITE paid

volunteer *VERB*
*No one **volunteered** to do the washing-up.*
• to offer, to put yourself forward, to be willing

vote *VERB*
*Everyone can **vote** in the election.*
• to cast your vote, to have a vote
➤ **to vote for someone** or **something**
*We **voted for** a new class captain.*
• to choose, to elect, to opt for, to nominate

vote *NOUN*
*The results of the **vote** will be known tomorrow.*
• an election, a poll, a survey
— A **referendum** is a vote on one question.

voucher *NOUN*
*You can exchange this **voucher** for a free drink.*
• a coupon, a ticket, a token

 Can you think of 3 different ways to say 'walk unsteadily'?

 Can you think of a word that means 'to walk proudly'?

 Check the thesaurus to find answers!

wag VERB
*The dog was eagerly **wagging** its tail.*
• to shake, to waggle, to move to and fro, to swing, to wave

wage NOUN
*Her weekly **wage** was barely enough to live on.*
• earnings, income, pay
— Someone's **salary** is the amount they are paid per year for work.

wage VERB
*The Greeks **waged** a long war against Troy.*
• to carry on, to conduct, to fight

wail VERB
*Upstairs, the baby began to **wail**.*
• to cry, to howl, to bawl, to moan, to shriek

wait VERB
❶ *Please **wait** here until I get back.*
• to stay, to remain, to stop, to linger, to hang on *(informal)*, to hold on *(informal)*
❷ *She **waited** for a moment before starting to speak.*
• to pause, to hesitate

wait NOUN
*There was a long **wait** before the show began.*
• a pause, a delay, an interval

wake (also **waken**) VERB wakes, waking, woke, woken
❶ *She **woke** early that morning.*
• to awake, to awaken, to wake up, to rise, to stir, to get up
❷ *The alarm **woke** me from a deep sleep.*
• to rouse, to awaken, to disturb, to wake someone up

walk VERB

😮 **OVERUSED WORD**

Try to use a more interesting word when you want to say **walk**. Here are some ideas and examples:

TO WALK SLOWLY OR REGULARLY:

• to amble, to plod, to trudge, to pace, to tread
— To **stroll**, to **saunter** or to **wander** is to walk slowly in a relaxed way.
— To **dawdle** or to **straggle** is to walk more slowly than other people.

TO WALK UNSTEADILY:

• to stagger, to stumble, to totter, to hobble, to limp, to lurch, to shamble, to shuffle, to waddle
Sleeping people are not fast. They stumble, they stagger; they move like children wading through rivers of treacle, like old people whose feet are weighed down by thick, wet mud.—THE SLEEPER AND THE SPINDLE, Neil Gaiman

TO WALK HEAVILY OR LOUDLY:

• to stamp, to tramp, to trudge, to plod
*We all **tramped** downstairs in our boots.*

TO WALK QUIETLY:

• to pad, to tiptoe, to slink, to steal, to creep, to prowl
[The wolves] were slinking along now, their emaciated bodies held low, moving towards Measle and Iggy and Tinker in a stealthy, hunting manner—and, all the time, in utter silence.—MEASLE AND THE DOOMPIT, Ian Ogilvy

TO WALK PROUDLY:

• to march, to stride, to stalk, to strut, to swagger
Cassie tossed her hair, gave a little wave and strutted off.—THE DAY OF THE PSYCHIC SOCK, Steve Cole

WALK IN WATER:

• to paddle, to wade
*We had to **wade** across a river.*

TO WALK A LONG DISTANCE:

• to hike, to trek, to ramble
*They **trekked** through the jungle.*

TO WALK IN A GROUP:

• to file, to troop
*The children **trooped** into the classroom.*

a
b
c
d
e
f
g
h
i
j
k
l
m
n
o
p
q
r
s
t
u
v
w
x
y
z

walk NOUN
*We went for a **walk** in the country.*
• a stroll, a ramble, a hike, a trek, a tramp, a trudge

wall NOUN
*A crumbling stone **wall** surrounded the cottage.*
• a barrier, a barricade
— A **partition** is a thin dividing wall inside a room.
— A **parapet** is a low wall along the edge of a bridge, roof or balcony.
— **Battlements** are the top part of a castle wall.
— A **dam** or a **dyke** is a wall built to hold back water.

wallow VERB
*Hippos like to **wallow** in mud.*
• to roll, to flounder, to wade, to lie, to loll

wander VERB
❶ *Sheep **wandered** about the hills.*
• to stray, to roam, to rove, to ramble, to meander
❷ *We must have **wandered** off the path.*
• to stray, to get lost, to straggle

want VERB
❶ *Do you **want** a drink?*
• to feel like, to fancy, to need, to wish for *(formal)*, to desire *(formal)*
— To **crave**, to **long for**, to **yearn for** or to **pine for** something is to want it very much.
❷ *He **wants** to play for Wales one day.*
• to hope, to wish
• to dream: *He **dreams** of playing for Wales.*

war NOUN
*The **war** between the two countries lasted many years.*
• fighting, warfare, conflict
OPPOSITE peace

wares NOUN
*The market traders displayed their **wares**.*
• goods, merchandise, produce, stock

warm ADJECTIVE
❶ *It was a **warm** spring day.*
• mild, pleasant
— **Humid** means warm and damp.
OPPOSITE cold
❷ *Sandy put on a **warm** jumper.*
• cosy, snug, thick, woolly
OPPOSITE thin
❸ *She gave us a **warm** smile.*
• friendly, enthusiastic, welcoming, kind, affectionate
OPPOSITE unfriendly

warn VERB
*The guide **warned** us to keep to the path.*
• to advise, to caution, to counsel, to alert, to remind

warning NOUN
❶ *There was no **warning** of the danger ahead.*
• a sign, a signal, an indication, notice
❷ *The traffic warden let him off with a **warning**.*
• a caution, a telling-off

wash VERB
*Don't forget to **wash** your hands.*
• to clean, to rinse
— To wash your hair is to **shampoo** it.
— To wash clothes is to **launder** them.
— To wash yourself all over is to **bath**, **bathe** or **shower**.
— To wash dishes and cutlery after a meal is to **wash up**.

waste VERB
*Let's not **waste** any more time.*
• to squander, to misuse, to throw away
OPPOSITE to save

waste NOUN
*A lot of household **waste** can be recycled.*
• rubbish, refuse, trash, garbage, junk, litter
— **Scrap** is waste metal or paper.

scrap

wasteful *ADJECTIVE*
It's wasteful to cook more food than you need.
• extravagant, uneconomical, lavish
OPPOSITE economical

watch *VERB*
❶ *I could sit and watch the sea for hours.*
• to gaze at, to look at, to stare at, to view,
to contemplate
❷ *Watch how the batsman holds the bat.*
• to observe, to take notice of, to pay attention to,
to attend to, to heed, to note
❸ *Could you watch my bag?*
• to keep an eye on, to guard, to mind, to look
after, to supervise
➤ **to watch out**
Watch out—there's a car coming!
• to be careful, to pay attention, to beware,
to take care

watch *NOUN*
» *For instruments used to measure time look at* **time**.

water *NOUN*

WORD WEB

SOME AREAS OF WATER:

• a brook, a canal, a lake, a loch *(Scottish)*,
an ocean, a pond, a pool, a reservoir, a river,
a sea, a stream
— Animals and plants which live in water are **aquatic**.

WRITING TIPS

Here are some useful words for writing about **water**:

TO DESCRIBE POURING OR FLOWING WATER:

• to cascade, to dribble, to drip, to flow, to gush,
to jet, to overflow, to run, to seep, to spill,
to spout, to spurt, to squirt, to stream, to trickle

TO DESCRIBE HOW A BODY OF WATER MOVES:

• to bubble, to foam, to flood, to froth, to gurgle,
to lap, to ripple, to rise, to roll, to surge,
to sweep, to swirl, to swish

TO DESCRIBE SPLASHING:

• to shower, to splash, to spray, to sprinkle
*From the bathroom comes the ominous sound of
running water. [I] find the plug in the washbasin,
the tap half on, and water lapping over the side
and flooding the floor.*—THE KISSING CLUB, Julia Clarke
» *Look at* **flow**.

wave *VERB*
❶ *She waved at me from across the street.*
• to signal, to gesture
❷ *The flags waved in the breeze.*
• to sway, to swing, to flap, to flutter,
to move to and fro
❸ *He waved a piece of paper in my face.*
• to shake, to brandish, to flourish, to wag, to waggle

wave *NOUN*
We played in the waves.
— The **surf** is waves breaking on the shore.
— A **breaker** is a wave breaking on the shore.
— A **roller** is a long rolling wave in the sea.
— A **ripple** is a very small wave.
— A **tidal wave** is a huge wave moving with the tide.
— A **tsunami** is a huge wave caused by an earthquake.
— The **crest** of a wave is the top.

WRITING TIPS

Here are some useful words for describing what
waves do:
• to billow, to break, to crash, to dash, to heave,
to lap, to pound, to roll, to slap against something,
to surge, to swell, to toss something, to wash
somewhere
*On the beach, waves crashed against the cliffs as the
wind howled like a wolf. Spray flung itself into the air
to dash on the pebbles at the girl's feet.*—MINES OF THE
MINOTAUR, Julia Golding

a wave breaking

way *NOUN*
❶ *What is the best way to measure the playground?*
• a method, a procedure, a process, a system,
a technique
❷ *She has done her hair in a nice way.*
• a manner, a fashion, a style
❸ *I'll show you the way to the park.*
• a route, a road, a path, a direction
❹ *Is your house a long way from here?*
• distance, journey
❺ *It's a good idea in some ways.*
• a respect, a feature, a detail, an aspect

a
b
c
d
e
f
g
h
i
j
k
l
m
n
o
p
q
r
s
t
u
v
w
x
y
z

weak ADJECTIVE
❶ *He was ill and very **weak**.*
• feeble, frail, sickly, delicate, puny, vulnerable
❷ *The footbridge was old and **weak**.*
• fragile, flimsy, rickety, shaky, unsteady, unsafe, brittle
❸ *That was a very **weak** argument.*
• lame, feeble, unconvincing
OPPOSITE strong

weaken VERB
❶ *Too much water will **weaken** the flavour.*
• to reduce, to lessen, to diminish
❷ *The storm had **weakened** overnight.*
• to decrease, to decline, to die down, to fade, to dwindle, to wane
OPPOSITE to strengthen

weakness NOUN
*He pointed out the **weakness** in their plan.*
• a fault, a flaw, a defect, an imperfection, a weak point
OPPOSITE a strength

wealth NOUN
*The family had got its **wealth** from coal mining.*
• fortune, money, riches, prosperity, affluence
OPPOSITE poverty

wealthy ADJECTIVE
*He came from a **wealthy** family.*
• rich, well-off, affluent, prosperous
OPPOSITE poor

weapon NOUN

⬡ **WORD WEB**

SOME TYPES OF WEAPON:

• an axe, a bayonet, a bomb, a cannon, a catapult, a club, a crossbow, a cutlass, a dagger, a gun, a harpoon, a mine, a missile, a musket, mortar, a pistol, a revolver, a rocket, a rifle, a sabre, a spear, a sword, a torpedo

a cutlass

wear VERB wears, wearing, wore, worn
❶ *I **wore** my new dress to the party.*
• to dress in, to be dressed in, to have on
❷ *The rug in the hallway is starting to **wear**.*
• to fray, to wear away, to wear out
— If rocks wear away, they **erode**.
➤ **to wear off**
*The pain will **wear off** soon.*
• to die down, to disappear, to ease, to fade, to lessen, to subside, to weaken

weather NOUN

 WRITING TIPS

Here are some useful words for describing **weather**:

TO DESCRIBE CLOUDY WEATHER:
• dull, dreary, grey, overcast, sunless

TO DESCRIBE WET WEATHER:
• damp, drizzly, rainy, showery, torrential
— Humid means wet and warm.

TO DESCRIBE COLD WEATHER:
• bitter, biting, bleak, chilly, frosty, icy, raw, snowy, wintry
Then one frosty evening when the stars were sparkling in the night sky and snowflakes were dancing past the windows, a little boy and his daddy came into the store.—WOLSTENCROFT THE BEAR, Karen Lewis

blowy

web NOUN
*A **web** of tunnels lay under the castle.*
• a net, a network, a mesh

wedding NOUN
*She was a bridesmaid at her cousin's **wedding**.*
• a marriage

⬡ **WORD WEB**

PEOPLE AT A WEDDING:
• the bride, the bridegroom or groom, the best man, a bridesmaid, the maid or matron of honour

weight NOUN
*Take care when lifting heavy **weights**.*
• a load, a mass, a burden

welcome VERB
❶ *An elderly butler **welcomed** us at the door.*
• to greet, to receive, to meet
❷ *We **welcome** suggestions from the public.*
• to appreciate, to accept, to like, to want

welcome NOUN
*The shopkeeper gave us a friendly **welcome**.*
• a greeting, a reception

welcome ADJECTIVE
*This sunny day makes a **welcome** change.*
• pleasant, pleasing, agreeable, appreciated, desirable
OPPOSITES unwelcome, unacceptable

TO DESCRIBE SUNNY WEATHER:

• bright, cloudless, clear, fair, fine, springlike, summery, sunny
— **Crisp** means sunny and cold.

TO DESCRIBE HOT WEATHER:

• baking, humid, melting, roasting, sizzling, sticky, sweltering

TO DESCRIBE STORMY WEATHER:

• rough, squally, turbulent, violent, wild

TO DESCRIBE WINDY WEATHER:

• blowy, blustery, breezy, gusty
» Look at **rain**, **sky**, **snow**, **storm**, **thunder** and **wind**.

blustery

well ADVERB
❶ *The whole team played* **well** *on Saturday.*
• ably, skilfully, expertly, effectively, efficiently, admirably, marvellously, wonderfully
OPPOSITE badly
❷ *It's cold outside, so wrap up* **well**.
• properly, correctly, thoroughly, carefully
❸ *I don't know him* **well**.
• closely, intimately, personally

well ADJECTIVE
He's been ill, but he looks very **well** *now.*
• healthy, fit, strong, lively, hearty
OPPOSITE ill

well-known ADJECTIVE
A **well-known** *athlete will open the new sports shop.*
• famous, celebrated, prominent, notable, renowned, distinguished, illustrious, legendary
— Use **notorious** or **infamous** if someone is well known for something bad.
OPPOSITES unknown, obscure

breezy

went (*past tense of* **go**)

wet ADJECTIVE
❶ *Take off your* **wet** *clothes.*
— **Damp** means slightly wet.
— **Soaked, soaking, dripping** or **drenched** means very wet.
— **Bedraggled** means dirty and wet.
❷ *The ground was too* **wet** *to play on.*
• muddy, boggy, marshy, soggy, waterlogged, saturated

❸ *What's this* **wet** *stuff on the table?*
• runny, sticky, moist
— A **sloppy** substance is wet and very soft.
— A **slimy** substance is unpleasantly wet and slippery.
— A **pulpy** substance is soft and wet.
❹ *It was a cold* **wet** *day.*
• rainy, showery, pouring, drizzly, misty
OPPOSITE dry

wet VERB wets, wetting, wet or wetted
Wet the clay before you start to mould it.
• to dampen, to moisten
— To **drench** or to **soak** something is to make it very wet.
OPPOSITE to dry

squally

while NOUN
You will have to wait a short **while** *for the next bus.*
• a period, a time

whirl VERB
The snowflakes **whirled** *in the icy wind.*
• to turn, to twirl, to spin, to twist, to circle, to spiral, to revolve, to rotate

whisper VERB
What are you two **whispering** *about?*
• to murmur, to mutter, to mumble
OPPOSITE to shout

white ADJECTIVE, NOUN

🌐 **WORD WEB**

SOME SHADES OF WHITE:

• cream, ivory, silvery, snow-white
— To **bleach** or to **fade** is to become whiter in colour.
— Common similes are **as white as a sheet**, **as white as chalk** and **as white as snow**.

gusty

whole ADJECTIVE
❶ *I haven't read the* **whole** *book yet.*
• complete, entire, full, total
OPPOSITE incomplete
❷ *The dinosaur skeleton appears to be* **whole**.
• in one piece, intact, unbroken, undamaged, perfect
OPPOSITES broken, in pieces

stormy

wicked ADJECTIVE
❶ *Snow White had a* **wicked** *stepmother.*
• evil, cruel, vicious, villainous, detestable, mean, corrupt, immoral, sinful
OPPOSITES good, virtuous
❷ *They had a* **wicked** *plan to take over the world.*
• evil, malicious, malevolent, diabolical, monstrous, shameful, foul, vile

a b c d e f i j k l m n p q r s u v w x y z

❸ She gave a *wicked* grin.
• mischievous, playful, naughty

wide ADJECTIVE
❶ The street is very *wide* here.
• broad, open, large, extensive, spacious, vast
OPPOSITE narrow
❷ They sell a *wide* range of books.
• comprehensive, vast, varied, diverse
OPPOSITE limited

width NOUN
The room is about three metres in *width*.
• breadth
— The width of a circle is its **diameter**.

wild ADJECTIVE
❶ There are *wild* animals in the forest.
• undomesticated, untamed, ferocious
OPPOSITE tame
❷ This is a *wild* and mountainous region.
• rough, rugged, natural, uncultivated,
uninhabited, desolate
OPPOSITE cultivated
❸ The crowd was *wild* with excitement.
• boisterous, uncontrollable, rowdy, unruly,
disorderly, noisy, hysterical
OPPOSITES calm, restrained

will NOUN
She had a strong *will* to win.
• determination, desire, wish, resolve

willing ADJECTIVE
❶ She is always *willing* to help.
• ready, eager, happy, glad, pleased, prepared
OPPOSITE unwilling
❷ I need a couple of *willing* volunteers.
• enthusiastic, helpful, cooperative, obliging

wilt VERB
The flowers *wilted* in the heat.
• to become limp, to droop, to flop,
to sag, to fade, to shrivel, to wither
OPPOSITE to flourish

win VERB wins, winning, won
❶ Who do you think will *win*?
• to come first, to be victorious, to succeed,
to triumph, to prevail
— To win against someone is also to **beat**,
to **conquer**, to **defeat** or to **overcome** them.
OPPOSITE lose
❷ She *won* first prize in the poetry competition.
• to get, to receive, to gain, to obtain, to secure,
to pick up (informal), to walk away with

wind (rhymes with **tinned**) NOUN
A cold *wind* blew.
— A **breeze** is a gentle wind.
— A **gale** or a **hurricane** is a very strong wind.
— A **cyclone** or a **tornado** is a very strong wind that
blows in a spiral.
— A **draught** is a current of air that blows through
a room.
— A **blast**, a **gust** or a **puff** of wind is a sudden
strong wind that blows for a few seconds.

😊 **WRITING TIPS**

Here are some useful words for writing about **wind**:

THINGS WIND MIGHT DO:

• to batter, to tear, to toss, to sweep, to blast,
to howl, to moan, to wail, to shriek, to scream,
to roar

SOME WORDS FOR DESCRIBING WIND:

• icy, freezing, chill, bitter, fierce, keen, howling,
shrieking, driving, gentle, soft, light, warm
*The ship was pitching and rolling, waves were
battering it and crashing over it, the rain lashed the
decks and the wind screamed.*—THE MAP OF MARVELS,
David Calcutt

wind *(rhymes with* **find***)* *VERB* **winds, winding, wound**
❶ *The road winds up the hill.*
• to bend, to curve, to twist, to twist and turn, to zigzag, to meander
❷ *She wound her scarf around her neck.*
• to twist, to wrap, to coil, to loop, to roll, to turn

window *NOUN*
— A **pane** is a sheet of glass in a window.
— A **hatch** is an opening in a wall, door or floor.
— A **skylight** is a window in a roof.
— A **porthole** is a small round window in a ship or aircraft.
— The **windscreen** is the front window in a car.

a porthole

windy *ADJECTIVE*
It was a cold windy day.
• breezy, blustery, gusty, squally, stormy
OPPOSITE **calm**

winner *NOUN*
The winner was presented with a silver cup.
• a victor, a champion
OPPOSITE **a loser**

wipe *VERB*
I wiped the floor with a cloth.
• to rub, to clean, to polish, to mop

wire *NOUN*
There are a lot of wires coming out of the back of the machine.
• a cable, a lead, a flex

wisdom *NOUN*
The old lady was known for her wisdom.
• judgement, sense, understanding, intelligence

wise *ADJECTIVE*
❶ *My grandad is very wise.*
• sensible, intelligent, perceptive, knowledgeable, thoughtful
❷ *I think you made a wise decision.*
• sensible, good, correct, just
OPPOSITE **foolish**

wish *VERB*
I wish that it would stop raining!
— If you wish something would happen, you can say that you **want** or **would like** it to happen.
➤ **to wish for**
You can have anything you wish for.
• to desire, to want, to fancy
— To **crave**, to **long for**, to **yearn for** or to **pine for** something is to want it very much.

wish *NOUN*
Her dearest wish was to see her home again.
• a desire, a longing, a yearning, an urge, a craving, a hope, an ambition

wit *NOUN*
❶ *The film is full of wit.*
• humour, comedy, jokes
❷ *He didn't have the wit to deal with the problem.*
• intelligence, cleverness, brains, sense

witness *NOUN*
A witness said that the car was going too fast.
• an observer, an onlooker, an eyewitness, a spectator

witty *ADJECTIVE*
He gave a witty account of his schooldays.
• humorous, amusing, comic, funny, clever
OPPOSITE **dull**

wobble *VERB*
❶ *The cyclist wobbled all over the road.*
• to sway, to totter, to teeter, to waver, to rock
❷ *The jelly wobbled as I carried the plate.*
• to shake, to tremble, to quake, to quiver, to vibrate

woman NOUN
— A **lady** is a polite word for a woman.
— A **wife** is a married woman.
— A **mother** is a woman who has children.
— A **spinster** is an old-fashioned word for an unmarried woman.
— A **fiancée** is a woman who is engaged to be married.
— A **bride** is a woman on her wedding day.
— A **widow** is a woman whose husband or wife has died.

won *(past tense of* **win***)*

wonder VERB
❶ *I wonder why she left in such a hurry.*
• to be curious about, to ask yourself, to ponder, to want to know
❷ *This waterfall is one of the wonders of the world.*
• a marvel, a miracle

wonder NOUN
The sight of the Taj Mahal filled them with wonder.
• admiration, awe, reverence, amazement, astonishment
— If something makes you feel wonder, you can say that you **marvel at** it.

wonderful ADJECTIVE
❶ *The Northern Lights are a wonderful sight.*
• amazing, astonishing, astounding, incredible, remarkable, extraordinary, marvellous, sensational, tremendous, breathtaking
❷ *We had a wonderful day.*
• excellent, fantastic, brilliant, fabulous, marvellous, splendid, superb, super, delightful

wood NOUN
❶ *The little hut was made of wood.*
• timber, lumber, logs

— A **beam** or a **rafter** is a long piece of wood holding up a roof.
— A **board**, a **plank**, a **panel** or a **slat** is a flat piece of wood.
— A **pole** is a long thin cylinder of wood.
— A **chip** or a **splinter** is a small piece of wood.
— **Kindling** is small pieces of wood for lighting fires.
❷ *We followed a path through the wood.*
• woodland, woods, forest, trees
» *Look at* **tree**.

woolly *ADJECTIVE*
*I wore a warm **woolly** jumper.*
• wool, woollen, fleecy, furry, thick, cuddly

word *NOUN*
❶ *What's the French **word** for 'birthday'?*
• an expression, a term
— Your **vocabulary** is all the words you know.
❷ *Can I have a **word** with you?*
• a chat, a talk, a conversation,
a discussion
❸ *You gave me your **word**.*
• a promise, an assurance,
a guarantee, a pledge, a vow

word *VERB*
*Can you **word** it differently?*
• to express, to phrase, to say
• to put into words: *Can you **put it into**
different **words**?*
— The way that you word something is the **wording**
or **phrasing**.

wore (past tense of **wear**)

work *VERB*
❶ *I've been **working** on my project all day.*
• to be busy, to labour, to toil
❷ *He **works** in the bookshop on Saturdays.*
• to be employed, to have a job, to go to work
❸ *The printer isn't **working**.*
• to function, to go, to operate
❹ *My plan didn't **work**.*
• to succeed, to work out, to be effective,
to be successful
➤ **to work something out**
*Can you **work out** how to do it?*
• to deduce, to infer, to conclude, to calculate,
to figure out, to solve, to explain

work *NOUN*
❶ *Mopping the floor is hard **work**.*
• effort, labour, toil

❷ *The teacher gave us some **work** to do.*
• a task, an assignment, a job
— **Homework** is schoolwork you have to do
at home.
❸ *What **work** does she do?*
• an occupation, an employment, a job,
a profession, a trade
》 *For some kinds of work look at* **job**.

world *NOUN*
❶ *Antarctica is a remote part of the **world**.*
• the earth, the globe
❷ *He knows a lot about the **world** of sport.*
• a subject, a field, an area

worn (past participle of **wear**)

worried *ADJECTIVE*
*You look **worried**. Is something wrong?*
• anxious, troubled, uneasy, distressed, disturbed,
upset, apprehensive, concerned, bothered,
preoccupied, tense, nervous
OPPOSITE relaxed

worry *VERB*
❶ *There's no need to **worry**.*
• to be anxious, to be troubled, to be uneasy,
to be disturbed, to brood, to fret
— To worry about something happening is to
dread it.
❷ *It **worried** her that he wasn't answering
his phone.*
• to trouble, to distress, to upset, to concern,
to disturb

worry *NOUN*
❶ *My main **worry** is the spelling test.*
• a concern, a trouble, a burden, a care, a problem
❷ *He's been a constant source of **worry** to her.*
• anxiety, concern, distress, uneasiness, trouble, care

worship *VERB*
*Ancient Egyptians **worshipped** the sun god, Ra.*
• to pray to, to glorify, to praise, to revere, to adore
》 *For places where people worship look at* **building**.

worth *NOUN*
*The ring was an object of great **worth**.*
• value, merit, quality, significance, importance

worthless *ADJECTIVE*
*It's nothing but a **worthless** piece of junk.*
• useless, valueless, pointless, insignificant
OPPOSITE valuable

a b c d e f g h i j k l m n o p q r s t u v w x y z

worthwhile ADJECTIVE
*It is always **worthwhile** learning new words.*
• helpful, useful, valuable, beneficial
OPPOSITE useless

wound *(rhymes with **sound***) *(past tense of **wind**)*

wound *(say* woond*)* NOUN
*He had to be treated in hospital for a head **wound**.*
• an injury, a cut, a gash, a graze, a scratch
» *For some types of wound look at **injury**.*

wound *(say* woond*)* VERB
*The soldier had been **wounded**.*
• to injure, to hurt, to harm

wrap VERB
*She **wrapped** the presents in shiny gold paper.*
• to cover, to pack, to enclose

wreck VERB
*He **wrecked** his bike by riding it into a tree.*
• to destroy, to demolish, to crush, to smash

wreckage NOUN
*Divers have discovered the **wreckage** of an old ship.*
• debris, fragments, pieces, remains
— Use **rubble** or **ruins** for the wreckage of a building.

wriggle VERB
*The prisoner managed to **wriggle** out of his bonds.*
• to twist, to writhe, to squirm, to wiggle, to worm your way

wrinkle NOUN
*The old man's face was covered in **wrinkles**.*
• a crease, a fold, a furrow, a line, a ridge, a crinkle

wrinkle VERB
*The creature **wrinkled** its nose and sniffed.*
• to pucker, to crease, to crinkle, to crumple
OPPOSITE to smooth

write VERB writes, writing, wrote, written
❶ *She **wrote** a letter to her friend.*
• to compose, to draw up
— To write letters or emails to someone is to **correspond** with them.
— To **draft** a letter or story is to write a rough version of it.
❷ *He **wrote** the address on a piece of paper.*
• to jot down, to note, to print, to put
— To **scrawl** or to **scribble** something is to write it down in a quick untidy way.
❸ *I've **written** a song.*
• to compose, to create

writer NOUN

WORD WEB

SOME TYPES OF WRITER:

— An **author** is someone who writes books.
— A **novelist** is someone who writes novels.
— A **playwright** is someone who writes plays.
— A **poet** is someone who writes poetry.
— A **scriptwriter** or a **screenwriter** is someone who writes stories for film or television.
— A **journalist**, a **reporter** or a **correspondent** is someone who writes news stories.
— A **blogger** is someone who writes a blog.

writing NOUN
❶ *Can you read the **writing** on the envelope?*
• handwriting
— **Scrawl** or **scribble** is untidy writing.
❷ *The **writing** on the stone was very faint.*
• inscription

WORD WEB

SOME FORMS OF WRITING AND LITERATURE:

• an article, an autobiography, a biography, a blog, a comic, a detective story, a diary, a drama or a play, an essay, a fable, a fairy story or fairy tale, a fantasy, a folk tale, a ghost story, a legend, a letter, lyrics, a myth, a novel, poetry or verse, a romance, a saga, science fiction, a script, a spy story, a thriller
— **Fiction** is writing about imaginary events.
— **Non-fiction** is writing containing information about real things and events.
— **Prose** is writing that is not poetry or a play.
» *For ways to describe a piece of writing look at **story**.*

written (past participle of **write**)

wrong ADJECTIVE
❶ It is **wrong** to cheat.
• bad, dishonest, immoral, wicked, sinful,
irresponsible, unfair, unjust
❷ Your answer was **wrong**.
• incorrect, mistaken, inaccurate, false, untrue
❸ Did I say something **wrong**?
• inappropriate, unsuitable
❹ There's something **wrong** with the TV.
• faulty, defective, not working, out of order
OPPOSITE right

wrote (past tense of **write**)

⚙ Do you know a
   word for
   a) a young plant
   b) a young tree
   c) a young bird?

⚙ Do you know a
   word for a family
   of young dogs
   or cats?

⚙ Check the thesaurus to find answers!

yard NOUN
A solitary tree stood in the middle of the **yard**.
• a courtyard, a patio, an enclosure

yearly ADJECTIVE
Your pets should have a **yearly** check-up.
• annual

yell VERB
I **yelled** to attract their attention.
• to shout, to call out, to cry out, to roar, to bawl,
to bellow
yell NOUN
The pirates gave a bloodcurdling **yell**.
• a cry, a roar, a shout, a bellow

yellow ADJECTIVE, NOUN

🕸 **WORD WEB**

SOME SHADES OF YELLOW:

• amber, gold, golden, lemon, primrose, tawny
*A crack of light showed primrose pale under the door
ahead of them, and the little room seemed very bright
as Justin raised the latch and went in.*—THE EAGLE OF
THE NINTH, Rosemary Sutcliff
— Something which is rather yellow is **yellowish**.

young ADJECTIVE
❶ I was too **young** to understand what was
happening.
• little, small
OPPOSITE old

a
b
c
d
e
f
g
h
i
j
k
l
m
n
o
p
q
r
s
t
u
v
w
x
y
z

❷ *I think this book is a bit* **young** *for you.*
• childish, babyish, immature, infantile, youthful
OPPOSITES adult, grown-up, mature

WORD WEB

— A **youngster** is a young person or child.
— An **adolescent** or a **juvenile** is a young person who is older than a child and not yet an adult.
— A **youth** is a boy or a young man.
— An **infant** is a baby or a very young child.
— A **toddler** is a young child who is just learning to walk.
— A **seedling** is a young plant.
— A **sapling** is a young tree.
» *For young animals and birds look at* **bear**, **bird**, **cat**, **cattle**, **deer**, **dog**, **horse**, **pig** *and* **sheep**.

young NOUN
The mother bird returned to feed her **young**.
• offspring, babies, family
— A family of young birds is a **brood**.
— A family of young cats or dogs is a **litter**.

a brood

a litter

youth NOUN
❶ *In her* **youth**, *she had been a keen tennis player.*
• childhood, boyhood or girlhood, adolescence, teens
❷ *A group of* **youths** *started fighting.*
• an adolescent, a youngster, a juvenile, a teenager, a boy, a young man

youthful ADJECTIVE
The magic potion was supposed to keep him **youthful**.
• young, young-looking, vigorous, sprightly

○ Can you think of two other words that mean 'zero'?

○ Do you know a word that means 'zero goals' or 'zero points'?

○ Check the thesaurus to find answers!

zap *VERB*
*You have to **zap** aliens in this game.*
• to blast, to shoot, to fire at, to hit, to destroy

zero *NOUN*
*Four minus four makes **zero**.*
• nothing, nought
– Nil means zero goals or points.

zigzag *VERB*
*The road **zigzags** up the hill.*
• to wind, to twist, to meander

zone *NOUN*
*You may not enter the restricted **zone**.*
• an area, a district, a region, a neighbourhood, a territory

zoo *NOUN*
*Which is your favourite animal in the **zoo**?*
• a menagerie, a safari park, a wildlife reserve, a nature reserve
» *For animals you might see in a zoo look at* **animal**.

zoom *VERB*
*Cars **zoomed** past us.*
• to rush, to fly, to tear, to speed, to streak, to race, to whizz, to shoot

a
b
c
d
e
f
g
h
i
j
k
l
m
n
o
p
q
r
s
t
u
v
w
x
y
z

Contents

Similes

Similes are comparisons using 'as' or 'like'. Some common similes with 'as' are listed in the thesaurus, for example:

as clear as a bell

as clear as crystal

as cold as ice

as cool as a cucumber

as fit as a fiddle

as flat as a pancake

as good as gold

as light as a feather

as quiet as a mouse

as regular as clockwork

as sly as a fox

as solid as a rock

as straight as an arrow

as strong as an ox

as stubborn as a mule

as thin as a rake

But you can make up your own, original similes. If you want to say that something is very tall or very cold, think of other tall or cold things you could compare it to—*as tall as a skyscraper, as cold as an ice lolly . . .*

» Try comparing things or people to animals, for example *as slow as a slug, as soft as a rabbit's ear* or *as bumpy as a crocodile's back*. You could describe the way someone moves by saying that they *scuttled like a spider* or *tottered like a baby giraffe*.

» Look at the entry for **animal** for some ideas on describing animals that you could use to inspire you.

Special names for things

A thesaurus can help you find the right names for certain things, which can make your writing more accurate and convincing. For example, if you are writing about young animals you could find exactly the right word here:

young NOUN
The mother returned to feed her **young**.
• offspring, babies, family
– A family of young birds is a **brood**.
– A family of young cats or dogs is a **litter**.

You can find special words for writing about planes at **aircraft**. Instead of writing:

> *Part of the plane was on fire. The pilot realised he would have to stop and grabbed the controls. The bottom of the plane scraped along the ground as it stopped.*

you could write:

> *One of the engines was on fire. The pilot realised he would have to land and grabbed the joystick. The undercarriage scraped along the runway as it screeched to a halt.*

Activity

Do you know the special name for a baby bird, a baby goose or a baby swan?
» Look at the entry for **bird** to find the answers!

Do you know a word for a male pig or sheep?
» Look at the entries for **pig** and **sheep** to check!

Do you know the special names for the front and back parts of a ship or boat? Look at the entry for **boat** to find out!

Activity

There are special names for some **groups** of animals, people and things, called **collective nouns**. Can you match these?

a batch		puppies
a colony		invaders
a crew		birds
a flight	of	seals
a flock		workers
a horde		stairs
a litter		biscuits

» Look at the entry for **group** to find the answers, and more examples.

» You can also make up your own collective nouns. Use the ways that animals move or sound to give you ideas, for example *a flutter of butterflies* or *a rumble of rhinoceroses*.

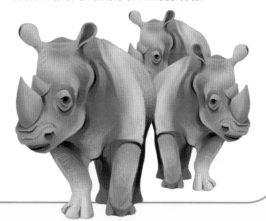

Sound effects

Some words, called **onomatopoeic** words, sound like the thing they are describing. These words can make your writing more descriptive and exciting. For example, you might say *his footsteps **crunched** on the gravel* or *Granny's teacup **chinked** in its saucer*.

Activity

Can you suggest some onomatopoeic words to go with the following noises?

- a machine making sounds
- a stream running over pebbles
- food frying in a pan
- someone coming through thick bushes
- someone walking along a muddy path
- traffic noises in a busy city

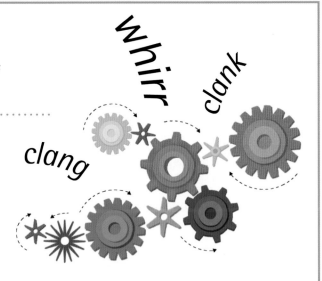

» Look at the entry for **sound** in the thesaurus for some ideas to help you.

Word building

Have you ever thought about making up a word? You can try building a new word by starting with a word you know, or one you have found in the thesaurus, and adding one of these suffixes (endings) to it:

-ish *shortish, greenish, hairyish*

-less *a moonless night, a flowerless garden*

-like *a giraffe-like neck, a ghost-like shadow*

-proof *a sword-proof shield, an ogre-proof castle*

-y *a fishy smell, a pinky colour, a lemony pudding*

You can also make new **compounds** by joining two whole words together. You could describe what something feels, looks, smells or sounds like using these endings:

-feeling *rough-feeling bark*

-looking *scary-looking teeth*

-smelling *a vile-smelling cave*

-sounding *an eerie-sounding wail*

To describe a unicorn, you could write:

*I approached the unicorn and it allowed me to stroke its **velvet-feeling, milk-like** skin. It had a **pearly, sharp-looking** horn, large **long-lashed** eyes that sparkled like jewels, and a garland of **sweet-smelling** flowers around its neck.*

Writing stories: Top 10 Tips

Before you write

1 **Plan your story**

» Use the question words **who**, **what**, **when**, **where**, **why** and **how** to help you. See the next section on **Planning and writing a story** for more details and ideas.

2 Tell your story to a friend before you write. Would you want to read this story? Would your friend? Change your plan if necessary.

While you are writing

3 Keep to your plan once you start writing.

4 Write in sentences and think about punctuation.

5 Don't forget paragraphs. If you need to begin a sentence with an adverbial of time (e.g. *Later that day . . . When it was all over . . .*) or place (e.g. *Outside . . . In the woods . . .*), you probably need to start a new paragraph.

After you have written the first draft

6 Use your *Oxford Primary Illustrated Dictionary* to check your spelling.

7 Use this thesaurus to make sure you have chosen the best words.

8 Look at the OVERUSED WORDS list on page viii. If you have used any of them, look at the entry in this thesaurus. Try to use other words if they can add meaning or excitement to your story.

9 Can you add some details about your characters to make them more interesting to your reader?

10 Can you add more information about your setting to help your reader to 'see' it in their mind?

289

Planning and writing a story

1. Setting

WHEN does the story take place?

Use adverbials such as *early one morning, on a beautiful spring day,* or *many years ago.*

WHEN do the different events happen?

Use time adverbials such as *earlier, meanwhile, later that night* or *the following day.*

WHERE do the events take place?

Use adverbials of place, for example *at sea, on a desert island, in an ancient castle, in outer space.*

WHAT is the place and its atmosphere like?

» Think about details such as **weather, trees, animals,** and **birds.** You can find interesting adjectives and nouns at these entries.

» Look at the list of WRITING TIPS on page x to see where you can find more ideas for writing about your setting. For example, you might want to look at the entry for **building** for ideas for types of building, **ghost** for some spooky places to set your story, **ice** and **snow** for a story set in a cold place, or **space** for a story set in space.

2. Characters

WHO are you writing about?

» If you want to write about a character such as a **detective, explorer, fairy, ghost, knight, pirate, robot,** or **superhero** look at the entry for this word in the thesaurus to find ideas. For example, the box at **pirate** will give you words for describing a pirate, and ideas for things a pirate might use or carry. It also has suggestions for other places you could look, for example at **boat** for lots of useful words for writing about the pirate's ship.

» If you want to write about magical creatures, look at the entries for **magic** and **myth** for some ideas for characters you could have in your story.

WHAT are the characters like?

Use interesting adjectives to describe:

. . . your characters' appearance. Are they *lean* or *squat*? Is their hair *bushy* or *straggly*? Is their face *chubby* or *gaunt*? Are their eyes *beady* or *blank*?

. . . your characters' personality and mood. Are they *monstrous* and *malevolent* or *honourable* and *true*? Are they *merry* and *light-hearted* or *dejected* and *downcast*? Are they *wily* and *cunning* or *foolish* and *unwise*?

» Instead of using a very common word such as **bad, good, nice, happy** or **small,** try to find more varied and exact adjectives. Look at the list to see more of OVERUSED WORDS on page viii.

» If you are writing about imaginary creatures, it is especially important to let your readers know how they look and sound. You could compare them to real animals to help form a picture in the reader's mind. Look at the sections on **Similes** and **Word building** for some ideas of how to do this.

The aliens had *insect-like* bodies, with legs *like beetles* and *spiky* antennae.
They spoke in *electronic-sounding* bleeps.

3. Action

WHAT does your character do?

HOW do they do it?

Use interesting verbs and adverbs to describe how your characters move and do things. Do they *scurry hastily*, *glide gracefully* or *slink stealthily*?

>> Look at the entries for **move**, **run** and **walk** to help you describe movement.

>> Look at the entries for **eat**, **drink**, **look**, and **hit** for more interesting action words.

WHY do they do it?
Use interesting adjectives to describe your characters' feelings when they do things.

>> Look at the entries for **angry**, **frightened**, **happy**, **pain**, **sad**, and **surprised** for some interesting ways of writing about emotions.

>> Use idioms (phrases) to describe what your character's feelings make them do. The entries for **angry**, **frightened** and **surprised** have some ideas.

4. Dialogue

WHAT do the characters say?

Lively dialogue can bring the characters in your story to life.

>> Try using exclamations at exciting moments in your story. Look at the entry for **exclamation** for some ideas.

HOW do they say it?

Try not to use the verb *say* every time you report what a character says.

>> Look at the entry for **say** for lots of different ways to say things, with examples from different stories.

TO SAY ANGRILY:

• to snap, to snarl, to growl, to thunder, to bark, to rant, to rave

'Shut your mouth, Gristle!' barked Cudgel and Griswold's voice stopped dead.—MEASLE: THE MONSTER OF MUCUS!, Ian Ogilvy

'Blithering barnacles!' thundered Captain Redbeard. 'What are you doing?'

'Great magical mousetraps!' declared Griselda, 'I've had an idea!'

Different types of writing: non-fiction

Whether you are writing fiction or non-fiction, it is important to think about *who* you are writing it for (your **audience**) and **why** you are writing it (your **purpose**). The thesaurus can help you find the best words to use.

An article or review. You might write an article for a school newsletter, in which you describe a recent trip to a theme park. You might write a description of a book you have read or a programme you have seen.

» Look at the entry for **story** for some ideas!

» To make your article or review interesting and entertaining, use the OVERUSED WORD boxes to find alternatives to very common words such as **nice** and **good**:

Activity

Try editing this report on a school trip by replacing the words in bold with some interesting alternatives from the thesaurus:

Year 3 enjoyed a nice trip to the safari park last week. They saw some good animals including a very big elephant, a scary tiger and some naughty monkeys. After that, some of the children had an exciting ride on a roller coaster.

An advertisement or a poster. You might be trying to persuade other pupils to join a new after-school club, or to persuade parents and friends to come to a school event.

» To make your writing persuasive, try using commands and questions. To make it fun, try using **alliteration** (words that start with the same sound). If you look up the word you were thinking of using, the thesaurus can help you find alternatives starting with the sound you want.

Come to our fun and fabulous Summer Fair on Saturday 18th June! Sample scrumptious home-made cakes and have your face perfectly painted! Or why not try your luck at some of our glorious games?

Activity

Use the thesaurus to find a different, alliterative adjective to replace the words in bold. The first one has been done for you:

• a **nice** day ⟶ a delightful day
• an **interesting** read
• **lovely** food
• some **good** music

Project work. You might want to write a blogpost, essay or project about a factual topic.

» Use the WORD WEBS in this thesaurus (see page ix) to help you. For example, the panel on **animals**, **farm** and **pet** will help you write about animals.

Writing letters

Formal letters

You might write a **formal letter** to someone you do not know, or someone who is important. This might be a letter of complaint, a request for a job or some information, or an invitation to a formal occasion.

In a formal letter, you should

- write in complete sentences

- avoid short forms like *don't* and *I'm* (use *do not* and *I am*)

- avoid informal words and phrases, such as *thanks*, and try to use more formal words such as *unable to* instead of *can't*

- avoid exclamation marks or block capitals

- begin with a formal salutation *Dear*... and the person's title and family name, e.g. *Mrs Davies, Dr Khan* (if you don't know their name, use *Sir* or *Madam*)

- end with *Yours sincerely* or *Yours truly* followed by the letter writer's name

> 5, Ugly Towers
>
> Dear Prince Charming,
>
> Thank you for your kind invitation to the Palace Ball on Saturday. Unfortunately I am unable to come, as I am obliged to stay at home all evening to sweep the floors.
> Please accept my apologies.
>
> Yours sincerely,
> Cinderella

» If a synonym is informal, this is stated in the thesaurus, so you know to avoid it in formal writing. For example:

abandon *VERB*
*His friends **abandoned him** and went home.*
- **to leave, to desert, to forsake, to dump** *(informal)*

Informal letters and emails

An **informal letter** or **email** is to someone you know well. It might sound chatty, as if you are speaking rather than writing.

In informal writing, you can

- use incomplete sentences

- use short forms like *don't* and *I'm*

- use informal words and phrases such as *thanks* or *drive you mad*

- use exclamation marks or block capitals to emphasise things

- begin with *Dear, Hello, Hi* and the person's first name or a nickname

- end with *Love, Lots of love* or, if you don't know the person quite so well, *Yours* or *Best wishes*

> Hi Cinders
>
> Just had a cool idea! Meet me at the kitchen door, 6 p.m. on Sat.
> Bring a pumpkin and a few mice.
>
> Love
> Your Fairy Godmother xxx

fish

a hummingbird

a unicorn

a buzzard

an echidna

effort

a chandelier

fangs

a scorpion

dive

a cheetah

cook

stew

a litter

eat